Film Review

1997-8

James Cameron-Wilson became a committed film buff when he moved to London at the age of seventeen. After a stint at the Webber Douglas Academy of Dramatic Art he joined *What's On In London* and took over from F. Maurice Speed as cinema editor. Later, he edited the trade newspaper *Showbiz*, was commissioning editor for *Film Review*, consultant and quizmaster for *The Movie Show* on BSkyB and a frequent presenter on the Radio 2 *Arts Programme*. He is also the author of the books *Young Hollywood* and *The Cinema of Robert De Niro*. He currently writes for *Film Review*, *Flicks*, *The Times*, *Midlands Zone*, *Fuji* and *London MAG*, and is film critic for the *What's On* magazine group, cinema correspondent for BBC Worldwide Television and Britain's resident dial-a-film critic (number available on request). Besides the cinema, James Cameron-Wilson's interests include the process of ageing, the discovery of America and the phenomenon of missing persons.

Film Review

1997-8

Including Video Releases

James Cameron-Wilson

TO MARK HARDY WITH
FOND MEMORIES OF FOREST ROW,
STEPHEN SONDHEIM
AND BRIAN DENNEHY

Acknowledgements

The author would like to impart his
eternal appreciation to the following,
without whom this book would not have
been possible (or at least a total mess):
Charles Bacon, Wendy Brown,
Ewen Brownrigg, Christopher Cameron,
Michael Darvell, Marianne Gray,
Karen Krizanovich, Nigel Mulock, my
mother, Frances Palmer, Gwyneth Paltrow
(for inspiration, among other things),
Virginia Palmer, Fred Price, David Quinlan,
Simon Rose, Mansel Stimpson, David Stoner
and Derek Winnert. Till next year ...

First published in Great Britain in 1997 by
VIRGIN BOOKS
an imprint of Virgin Publishing Ltd
332 Ladbroke Grove, London W10 5AH

A catalogue record for this book is available
from the British Library

ISBN 07535 01082

Designed and typeset by Fred Price

Printed in Great Britain by
Butler & Tanner Ltd

Contents

Introduction

James Cameron-Wilson

For a while there this annual was beginning to look redundant. That is, the most successful film of 1977 – which we covered twenty issues ago – was turning out to be the most successful film of 1997. With a growing number of pictures crowding our multiplexes, it's difficult enough to find adequate space in this book for the new films. As editor, I am determined that the increasing flow of product should not compromise the contents of this, the 53rd edition of the world's longest-running film annual. I intend the credits to be as comprehensive, the comment as detailed and the photographs as abundant as ever before. Because, if one starts cutting corners, this labour of love can only lose its value as an essential reference. But then, by definition, the annual is a record of twelve months of product. So at what point, if any, does one start to include coverage of re-releases? In my opinion, such a move can only lead to sacrifice. Having said that, 1997 turned out to be the year of the reissue.

Until *The Lost World: Jurassic Park* lumbered into the record books in late May (grossing an unheard-of $26.1 million in one day), the top-grossing movie release of 1997 was *Star Wars*. Rechristened *Star Wars: Episode IV – A New Hope*, the 1977 box-office behemoth arrived armed with an exorbitant marketing campaign and four extra highly publicised minutes. The latter material included a freshly conceived 'dewback lizard', the addition of a single black extra (political correctness will out), a meeting between Han Solo and a computer-generated Jabba the Hutt and a minor dialogue between Luke Skywalker and a chap called Biggs. Moreover, the film's sound and special effects had been given a thorough spring cleaning to bring it in line with the standards one expects from today's overpriced extravaganzas.

And yet, in spite of all this attention, *Star Wars* still looks awfully cheesy. Young Luke has lost none of the dampness behind his ears, and Princess Leia is just as irritating as she ever was, while the cast's predilection for seventies' sideburns dates the film terribly. The technology may have been well ahead of its time, but the hairstyles prove to be embarrassing fossils.

Notwithstanding, when *Star Wars* opened in the US on 31st January 1997, it held the number one position for three weeks – until being dethroned by *The Empire Strikes Back*. Then, another three weeks later, *Return of the Jedi* came along and snatched the top spot. Fired by such colossal box-office figures, Steven Spielberg promptly announced that he was planning to reissue *Jaws* – as soon as he had the rubber fish replaced by a digitally upgraded version.

Yet the *Star Wars* trilogy was merely the tip of the Death Star. On Friday 25th April 1997, London film critics found themselves reassessing the merits of not only *Return of the Jedi* but also of Robert Siodmak's *The Spiral Staircase* and Hitchcock's *Vertigo*. And it was only the previous week that they had reviewed *The Empire Strikes Back* and *Citizen Kane*! But don't get me wrong. I think it's wonderful that old films are being dusted off and introduced to a new generation. I'm just sorry that I can't include them within these pages. However, with new films of such eclectic calibre as *The Eighth Day*, *The English Patient*, *Fly Away Home*, *Kolya*, *Microcosmos*, *She's the One* and *Shine*, I hope you share my belief that current cinema still has so much to offer.

New wine into old bottles: A young Harrison Ford chats up the latest in computer imagery, in Star Wars: Episode IV - A New Hope

Top Twenty Box-Office Hits

(for the period July 1996–June 1997)

1 Independence Day
2 101 Dalmatians
3 Mission: Impossible
4 Star Wars
5 Evita
6 Twister
7 Ransom
8 The Nutty Professor
9 The English Patient
10 Trainspotting
11 Space Jam
12 Liar Liar
13 Matilda
14 Sleepers
15 Star Trek First Contact
16 The Hunchback of Notre Dame
17 Jerry Maguire
18 The Rock
19 Scream
20 The Empire Strikes Back

Prepare for impact! An alien ship hovers over Manhattan in Roland Emmerich's number one box-office hit Independence Day

Top dog: Pongo declares his box-office muscle in Stephen Herek's 101 Dalmatians

That familiar feeling: Mark Hamill, Carrie Fisher and Harrison Ford return for a few dollars more, in George Lucas's Star Wars: Episode IV - A New Hope

Tom Cruise, deciding to accept his assignment, in Brian De Palma's Mission: Impossible

Together at last! Antonio Banderas and Madonna as Ché Guevara and Eva Peron in Alan Parker's surprisingly popular Evita

Top Ten Box-Office Stars

There's no disputing this year's 'star of the year'. *Mission: Impossible*, which clocked up an outstanding £17 million at UK cinemas, squarely owes its success to its producer and leading man, Tom Cruise. And then, just to confirm the phenomenon, there's the £8.5m racked up by *Jerry Maguire*. Notwithstanding, the number one attraction of the last two years, Jim Carrey, is still exercising a strong grip on the chart thanks to the success of *Liar Liar*, making him the nearest thing to a box-office certainty.

More interesting is the unexpected popularity in the UK of *Roald Dahl's Matilda*, starring, produced and directed by Danny DeVito. A box-office disappointment in the States, this wickedly enjoyable family film found its true audience here, proving just how sophisticated British children really are. Yet even more surprising is how well *Space Jam* fared on these shores, in spite of its preponderance of basketball and unashamed deference to an all-American icon called Michael Jordan (who, in tabloid inches, can hardly compete with Gazza and Eric Cantona over here). Even taking into account the 250,000 Americans who live in the UK, *Space Jam* was a startling success, beating out such qualified contenders as *Star Trek First Contact*, *The Hunchback of Notre Dame* and *The Rock*. Fans of Danny DeVito will point out that the actor also supplied the voice of 'Swackhammer' in *Space Jam*, which, with his appearance in *Mars Attacks!* (which entered the list at 21), cements his position on this chart.

For the record, the runners-up this year include Harrison Ford, Robert De Niro, Bill Pullman, Madonna, Ralph Fiennes and Jack Nicholson.

STAR OF THE YEAR: TOM CRUISE

2 Jim Carrey

3 Mel Gibson

4 Eddie Murphy

5 Brad Pitt

6 Danny DeVito

7 Sean Connery

8 John Travolta

9 Arnold Schwarzenegger

10 Will Smith

Releases of the Year

In this section you will find details of all the films released in Great Britain from 1 July 1996 to the end of June 1997 – the period covered by all the reference features in the book.

The normal abbreviations operate as follows: Dir – for Director; Pro – for Producer; Assoc Pro – for Associate Producer; Ex Pro – for Executive Producer; Pro Ex – for Production Executive; Pro Sup – for Production Supervisor; Co-Pro – for Co-Producer; Pro Co-Ord – for Production Co-Ordinator; Ph – for Photographer; Ed – for Editor; Art – for Art Director; Pro Des – for Production Designer; M – for Music; and a few others which will be obvious.

Abbreviations for the names of film companies are also pretty obvious when used, such as Fox for 20th Century-Fox, Rank for Rank Film Distributors, and UIP for Universal International Pictures. Where known, the actual production company is given first, the releasing company last.

All films reviewed by James Cameron-Wilson unless otherwise specified. Additional contributors: Charles Bacon, Ewen Brownrigg, Simon Rose, Mansel Stimpson, Derek Winnert, Nigel Mulock and Marianne Gray.

Absolute Power

'All power corrupts and absolute power corrupts absolutely,' wrote Lord Acton to Bishop Mandell Creighton in 1887. Few people come more powerful than the president of the United States, and when Alan Richmond gets into a fight with the young wife of a rich mentor, she is unceremoniously executed by the secret service. But, unbeknownst to Richmond, a burglar – closeted behind a two-way mirror – has witnessed the entire scene. The latter, the highly efficient and diligent Luther Whitney, is now the most wanted man in the US, suspected of murder by the FBI and hunted both by the secret service and a hitman hired by the victim's husband... Working from a superlative script by William Goldman (based on the novel by David Baldacci), director Clint Eastwood is confident and wise enough to let the material work for itself. Unfolding his gripping story in simple, straightforward strokes, the filmmaker reveals a masterly touch, aided by seamless editing and a subtle, stealthy score by Lennie

Niehaus (accompanied by two instrumental themes composed by Eastwood himself). And, in a first-rate cast, only Gene Hackman, as the philandering president, seems ill suited for a part that demands greater youth and charisma.

Clint Eastwood (*Luther Whitney*), Gene Hackman (*President Alan Richmond*), Ed Harris (*Seth Frank*), Laura Linney (*Kate Whitney*), Judy Davis (*Gloria Russell*), Scott Glenn (*Bill Burton*), Dennis Haysbert (*Tim Collin*), E.G. Marshall (*Walter Sullivan*), Melora Hardin (*Christy Sullivan*), Ken Welsh, Penny Johnson, Richard Jenkins, Mark Margolis, Elaine Kagan, Alison Eastwood, Kimber Eastwood.
　Dir: Clint Eastwood. Pro: Eastwood and Karen Spiegel. Ex Pro: Tom Rooker. Screenplay: William Goldman. Ph: Jack N. Green. Pro Des: Henry Bumstead. Ed: Joel Cox. M: Lennie Niehaus; Eastwood. (Castle Rock/Malpaso–Rank–Castle Rock/Turner.) Rel: 30 May 1997. 121 mins. Cert 15. USA. 1996.

Acts of Love

Texas; today. In the autumn of his life, Joseph Svenden, a mediocre teacher and sorry excuse for a farmer, is on the verge of committing to the woman he has loved since he was 18, the widow Rosealee Henson. Just then he is seduced by the 17-year-old daughter of a new neighbour and finds himself transformed. Suddenly in possession of a new awareness and passion, Joseph both frightens and arouses Rosealee, but can he keep the agent of his psychological make-over a secret in the small, close community in which they live? While successfully capturing the visual landscape of Andrew Wyeth and Dorothea Lange, this dramatically static adaptation of Jim Harrison's novel, *Farmer*, fails to overcome the implausibilities of the original's scenario. It's hard to comprehend how a teenage sexpot could fall for a 47-year-old cripple at the best of times, but with Dennis Hopper (who's actually 61) cast as the doddery old codger the idea is ludicrous. The director's original choice, Ed Harris, would have made much more sense, but Hopper (who previously appeared in Barreto's intriguing TV movie *The Heart of Justice*) ill-advisedly persuaded him otherwise. Bruce Broughton's omnipresent and undistinguished

Power corrupts: Gene Hackman as President Richmond in Clint Eastwood's gripping Absolute Power (from Rank–Castle Rock/ Turner)

score merely aggravates matters. US title: *Carried Away*.

Dennis Hopper (*Joseph Svenden*), Amy Irving (*Rosealee Henson*), Amy Locane (*Catherine Wheeler*), Julie Harris (*Joseph's mother*), Gary Busey (*Major Nathan Wheeler*), Hal Holbrook (*Dr Evans*), Christopher Pettiet (*Robert Henson*), Priscilla Pointer (*Lily Henson*), Gail Cronauer (*Beverly Wheeler*), Alissa Alban, E.J. Morris, Joe Stevens.
　Dir: Bruno Barreto. Pro: Lisa M. Hansen and Paul Hertzberg. Ex Pro: Barreto, Amy Irving and Robert Dattila. Co-Pro:
Catalaine Knell. Screenplay: Ed Jones. Ph: Declan Quinn. Pro Des: Peter Paul Raubertas. Ed: Bruce Cannon. M: Bruce Broughton; Dvorak; numbers performed by Willie Nelson, Gene Austin, Cardboard, etc. Costumes: Grania Preston. Sound: Jay Boekelheide. (CineTel–First Independent.) Rel: 13 December 1996. 109 mins. Cert 18. USA. 1995.

The Addiction

A philosophy major at New York University, Kathleen Conklin is incensed by the capacity for evil in her fellow man. But no sooner has she attended a lecture on the atrocities of Vietnam, than she is summarily ambushed by a vampire and transformed into a member of

Blood lust: Christopher Walken and Lili Taylor haunt the streets of New York in Abel Ferrara's surrealistic exposé of evil, The Addiction *(from Guild)*

the walking dead. Torn between her former beliefs and her new hunger for blood, Kathleen is propelled into a physical and metaphysical nightmare... A visually arresting, almost poetic work (filmed in stark black and white), *The Addiction* promises much in its early stages as it captures the underbelly of New York in almost documentary-like surrealism. Then, trapped in the clichés of the vampire genre – the aversion to sunlight, need for blood, etc. – the film loses its innovative bite. With each of his features Abel Ferrara has sought to cross some threshold of taste, but here he goes too far. By juxtaposing photographs and newsreel footage of Holocaust slaughter to underscore his point (the innate evil of mankind), the director has exploited the suffering of

innocent victims to furnish his own fiction. This time his habitual get-out clause of final spiritual redemption just doesn't stick.

Lili Taylor (*Kathleen Conklin*), Christopher Walken (*Peina*), Annabella Sciorra (*Casanova*), Edie Falco (*Jean*), Paul Calderon, Fredro Starr, Kathryn Erbe, Lisa Casillo, Michael Imperioli, Heather Bracken, Father Robert Castle.
   Dir: Abel Ferrara. Pro: Denis Hann and Fernando Sulichin. Ex Pro: Russell Simmons and Preston Holmes. Line Pro: Margot E. Lulick. Screenplay: Nicolas St John. Ph: Ken Kelsch. Pro Des: Charles Lagola. Ed: Mayin Lo. M: Joe Delia; Vivaldi; numbers performed by Eddie Kendrix and David Ruffin, Onyx, Schooly D, Cypress Hill, Endira, etc. Costumes: Melinda Eshelman. (Fast Films Inc–Guild.) Rel: 18 April 1997. 82 mins. Cert 18. USA. 1994.

Adrenalin: Fear the Rush

Boston, Massachusetts; 2007 AD. In a world where 'crime, civil disobedience and deadly viruses are

the norm', a virulent plague has forged a divide between the healthy and the sick. The sick are rounded up and dumped in a quarantine camp, where the internees fall prey to a cannibalistic mental patient... Shot on a budget that couldn't feed a rat, this terminally unpleasant, repetitive thriller from the director of *Brain Smasher: A Love Story* and *Vicious Lips* is every bit as awful as you'd expect it to be. [*Ewen Brownrigg*]

Christopher Lambert (*Lemieux*), Natasha Henstridge (*Delon*), Norbert Weisser (*Cuzo*), Elizabeth Barondes (*Wocek*), Craig Davis, Xavier Declie, Nicholas Guest, Andrew Divoff, Jon Epstein.
   Dir and Screenplay: Albert Pyun. Pro: Tom Karnowski and Gary Schmoeller. Ex Pro: Barr. B. Potter and Paul Rosenblum. Co-Pro: Mark Scoon. Line Pro: Jessica G. Budin. Ph: George Mooradian. Pro Des: Nenad Pecur. Ed: Ken Morrisey. M: Tony Riparetti; 'I Wanna Be Sedated' performed by The Ramones. Costumes: Shelly Boies. (Largo Entertainment/Toga Prods/ Filmwerks–Columbia TriStar.) Rel: 6 June 1997. 76 mins. Cert 18. USA. 1995.

The Adventures of Pinocchio

Many, many years after he carved a heart to his love in the bole of a pine tree, the puppet maker Geppetto discovers that the trunk has acquired unusual powers. Fashioning the wood into a puppet that he names Pinocchio, Geppetto is further surprised to find that the puppet has a life of its own. A quick learner, Pinocchio pines to be nothing more than a real boy, but first he has to overcome his mischievous tendencies – leading to a series of hair-raising adventures – before he can realise his dream... Magnificently capturing the spirit of a bygone Italy, this unexpected version of Carlo Collodi's 1883 tale is an enchanting and moving antidote to the noisy and sentimental children's films of late. Juan Ruiz Anchia's golden-hued lighting, Rachel Portman's melodious score and the unobtrusive and sophisticated special effects add to the pleasure, while Martin Landau brings a commendable poignancy and dignity to his Geppetto. Only Bebe Neuwirth's conniving villainess and her bumbling henchman Rob Schneider usher in an element of Hollywood formula. Filmed on location in the Czech Republic.

Martin Landau (*Geppetto*), Jonathan Taylor
Thomas (*Pinocchio*), Rob Schneider (*Volpe*),
Udo Kier (*Lorenzini*), Bebe Neuwirth
(*Felinet*), David Doyle (*the voice of Pepe*),
Corey Carrier (*Lampwick*), Genevieve
Bujold (*Leona*), Dawn French, Griff Rhys
Jones, Marcello Magni, John Sessions,
Richard Claxton, Jean-Claude Drouot,
Jean-Claude Dreyfus.

Dir: Steve Barron. Pro: Raju Patel and
Jeffrey Sneller. Ex Pro: Sharad Patel, Peter
Locke and Donald Kushner. Co-Ex Pro:
Lawrence Mortorff. Co-Pro: Michael
MacDonald and Tim Hampton.
Screenplay: Barron, Sherry Mills, Tom
Benedek and Barry Berman. Ph: Juan Ruiz
Anchia. Pro Des: Allan Cameron. Ed: Sean
Barton. M: Rachel Portman; numbers
performed by Stevie Wonder, Brian May,
Jerry Hadley, etc. Costumes: Maurizio
Millenotti. Visual effects: Angus Bickerton.
Animatronics: Jim Henson's Creature
Shop. (Pangaea Holdings/Twin
Continental/Allied Pinocchio/Davis
Films/Deiter Geissler Filmproduktion/
Alta Vista Film–PolyGram.) Rel: 18
October 1996. 94 mins. Cert U. UK/
France/Germany/Czech Republic/USA.
1996.

Alaska

When the wife of Jake Barnes dies,
the 747 pilot attempts to put his past
behind him by moving from Chicago
to a remote Alaskan settlement.
Reduced to delivering loo paper to
outlying communities, Jake becomes
alienated from his 14-year-old son,
Sean, but still has the love and care of
his 12-year-old daughter, Jessie.
Then, when Jake goes missing during
an emergency drop-off, Sean and
Jessie forget bygones and combine
forces to find their father... A creaky
scenario is rendered insensible by a
frantic score, which seems to employ
a 2,000-man orchestra to accompany
Jessie rushing to her front door.
When the real excitement starts
(Jake's plane plummeting down a
cliff face, Jessie and Sean navigating
white-water rapids, Sean hurtling
down a mountainside) much of
the impetus would have been
squandered were it not for the calibre
of stunts and editing. Children
getting lost in the wilderness is now
becoming a genre unto itself, with
this one rather on the intense side for
younger cinemagoers.

Thora Birch (*Jessie Barnes*), Vincent
Kartheiser (*Sean Barnes*), Dirk Benedict
(*Jake Barnes*), Charlton Heston (*Perry*),
Duncan Fraser (*Mr Koontz*), Gordon
Tootoosis (*Ben*), Ben Cardinal (*Charlie*),

*Woodentop: The puppet that pines to be a real
boy in Steve Barron's enchanting* The
Adventures of Pinocchio *(from PolyGram)*

*Bearing witness: Agee as Cubby in Fraser C.
Heston's rather intense* Alaska *(from
Rank–Castle Rock/Turner)*

Dying to love you: Antony Sher and Jason Flemyng in Nancy Meckler's frank, sparkling Alive and Kicking *(from Channel Four Films)*

Ryan Kent (*Chip*), Don S. Davis, Dolly Madsen, Stephen E. Miller, Byron Chief Moon, Kristin Lehman, Agee (*Cubby, the polar bear cub*).
   Dir: Fraser C. Heston. Pro: Carol Fuchs and Andy Burg. Co-Pro: Gordon Mark. Screenplay: Burg and Scott Myers. Ph: Tony Westman. Pro Des: Douglas Higgins. Ed: Rob Kobrin. M: Reg Powell. Costumes: Monique Prudhomme. (Castle Rock–Rank–Castle Rock/Turner.) Rel: 18 October 1996. 109 mins. Cert PG. USA. 1996.

Alive and Kicking

London; today. With his lover dead a year and his best friend recently destroyed by Aids, Tonio, a talented modern dancer, refuses to face up to the realities of his own short life. HIV positive, he is determined to wear a brave face, but is confused by the advances of an older, healthier man. Rejecting the latter's offer of friendship, Tonio immerses himself into gruelling rehearsals for a controversial ballet (*Indian Summer*), but denies himself a true emotional outlet... A startlingly frank look at the dilemma of living with Aids, *Alive and Kicking*, like *Jeffrey* before it, confronts its traumatic subject through humour. Unlike *Jeffrey*, the film is an original project, the first screenplay by the American London-based dramatist Martin Sherman

(most famous for his homosexual-themed play *Bent*). While Sherman's sparkling dialogue betrays the hand of a seasoned playwright ('romance had a stroke a long time ago' is not a cinematic line), director Nancy Meckler (*Sister My Sister*) brings a naturalistic spontaneity to the material that is quite affecting. Jason Flemyng (a revelation), Antony Sher and Diane Parish are all top flight. Aka *Indian Summer*.

Jason Flemyng (*Tonio*), Antony Sher (*Jack*), Dorothy Tutin (*Luna*), Anthony Higgins (*Ramon*), Bill Nighy (*Tristan*), Philip Voss (*Duncan*), Diane Parish (*Millie*), Aiden Waters (*Vincent*), Natalie Roles, Freddy Douglas, Kenneth Tharp, Michael Keegan-Dolan, Linda Bassett, David Ashton, Annabel Leventon, Richard Hope, Martin Sherman (*man at pub*).
   Dir: Nancy Meckler. Pro: Martin Pope. Assoc Pro: Lorraine Goodman. Screenplay: Martin Sherman. Ph: Chris Seager. Pro Des: Cecelia Brereton. Ed: Rodney Holland. M: Peter Salem; Schubert. Costumes: Monica Howe. Choreographer: Liz Ranken. (M.P Prods–Channel Four Films.) Rel: 6 June 1997. 98 mins. Cert 15. UK. 1996.

All Things Fair

See *Love Lessons*.

American Buffalo

Donny Dubrow, the owner of a Chicago junk job, tells his friend 'Teach' that he has sold a buffalo head nickel for $90. Over the next few hours (of a remarkably

uneventful day), the two low-lives plot how to steal the nickel back... The big joke of this spectacularly boring film is that David Mamet is credited with 'adapting' it from his own stage play (which starred Al Pacino). Well, with nary a glimpse of another human being (not even a pedestrian) during the film's entire 90 minutes, this is hardly a cinematic modification. If Mamet (who scripted the thoroughly cinematic *The Untouchables*) were honest, he would admit to fine-tuning his extremely boring play for the camera, but not 'adapting' it. Even Dustin Hoffman, as the miserable and profane 'Teach', cannot breathe life into this welter of tired *non sequiturs*. Mamet's theme, it would seem, is that a lot of low-lives are just full of talk. Which is a shame as they are so inarticulate.

Dustin Hoffman (*Walter 'Teach' Cole*), Dennis Franz (*Donny Dubrow*), Sean Nelson (*Bob*).
   Dir: Michael Corrente. Pro: Gregory Mosher. Ex Pro: John Sloss. Co-Pro: Sarah Green. Screenplay: David Mamet. Ph: Richard Crudo. Pro Des: Daniel Talpers. Ed: Kate Sanford. M: Thomas Newman. Costumes: Deborah Newhall. (Capitol Films/Samuel Goldwyn/Channel Four/Punch Prods–Film Four.) Rel: 22 November 1996. 90 mins. Cert 15. USA. 1996.

L'Amore Molesto

Naples; today. When Delia, a comic-strip artist, receives a bizarre telephone call from her mother, she fears the worst. And sure enough, her mother's naked body is found washed up on the beach the following day. Determined to get to the bottom of her death, Delia embarks on a precarious investigation that throws fresh light on childhood traumas and reveals the powerful treachery of appearances. Life, Delia discovers, is less sinister but more bizarre than she had imagined... A subtle, intelligent drama, *L'Amore Molesto* is, within the confines of the mystery-thriller genre, a little too subtle and intelligent for its own good, frequently leaving the viewer both perplexed and distracted. While the film offers plenty of Neapolitan flavour, a sprinkling of humour (dark or otherwise) and a dash of suspense would have been most welcome.

Anna Bonaiuto (*Delia*), Angela Luce (*Amalia*), Carmela Pecoraro (*Delia as a child*), Licia Maglietta (*young Amalia*), Gianni Cajafa (*Uncle Filippo, Amalia's brother*), Anna Calato (*Madame De Riso*), Giovanni Viglietti (*Nicola 'Caserta' Polledro*), Peppe Lanzetta (*Antonio Polledro*), Italo Celoro (*Delia's father*).

Dir and Screenplay: Mario Martone, from the novel by Elena Ferrante. Pro: Angelo Curti, Andrea Occhipinti and Kermit Smith. Ph: Luca Bigazzi. Pro Des: Giancarlo Muselli. Ed: Jacopo Quadri. M: Steve Lacy and Alfred Schittke. Costumes: Metella Raboni. (Lucky Red/Teatri Unit–Arrow.) Rel: 13 September 1996. 91 mins. Cert 15. Italy. 1995.

Anaconda

In the heart of the Brazilian rainforest, a documentary film crew sets out to record the elusive Shirishama, a tribe of Amazonian natives that may or may not exist. Granting asylum to an enigmatic snake catcher along the way, the filmmakers find their agenda dramatically altered as they sail directly into the path of a 40-foot man-eating anaconda... Featuring an animatronic/computer-generated snake that looks like it's escaped from the set of *Toy Story*, this laughably melodramatic thriller is further stymied by a cast of ethnically balanced characters that are even caricatures by Hollywood standards. Any cinematic menace, whether it be shark, dinosaur or extraterrestrial, can only be as threatening as the lives of its victims are valued and sympathetic. But with this motley crew of idiots, one's only response to their systematic termination is one of relief. P.S. As a tribute to the mother of all monster movies – *Jaws* – there's even the old forward-zoom-reverse tracking shot (the 'oh my God' shot), now the most over-used cliché in the book.

Jennifer Lopez (*Terri Flores*), Ice Cube (*Danny Rich*), Jon Voight (*Paul Sarone*), Eric Stoltz (*Dr Steven Cale*), Jonathan Hyde (*Warren Westridge*), Owen Wilson (*Gary Dixon*), Kari Wuhrer (*Denise Kalberg*), Vincent Castellanos (*Mateo*), Danny Trejo (*poacher*).

Dir: Luis Llosa. Pro: Verna Harrah, Leonard Rabinowitz and Carole Little. Ex Pro: Susan Ruskin. Screenplay: Hans Bauer and Jim Cash & Jack Epps Jr. Ph: Bill Butler. Pro Des: Kirk M. Petruccelli. Ed: Michael R. Miller. M: Randy Edelman; Verdi. Costumes: Roberto Carneioro.

Serpent's kiss: The eponymous Anaconda gives Jon Voight something to think about in Luis Llosa's terrible thriller (from Columbia TriStar)

Visual effects: John Nelson. Animatronic effects: Walt Conti. Herpetologist: Steve Seccor. (Columbia/CL Cinema Line Films–Columbia TriStar.) Rel: 9 May 1997. 90 mins. Cert 15. USA. 1997.

Anna Karenina

Moscow/St Petersburg/Italy; 1880-1883. When the writer Constantine Levin comes to Moscow to propose to Kitty Scherbatsky, he is rejected in favour of the dashing Count Vronsky. But Vronsky himself is quickly distracted by the physical allures of Anna Karenina, the wife of

Grief encounter: Sophie Marceau threatens her station in life in Bernard Rose's unwieldy Anna Karenina *(from Warner)*

Georg Solti. Costumes: Maurizio Millenotti. (Icon/Warner–Warner.) Rel: 23 May 1997. 108 mins. Cert 15. USA. 1997.

Antonia's Line - Antonia

Rural Holland; 1945-1995. Returning to the village of her youth with her teenage daughter, Antonia quickly notes that nothing has changed before or since the Second World War. The same old eccentric characters follow their idiosyncratic ways; the same prejudices and small-minded attitudes prevail. Notwithstanding, Antonia continues with her life, tending to her growing family of direct offspring and adopted misfits to the best of her ability. Brimming with heart and wry humour, *Antonia's Line* is the lyrical, touching tale of the difference one woman in a community can make by standing up for her rights. Unfolded in bold, unhurried strokes, the film gathers a timeless charm as it builds its anecdotal tapestry, spiked with quirky detail and succinct insight. Yet in spite of its narrative complexity and ambitious time span (nearly 50 years), the film is a model of simplicity in its storytelling. FYI: The winner of the Oscar for best foreign language film, *Antonia's Line* is the first full-length feature directed

a well-connected, if detached, government minister. Thanks to his persistence and handsome jaw, Vronsky's overtures pay off and Anna risks everything – husband, son and inheritance – for a bit of slap and tickle. Meanwhile, Constantine continues to yearn for the hand of the straightforward Kitty and takes up scything... By attempting to incorporate the parallel love story of Constantine and Kitty, writer-director Bernard Rose has taken on more than he can agreeably process in 108 minutes. Edited together as if in a hurry to get to the action, the film does, periodically, throw up some splendid moments – only to be abruptly brushed aside by the story. Ultimately, however, the clash of French, English, Canadian and American accents and some stock Russian clichés – a steam train chugging across a snowy landscape, *Swan Lake* at the ballet – render this sub-mediocre.

Sophie Marceau (*Anna Karenina*), Sean Bean (*Count Vronsky*), Alfred Molina (*Constantine Dmitrich Levin*), Mia Kirshner (*Princess Ekaterina 'Kitty' Scherbatsky*), James Fox (*Alexei Alexandrovich Karenin*),

Fiona Shaw (*Lydia Ivanova*), Phyllida Law (*Countess Vronskaya*), Danny Huston (*Prince 'Stiva' Oblonsky*), Saskia Wickham (*Dolly*), David Schofield (*Nikolai*), Kseniya Rappaport, Anna Calder-Marshall, Justine Waddell, Jennifer Hall, Stefan Gryff, Anthony Calf, Niall Buggy, Vernon Dobtcheff.

Dir and Screenplay: Bernard Rose, based on the novel by Leo Tolstoy. Pro: Bruce Davey. Ex Pro: Stephen McEveety. Ph: Daryn Okada. Pro Des: John Myhre. Ed: Victor Du Bois. M: Tchaikovsky, Rachmaninov, Prokofiev, etc. M Director:

Dutch courage: Willeke van Ammelrooy and Jan Decleir in Marleen Gorris's lyrical, touching Antonia's Line *(from Guild)*

by a woman to receive a best picture Academy Award.

Willeke van Ammelrooy (*Antonia*), Els Dottermans (*Danielle*), Jan Decleir (*Bas*), Marina de Graaf (*Deedee*), Mil Seghers (*Crooked Finger*), Veerle van Overloop (*Therese*), Elsie de Brauw (*Lara*), Thyrza Ravesteijn (*Sarah*), Jan Steen (*Loony Lips*), Fran Waller Zeper (*Olga*), Wimie Wilhelm (*Letta*), Filip Peeters (*Pitte*), Dora van der Groen, Esther Vriesendorp, Carolien Spoor.
  Dir and Screenplay: Marleen Gorris. Pro: Hans de Weers. Co-Pro: Antonino Lombardo and Judy Counihan. Ph: Willy Stassen. Pro Des: Harry Ammerlaan. Ed: Michiel Reichwein and Wim Louwrier. M: Ilona Sekacz. Costumes: Jany Temime. (Bergen, Prime Time, Bard Entertainments/NPS Televisie/European Co-Production Fund–Guild.) Rel: 20 September 1996. 102 mins. Cert 15. Netherlands/Belgium/UK. 1995.

Les Apprentis

Antoine, a divorcee and dilatory playwright, finds himself forced to share a Paris apartment with Fred, a young man with a talent for doing nothing and stealing groceries. Over the years, as fate deals the two men increasingly hard blows, Fred and Antoine become inseparable – in spite of their remarkable differences. Although very funny in parts, *Les Apprentis* will prove a disappointment for those acquainted with Salvadori's last film, *Wild Target*. Even *Wild Target* ran out of steam near the end, but it did have the estimable Jean Rochefort distinguishing every scene. Here, Francois Cluzet and Guillaume Depardieu are not funny enough in their own right to salvage the material, although there are a number of priceless moments, some hilarious, others quite touching. But a series of skits is no excuse for a movie.

Francois Cluzet (*Antoine*), Guillaume Depardieu (*Fred*), Judith Henry (*Sylvie*), Claire Laroche (*Agnes*), Philippe Girard (*Nicolas*), Bernard Yerles (*Patrick*), Jean-Pol Brissard (*editor of Karate magazine*), Marie Trintignant (*Lorette*), Jean-Michel Julliard, Maryvonne Schlitz, Claude Aufaure, Helene Roussel, Jean-Baptiste Marcenac, Elisabeth Kaza, Philippe Duclos.
  Dir and Screenplay: Pierre Salvadori, from a story by Salvadori and Philippe Harel. Pro: Philippe Martin. Co-Pro: Gerard Louvin. Art: Francois Emmanuelli. Ed: Helene Viard. M: Philippe Eidel;

Mozart. Costumes: Valerie Pozzo di Borgo. (Les Films Pelleas/Glem Film/La Sept Cinema/Canal Plus, etc.–Gala.) Rel: 19 July 1996. 98 mins. Cert 15. France. 1995.

Fools of fortune: Guillaume Depardieu and Francois Cluzet face the music in Pierre Salvadori's Les Apprentis *(from Gala)*

The Associate

When top financial analyst Laurel Ayres is passed over for promotion in favour of her callow male partner, she sets up her own business at home. However, because she's a woman – without a male associate – nobody will even read her prospectus. So she invents her own partner who, thanks to Laurel's sharp business sense, becomes the talk of Wall Street. But Laurel's imaginary prodigy is still taking all the credit, while she's left out in the cold... A fabulous idea, borrowing elements of *Trading Places* and *Tootsie*, is given a brisk, slick reading here, aided by a winning turn from Whoopi Goldberg. And although it's all fairly predictable and derivative, it's nice to find a comedy with something to say. Interestingly, while much is made of Whoopi's gender, there is no allusion to her colour.

Whoopi Goldberg (*Laurel Ayres/Robert S. Cutty*), Dianne Wiest (*Sally*), Tim Daly (*Frank*), Bebe Neuwirth (*Camille*), Eli Wallach (*Fallon*), Austin Pendleton (*Aesop Franklin*), Lainie Kazan (*Cindy Mason*), George Martin (*Walter Manchester*), Johnny Miller (*himself*), Kenny Kerr, Lee Wilkof, Helen Hanft, George Morfogen, Zeljko Ivanek, Miles Chapin, Jean De Baer, Louis Turenne, William Hill, Colleen Camp Wilson, Jerry Hardin, Allison Janney, Vincent Laresca, Katherine Wallach, Sally Jessy Raphael, Rex Robbins, Ira Wheeler, Donald Trump.
  Dir: Donald Petrie. Pro: Frederic Golchan, Patrick Markey and Adam Leipzig. Ex Pro: Ted Field, Scott Kroope, Robert W. Cort and David Madden. Co-Pro: Rene Gainville and Michael A. Helfant. Screenplay: Nick Thiel. Ph: Alex Nepomniaschy. Pro Des: Andrew Jackness. Ed: Bonnie Koehler. M: Christopher Tyng; Mozart; numbers performed by Louise Hoffsten, Sophie B. Hawkins, LaShanda Reese, The Commodores, Salt 'N' Pepa, Kate Pierson and Cindy Wilson, The Pointer Sisters, Free and Queen Latifah, Linda Jack-son, Frankie, Dusty Springfield, David Farnon, Wynonna Judd, etc. Costumes: April Ferry. Special make-up: Greg Cannom. (Hollywood Pictures/Interscope Communications/PolyGram– PolyGram.) Rel: 13 June 1997. 113 mins. Cert PG. USA. 1996.

August

Transposing the story of *Uncle Vanya* to Wales (circa 1890), director Anthony Hopkins has fashioned a workmanlike adaptation of Chekhov's play, but has failed to rework it in cinematic terms (in spite of a dramatic digression involving an accident in a mine). This is unfortunate as *August* follows so closely on the heels of Louis Malle's *Vanya on 42nd Street* and Michael Blakemore's recent, lively interpretation, *Country Life*. Strangely, in spite of its ambling pace (and gloating eye for picturesque detail), the film feels oddly truncated, as if an entire act was lost in the cutting room. Not, sadly, Hopkins' *Dances With Wolves*, but a dreary, small-scale exercise that lurches between theatrical stasis and grotesque farce. Incidentally, the actor wrote the music himself, although its placement seems entirely arbitrary. Filmed on location on the Lleyn Peninsula in North Wales.

Anthony Hopkins (*Ieuan*), Leslie Phillips (*Professor Blathwaite*), Kate Burton (*Helen*), Gawn Grainger (*Dr Lloyd*), Hugh Lloyd

But is it art? David Bowie as Andy Warhol models the latest in designer millinery, in Julian Schnabel's Basquiat *(from Guild)*

(*Prosser*), Rhoda Lewis (*Mair*), Menna Trussler (*Gwen*), Rhian Morgan (*Sian*), Huw Garmon, Rhys Ifans, Susan Flynn, Victoria Pugh, Dylan Thomas.

Dir and M: Anthony Hopkins. Pro: June Wyndham Davies and Pippa Cross. Ex Pro: Steve Morrison and Guy East. Line Pro: Craig McNeil. Co-Pro: Janette Day. Screenplay: Julian Mitchell. Ph: Robin Vidgeon. Pro Des: Eileen Diss. Ed: Edward Mansell. Costumes: Dany Everett. (Granada Films/Majestic Films/ Newcomm–Film Four.) Rel: 9 August 1996. 89 mins. Cert PG. UK. 1995.

Basquiat

New York; 1981-1988. Embraced as the first black artist of any significance in the Western world, Jean Michel Basquiat was variously described as the James Dean and/or Eddie Murphy of art. Befriended by Andy Warhol and courted by the establishment, Basquiat tumbled deeper and deeper into drug abuse and delusions of grandeur until his death from a heroin overdose at the age of 27. Marking the directorial debut of New York artist Julian Schnabel (and friend of the subject), *Basquiat* is an honest, striking portrait of a victim of his own success. Illuminated by an engaging turn from Jeffrey Wright in the title role (and shaded by an amusing one from David Bowie as Andy Warhol), the

film at least reveals the attraction of the man (unlike *Surviving Picasso*) if not the process of his art.

David Bowie (*Andy Warhol*), Dennis Hopper (*Bruno Bischofberger*), Gary Oldman (*Albert Milo*), Jeffrey Wright (*Jean Michel Basquiat*), Benicio Del Toro (*Benny Dalmau*), Claire Forlani (*Gina Cardinale*), Michael Wincott (*Rene Ricard*), Parker Posey (*Mary Boone*), Elina Lowensohn (*Annina Nosei*), Courtney Love (*Big Pink*), Rockets Redglare (*Rockets*), Michael Chow (*himself*), Christopher Walken, Jean Claude Le Marre, Paul Bartel (*Henry Geldzahler*), Tatum O'Neal, Chuck Pfeifer, Esther G. Schnabel, Jack Schnabel, Lola Schnabel, Olatz Maria Schnabel, Stella Schnabel, Michael Badalucco, Vincent Laresca, Frederick Weller, Sam Rockwell.

Dir and Screenplay: Julian Schnabel, based on a story by Lech Majewski, developed by Michael Thomas Holman. Pro: Jon Kilik, Randy Ostrow and Joni Sighvatsson. Ex Pro: Peter Brant, Joseph Allen and Michiyo Yoshizaki. Ph: Ron Fortunato. Pro Des: Dan Leigh. Ed: Michael Berenbaum. M: John Cale; Verdi; numbers performed by The Pogues, The Modern Lovers, The Toadies, Iggy Pop, The Rolling Stones, Charlie Parker, Peggy Lee, Tom Waits, John Cale, Gavin Friday, Public Image Ltd, Nicholas Marion Taylor, Keith Richards, Electro Band, Van Morrison and Them, Miles Davis, Grandmaster Flash, Melle Mel, Psychedelic Furs, David Bowie, etc. Costumes: John Dunn. (Eleventh Street Prods/Miramax International–Guild.) Rel: 28 March 1997. 107 mins. Cert 15. USA. 1996.

Batman and Robin

Following both the death of his wife and an industrial accident necessitating the adoption of a bizarre deep-frozen suit of armour, molecular biologist Dr Victor Fries turns his anger and frustration on Gotham City. Attracted by his power, the poisonous flower child Poison Ivy sees this as a chance to rid the world of its human population and make way for a greener planet. Meanwhile, Batman is faced with problems at home when his loyal manservant, Alfred, contracts a fatal illness and the latter's niece drops in to play... Lacking the talent of Jack Nicholson, the sex appeal of Michelle

The ultimate cold shoulder: Mr Freeze (Arnold Schwarzenegger) gives his best icy stare in Joel Schumacher's underwhelming Batman and Robin *(from Warner)*

And mighty with the pen: Fabrice Luchini parries Jacques Weber in Edouard Molinaro's full-bodied Beaumarchais *(from Artificial Eye)*

Pfeiffer or the comic genius of Jim Carrey, Arnold Schwarzenegger weighs in as the most expensive ($20-25m) but least satisfying of all the Dark Night's adversaries, coming off as nothing more exciting than a Neanderthal icicle. And, in spite of an embarrassment of fantastical baddies, this fourth instalment in Warner's lucrative franchise is the weakest on villainy. Having beaten out both Demi Moore and Julia Roberts to the role of the venomous Poison Ivy, Uma Thurman lacks the sheer sex appeal and edge that the part demands and no end of Mae West put-downs can make a difference. In fact, it is George Clooney as The Caped Crusader who actually brings a modicum of charismatic dignity to the proceedings – but even he cannot overcome the sheer depression of continuous noise, empty effects and bad dialogue (Arnie: 'Allow me to break the ice'). In short, the film is so far removed from reality that it produces almost a narcoleptic effect, in which the audience is bludgeoned into a trance by an excess of garish, flashing images.

Arnold Schwarzenegger (*Mr Freeze/Dr Victor Fries*), George Clooney (*Batman/Bruce Wayne*), Chris O'Donnell (*Robin/Dick Grayson*), Uma Thurman (*Poison Ivy/Dr Pamela Isley*), Alicia Silverstone (*Batgirl/Barbara Wilson*), Michael Gough (*Alfred Pennyworth*), Pat Hingle (*Commissioner Gordon*), Elle Macpherson (*Julie Madison*), John Glover (*Dr Jason Woodrue*), Vivica A. Fox (*Ms B. Haven*), Vendela K. Thommessen (*Nora Fries*), Elizabeth Sanders, John Fink, Eric Lloyd, Joe Sabatino, Michael Paul Chan, Kimberly Scott, Senator Patrick Leahy, Jesse Ventura, Coolio, Nicky Katt.

Dir: Joel Schumacher. Pro: Peter MacGregor-Scott. Ex Pro: Benjamin Melniker and Michael E. Uslan. Co-Pro: William M. Elvin. Screenplay: Akiva Goldsman. Ph: Stephen Goldblatt. Pro Des: Barbara Ling. Ed: Dennis Virkler. M: Elliot Goldenthal; numbers performed by The Smashing Pumpkins, R. Kelly, Goo Goo Dolls, Moloko, and Underworld. Costumes: Ingrid Ferrin and Robert Turturice. Sound: Lance Brown. Visual effects: John Dykstra. Second unit director: Peter Macdonald. Mr Schwarzenegger's drama coach: Walter Von Huene. Principal Copsicals: Rick Baker. (Warner–Warner.) Rel: 27 June 1997. 130 mins. Cert PG. USA. 1997.

Beaumarchais - Beaumarchais l'Insolent

1773-1784; France/England. A watchmaker, inventor, teacher of the harp, stage director, judge, arms dealer, womaniser, adulterer, speculator, habitual convict, suspected murderer, defender of the poor and above all a masterful playwright, Pierre-Augustin Caron de Beaumarchais was seldom to be recalled in the same breath as Moliere or Voltaire because, in the words of one observer, 'He preferred his life to his work.' Constantly at odds with the nobility that variously condemned and championed him, Beaumarchais survived by his wits and his wit, turning out wicked theatrical assaults on the aristocracy (*The Barber of Seville*, *The Marriage of Figaro*) cloaked in broad humour and allegory. In the tradition of *Cyrano de Bergerac* and *La Reine Margot*, *Beaumarchais* competes for our attention with spectacular architecture, opulent costumes and lavish production design. Fabrice Luchini (who played the eminent lawyer Derville in *Le Colonel Chabert*) makes a wily and hypnotic Beaumarchais, distilling the colourful irony surrounding the 'scoundrel's life. And a starry cast and sumptuous score from Jean-Claude Petit (*Jean de Florette*) bring considerable flavour to a rewarding and full-bodied entertainment.

Fabrice Luchini (*Pierre-Augustin Caron de Beaumarchais*), Manuel Blanc (*Gudin*),

Sandrine Kiberlain (*Marie-Therese*), Jacques Weber (*Duc de Chaulnes*), Michel Piccoli (*Prince de Conti*), Claire Nebout (*Chevalier d'Eon*), Jean-Francois Balmer (*Sartine*), Florence Thomassin (*Marion Menard*), Michel Serrault (*Louis XV*), Dominique Besnehard (*Louis XVI*), Murray Head (*Lord Rochford*), Jeff Nuttall (*Benjamin Franklin*), Jean Yanne (*Louis Goezman*), Dominic Gould (*Arthur Lee*), Judith Godreche (*Marie-Antoinette*), Axelle Laffont, Maka Kotto, Jean-Claude Brialy, Patrick Bouchitey, Jay Benedict, Michel Aumont, Evelyne Bouix, Jose Garcia, Roger Brierley, Richard Durden, Guy Marchand, Alain Chabat.

Dir: Edouard Molinaro. Pro: Charles Gassot. Ex Pro: Dominque Brunner. Screenplay: Molinaro and Jean-Claude Brisville, freely adapted from the play by Sacha Guitry. Ph: Michel Epp. Pro Des: Jean-Marc Kerdelhue. Ed: Veronique Parnet. M: Jean-Claude Petit. Costumes: Sylvie de Segonzac. (Telema/France 2 Cinema/Canal Plus/France 3 Cinema–Artificial Eye.) Rel: 6 September 1996. 100 mins. Cert 15. France. 1996.

Beautiful Girls

In spite of the title, this is an ensemble dramatic comedy about a group of everyday guys getting their romantic act together. Victims of the twentieth-century precept that girls should be beautiful, well endowed and taut bunned, the lads of Knight's Ridge, Massachusetts, struggle to appreciate the love they already have in their lives – besides each other... Some strategically placed rock numbers, a few choice movie references ('Did you see *Misery*? You look just like Kathy Bates') and a roster of trendy actors cannot compensate for a lack of real wit or insight. A bunch of stock characters are wheeled out for us to chuckle over (such as Michael Rapaport's habitual knucklehead) but then, you know, guys are just guys. A lot of camaraderie goes a long way, man, but if these good ol' boys hugged one more time...

Matt Dillon (*Tommy 'Birdman' Rowland*), Noah Emmerich (*Michael 'Mo' Morris*), Annabeth Gish (*Tracy Stover*), Lauren Holly (*Darian Smalls*), Timothy Hutton (*Willie Conway*), Rosie O'Donnell (*Gina Barrisano*), Max Perlich (*Kev*), Martha Plimpton (*Jan*), Natalie Portman (*Marty*), Michael Rapaport (*Paul Kirkwood*), Mira Sorvino (*Sharon Cassidy*), Uma Thurman (*Andera*), Pruitt Taylor Vince (*Stanley 'Stinky' Womack*), Anne Bobby (*Sarah Morris*), Richard Bright (*Dick Conway*),

David Arquette (*Bobby Conway*), Sam Robards, Adam Le Fevre, Tom Gibis.

Dir: Ted Demme. Pro: Cary Woods. Ex Pro: Bob Weinstein, Harvey Weinstein and Cathy Konrad. Screenplay and Assoc Pro: Scott Rosenberg. Ph: Adam Kimmel. Pro Des: Dan Davis. Ed: Jeffrey Wolf. M: David A. Stewart; numbers performed by The Afghan Whigs, Pete Droge, Greg Kihn Band, Split Enz, Billy Preston, Chris Isaak, A Flock of Seagulls, Ween, The Diamonds, Jethro Tull, The Rolling Stones, Billy Paul, The Spinners, Morphine, Roland Gift, KISS, Neil Diamond, etc. Costumes: Lucy W. Corrigan. (Miramax/Woods Entertainment–Buena Vista.) Rel: 29 November 1996. 113 mins. Cert 15. USA. 1996.

Beavis and Butt-Head Do America

Two moronic teenagers obsessed by chicks and music videos go searching for their stolen TV set and end up in Las Vegas. There, they board a tour bus and get up to no end of trouble, while pursued by a redneck thug, a female arms dealer and the ATF... Basically a series of dumb misunderstandings in which our heroes believe they are finally going to 'score', Beavis and Butt-Head don't so much get to 'do' America as 'do it over' – destroying the Hoover Dam, causing a horrific motorway pile-up and inciting the wrath of Chelsea Clinton. The first full-length cartoon featuring Mike Judge's braindead, irreverent geeks showcased on MTV,

'Let me read your inner reality, babe': Peter Weller beds down with Fanny Ardant in Michelangelo Antonioni's enigmatic and inconclusive Beyond the Clouds *(from Artificial Eye)*

B&B Do America is neither daring enough nor funny enough. Anarchy is fine, but anarchy without a burp of wit is entirely tiresome. B&B fans may enjoy seeing their culturally challenged icons on the large screen, but this inane satire is not going to win over any converts.

Voices: Mike Judge (*Beavis/Butt-Head/Tom Anderson/Van Driessen/Principal McVicker*), Robert Stack (*Agent Flemming*), Cloris Leachman (*old woman on the plane and bus*), Jacqueline Barba, Pamela Blair, Eric Bogosian, Kristofor Brown, Tim Guinee, Toby Huss, Sam Johnson, Richard Linklater, Gail Thomas, and (*uncredited*) Bruce Willis (*Muddy*), Demi Moore (*Dallas*).

Dir: Mike Judge. Pro: Abby Terkuhle. Ex Pro: David Gale and Van Toffler. Line Pro: Winnie Chaffee. Screenplay: Judge and Joe Stillman. Animation Dir: Yvette Kaplan. M: John Frizzell; 'Two Cool Guys' performed by Isaac Hayes, 'Lesbian Seagull' performed by Engelbert Humperdinck, other numbers performed by Southern Culture On The Skids, No Doubt, Madd Head, Red Hot Chilli Peppers, AC/DC, White Zombie, Ozzy Osbourne, Butthole Surfers, LL Cool J, etc. (Paramount/Geffen Pictures/MTV–UIP.) Rel: 23 May 1997. 81 mins. Cert 12. USA. 1996.

Beyond the Clouds - Par Dela les Nuages

Ferrara, Italy/Portofino, Italy/Paris, France/Aix-en-Provence, France; today. A handsome drainage pump technician, turning to the beautiful young woman he barely knows, observes, 'There's always something left behind.' In reply, the woman

Food for thought: Stanley Tucci and Tony Shalhoub in Tucci and Campbell Scott's delicious Big Night *(from Electric)*

offers: 'Like dregs in a coffee cup.' In his first film for 13 years, the 83-year-old Michelangelo Antonioni rummages through the dregs of human alienation and attempts to spotlight the 'real' beneath the layers of 'public relationed' emotions we have affected for an expedient life. Aided by the guiding hand of fellow mystic Wim Wenders, Antonioni brings to light four stories from his book *That Bowling Alley On the Tiber*, all hinged on the encounter of strangers and of the emotional consequences. Inconclusive and enigmatic, the stories themselves shed little light on Antonioni's dilemma, a predicament he summarises with the observation, 'I always distrust what I see. As we go deeper, we probably arrive at the true reality of things.' Be that as it may, *Beyond the Clouds* is, if anything, most visually arresting, the female characters in particular being very physically alluring. Antonioni may be digging beneath the emotional surface, but he offers a very beguiling exterior one. More satisfactory is Wenders' linking narrative, in which John Malkovich, as the alter ego of

Antonioni, ruminates on the whole conundrum of 'reality' with lucid and fascinating insight.

John Malkovich (*the director*), Kim Rossi-Stuart (*Silvano*), Ines Sastre (*Carmen*), Sophie Marceau (*the young woman*), Chiara Caselli (*Olga*), Peter Weller (*Roberto*), Fanny Ardant (*Patrizia*), Jean Reno (*Carlo*), Jeanne Morreau (*woman*), Marcello Mastroianni (*maestro*), Irene Jacob (*young woman*), Vincent Perez (*Niccolo*), Enrica Antonioni, Veronica Lazar.
    Dir: Michelangelo Antonioni. Pro: Philippe Carcassone and Stephane Tchal Gadjieff. Ex Pro: Danielle Gegauff-Rosencranz, Brigitte Faure and Pierre Roitfeld. Co-Pro: Vittorio Cecchi Gori and Ulrich Felsberg. Assoc Pro: Felice Laudadio. Screenplay: Antonioni, Tonino Guerra and Wim Wenders. Ph: Alfio Contini. Pro Des: Thierry Flamand. Ed: Antonioni and Claudio Maro. M: Lucio Dalla, Laurent Petitgand and Van Morrison. Costumes: Esther Walz. Prologue, Interludes and Epilogue: Dir: Wim Wenders. Ph: Robby Muller. Ed: Peter Przygodda and Luciano Segura. (Sunshine/Cine B/France 3 Cinema/Road Movies Zweite/Canal Plus, etc.–Artificial Eye.) Rel: 10 January 1997. 109 mins. Cert 18. France/Italy/Germany. 1995.

Big Night

New Jersey; the late 1950s. The brothers Primo and Secondo Pilaggi, respectively a chef and manager, are Italian immigrants who have just opened a new restaurant, The Paradise. Unfortunately, Primo's

dedication to crafting authentic culinary masterpieces is not appreciated by an American public that prefers the spaghetti, meatballs and red chequered tablecloths of Pascal's, a more vulgar and expensive establishment across the street. However, in a surprising show of magnanimity, Pascal's owner volunteers to invite his old friend Louis Prima, the jazz legend, to The Paradise in order to attract some publicity. Sinking what they have left of their savings, hopes and dreams into one Big Night, Primo and Secondo prepare for the ultimate banquet... Marking the directorial debut of the actors Stanley Tucci and Campbell Scott, *Big Night* is an affectionate, touching and remarkably assured enterprise that has the maturity never to sell itself to its audience. From the low-key opening to the subdued, mesmerising finale, the film is a celebration of food, family and the pursuit of excellence. In short, this is a superbly underplayed, gentle entertainment, distinguished by beautifully nuanced performances and an evocative guitar-driven score.

Minnie Driver (*Phyllis*), Ian Holm (*Pascal*), Isabella Rossellini (*Gabriella*), Tony Shalhoub (*Primo Pilaggi*), Stanley Tucci (*Secondo Pilaggi*), Campbell Scott (*Bob*), Marc Anthony (*Cristiano*), Pasquale Cajano (*Alberto*), Allison Janney (*Ann*), Larry Block, Caroline Aaron, Andrei Belgrader, Peter McRobbie, Liev Schreiber, Christine Tucci, Gene Canfield, Tina Bruno, Peter Appel, Robert W. Castle.
    Dir: Campbell Scott and Stanley Tucci. Pro: Jonathan Filley. Ex Pro: Keith Samples and David Kirkpatrick. Co-Pro: Elizabeth W. Alexander, Peter Liguori and Oliver Platt. Screenplay: Tucci and Joseph Tropiano (Tucci's cousin). Ph: Ken Kelsch. Pro Des: Andrew Jackness. Ed: Suzy Elmiger. M: Gary DeMichele; numbers performed by Claudio Villa, Louis Prima, Rosemary Clooney, Keely Smith, etc. Costumes: Juliet A. Polcsa. (Rysher Entertainment/Timpano–Electric.) Rel: 30 May 1997. 109 mins. Cert 15. USA. 1995.

Bits and Pieces - Il Cielo e Sempre Piu Blu

Rome; today. A 17-year-old girl tells her 35-year-old cousin of her numerous sexual encounters; a Chinese restaurant is robbed at gunpoint, prompting one patron to die from a heart attack; an attractive traffic warden gleefully enters into the spirit of her job, distributing tickets with merciless abandon; a girl badgers her postman, complaining that she hasn't even received junk mail or a bill... A mosaic of interlinked stories of varying degrees of interest and consequence, *Bits and Pieces* is as much a vivid portrait of Rome and its denizens as it is a self-indulgent exercise in neo-realism. Lacking the thrust and cohesion of Robert Altman's comparable *Short Cuts*, the film attempts to tie together 30 vignettes featuring 65 characters but has the irritating habit of cutting from the chase, leaving stories abandoned halfway through. The effect is rather like tucking into a plate of spaghetti only to find that you've been shortchanged by a cup of minced noodles.

Asia Argento, Monica Bellucci, Margherita Buy, Enrico Lo Verso, Dario Argento, Daniele Luchetti, Ivano Marescotti, Federica Mastroianni, Francesca Neri, Jose Luis Puertas, Sergio Rubini, Gabriele Salvatores, Gianmarco Tognazzi, Leonardo Treviglio, Massimo Wertmuller, Massimiliano Aiello, Francesca Buy, Federica Rosellini, Giovanni Rosellini, etc.

Dir: Antonello Grimaldi. Pro: Domenico Procacci and Maurizio Totti. Line Pro: Gianluca Arcopinto. Screenplay: Daniele Cesarano and Paolo Marchesini. Ph: Alessandro Pesci. Pro Des: Giada Calabria. Ed: Angelo Nicolini. M: Enzo Favata and Jana Project. Costumes: Maria Camilla Righi, Alessandra Covelli and Antonella Amato. (Fandango/Colorado Film–Electric.) Rel: 11 April 1997. 109 mins. Cert 15. Italy. 1995.

Blood and Wine

Miami/the Florida Keys; the present. On the outside, Alex Gates would appear to lead an enviable life: a respectable figure in the community, he runs an up-market wine business, drives a red BMW convertible and entertains a sexy Latin mistress. Yet his second marriage is putrid to the core, his relationship with his stepson painfully strained and his finances all but shot. Then he conceives what should be the model solution: the perfectly straight-forward theft of a $1 million diamond necklace. But Alex hadn't bargained on the intervention of his wife... A dark, moody thriller that inhabits its own distinctive space with authority, *Blood and Wine* marks

Thicker than water: Jack Nicholson fools around with Jennifer Lopez in Bob Rafelson's moody and menacing Blood and Wine *(from Fox)*

the fifth collaboration between Bob Rafelson and Jack Nicholson as director and star. Beautifully nuanced and layered, the film displays yet again Rafelson's mastery at setting up a situation, with Nicholson perfectly credible as the cornered fox.

Jack Nicholson (*Alex Gates*), Stephen Dorff (*Jason*), Jennifer Lopez (*Gabriella*), Judy Davis (*Suzanne Gates*), Michael Caine (*Victor Spansky*), Harold Perrineau Jr (*Henry*), Robyn Peterson, Mike Starr, John Seitz, Mark Macaulay, Dan Daily.

Dir: Bob Rafelson. Pro: Jeremy Thomas. Ex Pro: Chris Auty and Bernie Williams. Screenplay: Nick Villiers and Alison Cross, from a story by Villiers and Rafelson. Ph: Newton Thomas Sigel. Pro Des: Richard Sylbert. Ed: Steven Cohen. M: Michal Lorenc; numbers performed by Celia Cruz, Grupo Niche, Victoria Shaw, etc. Costumes: Lindy Hemming. Sound: Leslie Shatz. Animatronic shark: Jim Henson's Creature Shop. (Blood and Wine/Marmont Prods/Recorded Picture Company/Majestic Films–Fox.) Rel: 7 March 1997. 100 mins. Cert 15. USA/UK. 1996.

Happy, shiny people: Michel Serrault, Sabine Azema and Francois Morel ponder the future in Etienne Chatiliez's captivating Le Bonheur *(from Guild)*

Le Bonheur... - Le Bonheur est dans le pre

Dole/Condom; France; today. Francis Bergeaud is at the end of his tether. The employees of his loo seat factory are on strike, the auditors are rifling through his accounts, his daughter is planning a wedding that he cannot afford and his spoilt wife has become intolerable. Just then, he is mistaken for the long-lost husband of a handsome Spanish woman (with two comely daughters) who runs a foie gras farm in the South of France... It's rare these days to find a film brimming with so much unapologetic bon homie, let alone one that flaunts such an unfashionable title (*The Happiness*, in English). Some may frown on the director's resolute refusal to introduce a note of cynicism, but this is feel-good fantasy that never pretends to be anything else. Michel Serrault is quite delightful as the testy victim of his own inadequacies, although it is Eddy Mitchell – as Francis's bruisingly forthright friend – who steals our affections. In short, it is a film like this that empowers one for real life – armed with a spring in one's step.

Michel Serrault (*Francis Bergeaud*), Eddy Mitchell (*Gerard Lesueur*), Sabine Azema (*Nicole Bergeaud*), Carmen Maura (*Delores Thivart*), Francois Morel (*Pouillaud*), Guilaine Londez ('*Zig*' *Thivart*), Virginie Darmon ('*Flea*' *Thivart*), Alexandra London (*Geraldine Bergeaud*), Christophe Kourotchkine (*Remi*), Jean Bousquet, Eric Cantona (*Lionel*), Joel Cantona (*Nono*), Catherine Jacob, Daniel Russo, Roger Gicquel, Patrick Bouchitey, Yolande Moreau, Seloua Hamse (*Yasmina*).

Dir: Etienne Chatiliez. Pro: Charles Gassot. Screenplay: Florence Quentin. Ph: Philippe Welt. Pro Des: Stephane Makedonsky. Ed: Anne Faure-Lafarge. M: Pascal Andreacchio. Costumes: Edith Vesperini. (Telema/Studio Canal Plus/France 3 Cinema/France 2, etc.–Guild.) Rel: 29 November 1996. 106 mins. Cert 15. France. 1995.

Boston Kickout

Following the suicide of his mother, Phil moves to Stevenage with his father to make a fresh start in a new town. Nine years later, aged 17, Phil is awaiting his exam results and contemplating his future when a rush of events conspire to shake him up for manhood... Any film set in Stevenage deserves some kind of credit, if only for its uniqueness. Semi-autobiographical and fiercely unsentimental, *Boston Kickout* reflects the upbringing of its young writer-director who had to fight the physical and metaphorical walls of concrete that suffocated him. The traditional ingredients of kitchen sink drama – drugs, pubs, sex, unemployment, alcoholism, violence and profanity – are given a fresh and honest reappraisal in a film that confronts its questions without resorting to melodrama or tidy solutions. Only the centre section, with its introduction of a romantic distraction, slows the narrative down and fails to ring entirely true. P.S. A 'Boston kickout' refers to the local practise of rampaging through back gardens and creating as much damage as possible.

John Simm (*Phil*), Emer McCourt (*Shona Murphy*), Marc Warren (*Robert*), Andrew Lincoln (*Ted*), Richard Hanson (*Steven*), Nathan Valente (*Matthew*), Derek Martin (*Ray*), Vincent Phillips (*Brad*), Natalie Davies (*Sue*), David Aldous, Sally Grace,

Concrete catharsis: Marc Warren doles out the hate in Paul Hills' fresh and honest Boston Kickout *(from First Independent)*

Julie Smith, Jeanette Driver, Suzanne Church, Anne Francoeur, Mary Healy.

Dir: Paul Hills. Pro: Hills and Tedi De Toledo. Ex Pro: Paul Trijbits and Danny Cannon. Line Pro: Michael Riley. Screenplay: Hills, Diane Whitley and Roberto Troni. Ph: Roger Bonnici. Pro Des: Simon Elliott. Ed: Melanie Adams. M: Robert Hartshorne; Vivaldi; numbers performed by Whiteout, Samantha Fox, Joy Division, Romeo's Daughter, The Velvet Underground, The Stone Roses, The Damned, Primal Scream, Oasis, etc. (Amaranth Film Partners/Trijbits & Worrell/Boston Films–First Independent.) Rel: 18 October 1996. 105 mins. Cert 18. UK. 1995.

Bound

Chicago; today. A prostitute, a lesbian and $2,176,000 in laundered 100 dollar bills. Or, to put it another way, a gangster's moll, an ex-con and a $2,176,000 ticket to a new life. Violet and Corky are as different as Tanqueray and Tennent's Extra, but they know what they want: and that doesn't include a man. However, Violet's guy, a Mafia agent, has acquired a large quantity of cash and the Mob are arriving to pick it up. Corky, a fix-it kinda girl, proposes the perfect plan. But will the participants stick to Corky's rules? Once one has got over the shock of seeing a breathy, sultry Jennifer Tilly seduce the sinewy, grease-stained Gina Gershon, this self-conscious thriller certainly hits its stride. The

Man trap: Gina Gershon holds her own in the Wachowski Brothers' toe-scrunching Bound *(from Guild)*

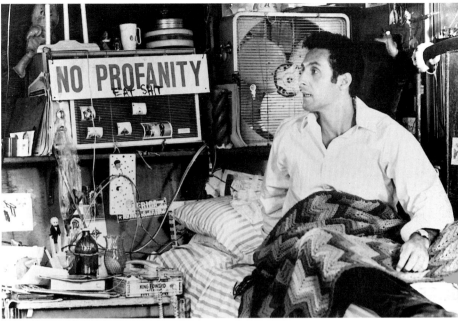

Catching the unobtainable: John Turturro in Tom DiCillo's self-consciously eccentric Box of Moonlight *(from First Independent)*

melodramatic music, slow motion and overhead shots aside, *Bound* is bound to attract a cult audience hungry for genuine toe-scrunching suspense and showy set pieces. Have the Coen brothers met their match?

Jennifer Tilly (*Violet*), Gina Gershon (*Corky*), Joe Pantoliano (*Caesar*), John P. Ryan (*Mickey Malnato*), Christopher Meloni (*Johnnie Marconi*), Richard C. Sarafian (*Gino Marzzone*), Barry Kivel (*Shelly*), Mary Mara, Susie Bright, Ivan Kane, Kevin M. Richardson, Gene Borkan.

Dir and Screenplay: Larry and Andy Wachowski. Pro: Andrew Lazar and Stuart Boros. Co-Pro: Jeffrey Sudzin. Ph: Bill Pope. Pro Des: Eve Cauley. Ed: Zach Staenberg. M: Don Davis; numbers performed by Aretha Franklin, The Hail Marys, Ray Charles, and Tom Jones. Costumes: Lizzy Gardiner. Sound: Dane Davis. (Dino De Laurentiis/Summit Entertainment/Newmarket Capital–Guild.) Rel: 28 February 1997. 109 mins. Cert 18. USA. 1996.

Box of Moonlight

In Tennessee to supervise the construction of a new windshield wiper factory, an anally retentive electrical engineer notices his first grey hair. In a subliminal endeavour to check the march of time, he starts hallucinating episodes backwards and takes off on a spontaneous cross-country drive to find himself. 'After all,' he reasons, 'it's not where you're going that counts, it's how you get there.' Or is it the other way round? A comic fable about an automaton stumbling across the magic of life, *Box of Moonlight* guides its message in a weird and wonderful way. In fact, it's the incidental detail – a God-fearing well-wisher toying with an axe, an aged receptionist reminiscing about the time he drowned a rat, an armchair burning by the side of the road – that truly enriches this incredible journey. Unfortunately, the protagonists themselves are so resolutely oddball that the collision of eccentricities does get a bit much. Besides, you can't nonplus the nonplussed.

John Turturro (*Al Fountain*), Sam Rockwell (*Bucky, 'Kid'*), Catherine Keener (*Floatie Dupre*), Lisa Blount (*Purlene Dupre*), Annie Corley (*Deborah Fountain*), Alexander Goodwin (*Bobby Fountain*), Dermot Mulroney (*Wick*), Mike Stanley (*Doob*), Rica Martens (*Doris*), Ray Aranha, Robert Wightman, James Richardson, Stephen Dupree.

Dir and Screenplay: Tom DiCillo. Pro: Marcus Viscidi and Thomas A. Bliss. Ex Pro: Michael Mendelsohn, Tom Rosenberg, Sigurjon Sighvatsson and Steven Sherman. Co-Pro: Meredith Zamsky and Taylor MacCrae. Ph: Paul Ryan. Pro Des: Therese DePrez. Ed: Camilla Toniolo. M: Jim Farmer; numbers performed by The Chantays, The Champs, Wall of Voodoo, Nick Cave and The Bad Seeds, The Chrome Cranks, T 'Smallbore' DiCillo, Elmore James, etc. Costumes:

No music to their ears: Stephen Tompkinson and Ewan McGregor drown their sorrows in Mark Herman's touching, beguiling Brassed Off *(from Film Four)*

Ellen Lutter. (Lakeshore Entertainment/ Large Entertainment/JVC Entertainment/ Lemon Sky–First Independent.) Rel: 18 April 1997. 112 mins. Cert 15. USA. 1996.

The Boy From Mercury

1960; Dublin. It is five years since his father died and eight-year-old Harry Cronin is finding it hard to adjust to reality. His only brother, Paul, has drifted on to girls and rock 'n' roll, which just leaves the highlight of the week: the Saturday morning trip to the picture house. There, Harry's imagination is fuelled by the exploits of Flash Gordon, leading to a serious identity disorder... Still enthralled by the idea that, as an eight-year-old boy, he believed that he was an alien from Mercury, first-time writer-director Martin Duffy has fashioned a somewhat static autobiographical fable earnestly in need of a story. Punctuated by endless clips from bad *Flash Gordon* movies, the film aims for charm but is undermined by uneven performances, particularly from the dog. Still, an ebullient score and some nice turns from Tom Courteney (as Harry's dotty uncle) and Sean O'Flanagain (as Harry's friend) shake up the monotony.

Hugh O'Conor (*Paul Cronin*), Tom Courteney (*Uncle Tony Cronin*), Rita Tushingham (*May Cronin*), James Hickey (*Harry Cronin*), Sean O'Flanagain (*Sean McCarthy*), Joanne Gerrard (*Sarah*), Ian McElhinney (*Brother Dowdall*), Kevin James, Brendan Morrissey, Kiaran O'Brien, Sandy (*Max, the dog*).
Dir and Screenplay: Martin Duffy. Pro: Marina Hughes. Ex Pro: Jo Manuel. Ph: Seamus Deasy. Pro Des: Tom Conroy. Ed: John Victor Smith. M: Stephen McKeon. Costumes: Lorna Mugan. (Mercurian Prods/Blue Dahlia/Blue Rose/Canal Plus, etc.–Blue Dolphin.) Rel: 2 May 1997. 87 mins. Cert PG. Ireland/France/UK. 1996.

Boys

The last thing Patty Vare expects when she falls off her horse is to wake up in the dorm room of a timid high school senior. The latter, John Baker Jr, doesn't have a clue what to do with his rescued maiden, but he's obviously smitten by the beauty of this 'older woman'. As it transpires, Patty is on the run from the police, yet this turn of events only adds to the excitement for Baker. The adrenaline produced by the unlikely scenario can only lead to one thing – and Baker is about to grow up fast... Some fine films have been developed from short stories, but *Boys*, blown up from James Salter's eight-page tale *Twenty Minutes*, is not one of them. Stacy Cochran, who previously directed the quirky and static *My New Gun*, fails to generate any

momentum with this dour, lethargic and improbable exercise. And the constant rumble of strategically placed rock numbers hardly helps.

Winona Ryder (*Patty Vare*), Lukas Haas (*John Baker Jr*), John C. Reilly (*Officer Kellogg Curry*), James LeGros (*Fenton Ray*), Skeet Ulrich (*Bud Valentine*), Chris Cooper (*John Baker Snr*), Jessica Harper (*Mrs John Baker*), Bill Sage (*Officer Bill Martone*), Wiley Wiggins (*John Phillips*), Russell Young (*John Van Slieder*), Charlie Hofheimer (*John Cooke*), Catherine Keener (*Jilly*), Marty McDonough, Vivienne Shub, Spencer Vrooman, Christopher Pettiet, Andy Davis, Gregorio Rosenblum, Angela Hall.
Dir and Screenplay: Stacy Cochran. Pro: Peter Frankfurt, Paul Feldsher and Erica Huggins. Ex Pro: Ted Field, Scott Kroopf and Robert W. Cort. Co-Pro: Rudd Simmons. Ph: Robert Elswit. Pro Des: Dan Bishop. Ed: Camilla Toniolo. M: Stewart Copeland; numbers performed by The Cruel Sea, Cast, Smoking Popes, Scarce, Paul Weller, Orbit, Sparklehorse, Kelly Willis, Del Amitri, Squeeze, Supergrass, Compulsion, Stone Roses, The Devlins, and Stewart Copeland. Costumes: Lucy W. Corrigan. (Interscope Communications–PolyGram.) Rel: 30 August 1996. 86 mins. Cert 15. USA. 1996.

Brassed Off

Music might not mean much to the members of Grimley's Colliery Brass Band, but for Danny it represents the pride of the community. When the local (and profitable) pit is threatened with closure by govern-ment cutbacks, Danny finds it even harder to rouse the spirit of his men. Until, that is, the arrival of a pretty young lass who blows a mean flugel... Mark Herman, who previously directed the frenetic Dudley Moore farce *Blame It On the Bellboy*, takes a dramatic U-turn with this touching tale of a community struggling to retain its dignity. A sublime cast brings warmth and candour to their roles, while the desolate locale of Grimley takes on a charm it doesn't know it has. An articulate attack on the ruthless tactics of Thatcher's government - and a call-to-arms for human solidarity – *Brassed Off* mixes humour and message to potent effect.

Pete Postlethwaite (*Danny*), Tara Fitzgerald (*Gloria*), Ewan McGregor (*Andy*), Stephen Tompkinson (*Phil*), Jim Carter (*Harry*), Mary Healey (*Ida*), Melanie Hill (*Sandra*), Philip Jackson (*Jim*), Sue

Johnston (*Vera*), Peter Martin (*Ernie*), Stephen Moore (*Mackenzie*), Lill Roughley (*Rita*), Kenneth Colley, Peter Gunn, Olga Grahame, Sky Ingram, Ronnie Stevens, Peter Wallis.

Dir and Screenplay: Mark Herman. Pro: Steve Abbott. Co-Pro: Olivia Stewart. Ph: Andy Collins. Pro Des: Don Taylor. Ed: Michael Ellis. M: Trevor Jones; numbers performed by The Grimethorpe Colliery Band. Costumes: Amy Roberts. (Channel Four/Miramax/Prominent Features–Film Four.) Rel: 1 November 1996. 107 mins. Cert 15. UK/USA. 1996.

Breaking the Waves

The early 1970s; the north coast of Scotland. A simple, protected girl from a remote fishing village, Bess is brought up to believe that music, dancing and alcohol are the instruments of the devil. Consequently, when she meets Jan, a happy-go-lucky oil-rig worker, she is drawn to his earthy 'worldliness' and he to her radiant innocence. Thus, against the wishes of the village elders, Bess and Jan marry, although the latter seems unaware of what he has taken on. Consumed by her love for Jan (and the new pleasures of the flesh), Bess is torn between the deeply entrenched tenets of her upbringing and the promise of an exciting new life... Voyeuristically dwelling on the dual themes of insanity and sexual humiliation, *Breaking the Waves* is not exactly a pleasant distraction. Furthermore, the film's considerable length, bleached-out colours and constant use of a jittery hand-held camera hardly sweeten the brew. Which just leaves the fascination of the film's subject – the austere lifestyle of Scotland's 'Free Church' – and Emily Watson's extraordinarily gruelling and selfless central performance.

Emily Watson (*Bess*), Stellan Skarsgard (*Jan*), Katrin Cartlidge (*Dodo*), Jean-Marc Barr (*Terry*), Udo Kier (*man on the trawler*), Adrian Rawlins (*Dr Richardson*), Sandra Voe (*Bess's mother*), Mikkel Gaup, Roef Ragas, Phil McCall, Robert Robertson, Sarah Gudgeon, Ray Jeffries (*man on bus*).

Dir: Lars von Trier. Pro: Vibeke Windelov and Peter Aalbaeck Jensen. Ex Pro: Lars Jonsson. Co-Pro: Axel Helgeland, Peter Van Vogelpoel, Rob Langesstraat and Marianne Slot. Screenplay: von Trier and Peter Asmussen. Ph: Robby Muller. Pro Des: Karl Juliusson. Ed: Anders Refn. M: Joachim Holbek; J.S. Bach; numbers

Something friendly in the attic: Pravesh Kumar sheds light on a gloomy situation in Udayan Prasad's compassionate Brothers in Trouble *(from BFI)*

performed by Mott the Hoople, Jethro Tull, Roxy Music, Procul Harum, T. Rex, Leonard Cohen, Elton John, Thin Lizzy, Deep Purple, David Bowie, etc. Costumes: Manon Rasmussen. Sound: Per Streit. (Zentropa Entertainments/Northern Lights/La Sept Cinema/Swedish Television Drama/Nordic Film/Danish Film Institute/Canal Plus, etc.–Guild.) Rel: 18 October 1996. 158 mins. Cert 18. Denmark/Sweden/France/Netherlands/Norway. 1996.

Brothers in Trouble

1966; Bradford. Leaving his wife, children and home behind him in Pakistan, Amir travels to the north of England in a fruit crate. After his nightmarish journey, he is deposited into a dingy house inhabited by shadowy illegal immigrants. The next day he works a 12-hour shift shovelling sheep excrement in a wool-washing factory. Every Sunday, he pays an exorbitant fee to the 'agent' who allowed him illegal entry into Britain. 'I sold all my wife's jewellery for this?' he mutters. But Amir becomes so absorbed in the everyday pressures of remaining invisible and making ends meet that he denies himself the experience of a country that has much more to offer than squalid urban sprawl and constant drizzle. Consequently, a visit to the local pub takes on all the excitement of a state ball... Revealing a side of Britain that few of us can realise ever existed, director Udayan Prasad and writer-producer Robert Buckler farm fertile dramatic territory. Yet it is the film's focus on the details of this humiliating existence that touches the heart (shopping for chilli powder, sharing a prostitute) – until a dramatic structure finally takes shape. Thought-provoking, compassionate and beautifully paced.

Om Puri (*Hussein Shah*), Angeline Ball (*Mary*), Pavan Malhotra (*Amir*), Pravesh Kumar (*Sakib*), Ahsen Bhatti (*Irshad*), Badi Uzzaman (*Old Ram*), Bhasker (*Gholam*), Kulvinder Ghir (*the agent*), Lesley Clare O'Neill (*prostitute*), Harmage Singh Kalirai (*Sher Baz*), Freddie Fletcher (*Mr Redway*), June Broughton (*Beryl*), Kumall Grewal, Omar Salimi, William Maxwell.

Dir: Udayan Prasad. Pro and Screenplay: Robert Buckler, from the novel *Wapsi Ka Safar (The Return Journey)* by Abdullah Hussein. Ex Pro: George Faber. Production Supervisor: Peter Jaques. Ph: Alan Almond. Pro Des: Chris Townsend. Ed: Barrie Vince. M: Stephen Warbeck; numbers performed by The Yardbirds, Loot, and Dusty Springfield. Costumes: Andrea Galer. (Renegade Films/BBC/Kinowelt Film/Mikado–BFI.) Rel: 11 October 1996. 102 mins. Cert 15. UK. 1995.

Friendly fire: Jim Carrey excels at 'porno password' in Ben Stiller's ferocious comedy, The Cable Guy *(from Columbia TriStar)*

The Cable Guy

Following a meltdown with his girlfriend, architect Steven Kovacs moves into a new apartment and engages the services of Chip Douglas to install his cable TV. Offering the latter a $50 bribe for free channels, Steven gets more than he bargained for: complimentary cable and friendship for life. But Chip turns out to be something of a loose cannon and Steven finds it increasingly difficult to shake him off... Anybody expecting the infantile lunacy of *Ace Ventura* or *Dumb and Dumber* is in for a shock. Here Jim Carrey, who was paid a record $20 million for his services, takes a brave swing towards the darker side, although his physical presence is as wacky and over-powering as ever. Black comedy is extremely difficult to pull off well (*Death Becomes Her* is a rare exception), but director Ben Stiller (*Reality Bites*) injects enormous style

and vigour into this rollercoaster ride of mayhem. Indeed, this is the first Carrey vehicle guided by a filmmaker of any recognised merit, and while the end result is not as likely to engender guffaws, it is none the less far more stylish. Above all, it serves as a shameless showcase for an extraordinary talent (Carrey's, that is).

Jim Carrey (*Ernie 'Chip' Douglas/ Larry Tate*), Matthew Broderick (*Steven Kovacs*), Leslie Mann (*Robin Harris*), George Segal (*Earl Kovacs*), Diane Baker (*Mrs Kovacs*), Jack Black (*Rick*), Ben Stiller (*Sam Sweet*), Eric Roberts (*himself*), Janeane Garofalo, Andy Dick, Harry O'Reilly, Amy Stiller, Owen Wilson, Misa Kaprova, Paul Greco, James O'Conell, Charles Napier, Bob Odenkirk, Julie Hayden, David Bowe.
Dir: Ben Stiller. Pro: Andrew Licht, Jeffrey A. Mueller and Judd Apatow. Ex Pro: Brad Grey, Bernie Brillstein and Marc Gurvitz. Co-Pro: William Beasley. Screenplay: Lou Holtz, Jr. Ph: Robert Brinkman. Pro Des: Sharon Seymour. Ed: Steven Weisberg. M: John Ottman; numbers performed by Jerry Cantrell, Primitive Radio Gods, Porno For Pyros, Cracker, Jim Carrey, Cypress Hill, Stabbing Westward, etc. Costumes: Erica Edell Phillips. (Columbia TriStar.) Rel: 12 July 1996. 95 mins. Cert 12. USA. 1996.

Carla's Song

Glasgow/Nicaragua; 1987. Stuck in a dead-end job driving his No. 72 bus down the crowded streets of Glasgow, George is drawn to the exotic, mysterious Carla who cannot pay her fare. Refusing to reveal anything about her past – let alone her nationality – Carla appears constantly on her guard and initially rebuffs George's advances. But, taking ever greater risks to his employment by the bus company, George finally bites off more than he can chew by falling in love with a victim of indescribable atrocities... The strength of Ken Loach's film is that it builds its reality before revealing its true dramatic agenda. Utilising a hand-held camera and an almost documentary film style, the director creates a very credible world in dingy, rain-swept Glasgow, yet never loses sight of the story's humanity. Even in the film's later, more dramatic passages in Nicaragua, there are some delightful surprises: George mending a petrol leak with a bar of soap, or arguing with a peasant over whether a line was spoken by Yul Brynner or Paul Newman. Angry, eloquent and very,

Blood and beer: Robert Carlyle and Oyanka Cabezas in Ken Loach's gritty, outraged Carla's Song *(from PolyGram)*

very real, *Carla's Song* is what cinema should be all about (but very seldom is).

Robert Carlyle (*George*), Oyanka Cabezas (*Carla*), Scott Glenn (*Bradley*), Louise Goodall (*Maureen*), Gary Lewis (*Sammy*), Norma Rivera (*Norma*), Salvador Espinoza, Richard Loza, Subash Sing Pall.
   Dir: Ken Loach. Pro: Sally Hibbin. Co-Pro: Ulrich Felsberg and Gerardo Herrero. Screenplay: Paul Laverty. Ph: Barry Ackroyd. Pro Des: Martin Johnson. Ed: Jonathan Morris. M: George Fenton. Costumes: Daphne Dare and Lena Mossum. (Channel Four/Glasgow Film Fund/Institute of Culture, Nicaragua/Parallax Pictures/Road Movies/Tornasol Films, etc.–PolyGram.) Rel: 31 January 1997. 125 mins. Cert 15. UK/Germany/Spain. 1996.

The Celluloid Closet

A documentary chronicling the portrayal of homosexuality in the movies from 1895 to 1995, *The*

Celluloid Closet is a treasure trove of insights, commentary and clips that should keep cineastes and gay activists glued. Narrated by co-executive producer Lily Tomlin, the film dips into the archives to show a clip from Thomas Edison's studio featuring two men dancing together, then skips through the decades to illustrate how the image of the gay character has changed from a joke to a victim to a villain and then on to something bordering on human. A host of writers and actors add their own observations, shedding some intriguing light on the shadowy subtext of old movies, such as the homosexual attraction Messala has for Judah in *Ben-Hur* (even though Charlton Heston had no idea that co-star Stephen Boyd was making eyes at him!). Not surprisingly, Hollywood has always been several strides behind the times, leaving Britain to come up with the first mainstream film featuring a sexually ambiguous hero played by a leading actor: Dirk Bogarde in *Victim* (1961). But, as the film points out, even in the enlightened nineties, mainstream Hollywood was still not prepared to feature a gay protagonist who lived

at the end. Unfortunately, since this fascinating documentary was made, the goalposts have moved faster than ever before, witnessed by the commercial success of *The Birdcage* and the controversy provoked by the British-made *Priest*.

Interviewees: Tony Curtis, Amistead Maupin, Susie Bright, Whoopi Goldberg, Jan Oxenberg, Harvey Fierstein, Quentin Crisp, Richard Dyer, Jay Presson Allen, Arthur Laurents, Gore Vidal, Farley Granger, Stewart Stern, Paul Rudnick, Shirley MacLaine, Barry Sandler, Mart Crowley, Antonio Fargas, Tom Hanks, Ron Nyswaner, Daniel Melnick, Harry Hamlin, John Schlesinger, Susan Sarandon. Narrator: Lily Tomlin.
   Dir and Pro: Rob Epstein and Jeffrey Friedman. Co-Pro: Michael Lumpkin. Ex Pro: Howard Rosenman. Co-Ex Pro: Lily Tomlin. Narration written by: Armistead Maupin, from a story by Epstein, Friedman and Sharon Wood, based on the book by Vito Russo. Ph: Nancy Schreiber. Art: Scott Chambliss. Ed: Friedman and Arnold Glassman. M: Carter Burwell; 'Secret Love' performed by k.d. lang. (Home Box Office/Channel Four/ZDF/arte/Brillstein–Grey Entertainment/Hugh M. Hefner/James C. Hormel/Steve Tisch–Electric.) Rel: 5 July 1996. 102 mins. Cert 15. USA. 1995.

Chain Reaction

Chicago/Washington DC; tomorrow. As the world's insatiable appetite for fossil fuel reaches crisis point, Eddie Kasalivich, a student machinist in Chicago, stumbles across a unique frequency with the power to transform the hydrogen in water into energy. Of course, the instant availability of cheap, clean fuel has its price. For Paul Shannon, a government-funded industrialist, the price is the prospect of a global economic meltdown which could lead to world war. Far better, he reasons, to siphon off the profits into his own bank account. And for young Eddie the price of his discovery is his life as a nefarious frame-up sends him running from the police, the FBI and a variety of corporate assassins... Kick-starting the action with the spectacular demolition of eight city blocks, *Chain Reaction* hurtles through its paces with stream-lined precision as Eddie/Keanu Reeves falls off a bridge, commandeers an ice-patrol boat, wades through freezing water, clambers through underground shafts and so on. Andrew Davis (*The Fugitive*), who knows a thing or two about directing a good manhunt, keeps the narrative both ballistic and uncluttered, while Jerry Goldsmith's breathless score fills in the blanks.

Keanu Reeves (*Eddie Kasalivich*), Morgan Freeman (*Paul Shannon*), Rachel Weisz

Bicycle beef: Keanu Reeves makes his first narrow escape in Andrew Davis's ballistic Chain Reaction *(from Fox)*

(*Lily Sinclair*), Fred Ward (*FBI Agent Ford*), Kevin Dunn (*FBI Agent Doyle*), Brian Cox (*Lyman Earl Collier*), Joanna Cassidy (*Maggie McDermott*), Nicholas Rudall (*Dr Alistair Barkley*), Tzi Ma (*Lu Chen*), Chelcie Ross, Nathan Davis, Johnny Lee Davenport, Ron Dean, Margaret Travolta, Rick LeFevour, Charley Sherman, Danny Goldring, Eddie Bo Smith Jr, Dick Cusack, Mark Morettini.

Dir: Andrew Davis. Pro: Davis and Arne L. Schmidt. Ex Pro: Richard D. Zanuck and Erwin Stoff. Screenplay: J.F. Lawton and Michael Boatman, from a story by Schmidt, Rick Seaman and Josh Friedman. Ph: Frank Tidy. Pro Des: Maher Ahmad. Ed: Donald Brochu, Dov Hoenig and Arthur Schmidt. M: Jerry Goldsmith; 'One Love' performed by Bob Marley and The Wailers. Sound: Randy Thom. (Fox/Zanuck Company/Chicago Pacific–Fox.) Rel: 25 October 1996. 106 mins. Cert 12. USA. 1996.

The Chamber

The gas chamber, to be exact, the small glass-and-steel cubicle that awaits one Sam Cayhall, convicted of the murder of two five-year-old boys in 1967. Since then he's been on Death Row and has lost every appeal thrown his way. A self-confessed bigot and Klansman, Cayhall doesn't make his case easy, as his last hope – idealistic Chicago greenhorn Adam Hall – discovers to his frustration. But young Hall has a driving motive of his own: Cayhall is his grandfather... Breaking away from the heart-thumping, plot-driven thrills of John Grisham's first four novels, *The Chamber* is a sombre character-orientated piece, albeit exploring similar legal ground (crusading young lawyer fights intractable system). Unfortunately, the lead protagonist is so bland and uninteresting that it is hard to get an emotional toe-hold, hardly helped by Chris O'Donnell's one-dimensional interpretation. Which leaves Gene Hackman to light the film's emotional fuse, which he does with startling conviction. However, by encroaching on subject matter already explored with such intelligence by *Dead Man Walking*, *The Chamber* merely offers familiarity with contempt of court.

Chris O'Donnell (*Adam Hall*), Gene Hackman (*Sam Cayhall*), Faye Dunaway (*Lee Bowen*), Lela Rochon (*Nora Stark*), Robert Prosky (*E. Garner Goodman*), Raymond J. Barry (*Rollie Wedge*), David Marshall Grant (*Governor McAllister*), Bo Jackson (*Sgt Clyde Packer*), Nicholas Pryor (*Judge Slattery*), Millie Perkins (*Ruth Kramer*), Harve Presnell, Richard Bradford, Greg Goossen, Seth Isler, Josef Sommer, Leonard Vincent, Jane Kaczmarek.

Dir: James Foley. Pro: John Davis, Brian Grazer and Ron Howard. Ex Pro: David Friendly, Ric Kidney and Karen Kehela. Assoc Pro: Karen Snow. Screenplay: William Goldman and Chris Reese. Ph: Ian Baker. Pro Des: David Brisbin. Ed: Mark Warner. M: Carter Burwell. Costumes: Tracy Tynan. (Universal/Imagine Entertainment/Davis–Entertainment–UIP.) Rel: 20 June 1997. 113 mins. Cert 12. USA. 1996.

Cold Comfort Farm

Recently orphaned, young Flora Poste must decide what to do with her life. While visiting her friend and mentor Mrs Mary Smiling, she is besieged by offers of hospitality from relatives and opts to move in with the Starkadders at Cold Comfort Farm. There she finds nothing but gloom, grime and poverty and so sets about dragging the whole boiling lot of her poor cousins into the twentieth century... Like the BBC's *Persuasion*, this costume outing did sufficiently well on American screens to warrant a theatrical release in Britain, even after its showing on British television. As it happens, Flora Poste owns up, 'When I'm 53 I mean to write a novel as good as *Persuasion*, but with a modern setting.' Indeed, Stella Gibbons (1902-1989) wrote *Cold Comfort Farm* as a light-hearted antidote to the solemn rural novels of her day. John Schlesinger, whose experience with comedy has proved

to be his undoing (witness the disastrous *Honky Tonk Freeway*) has attempted to steer Gibbons' 1932 novel into the realms of earthy, bucolic fun, but instead has created something that borders on *Carry On Farming* without the double entendres. Still, in spite of this misjudged approach, the director has coaxed a perfectly judged performance from Kate Beckinsale as the sensible and forthright Flora, while much rustic detail, a splendid score and the story itself constantly appeal.

Kate Beckinsale (*Flora Poste*), Eileen Atkins (*Judith Starkadder*), Sheila Burrell (*Ada Doom*), Stephen Fry (*Mybug*), Freddie Jones (*Adam Lambsbreath*), Joanna Lumley (*Mary Smiling*), Ian McKellen (*Amos Starkadder*), Miriam Margolyes (*Mrs Beetle*), Rufus Sewell (*Seth Starkadder*), Ivan Kaye (*Reuben Starkadder*), Maria Miles (*Elfine Starkadder*), Christopher Bowen (*Charles Fairford*), Sophie Revell (*Rennet*), Trevor Baxter (*Sneller*), Jeremy Peters, Louise Rea, Rupert Penry-Jones, Angela Thorne, Harry Ditson, Frederick Jaeger, Pat Keen, Robert James, Susannah Morley, Basil Hoskins.
  Dir: John Schlesinger. Pro: Alison Gilby. Ex Pro: Richard Broke and Antony Root. Assoc Pro: Joanna Gueritz. Screenplay: Malcolm Bradbury. Ph: Chris Seager. Pro Des: Malcolm Thornton. Ed: Mark Day. M: Robert Lockhart. Costumes: Amy Roberts. (BBC Television/Thames Television–Feature Film Company.) Rel: 25 April 1997. 104 mins. Cert PG. UK. 1995.

Con Air

Eight years ago, surrounded by three drunken thugs, army ranger Cameron Poe lost his cool and fought back. It cost him his job, his freedom and the chance to watch his unborn child grow into a beautiful eight-year-old girl. Sentenced to eight years for manslaughter, Poe made the most of his time inside, working hard on his bodybuilding, Spanish and origami. Then, on the day of his release, he finds himself sharing a 'con air' flight with the meanest, ugliest and deadliest criminals in the US penitentiary system – all on their way to a new supermax facility. Led by the brilliant but barbaric Cyrus 'The Virus', the cons take over the plane and head for freedom. But that wasn't Poe's plan... Adopting his customary in-your-face MTV style of filmmaking, producer Jerry Bruckheimer (*Top Gun, Bad Boys, The*

Not the world's favourite airline: John Malkovich takes over steward duty in Simon West's brutal Con Air *(from Buena Vista)*

Rock) loads his story with big explosions, colourful villains, polluted humour and loud, loud, driving music. He also stacks his deck by casting real actors in pivotal roles and by hiring a first-time director to add a freshness of vision. Unfortunately, *Con Air* is a sloppy movie, choked by its own eagerness to assault the ear drums and get on with the action. The jokes are not bad and the testosterone is willing, but ultimately it all feels like an extended commercial for brutality.

Nicolas Cage (*Cameron Poe*), John Cusack (*Vince Larkin*), John Malkovich (*Cyrus 'The Virus' Grissom*), Steve Buscemi (*Garland Greene*), Ving Rhames (*Diamond Dog*), Colm Meaney (*Duncan Malloy*), Mykelti Williamson (*Baby-O*), Rachel Ticotin (*Sally Bishop*), Monica Potter (*Tricia Poe*), David Chappelle (*Pinball*), M.C. Gainey (*Swamp Thing*), Nick Chinlund (*Billy Bedlam*), Angela Featherstone (*Ginny*), John Roselius, Renoly, Danny Trejo, Jesse Borrego, Jose Zuniga, Robert Stephenson, Brendan Kelly, Don Davis, Bill Cusack.
  Dir: Simon West. Pro: Jerry Bruckheimer. Ex Pro: Chad Oman, Jonathan Hensleigh, Peter Bogart, Jim Kouf and Lynn Bigelow. Screenplay: Scott

Rosenberg. Ph: David Tattersall. Art: Edward T. McAvoy. Ed: Chris Lebenzon, Steve Mirkovich and Glen Scantlebury. M: Mark Mancina and Trevor Rabin. Costumes: Bobbie Read. Visual effects: David Goldberg. (Touchstone Pictures–Buena Vista.) Rel: 6 June 1997. 115 mins. Cert 15. USA. 1997.

Courage Under Fire

Haunted by his order to fire on a tank that turned out to be one of his own during the Gulf War, Lieutenant Colonel Nathaniel Serling finds himself estranged from his family and increasingly reliant on the bottle for emotional support. But the fabric of heroism is a complex thing, as the officer discovers when he embarks on an investigation in order to honour the first female recipient of the Medal of Honor. Interviewing three soldiers present at her death, he receives differing reports on what actually happened during the heat of battle. For once, though, Serling is determined to get something right – to find out the truth – even if it means alienating his PR-conscious superiors... Shedding an intelligent perspective on the trials of the Gulf War, *Courage Under Fire* uncovers the heartache, but not the gut-wrenching horror, of America's involvement in Iraq. As always, Denzel Washington turns in a first-rate piece of acting

Rashomon returns: Denzel Washington out of order in Edward Zwick's contemplative Courage Under Fire *(from Fox)*

and is backed by a sterling supporting cast. As war films go, this is certainly one of the more reflective. P.S. It's interesting, particularly considering the number of films already made about Bosnia, that *Courage Under Fire* is only the first major picture to focus on the Gulf conflict.

Denzel Washington (*Lt Colonel Nathaniel Serling*), Meg Ryan (*Captain Karen Emma Walden*), Lou Diamond Phillips (*Monfriez*), Michael Moriarty (*General Hershberg*), Matt Damon (*Ilario*), Seth Gilliam (*Steve Altameyer*), Bronson Pinchot (*Bruno*), Scott Glenn (*Tony Gartner*), Regina Taylor (*Meredith Serling*), Zeljko Ivanek (*Banacek*), Ned Vaughn (*Chelli*), Michole White (*Maria*), Tim Guinee, Tim Ransom, Sean Astin, Armand Darrius, Manny Perez, Sean Patrick Thomas, Ken Jenkins, Kathleen Widdoes, Bruce McGill, Albert Hall, Richard Venture, Diane Baker.
   Dir: Edward Zwick. Pro: John Davis, Joseph M. Singer and David T. Friendly. Ex Pro: Joseph M. Caracciolo and Debra Martin Chase. Screenplay: Patrick Sheane Duncan. Ph: Roger Deakins. Pro Des: John Graysmark. Ed: Steven Rosenblum. M: James Horner. Costumes: Francine Jamison and Tan Chuck. (Fox 200 Pictures–Fox.) Rel: 4 October 1996. 116 mins. Cert 15. USA. 1996.

The Craft

Feeling ostracised at her new Los Angeles school, Sarah Bailey falls in with three tightly knit outsiders – 'the bitches of Eastwick' – who are looking for a fourth girl to complete their circle. It seems they're impressed with Sarah's knack for standing a pencil on its lead, and soon all four are embodying the forces of earth, air, fire and water. Starting out with simple spells like changing their hair colour on command, the girls quickly learn to appreciate the sweetness of criminal revenge... A satisfactory enough thriller for the Saturday night market, *The Craft* is serviced by decent performances and some neat special effects (watch that lavatory bowl overflow with bugs!). However, a sharper wit and credible characters could have levitated this to the status of a cult repertory performer.

Fairuza Balk (*Nancy*), Robin Tunney (*Sarah Bailey*), Neve Campbell (*Bonnie*), Rachel True (*Rochelle*), Skeet Ulrich (*Chris*), Christine Taylor (*Laura Lizzie*), Cliff De Young (*Mr Bailey*), Assumpta Serna (*Lirio*), Helen Shaver (*Grace*), Endre Hules (*Monsieur Thepot*), Tony Genaro (*bus driver*), Breckin Meyer, Nathaniel Marston, Jeanine Jackson, Brenda Strong, Elizabeth Guber, Jennifer Greenhut, Arthur Senzy, Mark Conlon, Brogan Roche, Janet Eilber.
   Dir: Andrew Fleming. Pro: Douglas

Wick. Ex Pro: Ginny Nugent. Co-Pro: Lisa Tornell. Screenplay: Fleming and Peter Filardi. Ph: Alexander Gruszynski. Pro Des: Marek Dobrowolski. Ed: Jeff Freeman. M: Graeme Revell; numbers performed by Our Lady Peace, Sponge, Love Spit Love, Jewel, Juliana Hatfield, Tripping Daisy, Letters To Cleo, Siouxsie & The Banshees, Connie Francis, Matthew Sweet, All Too Much, Portishead, Spacehog, Elastica, and Heather Nova. Costumes: Deborah Everton. (Columbia Pictures–Columbia TriStar.) Rel: 8 November 1996. 101 mins. Cert 15. USA. 1996.

Crash

When James Ballard, an advertising executive, survives a fatal head-on collision with another car, he finds himself inexplicably drawn to the wife of the dead driver. Soon, with the full cooperation of his own wife, Ballard enters a nether world where a group of people derive their sexual kicks from vehicular wreckage. Using car crashes as 'a metaphor for the collision of present technology and the human psyche,' David Cronenberg's adaptation of J.G. Ballard's controversial 1973 novel has been attacked both for not going far enough and for reaching new depths of depravity. In a characteristic flurry of hysteria, the British tabloids even went so far as to mobilise a campaign to have this 'pornographic' film banned in the UK. But pornography, like bourbon, is an acquired taste. Submit somebody often enough to images that are alien to their sensibility and they become desensitised to the effect. Eventually, they may even enjoy what they behold – savouring the stimulation left over from the bracing overture. However, *Crash* is not pornographic for it does not set out to titillate. On the contrary. Where the car crash featured in David Lynch's *Wild at Heart* was genuinely upsetting, the gynaecological detail that David Cronenberg lavishes on the automobile carnage here disinfects the horror. Be that as it may, *Crash* works better as a conversation piece and psychoanalytical tract than as a movie. While having lost none of the sickness that informed his earlier films (*Shivers*, *Rabid*, *Videodrome*), Cronenberg has certainly misplaced his vitality as a filmmaker. It does bring a whole new meaning to the term car sickness, though.

James Spader (*James Ballard*), Holly Hunter (*Helen Remington*), Elias Koteas (*Vaughan*), Deborah Kara Unger (*Catherine Ballard*), Rosanna Arquette (*Gabrielle*), Peter MacNeill (*Colin Seagrave*), Yolande Julian, Cheryl Swarts, Nicky Guadagni, Alice Poon.
    Dir, Pro and Screenplay: David Cronenberg. Ex Pro: Jeremy Thomas and Robert Lantos. Co-Pro: Stephane Reichel and Marilyn Stonehouse. Co-Ex Pro: Andras Hamori and Chris Auty. Ph: Peter Suschitzky. Pro Des: Carol Spier. Ed: Ronald Sanders.M: Howard Shore. Costumes: Denise Cronenberg. (Alliance Communications/Telefilm Canada/ TMN–Columbia TriStar.) Rel: 6 June 1997. 100 mins. Cert 18. Canada. 1996.

Crimetime

When out-of-work actor Bobby Mahon takes on the role of a real-life serial murderer (nicknamed The Stocking Killer) on a crime re-enactment TV show, his fortunes take an upward swing. The show's ratings increase three hundred per cent and Bobby's mail bag swells, but the actor can only sustain his celebrity for as long as the killer continues his reign of terror. Luckily for Bobby, though, his real-life counterpart is relishing the spotlight and cannot supply enough raw

Car sickness: James Spader and Holly Hunter in David Cronenberg's clinical chrome dream, Crash *(from Columbia TriStar)*

material for the show... Yet another satire on the accountability of the media for promoting violence, *Crime Time* occasionally recalls the macabre touch that director George Sluizer displayed so effectively in his award-winning film *The Vanishing*. However, too many silly plot devices and some uneven performances conspire to undermine both the film's credibility as a thriller and potency as an argument.

Stephen Baldwin (*Bobby Mahon*), Pete Postlethwaite (*Sidney*), Sadie Frost (*Val*), Geraldine Chaplin (*Thelma*), Karen Black (*Millicent Hargreave*), James Faulkner (*Crowley*), Philip Davis (*Simon*), Marianne Faithfull, Emma Roberts, Anne Lambton, Suzanne Bertish, Stephanie Buttle, Caroline Langrishe, Orla Charlton, Ron Berglas, Matyelock Gibbs, Pete Lee Wilson, Jeff Nuttal, Pippa Hinchley, Gwyneth Strong, Frances Grey, George Sluizer, Laura Brattan.
    Dir and Co-Ex Pro: George Sluizer. Pro: David Pupkewitz. Ex Pro: Philip Alberstat, Barry Barnholtz and Marc Vlessing. Co-Pro: Rainer Kolmel. Line Pro: Raymond Day. Screenplay: Brendan Somers. Ph: Jules Van Den Steenhoven. Pro Des: Bernd Lepel. Ed: Fabienne Rawley. M: David A. Stewart; numbers performed by

David A. Stewart and Marianne Faithfull, Lightning Seeds, Leftfield, Roy Orbison, and Lyle & McGuiness. Costumes: Jany Temime. Lottery officer: Mark Dunford. (The National Lottery/Arts Council of England/Degeto Film/Club D'Investissement Media/Bavarian Fund for Film and Television/Euroimages Fund/Channel Four/Pandora Cinema/ Trimark Pictures/Focus Films/Kinowelt– First Independent.) Rel: 29 November 1996. 118 mins. Cert 18. UK/USA/ Germany. 1996.

The Crossing Guard

The story of three characters torn apart by their inability to reconcile their grief over the death of a little girl, *The Crossing Guard* is a work of enormous intelligence and maturity. Freddy Gale is the father who harbours a terrible plan of revenge and takes solace in prostitutes and drink. May is the mother who cannot comprehend her husband's incapacity to face his suffering. And John Booth is the man who goes down for manslaughter and is racked by guilt. Somehow, someday, they will all have to come to terms with their sense of loss... Following his directorial debut with *The Indian Runner* in 1991, writer, director and co-producer Sean Penn here confirms his talent as a first-rate filmmaker with an extraordinary grasp of

Witchfinder priest: Bruce Davison and Winona Ryder get caught up in the hysteria in Nicholas Hytner's stirring, literate The Crucible *(from Fox)*

character and psychological subtext, plus an ability to elicit remarkably naked performances from his powerhouse cast. He's also well served by Vilmos Zsigmond's sharp, atmospheric lighting and Jack Nitzsche's evocative score, combining to produce a film of unusual depth and nuance.

Jack Nicholson (*Freddy Gale*), David Morse (*John Booth*), Robin Wright (*JoJo*), Piper Laurie (*Helen Booth*), Richard Bradford (*Stuart Booth*), Robbie Robertson (*Roger*), Anjelica Huston (*Mary*), John Savage (*Bobby*), Priscilla Barnes, David Baerwald, Kari Wuhrer, Jennifer Leigh Warren, Richard Sarafian, Joe Viterelli, Eileen Ryan, Michael Ryan, Matthew Ryan, Penny Allen, Nicky Blair (*herself*), Leo Penn, Dr William Dignam (*the crossing guard*).
Dir and Screenplay: Sean Penn. Pro: Penn and David S. Hamburger. Ex Pro: Bob Weinstein, Harvey Weinstein and Richard Gladstein. Ph: Vilmos Zsigmond. Pro Des: Michael Haller. Ed: Jay Cassidy. M: Jack Nitzsche and Joseph Vitarelli;

numbers performed by Bruce Springsteen ('Missing'), Adam Ant, Hadda Brooks, Salt 'N' Pepa, Dead Can Dance, David Baerwald, Jewel, Kari Wuhrer, etc. Costumes: Jill Ohanneson. (Miramax–Buena Vista.) Rel: 16 August 1996. 115 mins. Cert 15. USA. 1995.

The Crow City of Angels

French pin-up Vincent Perez (*Indochine, La Reine Margot*) gleefully hurls himself into the wake of the late Brandon Lee as another murder victim of the scum of society. Again, the victim is resurrected by the mysterious powers of The Crow (a big black bird of the genus Corvus) and again he metes out his revenge in a variety of nasty ways set to heavy metal music... A sadistic, repetitive and visually uninspired sequel to the sadistic, repetitive and visually inspired film of 1994. Even fans of the original were mortified by this fiasco. [*Charles Bacon*]

Vincent Perez (*Ashe*), Mia Kirshner (*Sarah*), Iggy Pop (*Curve*), Richard Brooks (*Judah*), Thomas Jane (*Nemo*), Vincent Castellanos (*Spider Monkey*), Thuy Trang (*Kali*), Ian Dury (*Noah*), Tracey Ellis

(*Sybil*), Eric Acosta, Beverley Mitchell.
Dir: Tim Pope. Pro: Edward R. Pressman and Jeff Most. Co-Pro: Michael Flynn. Screenplay: David Goyer, based on the comic book series by James O'Barr. Ph: Jean Yves. Pro Des: Alex McDowell. Ed: Anthony Redman. M: Graeme Revell; numbers performed by Bush, Above the Law, The Toadies, White Zombie, Hole, Tricky, Iggy Pop, Grace Slick, NY Loose, Deftones, etc. Costumes: Kirsten Everberg. (Bad Bird Prods/Miramax/Dimension Films/Cowboy Films–Buena Vista.) Rel: 22 November 1996. 85 mins. Cert 18. USA/UK. 1996.

The Crucible

Salem, Massachusetts; 1692. When a group of girls are caught in the woods letting off steam, their Puritan elders read more into their frolics than mere sexual abandon. Faced with the prospect of hanging, the girls confess to demonic possession and start pointing their collective finger at harmless neighbours. In addition, ringleader Abigail Williams sees this as a chance to dispose of her lover's wife and soon the accusation of witchcraft becomes an indiscriminate cure-all for the community's discontents... While Arthur Miller wrote *The Crucible* in 1953 as an allegory for the Communist witch hunts of Senator McCarthy (of which he himself became a victim in 1957), the writer doesn't stint from historical accuracy. Indeed, Nicholas Hytner's handsome production rigorously captures the period, complete with 17th-century nails for the houses and authentic stitching for the costumes – while Daniel Day-Lewis pitched in with the construction crew to build his own clapboard house. Although less immediately cinematic than Roland Joffe's *The Scarlet Letter* (which covered similar terrain), this is still a fiercely intelligent adaptation of one of the greatest plays of the twentieth century.

Daniel Day-Lewis (*John Proctor*), Winona Ryder (*Abigail Williams*), Paul Scofield (*Judge Danforth*), Joan Allen (*Elizabeth Proctor*), Bruce Davison (*Reverend Parris*), Rob Campbell (*Reverend Hale*), Jeffrey Jones (*Thomas Putnam*), Peter Vaughan (*Giles Corey*), Karron Graves (*Mary Warren*), Charlayne Woodard (*Tituba*), Elizabeth Lawrence (*Rebecca Nurse*), Rachael Bella (*Betty Parris*), Tom McDermott (*Francis Nurse*), Ruth Maleczech (*Goody Osborne*), Frances

Conroy, George Gaynes, Mary Pat Gleason, Robert Brueler, Ashley Peldon, John Griesemer, Michael Gaston, William Preston.

Dir: Nicholas Hytner. Pro: Robert A. Miller and David V. Picker. Co-Pro: Diana Pokorny. Screenplay: Arthur Miller, adapted from his play. Ph: Andrew Dunn. Pro Des: Lilly Kilvert. Ed: Tariq Anwar. M: George Fenton. Costumes: Bob Crowley. (Fox–Fox.) Rel: 28 February 1997. 123 mins. Cert 12. USA. 1996.

Crying Freeman

San Francisco/Vancouver/ Hokkaido/Shanghai/Tokyo; the present. Unlike his peers of sword- and-sorcery hokum, Zen potter-cum- underworld assassin 'Yo' gets a bit of the old wet eye whenever he slices a victim to kingdom come. Hence he is identified by one Emu O'Hara, a virginal painter who fears for her life having witnessed his brutally efficient disposal of a Yakuza gangster and his bodyguards. But, heh, Yo and Emu are far too gorgeous not to blend their bodily fluids and so Yo finds himself a marked man for disobeying the orders of the 108 Sons of the Dragon to kill her... A painstaking recreation of the Manga comic book by Kazuo Koike and Ryoichi Ikegami, *Crying Freeman* takes itself terribly seriously while borrowing generously from other movies for its gutsy style. Still, it's highly entertaining at times, even if it lacks the edge and humour it so desperately calls out for. [*Ewen Brownrigg*]

Mark Dacascos (*Yo Hinomura/The Freeman*), Julie Condra (*Emu O'Hara*), Tcheky Karyo (*Inspector Netah*), Rae Dawn Chong (*Inspector Forge*), Byron Mann (*Koh*), Masaya Kato (*Ryuji Hanada*), Yoko Shimada (*Lady Hanada*), Mako (*Shudo Shimazaki*), Deborah Unger (*narrator*).

Dir: Christophe Gans. Pro: Samuel Hadida and Brian Yuzna. Ex Pro: Taka Ichise and Victor Hadida. Screenplay: Gans and Thierry Cazals. Ph: Thomas Burstyn. Pro Des: Douglas Higgins and Alex McDowell. Ed: David Wu and Chris Roth. M: Patrick O'Hearn; Verdi. Costumes: Toni Burroughs-Rutter. (Toei Video/Fuji Television/Davis Film/Ozla Pictures/Yuzna Films–Guild.) Rel: 9 May 1997. 102 mins. Cert 18. France/Canada/ USA/Japan. 1995.

Dangerous Ground

Twelve years after fleeing South Africa for the safety of America,

In a lava: Pierce Brosnan and Linda Hamilton run for their lives in Roger Donaldson's stirring Dante's Peak *(from UIP)*

aspiring drug counsellor 'Vusi' returns to bury his father. There, in Soweto, he is surprised to find that 'drugs have taken over where apartheid left off.' Promising his mother to locate his missing younger brother, Vusi is reluctantly thrust into the drug underworld of Johannesburg and the company of a stripper with a strange accent... A painfully mediocre, hackneyed action-melodrama, *Dangerous Ground* dresses itself up as social commentary in a misguided attempt to blend Ken Loach with blaxploitation. Violence parading as entertainment is one thing, but violence parading as social analysis is downright dishonest. Even the normally reliable Ving Rhames can make little of his crime lord who is stuck with lines like 'I like to fuck shit up.'

Ice Cube (*Vusi*), Elizabeth Hurley (*Karen*), Sechaba Morojele (*Ernest*), Eric 'Waku' Miyeni (*Steven*), Ving Rhames (*Muki*), Peter Kubheka, Roslyn Morapedi, Fana Mokoena, Anthony Bishop.

Dir: Darrell James Roodt. Pro: Roodt and Gillian Gorfil. Ex Pro: Ice Cube and Pat Charbonnet. Assoc Pro: Helena Spring. Screenplay: Roodt and Greg Latter. Ph: Paul Gilpin. Pro Des: Dimitri Repanis. Ed: David Heitner. M: Stanley Clarke. Costumes: Ruy Filipe. (Investec Merchant Bank/New Line–Entertainment.) Rel: 16 May 1997. 95 mins. Cert 18. South Africa/USA. 1996.

Dante's Peak

Colombia/Dante's Peak, Northern Cascades, the Pacific Northwest; 1992/1996. The problem with volcanoes is that they're still pretty hard to predict, and with 550 fully operative terrestrial mothers scattered across the globe (not counting many more than that under the sea), they are becoming a real menace. Worse still, as human colonisation expands the fatality rate is increasing, with 29,000 volcano- related deaths recorded in the last 15 years. And then there's that little matter of international climactic upheaval, in which a single eruption can turn summer into winter. Harry Dalton, volcanologist for the United States Geological Institute, knows the facts and is irked when the financial

The Hudson Adventure: Sylvester Stallone (right) comforts Amy Brenneman in Rob Cohen's thrilling Daylight *(from UIP)*

interests of the sleepy idyllic community of Dante's Peak is put above the welfare of its 7,400 citizens. He believes they should be warned about the acidity in the water supply, but such information could frighten off the tourist trade. So what about that naked couple boiled alive in the local hot spring? Leaping into the geologically cataclysmic wake of *Twister*, *Dante's Peak* piles on the suspense and computer-generated effects with aplomb, fulfilling its dictate very nicely, thank you. Formulaic, yes, but what do you expect from a disaster movie? *The English Patient*?

Pierce Brosnan (*Harry Dalton*), Linda Hamilton (*Rachel Wando*), Charles Hallahan (*Paul Dreyfus*), Grant Heslov (*Greg*), Elizabeth Hoffman (*Ruth*), Jamie Renee Smith (*Lauren Wando*), Jeremy Foley (*Graham Wando*), Walker Brandt (*Marianne*), Kirk Trutner, Arabella Field, Tzi May, Brian Reddy, Lee Garlington, Bill Bolender, Carol Androsky, Marilyn Leubner.
  Dir: Roger Donaldson. Pro: Gale Anne

Hurd and Joseph M. Singer. Ex Pro: Ilona Herzberg. Assoc Pro and second unit dir: Geoff Murphy. Screenplay: Leslie Bohem. Ph: Andrzej Bartkowial. Pro Des: Dennis Washington. Ed: Howard Smith, Conrad Buff and Tina Hirsch. M: John Frizzell; theme by James Newton Howard; 'Blue Moon Revisited' performed by Cowboy Junkies. Costumes: Isis Mussenden. Visual effects: Patrick McClung. (Universal/ Pacific Western–UIP.) Rel: 28 March 1997. 108 mins. Cert 12. USA. 1997.

Daylight

When a runaway car careens through the rush-hour traffic in the 80-year-old Manhattan Tunnel, its high-speed collision into a convoy of trucks carrying toxic waste sparks a devastating fireball. Burying between 200 and 300 commuters beneath the Hudson River, the accident abruptly cuts Manhattan off from New Jersey. But can there be any survivors? Kit Latura, the disgraced former head of New York's Emergency Medical Services, thinks so – and is willing to risk his neck to prove it... After deftly introducing its varied *dramatis personae*, *Daylight* buckles down to its white-knuckle objective. From the

popcorn-spilling showpiece – in which the explosion shatters concrete and flips cars like tiddlywinks – the film establishes its grip. And this is only the beginning. Such hazards as giant ventilation fans, frisky live cables, belching balls of fire, wind tunnels, freezing water, a dwindling oxygen supply and armies of rats collude to oil the chain of heart-stopping moments. An extremely efficient return to the *oeuvre* of *Earthquake* and *The Poseidon Adventure*, *Daylight* delivers with all the state-of-the-art muscle of Industrial Light & Magic and then some.

Sylvester Stallone (*Kit Latura*), Amy Brenneman (*Madelyne Thompson*), Viggo Mortensen (*Roy Nord*), Dan Hedaya (*Deputy Chief Frank Kraft*), Jay O. Sanders (*Stephan Crighton*), Karen Young (*Sarah Crighton*), Claire Bloom (*Eleanor Trilling*), Barry Newman (*Norman Bassett*), Stan Shaw (*George Tyrell*), Vanessa Bell Calloway (*Grace*), Colin Fox (*Roger Trilling*), Danielle Harris (*Ashley Crighton*), Renoly Santiago, Trina McGee-Davis, Marcello Thedford, Sage Stallone (*Vincent*), Jo Anderson, Mark Rolston, Rosemary Forsyth, Tony Munafo, Nestor Serrano, Dan Daily, John Lees.
  Dir: Rob Cohen. Pro: John Davis, Joseph

M. Singer and David T. Friendly. Ex Pro: Raffaella De Laurentiis. Co-Pro: Hester Hargett. Assoc Pro: Tony Munafo. Screenplay: Leslie Bohem. Ph: David Eggby. Pro Des: Benjamin Fernandez. Ed: Peter Amundsen. M: Randy Edelman. Costumes: Thomas Casterline. Special effects: Kit West. Stunts: Paul Weston. Visual effects: Scott Farrar. (Universal–UIP.) Rel: 26 December 1996. 114 mins. Cert 12. USA. 1996.

The Day of the Beast - El Dia de la Bestia

Having cracked the code of the Apocalypse, Angel Berriartua, a frail little professor of theology, is convinced that the Antichrist is due to be born on Christmas day. But in order to do battle with Satan, Angel feels that he must be admitted to the ranks of the diabolic and so embarks on a path of wickedness; stealing from the poor, scratching the paint-work of brand-new cars and indulging in heavy metal music... Approaching producer Andres Vicente Gomez for finance, writer-director Alex de la Iglesia warned him that *The Day of the Beast* 'is going to be a very unpleasant film'. Unperturbed, Gomez replied, 'It doesn't matter. The more unpleasant the better.' Presumably, Gomez had already seen de la Iglesia's first film, the utterly tasteless *Accion Mutante* (1993), and knew what to expect. As it happens, *The Day of the Beast* – in spite of its demonic subject matter – is nowhere near as offensive. In fact, while the film is constantly engaging, it is neither particularly frightening nor very funny. However, the concept of a Don Camillo figure teaming up with an overweight Hell's Angel and a satanic TV presenter on the trail of the Antichrist may have seemed funny enough for de la Iglesia.

Alex Angulo (*Angel Berriartua*), Armando De Razza (*Ennio Lombardi, 'Professor Cavan'*), Santiago Segura (*Jose Maria*), Terele Pavez (*Rosario*), Nathalie Sesena (*Mina*), Maria Grazia Cucinotta (*Susana*), Gianni Ippoliti, Saturnino Garcia.
   Dir: Alex de la Iglesia. Pro: Antonio Saura and Claudio Gaeta. Ex Pro: Andres Vicente Gomez. Screenplay: de la Iglesia and Jorge Guerricaechevarra. Ph: Flavio Martinez Labiano. Pro Des: Jose Luis Arrizabalaga and Biaffra. Ed and Sound: Teresa Font. M: Battista Lena. Costumes: Estibaliz Markiegi. (Iberoamericana-Sogetel/M.G. ALR/Canal Plus–Metro

Tartan.) Rel: 6 December 1996. 110 mins. Cert 18. Spain/Italy. 1995.

The Day the Sun Turned Cold - Tianguo Niezi

Hong Kong-born writer-director Yim Ho amply demonstrates his cinematic skills in this gripping, atmospheric drama based on real events. Set in Northern China, it concerns a son's accusation that his mother, who has subsequently remarried, had poisoned his father ten years previously. The belated investigation is as absorbing as a good thriller, and not without surprises. But the film is also a subtle study of rural life, and a fascinating exploration of a mother/child relationship in which the characters have rare depth and complexity. The leading players are fully persuasive and the technical credits impressive. This double award winner can be strongly recommended. [*Mansel Stimpson*]

Siqin Gowa (*mother*), Tuo Zhong Hua (*the son*), Ma Jing Wu (*father*), Wai Zhi (*lover*), Shu Zhong, Li Hu.
   Dir, Pro and Screenplay: Yim Ho. Ex Pro: Ann Hui. Ph: Hou Yong. Pro Des: Jessinta Liu. Ed: Wong Yee-shun. M: Otomo Yoshihide and Na Bing Chen. Costumes: Zhang Shu Fang. (Pineast Pictures–Artificial Eye.) Rel: 15 November 1996. 99 mins. Cert 12. Hong Kong. 1994.

Dead Man

When a mild-mannered accountant from Cleveland arrives in the Wild, Wild West, he is forced to re-evaluate his life... Few genres have been so entrenched in myth than the Western, so it was a natural target for that most individual of directors, Jim Jarmusch. Here, he wipes away the 'dusty colour palette' associated with the films of Leone and Peckinpah, and replaces it with his more singular black and white (which he used in *Stranger Than Paradise* and *Down By Law*). Jarmusch also draws peculiar attention to bizarre detail denied us by Clint Eastwood (like a horse urinating in the street). None the less, the director has allowed a few clichés to remain, if only to give his odyssey some cinematic perspective. But for every close-up of the wheels of a train, there is a bounty hunter jealously guarding his

The icon and the iconoclast: The late Robert Mitchum plays mean for Jim Jarmusch in the latter's delightfully bizarre Dead Man *(from Electric)*

teddy bear. Jarmusch fans won't be disappointed.

Johnny Depp (*William Blake*), Gary Farmer (*Nobody*), Lance Henriksen (*Cole Wilson*), Michael Wincott (*Conway Twill*), Gabriel Byrne (*Charlie Dickinson*), John Hurt (*John Scholfield*), Alfred Molina (*trading post missionary*), Robert Mitchum (*John Dickinson*), Mili Avital (*Thel Russell*), Eugene Byrd (*Johnny 'The Kid' Pickett*), Iggy Pop (*Salvatore 'Sally' Jenko*), Crispin Glover, John North, Billy Bob Thornton, Jared Harris, Jimmie Ray Weeks, Mark Bringleson, Michelle Thrush.
   Dir and Screenplay: Jim Jarmusch. Pro: Demetra J. MacBride. Co-Pro: Karen Koch. Ph: Robby Muller. Pro Des: Bob Ziembicki. Ed: Jay Rabinowitz. M: Neil Young. Costumes: Marit Allen. Elk wrangler: Jeffrey King. (12 Gauge Productions/Pandora Film/FFA Berlin Filmboard–Electric.) Rel: 5 July 1996. 120 mins. Cert 18. USA/Germany. 1995.

Dead Presidents

North-east Bronx, New York; 1968-73. A dead president, as any follower of 1940s' black slang will tell you, is a US bank note. And the terrific opening of this dynamic social thriller presages the fatal allure of this symbol of white, capitalist America. In extreme close-up a burning note peels back to reveal another, and then another, each exposing the image of a bygone president, each pushing home the transitory nature of paper money – and all that it represents. Anthony Curtis, a student from the north-east Bronx, has a good heart but is more interested in a career in the army than in further education. However, Curtis's determination to make a man of himself exposes him to unthinkable brutality in Vietnam, which ill prepares him for life as a husband and father back in New York... Resembling *The Deer Hunter* in theme and its three-part structure, *Dead Presidents* is a phenomenal achievement for its 22-year-old twin directors, Allen and Albert Hughes. Following the critical and commercial success of their first film, *Menace II Society*, the Hughes Brothers confirm their stature as the most significant Afro-American filmmakers of their generation. Stylish, credible, funny and exceptionally violent, *Dead Presidents* tackles the dilemmas of black American life in the late sixties and early seventies with extraordinary maturity.

Larenz Tate (*Anthony Curtis*), Keith David (*Kirby*), Chris Tucker (*Skippy*), N'Bushe Wright (*Delilah Benson*), Freddy Rodriguez (*Jose*), Rose Jackson (*Juanita Benson*), Bokeem Woodbine (*Cleon*), Alvaletah Guess (*Mrs Benson*), James Pickens Jr (*Mr Curtis*), Jenifer Lewis (*Mrs Curtis*), Clifton Powell (*Cutty*), Sticky Fingaz (*Martin*), Jaimz Woolvett (*Lt Dugan*), Seymour

Warfare in the blood: Freddy Rodriguez in Allen and Albert Hughes' dynamic Dead Presidents *(from Buena Vista)*

Cassel (*Saul*), Martin Sheen (*judge*), Elizabeth Rodriguez, Terrence Howard, Ryan Williams, Rodney Winfield, David Barry Gray, Michael Imperioli, Daniel Kruse.

Dir and Pro: Albert and Allen Hughes. Co-Pro: Michael Bennett. Ex Pro: Darryl Porter. Screenplay: Michael Henry Brown, from a story by Brown and Albert and Allen Hughes, itself suggested by the story *Specialist No. 4 Haywood T. 'The Kid' Kirkland* by Wallace Terry. Ph: Lisa Rinzler. Pro Des: David Brisbin. Ed: Dan Lebental. M: Danny Elfman; numbers performed by Stevie Wonder, Otis Redding, James Brown, The Impressions, The O'Jays, Sly and The Family Stone, Marvin Gaye, Andy Williams, Barry White, Edwin Starr, Aretha Franklin, The Temptations, The Dramatics, The Spinners, Isaac Hayes, Curtis Mayfield, Harold Melvin & The Blue Notes, The Cadillacs, Al Green, Jesse & Trina B, etc. Costumes: Paul A. Simmons. (Hollywood Pictures/Caravan Pictures/Underworld Entertainment–Buena Vista.) Rel: 6 September 1996. 119 mins. Cert 18. USA. 1995.

Denise Calls Up

In an age of the home shopping channel, call waiting, fax machines, e-mail, conference calls and other modem gymnastics, it has become increasingly easy for the human race to isolate themselves from each other. When writer-director Hal Salwen bumped into a close friend at a party, he was shocked by the latter's appearance: his weight gain, hair loss and so on. Yet through the miracles of modern tele-communications Salwen knew every detail of this man's life except for what he looked

like. They hadn't actually met for over three years! Scary. Taking this one step further, Salwen has fashioned a techno *Big Chill* without the reunion. Ten characters meet, interact, squabble, have sex, introduce each other and even die on the phone, while never actually coming face to face. One man even becomes a father by proxy (courtesy of the sperm bank) and is in at the birth of his son via cellular phone. While essentially a one-joke film, *Denise Calls Up* is plotted with some ingenuity, peppered with occasional wit and convincingly played by a deadpan cast. Furthermore, the film never strays from the boundaries it has set itself.

Tim Daly (*Frank*), Caroleen Feeney (*Barbara*), Dan Gunther (*Martin*), Dana Wheeler Nicholson (*Gale*), Liev Schreiber (*Jerry*), Aida Turturro (*Linda*), Alanna Ubach (*Denise*), Sylvia Miles, Jean Lamarre, Mark Blum, and a photograph of Hal Salwen.

Dir and Screenplay: Hal Salwen. Pro: J. Todd Harris. Ex Pro: John Davis and Stephen Nemeth. Co-Pro: Michael Cozell. Ph: Michael Mayers. Pro Des: Susan Bolles. Ed: Gary Sharfin. Music supervisor: Lynn Geller; numbers performed by The Fabulous Thunderbirds, Muddy Waters, Otis Redding, etc. Costumes: Edi Giguere. (Off the Hook/Davis Entertainment/Skyline Entertainment/Dark Matter–Artificial Eye.) Rel: 26 July 1996. 79 mins. Cert 15. USA. 1995.

The Devil's Own

Belfast/New York; 1972/1992-1993. When Tom O'Meara's partner shoots a fleeing thief in the back, Tom snaps: 'We're in the police business, Eddie, not the revenge business.' Conversely, over in Ireland, IRA foot soldier Frankie McGuire observes, 'They [the British] talk about peace, but all they want is surrender.' It is these two key sentences that set the moral tone of this gripping, conscientious and extremely well-written thriller, in which a New York cop unknowingly offers shelter to an Irish terrorist. By making the IRA 'villain' sympathetic and then filtering the alternative view through the eyes of an upstanding officer of the law, *The Devil's Own* sheds a fresh perspective on the cycle of violence that has dogged Northern Ireland for most of this century. While McGuire's acts of terrorism

should not be condoned, they are at least explicable. Indeed, they are a good deal more rational than the revenge motive of Sean Bean's IRA man in *Patriot Games*, which also starred Harrison Ford. Consequently, the tug of audience loyalty between the two characters becomes, at times, almost unbearable. FYI: Due to the enormous cost of its two stars (Harrison Ford: $20 million; Brad Pitt: $8m), this fairly standard thriller ended up costing Sony Pictures somewhere between $90m and $100m!

Harrison Ford (*Tom O'Meara*), Brad Pitt (*Frankie McGuire/Rory Devaney*), Margaret Colin (*Sheila O'Meara*), Ruben Blades (*Edwin Diaz*), Treat Williams (*Billy Burke*), George Hearn (*Peter Fitzsimmons*), Mitchell Ryan (*Chief Jim Kelly*), Natascha McElhone (*Megan Doherty*), Paul Ronan (*Sean Phelan*), Simon Jones (*Harry Sloan*), Julia Stiles (*Bridget O'Meara*), Ashley Carin (*Morgan O'Meara*), Kelly Singer (*Annie O'Meara*), David O'Hara (*Martin MacDuff*), David Wilmot, Anthony Brophy, Jonathan Earl Peck, Brendan Kelly, Jack McKillop, Victor Slezak.
  Dir: Alan J. Pakula. Pro: Lawrence Gordon and Robert F. Colesberry. Ex Pro: Lloyd Levin and Donald Laventhall. Screenplay: David Aaron Cohen & Vincent Patrick and Kevin Jarre. Ph: Gordon Willis. Pro Des: Jane Musky. Ed: Tom Rolf and Dennis Virkler. M: James Horner; numbers performed by Dolores O'Riordan, Color Me Badd, The Hues Corporation, Boz Scaggs, The Righteous Brothers, Melissa Etheridge, etc. Costumes: Bernie Pollack. (Columbia Pictures–Columbia TriStar.) Rel: 20 June 1997. 111 mins. Cert 15. USA. 1997.

Diabolique

At a somewhat dour boarding school outside Pittsburgh, two school teachers, Nicole Horner and Mia Baran, plot to rid themselves of the headmaster. A charismatic, arrogant man, the latter is married to Mia, a former nun, and is fooling around with Nicole, a woman who knows her own mind. Nicole arranges the murder, Mia carries it out and the poisoned body of Guy Baran ends up in the school swimming pool. But not for long... Although a slick and superficially entertaining film, *Diabolique* fails as both a thriller and a human drama. This is because the main protagonists are drawn as broad caricatures, with little detail, subtlety or shading to their

personalities. Only Kathy Bates' wry detective – who locks wills with Sharon Stone – activates our sympathy, although, sadly, the film is not her's. P.S. Cinemagoers who recall the compelling French original of 1955 – or even the effective TV version starring Tuesday Weld and

Ringing in the rain: Liev Schreiber on call waiting in Hal Salwen's amusing Denise Calls Up *(from Artificial Eye)*

The revenge business: Natascha McElhone and Brad Pitt share an illicit rendezvous in Alan J. Pakula's gripping, well-written The Devil's Own *(from Columbia TriStar)*

Wise guys: Johnny Depp, Al Pacino, Michael Madsen and James Russo plan direct action in Mike Newell's Donnie Brasco *(from Entertainment)*

Joan Hackett – will no doubt be incensed by this silly, glossy variation.

Sharon Stone (*Nicole Horner*), Isabelle Adjani (*Mia Baran*), Chazz Palminteri (*Guy Baran*), Kathy Bates (*Shirley Vogel*), Spalding Gray (*Simon Veatch*), Shirley Knight (*Edie Danziger*), Allen Garfield (*Leo Katzman*), Adam Hann-Byrd (*Erik Pretzer*), Donal Logue, Diana Bellamy, Clea Lewis, Jeffrey Abrams, O'Neal Compton, Stephen Liska, Hank Stohl.
  Dir: Jeremiah Chechik. Pro: Marvin Worth and James G. Robinson. Ex Pro: Gary Barber, Bill Todman Jr, Jerry Offsay and Chuck Binder. Co-Pro: Gary Daigler. Screenplay: Don Roos, based on the novel *Celle Qui n'Etait Plus* by Pierre Boileau and Thomas Narcejec. Ph: Peter James. Pro Des: Leslie Dilley. Ed: Carol Littleton. M: Randy Edelman; 'In The Arms Of Love' performed by Sherry Williams. (Morgan Creek/ABC Prods–Warner.) Rel: 6 September 1996. 107 mins. Cert 18. USA. 1996.

Donnie Brasco

When FBI agent Joe Pistone adopts the monicker of Donnie Brasco and infiltrates the Mafia, he forms an unusual bond with the proud and wily hitman Lefty Ruggiero. Drawn deeper and deeper into the fraternity of The Mob, Pistone finds himself torn between duty, his love of Lefty (whom he must betray) and the wife and children he has to exclude from his life... Based on Joseph D. Pistone's autobiography *Donnie Brasco: My Undercover Life in the Mafia*, Mike Newell's film is an intelligent, emotionally nuanced drama crafted from a terrific screenplay by Paul Attanasio (*Quiz Show, Disclosure*). While inevitably sharing comparisons with a number of other Mafia epics (accentuated by the presence of Al Pacino), *Donnie Brasco* is mercifully free of the stylistic excess and gratuitous brutality associated with the genre. Thus, when the (required) violence does come, it hits all the harder – such as in the scene when Donnie's refusal to take his boots off in a Japanese restaurant (so as not to reveal his hidden tape recorder) leads to the manager being beaten to a pulp. Interesting, too, to see Pacino in a role so diametrically opposed to the undercover cop he played in *Serpico* and the shrewd, ruthless Mafia don in the *Godfather* films. And Johnny Depp as the haunted, volatile Donnie has never been better, with excellent support from Anne Heche as his wife.

Al Pacino (*Lefty Ruggiero*), Johnny Depp (*Joe Pistone/Donnie Brasco*), Michael Madsen (*Sonny Black*), Bruno Kirby (*Nicky*), James Russo (*Paulie*), Anne Heche (*Maggie Pistone*), Zeljko Ivanek (*Tim Curley*), Gerry Becker (*Dean Blandford*), Zach Grenier (*Dr Berger*), Brian Tarantina, Robert Miano, Rocco Sisto, Ronnie Farer, Terry Serpico, Gretchen Mol, Val Avery, Frank Pesce.
  Dir: Mike Newell. Pro: Louis DiGiaimo, Gail Mutrux, Mark Johnson and Barry Levinson. Ex Pro: Patrick McCormick and Alan Greenspan. Screenplay: Paul Attanasio, based on the book by Joseph D. Pistone and Richard Woodley. Ph: Peter Sova. Pro Des: Donald Graham Burt. Ed: Jon Gregory. M: Patrick Doyle; numbers performed by Dinah Washington, Lou Monte, Herbie Hancock, Blondie, Johnny Mathis, Jerry Vale, Vic Damone, The Spinners, Neil Diamond, The Pointer Sisters, Electric Light Orchestra, The Miracles, The Trammps, The Alan Parsons Project, Dean Martin, Curt Sobel, etc. Costumes: Aude Bronson-Howard and David Robinson. (Mandalay Entertainment/Baltimore Pictures–Entertainment.) Rel: 2 May 1997. 126 mins. Cert 18. USA. 1997.

Don't Forget You're Going To Die - N'oublie Pas Que Tu Vas Mourir

The clue is in the title. However, little else is quite so obvious in this bold, confident, beguiling, disturbing, honest, anarchic, poetic, ironic, shocking, eye-opening and ultimately deeply haunting film. Faced with military service, art student Benoit embarks on a number of ploys to evade the draft, yet none of his cunning, lies or even a fake suicide attempt can sway the army's resolve. Then, out of the blue, Benoit stumbles on to something far more terrible than ten months in the military... The power of Xavier Beauvois's second film is that the 29-year-old writer-director-actor (who looks like an adolescent cross between John Cusack and Martin Donovan) refuses to resort to treacly compassion or in-your-face histrionics (à la *Savage Nights*). On the contrary, Beauvois presents his protagonist as a credible mix of amiability, reserve, intelligence and naivety who tumbles secretively into his own private hell.

Xavier Beauvois (*Benoit*), Roschdy Zem (*Omar*), Chiara Mastroianni (*Claudia*), Bulle Ogier (*Benoit's mother*), Jean-Louis Richard (*Benoit's father*), Jean Douchet, Emmanuel Salinger, Pascal Bonitzer, Cedric Kahn, Stanislas Nordey.
   Dir: Xavier Beauvois. Ex Pro: Jean-Marc Henchoz. Screenplay: Beauvois, Anne-Marie Sauzeau, Emmanuel Salinger and Zoubir Tligui. Ph: Caroline Champetier. Pro Des: Denis Barbier. Ed: Agnes Guillemot. M: John Cale. Costumes: Olga Pelletier and Laura Perez-Cobain. (Why Not Productions/La Sept Cinema/Canal Plus–ICA.) Rel: 27 September 1996. 118 mins. Cert 18. France. 1995.

Dracula Dead and Loving It

Mel Brooks revisits one of his finest hours – the 1974 *Young Frankenstein* – for a belated companion piece that has enough good humour and amusing jokes for tolerant Brooks aficionados to call this a slight return to form after the terrible *Robin Hood* spoof. Mel's best idea was to cast the deadpan Leslie Nielsen as the man with the fangs (with a perfect vocal impersonation of the original 1931 count, Bela Lugosi), and to let both his star and script treat the Bram Stoker story as seriously as possible in a comedy. Talking of impersonations, Harvey Korman does a great Nigel Bruce and Peter MacNicol a silly but funny version of Dwight Frye's role as the loopy Renfield. A likeable picture. All it needs is a team of TV gagpersons to write in a sprinkle of really funny jokes. [Derek Winnert]

Leslie Nielsen (*Count Dracula*), Peter MacNicol (*Renfield*), Steven Weber (*Jonathan Harker*), Amy Yasbeck (*Mina*), Lysette Anthony (*Lucy*), Harvey Korman (*Dr Seward*), Mel Brooks (*Professor Van Helsing*), Anne Bancroft (*Madame Ouspenskaya*), Mark Blankfield, Megan Cavanagh, Clive Revill, Chuck McCann, Avery Schreiber, Ezio Greggio, Rudy De Luca, Maura Nielsen, Thea Nielsen, David DeLuise.
   Dir and Pro: Mel Brooks. Ex Pro: Peter Schindler. Screenplay: Brooks, Rudy De Luca and Steve Haberman. Ph: Michael D. O'Shea. Pro Des: Roy Forge Smith. Ed: Adam Weiss. M: Hummie Mann. Costumes: Dodie Shepard. Visual effects: Dream Quest Images. (Castle Rock Entertainment/Gaumont/Brooksfilms–PolyGram.) Rel: 25 October 1996. 90 mins. Cert PG. USA. 1995.

DragonHeart

The tenth century; Europe. When the earnest Prince Einon is fatally wounded in a peasant revolt against his father, a kindly dragon restores

A positive future?: Xavier Beauvois in his own harrowing, unforgettable Don't Forget You're Going To Die *(from ICA Projects)*

Sean the magic dragon: Draco tests his halitosis in Rob Cohen's toothsome DragonHeart *(from UIP)*

his life by bequeathing half of his own heart. The Promethean beast, mortified by the reign of tyranny of the boy's father, hopes that by contributing his heart to the monarchy a new cycle of peace will prevail. However, the prince grows into a king even more unscrupulous than his forebear, his strength augmented by the dragon's, thus prompting good and evil to thrive to the beat of one heart... Filmed in the breathtaking mountainside of Slovakia and several years in pre-production, *DragonHeart* is a handsome production that pushes the marvels of computer-generated imagery to new heights (you'll believe a dragon can fly, etc. etc.). Dennis Quaid invests his 'knight of the old order' with welcome sincerity and irony (showing up the throw-away performance of Kevin Costner in the vaguely similar *Robin Hood: Prince of Thieves*), while Sean Connery, as the voice of the dragon, enjoys himself enormously. How-ever, it's a shame that some of the old clichés of the genre – the medieval hero with an American accent, the villain with an English one – remain. Besides, I'm sure that the homesteads of yore were never quite so inflammable (as repeatedly depicted in movies like this). FYI: In the interests of authenticity, many of the costumes were actually woven on looms from the tenth century.

Utter Misery: James Spader with Anne Brochet, his alluring, enigmatic captor, in Ronan O'Leary's Driftwood *(from Blue Dolphin/Goldcrest)*

Dennis Quaid (*Bowen*), David Thewlis (*Einon*), Sean Connery (*the voice of Draco*), Pete Postlethwaite (*Gilbert*), Dina Meyer (*Kara*), Julie Christie (*Queen Aislinn*), Jason Isaacs (*Felton*), Brian Thompson (*Brok*), Lee Oakes (*young Einon*), Peter Hric (*King Freyne*), John Gielgud (*the voice of King Arthur*), Wolf Christian, Terry O'Neill, Eva Vejmelkova.

Dir: Rob Cohen. Pro: Raffaella De Laurentiis. Ex Pro: David Rotman and Patrick Read Johnson. Co-Pro: Hester Hargett. Screenplay: Charles Edward Pogue, from a story by Johnson and Pogue. Ph: David Eggby. Pro Des: Benjamin Fernandez. Ed: Peter Amundson. M: Randy Edelman. Costumes: Thomas Casterline. Special effects: Kit West. Visual effects: Scott Squires; Industrial Light & Magic. (Universal–UIP.) Rel: 18 October 1996. 103 mins. Cert PG. USA. 1996.

Drifting Clouds – Kausas Pilvet Karkaavat

Helsinki, Finland; today. Ilona and Lauri Koponen are a middle-aged couple with no pretensions and precious few extravagances. They are still paying for their sofa, TV and bookshelf and when they've paid those off they intend to buy some books. Then Lauri, a tram driver, loses his job. Shortly afterwards, the restaurant at which Ilona works as head waiter closes down. This is, not to put too fine a point on it, no laughing matter... Writing in *Sight and Sound*, Jonathan Romney described the humour of Aki Kaurismaki as 'so acute and economic that laughter seems a

superfluous extravagance'. Economic, certainly. But acute? Large numbers of people who find themselves in a cinema showing a Kaurismaki picture (*Ariel, I Hired a Contract Killer*) aren't even aware they're watching a comedy. And that in itself is like an in-joke shared by Kaurismaki's disciples. Indeed, the merit of Finland's one-man film industry is that he doesn't stray from this extended inside gag – even if he does, finally, inject a little 'Frank Capra-like hyper-optimism' into *Drifting Clouds*. Accepted as a wry comment on Finnish society, the film certainly has its pleasures, but is its low-key, studied nonchalance worth the price of a cinema ticket?

Kati Outinen (*Ilona Koponen*), Kari Vaananen (*Lauri Koponen*), Elina Salo (*Mrs Sjoholm*), Sakari Kuosmanen (*Melartin*), Markku Peltola (*Lajunen*), Matti Onnismaa, Mustafa Altin, Outi Maenpaa.

Dir, Pro, Screenplay and Ed: Aki Kaurismaki. Ph: Timo Salminen. Art: Markku Patila and Jukka Salmi. M: Tchaikovsky, Handel, Shelley Fisher, etc. (Sputnik Oy/YLE TV-1/Eila Werning/ Pandora Film/The Finnish Film Foundation, etc.–Metro Tartan.) Rel: 6 June 1997. 96 mins. Cert PG. Finland/ Germany/France. 1996.

Driftwood

On a remote, windswept island off the west coast of Ireland, a solitary French woman, a wood carver, discovers the body of an American amnesiac washed up on the beach. Dragging him back to her ramshackle wooden abode, she nurtures him back to health and gradually becomes obsessed with her handsome new possession. He, on the other hand, while returning his captor's affections, yearns for his freedom and wants to discover his identity... Lacking narrative thrust, suspense, humour or even novelty (remember *Misery*?), *Driftwood* drifts from start to finish with little purpose. Throwing up a number of intriguing questions – What is a French woman doing in Ireland? Why does she have an English mother? Why is an American lying on her beach? – the film fails to answer any of them. Instead, it presents claustrophobia, stagnation and yet another opportunity to listen to the sound of uillean pipes on the soundtrack of an Irish film.

James Spader (*The Man*), Anne Brochet (*Sarah*), Barry McGovern (*Mr TcTavish*), Anna Massey (*Mother*), Kevin McHugh.

Dir: Ronan O'Leary. Pro: Mary Breen-Farrelly. Ex Pro: John Quested and Guy Collins. Line Pro: Moira Kelly. Screenplay: Richard M.N. Waring (and O'Leary). Ph: Billy Williams. Pro Des: Tim Hutchinson. Ed: Malcolm Cooke. M: John Cameron. Costumes: Bronwen Casson. (Deadwood Limited/Goldcrest Films/Setanta–Blue Dolphin/Goldcrest.) Rel: 28 March 1997. 100 mins. Cert 18. Ireland/United Kingdom. 1996.

Eddie

Eddie Franklin is an exuberant fan of The Knicks, New York's ailing basketball team, and is signed on as their coach – as a joke... Not since the early days of *Burglar* and *The Telephone* has Whoopi Goldberg succumbed to such mediocre material. The film may content itself with a string of glib cameos and the apparently enthusiastic cooperation of the NBA, but the jokes are embarrassingly limp and the story predictable and barren – not to mention the slapdash continuity, flabby editing, careless casting, etc, etc. Amazingly, the film's story and screenplay is credited to six different writers. FYI: Whoopi was paid $10 million and ran off with her leading man (a seriously miscast Langella).

Whoopi Goldberg (*Edwina 'Eddie' Franklin*), Frank Langella ('*Wild' Bill Burgess*), Dennis Farina ('*Coach' John Bailey*), Richard Jenkins (*Zimmer*), Lisa Ann Walter (*Claudine*), Malik Sealy (*Stacy Patton*), Dwayne Schintzius (*Ivan Radovadovitch*), Marv Albert (*himself*), Chris Berman (*himself*), Ebony Jo-Ann (*Mrs Patton*), John Benjamin Hickey, Troy Beyer, John Salley, Rick Fox, Mark Jackson, Greg Ostertag, Vernel Singleton, Aasif Mandvi, and as themselves: Edward Koch, Donald Trump, Mujibur Rahman, Sirajul Islam, Fabio, David Letterman.

Dir: Steve Rash. Pro: David Permut and Mark Burg. Ex Pro: Ron Bozman, Steve Zacharias and Jeff Buhai. Screenplay: Jon Connolly & David Loucka, and Eric Champnella & Keith Mitchell, and Steve Zacharias & Jeff Buhai. Ph: Victor Kemper. Pro Des: Dan Davis. Ed: Richard Halsey. M: Stanley Clarke; numbers performed by Coolio, House of Pain, Luke, Lady Soul, EMF, Myron, Darcus, Gary Glitter, Steam, etc. Costumes: Molly Maginnis. (Hollywood Pictures/PolyGram/Island Pictures–First Independent.) Rel: 25 April 1997. 101 mins. Cert 12. USA. 1996.

When worlds collide: Daniel Auteuil and Pascal Duquenne in their Cannes award-winning roles in Jaco Van Dormael's inventive, provocative The Eighth Day *(from PolyGram)*

The Eighth Day - Le Huitieme Jour

According to the gospel of Georges, an orphan with Down's syndrome, in the beginning there was nothing but music. Then on the first day God made the sun. On the second, the sea, then records, television, and so on. On the eighth day, He made Georges. There was also Harry, a high-powered sales consultant who advises his clients to surreptitiously adopt the mannerisms of their customers, as anything 'different' shocks people. Harry is up to his neck in work and has already lost his wife and two young daughters because of it. The last thing he needs is a crazy guy with Down's syndrome to look after. Or is it? Writer-director Jaco Van Dormael first met the Down's syndrome actor Pascal Duquenne on his last film, *Toto the Hero*. Finding himself totally at ease with these special people, the filmmaker relates, 'They have a talent for life, for loving life and the present moment that we often lack. Their world exists just alongside ours and yet we know nothing about it. Every

country has been explored; the whole surface of the earth has been mapped. Yet there remain unknown worlds just next to us, if we can be bothered to see them. For me, they symbolise difference – another way of seeing the world.' Van Dormael's film has plenty to say and does so in a dynamic, inventive and totally surprising way. Yet while punching a number of emotional buttons, *The Eighth Day* doesn't always connect. It does, though, force one to stop and think for a moment, and anything that achieves that with such style and distinction deserves a rousing ovation. FYI: Duquenne and Daniel Auteuil shared the best actor award at the 1996 Cannes film festival.

Daniel Auteuil (*Harry*), Pascal Duquenne (*Georges*), Miou-Miou (*Julie*), Isabelle Sadoyan (*Georges' mother*), Michele Maes (*Nathalie*), Laszlo Harmati (*Luis Mariano*), Alice Van Dormael (*Alice*), Juliette Van Dormael (*Juliette*), Henri Garcin, Helene Roussel, Fabienne Loriaux, Dominic Gould, Didier de Neck.

Dir and Screenplay: Jaco Van Dormael. Pro: Philippe Godeau. Line Pro: Eric Rommeluere and Dominique Josset. Ph: Walther Vanden Ende. Pro Des: Hubert Pouille. Ed: Susana Rossberg. M: Pierre Van Dormael; Moazart; numbers performed by Luis Mariano, Genesis, etc. Costumes: Yan Tax. (Pan Europeenne Prods/Homemade Films/TF1 Films/ Working Title/Canal Plus, etc.–Poly-Gram.) Rel: 8 November 1996. 118 mins. Cert PG. France/Belgium/UK. 1996.

Negotiations in love: Gwyneth Paltrow and Greta Scacchi chew the fat in Douglas McGrath's heavenly Emma *(from Buena Vista)*

Emma

Thrilled that her matchmaking of a wealthy neighbour with her governess has paid off, Emma Woodhouse embarks on finding a suitable mate for her new intimate, Harriet Smith. Emma, who lives in comfortable splendour with her amiably widowed father, is far too happy to worry about men in her own life. Besides, she has dear Mr Knightley to confide in, who is like an older brother to her. But when her well-intentioned scheming starts to unravel, Emma finds herself abandoned and her emotional support system crumbling... It's hard to believe that the journalist, playwright and co-scenarist of *Bullets Over Broadway*, Douglas McGrath, cut his directorial milk teeth on this Jane Austen adaptation, but it's true. Furthermore, he's given it a wit, power and flourish that elevates it above all previous Austen adaptations, including *Sense and Sensibility*. The Californian-born Gwyneth Paltrow, while obviously too thin for the role, captures the frail beauty and obsessive altruism of Emma perfectly and passes off a flawless English accent. In fact, a wonderful cast rises immaculately to the occasion, with Jeremy Northam particularly convincing as Mr Knightley, and Juliet Stevenson stealing every scene she's in as the insufferably arrogant Mrs Elton. Filmed on location in London and Dorset.

Gwyneth Paltrow (*Emma Woodhouse*), Toni Collette (*Harriet Smith*), Alan Cumming (*Mr Elton*), Ewan McGregor (*Frank Churchill*), Jeremy Northam (*George Knightley*), Greta Scacchi (*Anne Weston née Taylor*), Juliet Stevenson (*Augusta Elton*), Polly Walker (*Jane Fairfax*), Sophie Thompson (*Miss Bates*), Phyllida Law (*Mrs Bates*), James Cosmo (*Mr Weston*), Denys Hawthorne (*Mr Woodhouse*), Edward Woodall (*Robert Martin*), Kathleen Byron (*Mrs Goddard*), Brett Miley, Brian Capron, Karen Westwood, Rebecca Craig, Angela Down, John Franklyn Robbins.
Dir and Screenplay: Douglas McGrath. Pro: Patrick Cassavetti and Steven Haft. Ex Pro: Bob Weinstein, Harvey Weinstein and Donna Gigliotti. Assoc Pro: Donna Grey. Ph: Ian Wilson. Pro Des: Michael Howells. Ed: Lesley Walker. M: Rachel Portman; Handel. Costumes: Ruth Myers. (Matchmaker Films/Miramax–Buena Vista.) Rel: 13 September 1996. 120 mins. Cert U. UK/USA. 1996.

The English Patient

1938-1945; North Africa/Tuscany. Recovered from the wreck of his burned-out plane, Count Laszlo Almasy is tended in a Tuscan monastery by a Canadian nurse, Hana, who believes she is cursed. Yet as Laszlo recalls the passion and betrayal that brought him to this vegetative state, a bond of emotional healing unites the two victims of the war. But who is Hana's English patient? A visiting Canadian spy believes he knows the invalid's true identity, but then nothing is as it seems... From the very start, *The English Patient* exercises a striking command of its material. A primitive painting is daubed over the opening credits, the landscape of the paper then transfigured into a carpet of sand dunes, and the shadow of the painting – briefly reflected on the dunes – replaced by the shadow of a bi-plane. Cut to a shot of the plane being downed by Arab snipers, and the film's elaborate structure of flashbacks begins its sweeping revelation. Powerful, passionate and intelligent, *The English Patient* is a masterful interpretation of Michael Ondaatje's multi-layered Booker Prize-winning novel of 1992. P.S. Fiennes and Binoche previously played Heathcliff and Cathy in the ill-fated *Emily Bronte's Wuthering Heights*.

Ralph Fiennes (*Count Laszlo Almasy*), Juliette Binoche (*Hana*), Willem Dafoe (*David Caravaggio*), Kristin Scott-Thomas (*Katharine Clifton*), Naveen Andrews (*Kip*), Colin Firth (*Geoffrey Clifton*), Julian Wadham (*Madox*), Jurgen Prochnow (*Major Muller*), Kevin Whately (*Hardy*), Clive Merrison (*Fenelon-Barnes*), Nino Castelnuovo (*D'Agostino*), Hichem Rostom, Peter Ruhring, Geordie Johnson, Torri Higginson, Lisa Repo-Martell, Raymond Coulthard, Lee Ross, Amanda Walker.

Dir and Screenplay: Anthony Minghella. Pro: Saul Zaentz. Ex Pro: Bob Weinstein, Harvey Weinstein and Scott Greenstein. Line Pro: Alessandro von Normann. Ph: John Seale. Pro Des: Stuart Craig. Ed: Walter Murch. M: Gabriel Yared; numbers performed by Muzsikas and Marta Sebestyen, Fred Astaire, Ella Fitzgerald, and Benny Goodman. Costumes: Ann Roth. (Miramax/Tiger Moth Prods–Buena Vista.) Rel: 14 March 1997. 162 mins. Cert 15. USA. 1996.

Entertaining Angels: The Dorothy Day Story

1917-1963; New York City. Latterly dubbed 'the Mother Teresa of New York', Dorothy Day was a Marxist suffragette who punctuated her passion for causes with alcohol-fuelled romps with the literary glitterati of her day. Then, in 1927, she saw the light, converted to Catholicism and devoted the rest of her life to championing the poor, establishing a string of soup kitchens and founding the anarchic *Catholic Worker* newspaper... Set up to produce 'features about human values', Paulist Pictures previously greenlit *Romero*, a plodding biography of the Archbishop of San Salvador. But 'worthy' and 'inspirational' seldom go hand in hand, and while Moira Kelly gives a performance of inner resolve and quiet strength as the doggedly stubborn Day, Michael Ray Rhodes' leaden direction chokes the life out of the material. Resorting to such

clichés as the flashback format and the standard 'smashing up the furniture' scene of frustration, Rhodes should have heeded the warning of Lenny Von Dohlen's Forster Batterham who observes that religion sucks all the joy out of life. Forster is wrong, of course, but this sanitised trudge through Day's life goes a long way to proving him right.

Moira Kelly (*Dorothy Day*), Martin Sheen (*Peter Maurin*), Heather Graham (*Maggie*), Melinda Dillon (*Sister Aloysius*), Lenny Von Dohlen (*Forster Batterham*), Boyd Kestner (*Lionel Moise*), James Lancaster (*Eugene O'Neill*), Paul Lieber (*Mike Gold*), Brian Keith (*The Cardinal*), Tracey Walter (*Joe Bennett*), Geoffrey Blake (*Floyd Dell*), Allyce Beasley (*Frankie*), Heather Smerling

In love and war: Ralph Fiennes and Kristin Scott-Thomas pick up Oscar nominations in Anthony Minghella's masterly The English Patient *(from Buena Vista)*

(*Tamar*), Samantha MacLachlan (*Annie*), Mary Greening (*Eleanor*), Marianne Muellerleile, Renee Estevez.

Dir: Michael Ray Rhodes. Pro: The Rev. Ellwood E. Kieser. Co-Pro: Peter Burrell and Chris Donahue. Screenplay: John Wells. Ph: Michael Fash. Pro Des: Charles Rosen. Ed: George Folsey Jr and Geoffrey Rowland. M: Bill Conti and Ashley Irwin. Costumes: Gayle Evans-Ivy. (Paulist Pictures–Warner.) Rel: 6 June 1997. 111 mins. Cert 12. USA. 1996.

Eraser

John Kruger is an eraser and is the best in the business. Working strictly on his own, he takes subjects in the Federal Witness Protection Program and completely erases their identity. When Lee Cullen discovers that high-ranking officials are selling a prototype weapon to international terrorists – the thermal-powered and pulse-effective rail gun – she copies evidence on to a compact disc. Now certain big guns in the government

Blot on the landscape: Arnold Schwarzenegger rubs up against Vanessa Williams in Charles Russell's action-crammed Eraser *(from Warner)*

want her eliminated – at any cost. But then they hadn't reckoned on Kruger's obligation to his duty... As to be expected from the director of *The Mask*, much of *Eraser* is of a cartoonish quality, although this will hardly detract from the entertainment value for most Schwarzenegger fans. However, the old close-ups of Arnie preparing for battle (zipping up, thrusting knives into place), the limp one-liners and some impossible escapes from death will try the patience of many

action fans. Still, the hardware is impressive, James Caan makes a suitably hissable villain and the pace is kept at a merciless clip. FYI: Reputedly costing a bank-busting $120 million, *Eraser* goes down in the history books as the second most expensive movie ever made – not that you'd think it from some of the tacky back projection.

Arnold Schwarzenegger (*John Kruger*), James Caan (*Robert Deguerin*), Vanessa Williams (*Lee Cullen*), James Coburn

Down memory pain: Shirley MacLaine reminisces on her 1983 Oscar in Robert Harling's hollow The Evening Star *(from Entertainment)*

(*Beller*), Robert Pastorelli (*Johnny C.*), James Cromwell (*Donahue*), Danny Nucci (*Monroe*), Andy Romano (*Harper*), Olek Krupa (*Sergei*), Nick Chinlund, Michael Papajohn, Joe Viterelli, Mark Rolston, John Slattery, Robert Miranda, Roma Maffia, Tony Longo, Gerry Becker, John Snyder, Melora Walters, Cylk Cozart.

Dir: Charles 'Chuck' Russell. Pro: Arnold Kopelson and Anne Kopelson. Ex Pro: Russell and Michael Tadross. Co-Pro: Stephen Brown and Caroline Pham. Screenplay: Tony Puryear and Walon Green, from a story by Puryear, Green and Michael S. Chernuchin. Ph: Adam Greenberg. Pro Des: Bill Kenney. Ed: Michael Tronick. M: Alan Silvestri; numbers performed by Vanessa Williams, Dean Martin, and The Weather Girls. Costumes: Richard Bruno. (Warner– Warner.) Rel: 23 August 1996. 114 mins. Cert 18. USA. 1996.

Escape From L.A.

See *John Carpenter's Escape From L.A.*

The Evening Star

Houston, Texas; the recent past/ today. In the fifteen years since Emma Greenway Horton (Debra Winger) died at the end of *Terms of Endearment*, her mother's life has been locked in a downward spiral. Aurora Greenway's doting attempts at bringing up her daughter's children have, characteristically, pushed them from the nest. Tommy is in prison for the third time and has turned terminally bitter; Melanie has run off to LA after being caught *in flagrante delicto* with her boyfriend, Bruce; and Teddy has sired a toddler from hell. Which just leaves Aurora's mutinous maid, Rosie, and her on-going rivalry with Emma's old friend Patsy... As scenarist and playwright Robert Harling proved with his scripts for *Steel Magnolias* and *The First Wives Club*, he is a past master of the *bon mot*. However, his dialogue is so loaded towards the punchline that it carries an empty echo after the laughter has died. Thus, his characters become mere stand-up comics on the stage of his drama and fail to inhabit a world that we can either believe in or care about. Shirley MacLaine, while making the most of a line like 'Garrett Breedlove possessed every single quality I find repellent in a man,' has become a strutting caricature, whereas Juliette Lewis – as the alter ego of Debra Winger – cannot shake off the white

Crocodile smiles? Jonathan Pryce and Madonna grin for Argentina in Alan Parker's stylish Evita *(from Entertainment)*

trash roles that she has made her own. Ultimately, then, *The Evening Star* feels like *Terms of Endearment* flossed by *Steel Magnolias*.

Shirley MacLaine (*Aurora Greenway*), Bill Paxton (*Jerry Bruckner*), Juliette Lewis (*Melanie Horton*), Miranda Richardson (*Patsy Carpenter*), Ben Johnson (*Arthur Cotton*), Scott Wolf (*Bruce*), George Newbern (*Tommy Horton*), Marion Ross (*Rosie Dunlop*), Mackenzie Astin (*Teddy Horton*), Donald Moffat (*Hector Scott*), Jack Nicholson (*Garrett Breedlove*), Jennifer Grant (*Ellen*), Clement von Franckenstein (*Pascal Ferney*), China Kantner, Shawn Taylor Thompson, Jake Langerud, Antonia Bogdanovich, Mary Gross, Don Burgess.

Dir and Screenplay: Robert Harling, based on the novel by Larry McMurtry. Pro: David Kirkpatrick, Polly Platt and Keith Samples. Co-Pro: Dennis Bishop. Ph: Don Burgess. Pro Des: Bruno Rubeo. Ed: Priscilla Nedd-Friendly and David Moritz. M: William Ross. Costumes: Renee Kalfus. (Paramount/Rysher Entertainment–Entertainment.) Rel: 14 March 1997. 129 mins. Cert 15. USA. 1996.

Everyone Says I Love You

Park Avenue, Manhattan/Paris/Venice; today. An extended family living on Park Avenue – 'not the typical family you'd find in a musical comedy,' observes Natasha Lyonne, the film's narrator – find their romantic lives transformed with the onset of spring. There are two things that make this a unique Woody Allen enterprise. One, it is his first film not solely set in and around New York. And two, it has songs. Yet, while the sight of Woody having a seizure in Venice may have a certain curiosity value, the poorly executed musical numbers quickly lose their novelty. It was as if, strapped for a decent story and the usual roster of wisecracks, the filmmaker slipped in some songs so that nobody would notice the creative deficit. Unfortunately, by choosing a cast that cannot sing (with the exception of Goldie Hawn) and filming the numbers with all the exuberance of Godard on Valium, Woody has converted a silk purse into a cloth ear. At most, there are three or four smiles in the whole movie.

Alan Alda (*Bob*), Woody Allen (*Joe*), Drew Barrymore (*Skylar*), Lukas Haas (*Scott*), Goldie Hawn (*Steffi*), Gaby Hoffman (*Lane*), Natasha Lyonne (*DJ*), Edward Norton (*Holden*), Natalie Portman (*Laura*), Julia Roberts (*Von*), Tim Roth (*Charles Ferry*), David Ogden Stiers (*Holden's father*), Patrick Cranshaw (*Grandpa*), Robert Knepper (*Greg*), Billy Crudup (*Ken*), Trude Klein, Itzhak Perlman (*himself*), Navah Perlman, Edward Hibbert, Paolo Seganti, Andrea Piedimonte, Scotty Bloch.

Dir and Screenplay: Woody Allen. Pro: Robert Greenhut. Ex Pro: Jean Doumanian and J.E. Beaucaire. Co-Ex Pro: Jack Rollins, Charles H. Joffe and Letty Aronson. Co-Pro: Helen Roth. Ph: Carlo DiPalma. Pro Des: Santo Loquasto. Ed: Susan E. Morse. M: Dick Hyman; numbers performed by Edward Norton, Olivia Hayman, Natasha Lyonne, Edward Hibbert, Woody Allen, Natalie Portman, Alan Alda, Goldie Hawn, Julia Roberts, Billy Crudup, Tim Roth, Patrick Cranshaw, The Helen Singers, Dick Hyman and The New York Studio Players, etc. Costumes: Jeffrey Kurland. Choreographer: Graciela Daniele. (Magnolia Prods/Sweetland Films–Buena Vista.) Rel: 18 April 1997. 91 mins. Cert 12. USA. 1996.

Evita

The illegitimate daughter of a poor farmer, Maria Eva Duarte is determined to improve her lot. Attaching herself to a local singer, she persuades the latter to take her to Buenos Aires, where she begins to sleep her way up the ladder of Argentinean society. By the time she meets Colonel Juan Peron, she is already an established actress and, as

Would you let this man cut you open? Hugh Grant doctors his frivolous image in Michael Apted's ripping Extreme Measures *(from Rank–Castle Rock/Turner)*

First Lady, goes on to become the glamorous lifeblood of the Péronist party... After 14 years of false starts, the job of directing Sir Tim Rice and Lord Lloyd Webber's phenomenally successful opera falls to Alan Parker, the Islington-born filmmaker who brought us *Bugsy Malone*, *Fame* and *Pink Floyd – The Wall*. And so Parker – working from a script he adapted from Oliver Stone's – empowers the material with his characteristic flair, bringing epic grandeur to a relatively modest budget ($59 million at the last count). But it is Madonna, who fought for the part tooth and nail, who truly distinguishes this rousing, thrilling motion picture event with the performance of her life. When she's not on screen, the endless rallies, riots and marches threaten to overwhelm the patience. Filmed in Hungary, Argentina and at Shepperton Studios in London. FYI: Various performers discussed to play Evita include Kim Wilde, Olivia Newton-John, Diane Keaton, Elaine Paige, Barbra Streisand, Bette Midler, Gloria Estefan, Liza Minnelli, Meryl Streep and Michelle Pfeiffer.

Madonna (*Maria Eva Duarte Peron*), Antonio Banderas (*Ernesto Guevara de la Serna, aka Ché*), Jonathan Pryce (*Juan Domingo Peron*), Jimmy Nail (*Augustin Magaldi*), Victoria Sus (*Dona Juana*), Julian Littman (*Brother Juan*), Olga Merediz (*Blanca*), Laura Pallas (*Elisa*), Julia Worsley (*Erminda*), Maria Lujan Hidalgo, Servando Villamil, Andrea Corr, Peter Polycarpou, Gary Brooker, Mark Ryan, Gordon Neville, Frederick Warder, Nickolas Grace.
   Dir: Alan Parker. Pro: Parker, Robert Stigwood and Andrew G. Vajna. Line Pro: David Wimbury. Assoc Pro: Lisa Moran. Screenplay: Parker and Oliver Stone. Ph: Darius Khondji. Pro Des: Brian Morris. Ed: Gerry Hambling. M: Andrew Lloyd Webber; lyrics: Tim Rice. Costumes: Penny Rose. Choreographer: Vincent Paterson. (Cinergi Pictures/Dirty Hands–Entertainment.) Rel: 20 December 1996. 134 mins. Cert PG. USA. 1996.

Extreme Measures

Sometimes, doing what seems to be the right thing is not always the right thing. With ten seconds to choose between the fate of an injured cop and the critically wounded gunman who shot him, English ER physician Guy Luthan favours the cop. It's an ethical dilemma that the medical staff of New York's busy Gramercy Hospital face daily – however, by rights, morality should not be part of a doctor's kitbag. But this is only the starting point in a much bigger issue, one involving human experiments for the greater good of mankind... A ripping yarn with its fair share of suspenseful moments, *Extreme Measures* works as both a conspiracy thriller and talking point. Although unlikely casting as the driven, conscientious doctor, Hugh Grant is actually very good, introducing a welcome touch of humour to an unrelentingly grim scenario – particularly needed as Danny Elfman's overactive score allows the film little dramatic light and shade.

Hugh Grant (*Dr Guy Luthan*), Gene Hackman (*Dr Lawrence Myrick*), Sarah Jessica Parker (*Jodie Trammel*), David Morse (*Frank Hare*), Bill Nunn (*Burke*), John Toles-Bey (*Bobby*), Paul Guilfoyle (*Dr Jeffery Manko*), Debra Monk (*Dr Judith Gruszynski*), Peter Appel (*Det. Stone*), Shaun Austin-Olsen (*Claude Minkins*),

André De Shields, J.K. Simmons, Diana Zimmer, Nancy Beatty, Gerry Becker, Bill MacDonald, Peter Maloney, Ross Petty, Raynor Scheine, David Cronenberg (*hospital lawyer*), Marilyn McDonald.

Dir: Michael Apted. Pro: Elizabeth Hurley. Ex Pro: Andrew Scheinman. Screenplay: Tony Gilroy, based on the book by Michael Palmer. Ph: John Bailey. Pro Des: Doug Kraner. Ed: Rick Shaine. M: Danny Elfman; 'On My Mind' performed by Hoi Polloy. Costumes: Susan Lyall. (Columbia/Castle Rock/ Simian Films–Rank–Castle Rock/Turner.) Rel: 31 January 1997. 118 mins. Cert 15. USA/UK. 1996.

Fallen Angels - Duoluo Tianshi

Five characters inhabiting the labyrinthine corridors and boxy rooms of a nocturnal Hong Kong, slip in and out of madness as they strive to find a semblance of reason and hope in their lives... While Wong Kar-wai's *Chungking Express* was embraced by critics for its daring and innovative manipulation of cinematic technique, a repeat performance quickly loses its allure. Again the filmmaker populates his nihilistic perspective of Hong Kong with a variety of hopeless characters living on the edge of insanity. And, indeed, Wong Kar-wai's neon-washed vision – utilising wide-angle lenses, hand-held camera, frenetic cutting, speeded-up film, primary colours and brief sorties into black and white – is seductive, up to a point. But for a film to hold any grip on an audience it must have some cohesive story and characters to care for. *Fallen Angels*, however, is nothing but a masturbatory exercise in style.

Leon Lai Ming (*Wong Chi-Ming, the killer*), Takeshi Kaneshiro (*Ho*), Charlie Young (*Cherry*), Michele Reis (*agent*), Karen Mok (*Punkie*), Chan Fai-Hung, Chen Wanlei, Toru Saito.

Dir, Ex Pro and Screenplay: Wong Kar-wai. Pro: Jeff Lau. Line Pro: Jacky Pang Yee-Wah. Ph: Christopher Doyle. Pro Des and Ed: William Chang. M: Frankie Chan and Roel A. Garcia; numbers performed by Massive Attack, The Flying Pickets, Marianne Faithfull, Laurie Anderson, Shirley Kwan, and Chyi Chin. (Jet Tone Prods–Electric.) Rel: 6 September 1996. 95 mins. Cert 15. Hong Kong. 1995.

The Fan

San Francisco; the present. What happens when a man who has failed as a husband and parent – and who loses his job in the company founded by his own father – decides that he can help a national hero? Gil Renard, knife salesman and committed baseball fan, believes he has the answer when local baseball champ Bobby Rayburn – who's been bought by the San Francisco Giants for a cool $40m – hits a slump. Rayburn, Renard reasons, just needs his lucky number back, even if it is tattooed on the shoulder of a rival player... Abandoning his Armani and Versace threads, Robert De Niro dons baseball cap and trainers to play a bastard several rungs down the corporate criminal ladder. Here, twenty years on, the actor is back in *Taxi Driver* mode, as an irrational, obsessed outsider climbing out of the gutter to make 'a difference'. However, under the meretricious direction of Tony Scott this is not really a De Niro movie – although it's certainly a Wesley Snipes one. Obviously the critics (who damned the film to a man) were expecting something special, but as a piece of garish, pulse-quickening escapism, *The Fan* hits all the right marks with aplomb. Only near the ending does the film becomes so stylised that it finally loses its emotional grip.

Robert De Niro (*Gil Renard*), Wesley Snipes (*Bobby Rayburn*), Ellen Barkin (*Jewel Stern*),

The Number One Disciple: Robert De Niro flexes his adulation in Tony Scott's gripping The Fan *(from Entertainment)*

John Leguizamo (*Manny*), Benicio Del Toro (*Juan Primo*), Patti D'Arbanville-Quinn (*Ellen Renard*), Chris Mulkey (*Tim*), Andrew J. Ferchland (*Richie Renard*), Charles Hallahan (*Coop*), Brandon Hammond, Dan Butler, Kurt Fuller, Michael Jace, Frank Medrano, Don S. Davis, John Kruk, Stoney Jackson, Drew Snyder, Edith Diaz, Tuesday Knight, Marjorie Lovett, M.C. Gainey, Aaron Neville, Paul Herman, Richard Riehle.

Dir: Tony Scott. Pro: Wendy Finerman. Ex Pro: Bill Unger, James W. Skotchdopole and Barrie M. Osborne. Co-Pro: Margaret French Isaacs. Screenplay: Phoef Sutton, based on the book by Peter Abrahams. Ph: Darius Wolski. Pro Des: Ida Random. Ed: Christian Adam Wagner and Claire Simpson. M: Hans Zimmer; numbers performed by Black Grape, Terence Trent D'Arby, Foreskin 500, Honky, Massive Attack, Aaron Neville, Nine Inch Nails, The Rolling Stones, etc. Costumes: Rita Ryack and Daniel Orlandi. Stalking consultants: Lt John Lane and Dr Michael Zona. (Scott Free/TriStar/Mandalay Entertainment–Entertainment.) Rel: 1 November 1996. 115 mins. Cert 18. USA. 1996.

Fear

Seattle; now. All is not well in the comfortable lap of the Walker family, a nuclear household straining at the seams to stay in one piece. Steve Walker is working too hard and is missing out on quality time with his kids; his new wife, Laura, is finding it tough coming to terms with her stepdaughter, Nicole; and Nicole herself, at 16, is just beginning to flex the strings of rebellion. Then along comes David, a sweet, strong, gentle

and streetwise young man who falls head over heels for Nicole. Quickly sussing out the cracks in the Walker fabric, he moves in for the kill, so to speak... Starting out as a slickly made companion piece to *Fatal Attraction*, *The Hand That Rocks the Cradle*, *Single White Female* and company, this variation on the theme of the icon from hell trots along very nicely, sowing all the right seeds for a predictable showdown. But then the last third of the movie turns into something entirely more upsetting. Without giving too much away, the climax is a corker. James Foley, who's earned his stripes on *At Close Range* and *Glengarry Glen Ross*, guides the action with his usual integrity, while Alyssa Milano (Schwarzenegger's little girl in *Commando*) steals the acting honours as Nicole's spunky best friend.

Mark Wahlberg (*David McCall*), Reese Witherspoon (*Nicole Walker*), William Petersen (*Steve Walker*), Alyssa Milano (*Margo Masse*), Amy Brenneman (*Laura Walker*), Todd Caldecott (*Gary Rohmer*), Banner (*Kaiser*), Christopher Gray, Tracy Fraim, Gary John Riley, John Oliver, David Fredericks, Andrew Airlie.
   Dir: James Foley. Pro: Brian Grazer and Ric Kidney. Ex Pro: Karen Kehela. Assoc Pro: Karen Snow. Screenplay: Christopher Crowe. Ph: Thomas Kloss. Pro Des: Alex McDowell. Ed: David Brenner. M: Carter Burwell; numbers performed by The

Perverse charge: Tilda Swinton and Frances Fisher in Susan Streitfeld's stilted Female Perversions *(from Feature Film Company)*

Allman Brothers Band, Dink, Bush, The Sundays, Toad The Wet Sprocket, Prick, Marky Mark, and One Love. Costumes: Kirsten Everberg. (Imagine Entertainment/Universal–UIP.) Rel: 29 November 1996. 97 mins. Cert 18. USA. 1996.

Feast of July

Promised marriage by the dashing Arch Wilson, Bella Ford finds herself abandoned and pregnant. Reduced to giving birth to a stillborn child in a derelict cabin, she sets out to find the man who shamed her. Arriving sick and exhausted to the town of Addisford, Bella is taken pity on by Ben Wainwright, a kindly lamplighter, who takes her in. There, Wainwright's three strapping sons each makes a play for the woman's affections... A handsome adaptation of H.E. Bates' little-known novel, *Feast of July* steers away from the usual flourishes of period drama and focuses on the complexity and claustrophobia of the characters that drive the story. This is where the film is most successful, aided by some wonderful playing, notably from Gemma Jones as the down-to-earth Mrs Wainwright and Ben Chaplin as her shy, tortured son. However, the film does take far too long to hit its stride and suffers from deadly pacing and an undistinguished score (from the normally accomplished Zbigniew Preisner). Christopher Menaul, who directed *Prime Suspect* on television, makes his feature film debut.

Embeth Davidtz (*Bella Ford*), Tom Bell (*Ben Wainwright*), Gemma Jones (*Mrs Wainwright*), James Purefoy (*Jedd Wainwright*), Greg Wise (*Arch Wilson*), Kenneth Anderson (*Matty Wainwright*), Ben Chaplin (*Con Wainwright*), Charles De'ath (*Billy Swaine*), David Neal, Daphne Neville, Tim Preece, Richard Hope, Paddy Ward, Arthur Kelly, Mark Bazeley, Frederick Warder.
   Dir: Christopher Menaul. Pro: Henry Herbert and Christopher Neame. Ex Pro: Ismail Merchant and Paul Bradley. Assoc Pro: Jane Cussons and Donald Rosenfeld. Screenplay: Neame. Ph: Peter Sova. Pro Des: Christopher Robilliard. Ed: Chris Wimble. M: Zbigniew Preisner. Costumes: Phoebe De Gaye. (Touchstone Pictures/Merchant Ivory/Peregrine Prods–Buena Vista.) Rel: 12 July 1996. 118 mins. Cert 15. UK. 1995.

Feeling Minnesota

Minnesota; the 1970s/the present. Ambitious and complex, if flawed and muddled, this is a feel-bad melodrama about grungy sibling rivals who fight to the death after ex-con Keanu Reeves has sex with his brother's bride (Cameron Diaz) on their wedding day. The heady mix of violence, black jokes and a touch of true romance recalls Tarantino, and though director Stephen Baigelman cannot marshal his resources as incisively, nevertheless the resources are there. Baigelman has romance in his soul, looking for a happy love story in his dark tale of lives tarnished by society. A lot of wide-open gaps in the script are left to the actors to fill in and Keanu, apparently stretched by and involved in the material, acts rather well, making something out of his unshaven, inarticulate character. The horrible title is explained by the lines in a song: 'I just looked in the mirror/Things aren't looking so good/I'm looking California and feeling Minnesota.' [*Derek Winnert*]

Keanu Reeves (*Jjacks Clayton*), Vincent D'Onofrio (*Sam Clayton*), Cameron Diaz (*Freddie*), Delroy Lindo (*Red*), Courtney Love (*Rhonda*), Tuesday Weld (*Nora Clayton*), Dan Aykroyd (*Ben Costikyan*), Levon Helm, Drew DesMarais, Aaron Michael Metchik, Paul Smith, Michael Rispoli, Arabella Field, John Carroll Lynch, Max Perlich, Rocca (*the dog*).
   Dir and Screenplay: Stephen Baigelman. Pro: Danny DeVito, Michael Shamberg and Stacey Sher. Ex Pro: Erwin Stoff. Assoc Pro: Carla Santos Macy. Ph: Walt Lloyd. Pro Des: Naomi Shohan. Ed: Martin

Walsh. M: numbers performed by Johnny Cash, Bob Dylan, The Temptations, Helmet, The Rockin' Hollywoods, The Replacements, Nancy Sinatra, Wilco, The Righteous Brothers, Son Volt, etc. Costumes: Eugenie Bafaloukos. (New Line Cinema/Jersey Films/Sundance Institute–Entertainment.) Rel: 6 December 1996. 99 mins. Cert 18. USA. 1996.

Female Perversions

Not to be confused with the exclusively sexual perversions indulged in by some women, Susan Streitfeld's intrepid, fiercely individual adaptation of Louise J. Kaplan's psychoanalytical text (*Female Perversions: The Temptations of Emma Bovary*) is a study of the perversion of women's role in society. Having said that, a number of sexual idiosyncrasies are on display here, woven into the story of a female attorney and her kleptomaniacal sister. While the former is forced to bail the latter out of prison at a professionally crucial time in both their lives, homosexuality, masochism and depilation do make their entrance. Although the film explores some interesting ideas, Streitfeld's direction is so stilted that it deprives the audience of any emotional involvement. Basically a series of ideas threaded into the semblance of a plot, this bleak feminist tract has the appeal of staring into the eyes of a cobra for two hours. Tilda Swinton's performance as the neurotic, nymphomaniacal attorney is admirable in its nakedness and commitment, but cannot disguise the fact that this is a most unappealing, strident and downright unattractive character.

Tilda Swinton (*Evelyn 'Eve' Stephens*), Amy Madigan (*Madelyn Stephens*), Karen Sillas (*Renee*), Frances Fisher (*Annunciata*), Laila Robins (*Emma*), Clancy Brown (*John*), Paulina Porizkova (*Langley Flynn*), Dale Shuger (*Edwina, 'Ed'*), Lisa Jane Persky, John Diehl, John Cassini, Marcia Cross, Shawnee Smith, J. Patrick McCormick (*Wallace*), Don Gettinger.
Dir: Susan Streitfeld. Pro: Mindy Affrime. Ex Pro: Zalman King, Gina Resnick and Rena Ronson. Line Pro: Rana Joy Glickman. Screenplay: Streitfeld and Julie Hebert. Ph: Teresa Medina. Pro Des: Missy Stewart. Ed: Curtiss Clayton and Leo Trombetta. M: Debbie Wiseman. Costumes: Angela Billows. (MAP Films/Transatlantic Entertainment, etc.–Feature

Football lazy: Colin Firth and Mark Strong obsess over Arsenal in David Evans' winning Fever Pitch *(from Film Four)*

Film Co.) Rel: 2 May 1997. 113 mins. Cert 18. USA/Germany. 1996.

Fever Pitch

1968-72, Maidenhead, Berkshire/1988-9, North London. Arsenal Football Club was the first thing Paul Ashworth ever cared about and for 21 years he has been waiting for his team to capture the League Championship. Now a carefree but popular comprehensive teacher of English Lit, Paul finds he can worm his way into people's affections through his passion for and knowledge of football. In stark contrast, Sarah Hughes is a conscientious, hard-working history teacher who finds herself reluctantly attracted to Paul's popularity and devil-may-care attitude. But can she supplant Paul's first love? And can he ever come to the realisation that football is, after all, just a game? Adapting his own best-selling autobiography to the screen, Nick Hornby has fashioned an enjoyable

romantic comedy with something significant to say. While it's hard to identify with the total fixation of Paul Ashworth, it's not impossible – thanks to Colin Firth's credible reading of the part. As much about obsession as it is about football, *Fever Pitch* will none the less be enjoyed more by those who know something about the sport.

Colin Firth (*Paul Ashworth*), Ruth Gemmell (*Sarah Hughes*), Neil Pearson (*Paul's dad*), Lorraine Ashbourne (*Paul's mum*), Mark Strong (*Steve*), Holly Aird (*Jo*), Ken Stott (*Ted, headmaster*), Stephen Rea (*Ray, the governor*), Luke Aikman (*young Paul Ashworth*), Richard Claxton (*Robert*), Beau Guard, Annette Ekblom, Peter Quince, Emily Conway, Tony Longhurst.
Dir: David Evans. Pro: Amanda Posey. Ex Pro: Stephen Woolley and Nik Powell. Line Pro: Nick O'Hagan. Screenplay: Nick Hornby. Ph: Chris Seager. Pro Des: Michael Carlin. Ed: Scott Thomas. M: Neill MacColl and Boo Hewerdine; numbers performed by The Pretenders, The La's, The Bible, Tommy Steele, Harry J. Allstars, Lloyd Cole & The Commotions, The Smiths, Aztec Camera, Slade, Paul Hardcastle, New Order, The Who, The Jesus and Mary Chain, The Pogues, Tim Hardin, Fine Young Cannibals, Lisa Stansfield, and Van Morrison. Costumes: Mary-Jane Reyner. (Channel Four/Wildgaze Films–Film Four.) Rel: 4 April 1997. 102 mins. Cert 15. UK. 1996.

Fierce or cuddly? Kevin Kline panders to commercialism in Robert Young and Fred Schepisi's very, very funny Fierce Creatures *(from UIP)*

Fierce Creatures

When Antipodean media tycoon Rod McCain buys up the quiet provincial Marwood Zoo in England, he demands a 20 per cent return on his investment. So the zoo's new director, Rollo Lee – an ex-cop from Hong Kong – decides to dispense with all the cuddly, uninteresting animals and replace them with exciting, fierce creatures... While much publicity was mined from the clash of wills of the original stars of *A Fish Called Wanda* – not to mention the expensive re-shoots under the direction of Fred Schepisi (who added an additional 45 per cent of material) – the result is enormously funny. Like *Wanda*, this is a superbly crafted farce, crammed with in-jokes and priceless sight gags, as well as a series of running gags that help build the comic momentum. Cleese is on splendid form as the anarchic, flustered Rollo, while Kevin Kline valiantly attempts to steal the movie

in the dual role of the ruthless, flatulent Rod McCain ('Rod Almighty') and his grabbing, libidinous son Vince. Terrific dialogue, too (see Movie Quotations of the Year elsewhere in this book). Inspired by an idea for an unrealised TV sitcom dreamed up by Terry Jones and Michael Palin in 1968.

John Cleese (*Rollo Lee*), Jamie Lee Curtis (*Willa Weston*), Kevin Kline (*Vince McCain/Rod McCain*), Michael Palin (*Bugsy Malone*), Ronnie Corbett (*Reggie Sealions*), Carey Lowell (*Cub Felines*), Robert Lindsay (*Sydney Small Mammals*), Billie Brown (*Neville Coltrane*), Cynthia Cleese (*Pip Small Mammals*), Maria Aitken (*Di Admin*), Derek Griffiths, Richard Ridings, Michael Percival, Fred Evans, Lisa Hogan, Kim Vithana, Susie Blake, Pat Keen, Denis Lil, Gareth Hunt, Kerry Shale, Amanda Walker, Tom Georgeson.
  Dir: Robert Young and Fred Schepisi. Pro: Michael Shamberg and John Cleese. Ex Pro: Steve Abbott. Co-Pro: Patricia Carr. Screenplay: Cleese and Iain Johnstone. Ph: Adrian Biddle and Ian Baker. Pro Des: Roger Murray-Leach. Ed: Robert Gibson. M: Jerry Goldsmith. Costumes: Hazel Pethig. Gorillas: Animated Extras. (Universal Pictures/Fish Prods/Jersey Films–UIP.) Rel: 14 February 1997. 93 mins. Cert PG. USA. 1996.

The Fifth Element - Le Cinquieme Element

New York City; 2214. Every five thousand years a fifth element is needed to complete the holy quintet of earthly substances known to man. The key is discovering what the fifth element is and how to unite it with the other four: earth, air, fire and water. Without it, a catastrophic evil force will be able to cross over the threshold of our own universe and extinguish all known forms of life. Only one mysterious woman, with the element tattooed on her wrist, can save the world. But can she learn our language in time to save us? And does she believe the world is worth saving? One man, a cab driver from the 23rd century, has just a few hours to convince her that the answer is 'yes'. Employing his singular visual style to illuminate a daring premise, the iconoclastic French filmmaker Luc Besson (*Subway, Nikita, Leon*) takes on the sci-fi genre and injects it with a comic-book sensibility that is irresistible. Tossing the conventions of the genre on their head, Besson repeatedly takes us by surprise and delivers a sexy, funny and thought-provoking slice of escapism that should delight devotees of the absurd. Standout scene: an extra-terrestrial diva delivers a heart-rending aria intercut with a balletic skirmish between Milla Jovovich and a mob of ugly alien thugs. FYI: At a reported cost of $90 million, this is the most expensive production ever financed by a French company.

Bruce Willis (*Korben Dallas*), Gary Oldman (*Zorg*), Ian Holm (*Cornelius*), Milla Jovovich (*Leeloo*), Chris Tucker (*Ruby Rhod*), Luke Perry (*Billy*), Brion James (*General Munro*), Tommy 'Tiny' Lister Jr (*President Lindberg*), Maiwenn Le Besco (*Diva*), Lee Evans, Charlie Creed Miles, Tricky, John Neville, John Bluthal, Mathieu Kassovitz, Christopher Fairbank, Julie T. Wallace, Al Matthews, John Bennett, Sonita Henry, George Khan, John Hughes, Roger Monk, Indra Ove, Stanley Kowalski.
  Dir: Luc Besson. Pro: Patrice Ledoux. Co-Pro: Iain Smith. Screenplay: Besson and Robert Mark Kamen. Ph: Thierry Arbogast. Pro Des: Dan Weil. Ed: Sylvie Landra. M: Eric Serra, Cliff Martinez and Mark Mangini; numbers performed by Eric Serra, Khaled, Inva Mulla Tchako, RXRA, and Chris Tucker. Costumes: Jean-Paul Gaultier. Sound: Mangini. Visual effects: Mark Stetson. (Gaumont–Guild.)

Rel: 6 June 1997. 126 mins. Cert PG.
France. 1997.

The First Wives Club

A Jewish housewife, a resolutely
cheerful mother with a lesbian
daughter and a cosmetically
preserved movie star (a 'Beverly
Hills science project') are reunited at
the funeral of a fellow college
graduate after an interval of 27 years.
Discovering that they have all been
jilted by their husbands for younger
women, the former friends resolve to
see justice done... With a script
provided by Robert Harling, he who
furnished divine parts for the
predominantly female cast of *Steel
Magnolias*, *The First Wives Club* is off
to a running start (Goldie Hawn:
'You think because I'm a movie star I
don't have feelings? I'm an actress. I
have all of them'; Ivana Trump: 'And
remember. Don't get mad. Get
everything'). Yet, under the strident
direction of Hugh Wilson (*Police
Academy*), the film provides little bite,
let alone any insight into the war of
the sexes. Thus, three of the finest
comediennes in Hollywood are
reduced to squabbling, screaming
and giggling like over-pampered
banshees. Incidentally, all five
actresses are 50 years old. Goldie
Hawn was born in November of
1945, Bette Midler in December and
Diane Keaton a month after that.

Bette Midler (*Brenda Morelli Cushman*),
Goldie Hawn (*Elise Elliot Atchison*), Diane
Keaton (*Annie MacDuggan Paradise*),
Maggie Smith (*Gunilla Garson Goldberg*),
Sarah Jessica Parker (*Shelly*), Dan Hedaya
(*Morty Cushman*), Bronson Pinchot (*Duarto
Feliz*), Marcia Gay Harden (*Dr Leslie
Rosen*), Victor Garber (*Bill Atchison*),
Stephen Collins (*Aaron Paradise*), Elizabeth
Berkley (*Phoebe LaVelle*), Jennifer Dundas
(*Chris Paradise*), Eileen Heckart (*Catherine
MacDuggan*), Stockard Channing (*Cynthia
Swann Griffin*), Philip Bosco, Rob Reiner,
James Naughton, Ari Greenberg, Ivana
Trump (*herself*), Gloria Steinem (*herself*), Ed
Koch (*himself*), Kathie Lee Gifford (*herself*),
Edward Hibbert (*Maurice*), J. Smith-
Cameron, Kate Burton, Gregg Edelman,
Stephen Mendillo, Robin Morse, Peter
Frechette, Debra Monk, Nancy Ticotin,
Heather Locklear.
 Dir: Hugh Wilson. Pro: Scott Rudin. Ex
Pro: Ezra Swerdlow and Adam Schroeder.
Screenplay: Robert Harling, from the novel
by Olivia Goldsmith. Ph: Donald Thorin.
Pro Des: Peter Larkin. Ed: John Bloom. M:
Marc Shaiman; numbers performed by
Dionne Warwick, The Rascals, Puff

Johnson, Diana King, Brownstone, Billy
Porter, Eurythmics, Aretha Franklin,
Dionne Farris, Chantay Savage, M People,
Martha Wash, and Bette Midler, Goldie
Hawn and Diane Keaton. Costumes:
Theoni V. Aldredge. (Paramount–UIP.)
Rel: 15 November 1996. 102 mins. Cert PG.
USA. 1996.

Fled

'Who fled?' asks detective Matthew
Gibson following the bloody break-

*Saving the planet: Milla Jovovich and Bruce
Willis buckle down to a bit of technology in
Luc Besson's daring, playful and visually
intoxicating* The Fifth Element *(from Guild)*

*Now and them: Goldie Hawn, Diane Keaton
and Bette Midler plot their husbands' come-
uppance in Hugh Wilson's glossy, superficial
and strident* The First Wives Club *(from
UIP). Watch out for the actresses in their next
vehicle,* Avon Ladies of the Amazon *(no
kidding!)*

Happy times are here again: Stephen Baldwin and Laurence Fishburne share a joke in Kevin Hooks' tough, slick Fled *(from UIP)*

out from a Georgia prison. Not who he'd think, as the two convicts on the run – chained together by the wrist – are the least dangerous on the chain gang. They're tough, but not dangerous. It transpires that Luke Dodge was sent down for hacking into the computer of a crime syndicate and for transferring a cool $25 million into his own account. Now he's the sole possessor of incriminating evidence in a major trial and the Cuban mafia and some corrupt cops want him for breakfast. But they hadn't bargained on his fellow convict, the enigmatic and no-nonsense Charles Piper... A tough, slick wedge of escapism, *Fled* wears its machismo (and misogyny) on its sleeve. It is, however, undeniably stylish, and Laurence Fishburne contributes some weight as a man's man in a politically conventional universe, while Will Patton – as the 'country boy' detective on his tail – proves yet again that he is incapable of turning in an uninteresting performance. The trucker crowd will love it.

Laurence Fishburne (*Charles Piper*), Stephen Baldwin (*Luke Dodge*), Will Patton (*Matthew Gibson*), Robert John Burke (*Pat Schiller*), Salma Hayek (*Cora*), Robert Hooks (*Lt Clark*), Victor Rivers (*Rico Santiago*), David Dukes (*Chris Paine*), Ken Jenkins (*Warden Nichols*), Michael Nader (*Frank Mantajano*), Brittney Powell (*Faith/Cindy*), RuPaul (*himself*), Steve Carlisle, Brett Rice, J. Don Ferguson, Kathy Payne, Bob Apisa, Gary Yates, Jon Huffman, Michael Hooks, K. Addison Young.

Dir: Kevin Hooks. Pro: Frank Mancuso Jr. Ex Pro and Screenplay: Preston A. Whitmore II. Assoc Pro: Vikki Williams. Ph: Matthew F. Leonetti. Pro Des: Charles Bennett. Ed: Richard Nord and Joseph Gutowski. M: Graeme Revell; numbers performed by T. Smith, Planet Control, Fishbone, James Brown, Joi, Monica, For Real, Lou, Salt 'N' Pepa, God's Gift to God, Royal C, etc. Costumes: Jennifer Bryan. (MGM–UIP.) Rel: 8 November 1996. 98 mins. Cert 18. USA. 1996.

Flipper

Splashing cheekily in the wake of *Free Willy* and its sequel, this nth big-screen modification of a TV phenomenon (the 1964-67 NBC series) is a pretty mediocre affair. Besides its similarity to the whale tale (boy from a broken home falls in love with a friendly sea creature, then fights to save his new friend from human villains more interested in profit than marine altruism), this *Flipper* lacks charm, wit and direction. As the boy's salty uncle, Paul Hogan struggles unsuccessfully to engender laughs (blow-torching his toast, smoking cigars underwater), while much of the painterly photography is wasted on cheap film stock. Yet again it's Flipper himself who steals the show.

Paul Hogan (*Uncle Porter*), Elijah Wood (*Sandy Ricks*), Chelsea Field (*Cathy*), Isaac Hayes (*Buck*), Jonathan Banks (*Dirk Moran*), Jason Fuchs (*Marvin*), Jessica Wesson (*Kim*), Jake/Fat Man/McGuyver (*Flipper*), Luke Halpin, Bill Kelley, Mal Jones, Louis Seeger Crume, Mary Jo Faraci.

Dir and Screenplay: Alan Shapiro, based on the screenplay by Arthur Weiss and a story by Ricou Browning and Jack Cowden. Pro: James J. McNamara and Perry Katz. Ex Pro: Lance Hool. Co-Pro: Conrad Hool and Darlene Spezzi. Ph: Bill Butler. Pro Des: Thomas A. Walsh. Ed: Peck Prior. M: Joel McNeely; numbers performed by Matthew Sweet, Shaggy, Tom Jones, The Heptones, The Beach Boys, Professor Longhair, Laika and The Cosmonauts, Crosby, Stills and Nash, etc. Costumes: Matthew Jacobsen. Animatronics: Walt Conti. (Universal/The Bubble Factory/American Film–UIP.) Rel: 2 August 1996. 95 mins. Cert PG. USA. 1996.

Flirt

New York; February 1993/Berlin; October 1994/Tokyo; March 1995. A promiscuous New York bachelor, a black homosexual living in Berlin and a Japanese dance student in Tokyo are all given a 90-minute ultimatum in which to permanently commit to their respective lovers. It's the same story and the protagonists largely speak the same dialogue ('You don't need to see it if you know it's there'). However, because of the characters' respective milieux and sexual orientation, do the universal themes of love, commitment and indecision significantly diverge? Acknowledging that his film is nothing more than the cinematic equivalent of a flirt – 'a chaste, amorous relationship devoid of deep feelings' – writer-director Hal Hartley toys with his medium without committing to a serious relationship. Thus, whereas his last film, *Amateur,* acted as an engrossing platform on which to perch his eccentricities, *Flirt* is merely a one-night stand in which, for the most part, Hartley is playing with himself.

New York: Bill Sage (*Bill*), Parker Posey (*Emily*), Martin Donovan (*Walter*), Hannah Sullivan (*Margaret*), Paul Austin, Robert Burke, Erica Gimpel, Michael Imperioli, Harold Perrineau, Karen Sillas, Jose Zuniga. Berlin: Dwight Ewell (*Dwight*), Dominik Bender (*Johann*), Geno Lechner (*Greta*), Peter Fitz (*the doctor*), Maria Schrader (*girl in phone booth*), Elina Lowensohn (*nurse*). Tokyo: Miho Nikaidoh (*Miho*), Toshizo Fujisawa (*Ozu*), Chikako Hara (*Yuki*), Masatoshi Nagase, Hal Hartley.
    Dir and Screenplay: Hal Hartley. Pro: Ted Hope. Ex Pro: Reinhard Brundig, Satoru Iseki and Jerome Brownstein. Ph: Michael Spiller. Pro Des: Steven Rosenzweig. Ed: Hartley and Steve Hamilton. M: Ned Rifle (aka Hal Hartley) and Jeffrey Taylor; numbers performed by Lost, Lonely & Vicious, She Never Blinks, The Miss Alans, etc. Costumes: Alexandra Welker and Ulla Gothe. Casting director (New York): Billy Hopkins. (True Fiction/Pandora Films/Nippon Film/Miramax–Artificial Eye.) Rel: 21 February 1997. 84 mins. Cert 15. USA/Germany/Japan. 1995.

Flirting With Disaster

When New York entomologist Mel Coplin becomes the proud father of a baby boy, he feels an urgent need to discover the identity of his own

Parental pursuits: Mary Tyler Moore and George Segal find themselves in another fine mess in David O. Russell's rib-aching Flirting With Disaster *(from Buena Vista)*

biological parents. Allowing adoption agency psychologist Tina Kalb to record the reunion for her research in return for locating his folks, Coplin embarks on a chaotic journey of confusion and self-discovery. Dragging his wife along for the ride, the abandoned son begins to realise that human identity is a delicate thing... A film that derives its comic mileage from both its characters and escalating plot, *Flirting With Disaster* elevates farce to an art form. From the hilarious prologue featuring a montage of Coplin's potential parents to the final, frenetic resolution, the film fails to lose a stroke of wit or ingenuity. A wonderful cast of actors invest their roles with surprising conviction, even as events hurtle into absurdity, while writer-director David O. Russell's grasp of his script constantly retains its edge and momentum. A comedy this fresh and funny comes but once in a lifetime. P.S. Russell previously wrote and directed the low-budget *Spanking the Monkey,* which won an unprecedented number of prizes for a debut feature at the Independent Spirit Awards.

Ben Stiller (*Mel Coplin*), Patricia Arquette (*Nancy Coplin*), Tea Leoni (*Tina Kalb*), Mary Tyler Moore (*Mrs Coplin*), George Segal (*Mr Coplin*), Alan Alda (*Richard Schlicting*), Lily Tomlin (*Mary Schlicting*), Josh Brolin (*Tony*), Richard Jenkins (*Paul*), Celia Weston (*Valerie Swaney*), Glenn Fitzgerald (*Lonnie Schlicting*), David Patrick Kelly (*Fritz Boudreau*), John Ford Noonan (*Mitch*), Charlet Oberly (*B&B landlady*), Beth Ostrosky, Cynthia Lamontagne.
    Dir and Screenplay: David O. Russell. Pro: Dean Silvers. Ex Pro: Bob Weinstein and Harvey Weinstein. Co-Ex Pro: Trea Hoving. Co-Pro: Kerry Orent. Ph: Eric Edwards. Pro Des: Kevin Thompson. Ed: Christopher Tellefsen. M: Stephen Endelman. Costumes: Ellen Lutter. (Miramax–Buena Vista.) Rel: 24 January 1997. 92 mins. Cert 15. USA. 1996.

Fly Away Home

New Zealand/Ontario/North Carolina; the present. Eccentric inventor and sculptor Thomas Alden is working against the clock to meet some tough deadlines when, following the death of his ex-wife, his 13-year-old daughter Amy comes to live with him. Unable to reconcile their grief, father and daughter get off to a shaky start until Amy discovers 16 abandoned goose eggs. Required by law to clip their wings, Alden decides to take on the responsibility of teaching the birds to migrate, a move that unites father and daughter in their quest to beat seemingly insurmountable odds...

Daughter goose: Anna Paquin and friends in Carroll Ballard's captivating Fly Away Home *(from Columbia TriStar)*

Halfway through watching this enchanting film – when things begin to get extremely far-fetched – I got the peculiar sensation that it had to be all true. In fact, not only is *Fly Away Home* inspired by real events, but the man on whose autobiography this is based – Bill Lishman – did Jeff Daniels' stunt flying and fashioned Alden's bizarre sculptures. Director Carroll Ballard, who previously brought enormous visual poetry to the wildlife films *The Black Stallion* and *Never Cry Wolf*, tops his own record with this exquisite tale of man's triumphant collaboration with nature. Staging his film like a ballad, the director forewarns us of the story's inevitable outcome, but still manages to induce the most powerful emotions, enhanced by a wonderful score and some simply stunning photography.

Jeff Daniels (*Thomas Alden*), Anna Paquin (*Amy Alden*), Dana Delany (*Susan Barnes*), Terry Kinney (*David Alden*), Holter Graham (*Barry Strickland*), Jeremy Ratchford (*Glen Seifert*), David Hemblen (*Dr Killian*), Deborah Verginella, Michael J. Reynolds, Ken James, Nora Ballard, Sarena Paton, Carmen Lishman.

Dir: Carroll Ballard. Pro: John Veitch and Carol Baum. Ex Pro: Sandy Gallin. Screenplay: Robert Rodat and Vince McKewin, based on the autobiography by Bill Lishman. Ph: Caleb Deschanel. Pro Des: Seamus Flannery. Ed: Nicholas C. Smith. M: Mark Isham; '10,000 Miles' performed by Mary Chapin Carpenter. Costumes: Marie-Sylvie Deveau. (Columbia/Sandollar–Columbia TriStar.) Rel: 7 February 1997. 107 mins. Cert U. USA. 1996.

The Frighteners

Somewhere in the US (looking remarkably like New Zealand); the present. Unlike Whoopi Goldberg in *Ghost*, Frank Bannister is a psychic conman with a genuine rapport with the otherworldly. Capable of seeing and communicating with the dead, Bannister persuades a trio of spooks to haunt houses of his choosing so that he can collect a fat fee for getting rid of them. Then he comes up against a truly malevolent spirit that frames him for a series of inexplicable murders... Having exorcised his blood lust with *Bad Taste* and *Braindead*, and then bought his ticket to international recognition with *Heavenly Creatures*, Kiwi writer-director Peter Jackson tackles the cinematic minefield of comic horror. With the presence of Michael J. Fox dispelling any sense of real unease and some shameful mugging throttling the comedy, *The Frighteners* fails on both fronts. However, the elaborate special effects – in particular some sensational morphing – prevents this from being a total turkey. FYI: The name of Trini Alvarado's character Lucy Lynskey is presumably an in-joke, as Melanie Lynskey was the star of Jackson's *Heavenly Creatures* and has a brief cameo here.

Michael J. Fox (*Frank Bannister*), Trini Alvarado (*Lucy Lynskey*), Peter Dobson (*Ray Lynskey*), John Astin (*The Judge*), Jeffrey Combs (*Milton Dammers*), Dee Wallace Stone (*Patricia Bradley*), Jake Busey (*Johnny Bartlett*), Chi McBride, Jim Fyfe, Troy Evans, Julianna McCarthy, R. Lee Ermey, Elizabeth Hawthorne, Angela Bloomfield, Melanie Lynskey (*police deputy*), Peter Jackson.

Dir: Peter Jackson. Pro: Jackson and Jamie Selkirk. Ex Pro: Robert Zemeckis. Assoc Pro: Fran Walsh. Screenplay: Jackson and Walsh. Ph: Alun Bollinger and John Blick. Pro Des: Grant Major. Ed: Selkirk. M: Danny Elfman; numbers performed by The Mutton Birds, and Sonic Youth. Costumes: Barbara Darragh. Judge make-up design: Rick Baker. (Wingnut Films/Universal–UIP.) Rel: 24 January 1997. 110 mins. Cert 15. New Zealand/USA. 1996.

The Funeral

New York; the 1930s. At the funeral of his kid brother Johnny, gangland racketeer Ray Tempio seems more preoccupied with revenge than grief. And, in spite of protestations from his long-suffering wife, Ray sets in motion a bloody cycle of violence as he seeks retribution... Exploring his favourite themes of violence, Catholic guilt and the hope of salvation through the fairer sex, director Abel Ferrara tries on the gangster thriller for size but cannot shake off the precedents of the genre. Lacking both the garish verve of Scorsese and the grandiose sweep of Coppola, *The Funeral* is small scale, sluggish and ponderous. Notwithstanding, there are some nice turns from Walken, Penn and Del Toro and one or two scenes (near the end) that remind one of Ferrara's earlier brilliance.

Christopher Walken (*Ray Tempio*), Benicio Del Toro (*Gaspare Spoglia*), Vincent Gallo (*Johnny Tempio*), Paul Hipp (*Ghouly*), Chris Penn (*Chez Tempio*), Isabella Rossellini

A free man – for now: James Woods in his Oscar-nominated performance as the white supremacist Byron De La Beckwith in Ghosts From the Past *(from Rank). Says Woods: 'He [Byron] doesn't know he's the bad guy. He just does what he does.'*

(*Clara Tempio*), Annabella Sciorra (*Jeanette Tempio*), Gretchen Mol (*Helen*), John Ventimiglia (*Sali*), Victor Argo, Gian Di Donna, Frank John Hughes, Robert Castle, Edie Falco, David Patrick Kelly, Patrick McGraw, Heather Bracken, Chuck Zito.
   Dir: Abel Ferrara. Pro: Mary Kane. Ex Pro: Michael Chambers and Patrick Panzarella. Co-Pro: Randall Sabusawa. Assoc Pro: Russell Simmons, Jay Cannold and Annabella Sciorra. Ph: Ken Kelsch. Pro Des: Charles M. Lagola. Ed: Bill Pankow and Mayin Lo. M: Joe Delia; numbers performed by Billie Holiday, Sonny Boy Williamson, Killer Joe, Chris Penn, etc. Costumes: Melinda Eschelman. (October Film/MDP Worldwide/C&P– Guild.) Rel: 18 April 1997. 99 mins. Cert 18. USA. 1996.

The Ghost and the Darkness

In 1896 two lions were held responsible for halting production on the Tsavo Bridge in East Africa, one of the most ambitious engineering endeavours in British colonial rule. Dubbed The Darkness and The Ghost by the natives, the lions acted relentlessly out of character, artfully dodging traps laid by big game

hunters and claiming more than 130 fatalities in a matter of months. Sticking largely to these facts, scenarist William Goldman (*Butch Cassidy and the Sundance Kid*, *All the President's Men*) has composed a story of mythological import, punctuated by 'significant' dialogue ('the struggle is the glory') and some awkward dramatic effects. But the fundamental problem with the film is that the characters are too one-dimensional for us to care about, while the lion attacks are so hokily staged that they bear all the horror of a kabuki pageant. School children may thrill at the exotic grandeur and throwaway facts, but adults won't be counting the days till *Claws II*. Daftest line: 'I love Africa. I've always wanted to go there.' Filmed on the Songimelvo Game Reserve, on the border of South Africa and Swaziland.

Michael Douglas (*Remington*), Val Kilmer (*Lt Colonel John H. Patterson*), Bernard Hill (*Dr Hawthorne*), John Kani (*Samuel*), Tom Wilkinson (*Beaumont*), Brian McCardie (*Angus Starling*), Henry Cele (*Mahina*), Om Puri (*Abdullah*), Emily Mortimer (*Helena Patterson*).
   Dir: Stephen Hopkins. Pro: Gale Anne Hurd, Paul Radin and A. Kitman Ho. Ex Pro: Michael Douglas and Steven Reuther. Co-Pro: Grant Hill. Ph: Vilmos Zsigmond. Pro Des: Stuart Wurtzel. Ed: Robert Brown and Steve Mirkovich. M: Jerry Goldsmith;

numbers performed by The Worldbeaters. Costumes: Ellen Mirojnick. Live effects: Stan Winston. (Constellation Films/ Paramount–UIP.) Rel: 17 January 1997. 110 mins. Cert 15. USA. 1996.

Ghosts From the Past

Mississippi; 1963-1995. As John F. Kennedy makes his landmark civil rights speech on the night of 12 June, 1963, the well-connected white

Inviting death: Christopher Walken in Abel Ferrara's ponderous The Funeral *(from Guild)*

supremacist Byron De La Beckwith shoots a hole in the back of black activist Medgar Evers. As Evers dies in the arms of his wife, Myrlie – in front of his three young children – Myrlie resolves to bring her husband's assassin to justice. But white juries, civic indifference and vanishing evidence conspire to sabotage Myrlie's efforts until, 25 years later, she meets up with Assistant DA Bobby DeLaughter... With all the good intentions in the world, a heart-stirring true story and a first-rate cast cannot make a great film from a poorly constructed script. A flipside to the law and race themes explored in *A Time to Kill* (itself inspired by an amalgam of real events, set in Mississippi and featuring a crusading lawyer trapped in a disintegrating marriage), *Ghosts From the Past* falls foul of clumsy exposition and forced comic relief. Furthermore, while the facts themselves are fascinating, the story that connects them provides little narrative momentum. Original US title: *Ghosts of Mississippi*.

Alec Baldwin (*Bobby DeLaughter*), Whoopi Goldberg (*Myrlie Evers*), James Woods (*Byron De La Beckwith*), Craig T. Nelson (*Ed Peters*), Diane Ladd (*Caroline Moore*), Bonnie Bartlett (*Billie DeLaughter*), Bill Cobbs (*Charlie Evers*), William H. Macy (*Charlie Crisco*), Virginia Madsen (*Dixie DeLaughter*), Michael O'Keefe (*Merrida Coxwell*), Susanna Thompson (*Peggy Lloyd*), Joseph Tello (*Drew DeLaughter*), Lloyd 'Benny' Bennett (*Benny Bennett*), Yolanda King (*Reena Evers*), Darrell Evers (*Darrell Evers*), James Van Evers (*Van Evers*), Jerry Levine (*Jerry Mitchell*), Margo Martindale (*Clara Mayfield*), Jerry Hardin (*Barney DeLaughter*), Ramon Bieri (*James Holley*), Lucas Black, Alex Vega, Bill Smitrovich, Terry O'Quinn, Rex Linn, James Pickens Jr., Richard Riehle, Jim Harley, Brock Peters, Wayne Rogers, Finn Carter, Andy Romano, David Carpenter, Jordan Lund, Rance Howard, Louis E. Armstrong, Ed Bryson, Maggie Wade, Keanan K. Evers, Nicole Evers-Everette, Tracey Costello.
   Dir: Rob Reiner. Pro: Reiner, Frederick Zollo, Nicholas Paleologos and Andrew Scheinman. Ex Pro: Jeffrey Scott and Charles Newirth. Co-Pro: Frank Capra III. Screenplay: Lewis Colick. Ph: John Seale. Pro Des: Lilly Kilvert. Ed: Robert Leighton. M: Marc Shaiman; Vivaldi; numbers performed by Dionne Farris, Nina Simone, Tony Bennett, Muddy Waters, B.B. King, etc. Costumes: Gloria Gresham. (Castle Rock–Rank.) Rel: 9 May 1997. 130 mins. Cert 15. USA. 1996.

Ghosts of Mississippi

See *Ghosts From the Past*.

The Glimmer Man

Los Angeles; today. A Buddhist cop and his terminally bewildered partner are assigned to track down a serial killer who specialises in knocking off whole families, thus acquiring the witty monicker of The Family Man. But, low and behold, there's more to this than meets the eye, as the Russian mafia, CIA and various corrupt government officials also seem to be involved... Cashing in on the racially interactive buddy genre facilitated by *48 HRS*, *Lethal Weapon* and *The Last Boy Scout*, this low-IQ shambles pairs a pony-tailed, calorie-enhanced Steven Seagal with a hard-drinking Keenen Ivory Wayans to little effect. Coherence and originality are not an option. [*Ewen Brownrigg*]

Steven Seagal (*Jack Cole*), Keenen Ivory Wayans (*Jim Campbell*), Bob Gunton (*Frank Deverell*), Brian Cox (*Mr Smith*), Michelle Johnson (*Jessica Cole*), John M. Jackson (*Donald*), Stephen Tobolowsky, Peter Jason, Ryan Cutrona, Richard Gant, Johnny Strong, Wendy Robie.
   Dir: John Gray. Pro: Steven Seagal and Julius R. Nasso. Ex Pro: Michael Rachmil. Screenplay: Kevin Brodbin. Ph: Rick Bota. Pro Des: William Sandell. Ed: Donn Cambern. M: Trevor Rabin; numbers performed by Taj Mahal, and The Jeff Healey Band. Costumes: Luke Reichle. (Seagal/Nasso–Warner.) Rel: 1 November 1996. 91 mins. Cert 18. USA. 1996.

A Goofy Movie

The concept of turning Disney's 1932 creation into a leading character in this tiresome waste of time underlines Hollywood's current obsession with the cerebrally challenged. Here Goofy plays a department store photographer who fears for his son's future. But young Max is just an ordinary high school kid finding his feet in a modern world. When Max finally plucks up the courage to invite his dream date out, Goofy bundles him off on a fishing holiday 'to get away from it all'. This inevitably produces friction between father and son as all the latter wants to do is get to see his rock idol, Powerline, a Michael Jackson shuffle-like. Mawkish and

charmless, this crude addition to the Disney canon will have Goofy's original creator, Art Babbitt, reeling in his grave. FYI: Goofy first appeared in the 1932 Mickey Mouse short *Mickey's Revue*.

Voices: Bill Farmer (*Goofy*), Jason Marsden (*Max*), Jim Cummings (*Pete*), Kellie Martin (*Roanne*), Rob Paulsen (*P.J.*), Wallace Shawn (*Principal Mazur*), Jenna Von Oy, Frank Welker, Florence Stanley, Jo Anne Worley, Julie Brown.
   Dir: Kevin Lima. Pro: Dan Rounds. Screenplay: Jymm Magon, Chris Matheson and Brian Pimental. Pro Des: Fred Warter. Ed: Gregory Perler. M: Carter Burwell and Don Davis; 'Stayin' Alive' performed by The Bee Gees. (Walt Disney–Buena Vista.) Rel: 11 October 1996. 77 mins. Cert U. USA. 1995.

Grace of My Heart

Just as the era of Peggy Lee and Patti Page is drawing to a close, talented singer/songwriter Edna Buxton wins a ticket to New York after coming first in a Philadelphia talent show. However, Edna's manager is more interested in her prowess as a songwriter than singer and sets her up with a microscopic office at the legendary Brill Building to pen a string of hits for other artists. Over the next ten years, Edna – now famous under her nom de plume of Denise Waverly – draws on her emotional experiences with a number of men to fuel her work, while still pining to find her own voice... For anybody with a love of the golden age of pop, *Grace of My Heart* is a nostalgic gold mine. A superb score of new numbers composed by original Brill songwriters in collaboration with contemporary writers – such as the unique partnership of Burt Bacharach and Elvis Costello, and Carole Bayer Sager and Dave Stewart – supplies the irresistible musical backbone of the film. Unfortunately, the story's overly ambitious reach – stretching from 1958 to the psychedelic era of the late sixties – does ultimately test the patience.

Illeana Douglas (*Denise Waverly/Edna Buxton*), Matt Dillon (*Jay Phillips*), Eric Stoltz (*Howard Caszatt*), Bruce Davison (*John Murray*), Patsy Kensit (*Cheryl Steed*), Jennifer Leigh Warren (*Doris Shelley*), John Turturro (*Joel Millner*), Bridget Fonda (*Kelly Porter, reputedly modelled on Lesley*

Gore), David Clennon (*Dr Jones, 'Jonesy'*), Peter Fonda (*voice of Guru Dave*), Kristen Vigard (*the singing voice of Denise Waverly*), Christina Pickles, Jill Sobule, Richard Schiff, Natalie Venetia Belcon, Kathy Barbour, Drena De Niro, Amanda De Cadenet, For Real, Larry Klein, Chris Isaak, Lucinda Jenney, Shawn Colvin.

Dir and Screenplay: Allison Anders. Pro: Ruth Charny and Daniel Hassid. Ex Pro: Martin Scorsese. Line Pro: Elliot Rosenblatt. Ph: Jean Yves Escoffier. Pro Des: Francois Seguin. Ed: Thelma Schoonmaker, James Kwei and Harvey Rosenstock. M: Larry Klein; numbers performed by Wendy Williams, Kristen Vigard, For Real, The Williams Brothers, Jill Sobule, Flea, J. Mascis, Sonic Youth, Shawn Colvin, Burt Bacharach and Elvis Costello, etc; songs composed by Elvis Costello, Burt Bacharach, Gerry Goffin, Louise Goffin, David Baerwald, etc. M Supervisor: Karyn Rachtman. Costumes: Susan Bertram. (Universal/Gramercy Pictures/Gappa Prods–UIP.) Rel: 21 February 1997. 115 mins. Cert 15. USA. 1996.

The Great White Hype

With attendances dwindling and the financial demands of his pet heavyweight champion – James 'The Grim Reaper' Roper – escalating, extravagant boxing promoter Reverend Fred Sultan must find a way of regenerating interest in the game. Discovering that Roper was once beaten in an amateur bout by a white boy, Sultan sets about rigging a re-match between the champ and his great white hope, the rather dumb but earnest Terry Conklin (now lead singer with the heavy metal band Massive Head Wound). Roper is insulted by Sultan's publicity-seeking scam and embarks on an orgy of eating and smoking, while Conklin goes into serious training... Opening with a shot of two scorpions duelling on a desert road – seconds before being summarily crushed under the wheels of Sultan's limousine – *The Great White Hype* sets the tone for its broad satirical undercut to *Rocky*. Indeed, much of it is very, very funny, sharpened by the barbed pen of Ron Shelton (*Bull Durham, Tin Cup*) and buttressed by a stalwart supporting cast. The Reverend himself, obviously modelled on real-life boxing promoter (and convicted killer) Don King, allows Samuel L. Jackson another opportunity to

It's their party: Patsy Kensit, Bridget Fonda (in a part modelled on Lesley Gore) and Illeana Douglas in Allison Anders' affectionate, ambitious Grace of My Heart *(from UIP)*

extend his considerable range, while the role of the silver-tongued opportunist Mitchell Kane permits Jeff Goldblum to maintain his persona as the knowing smart-ass.

Samuel L. Jackson (*Reverend Fred Sultan*), Jeff Goldblum (*Mitchell Kane*), Peter Berg (*Terry Conklin*), Jon Lovitz (*Sol*), Corbin Bernsen (*Peter Prince*), Cheech Marin (*Julio Escobar*), Jamie Foxx (*Hassan El Ruk'n*), Damon Wayans (*James 'The Grim Reaper' Roper*), John Rhys-Davis (*Johnny Windsor*), Salli Richardson (*Bambi*), Rocky Carroll (*Artemus St John Saint*), Michael Jace (*Marvin Shabazz*), Albert Hall, Susan Gibney, Duane Davis, Lamont Johnson, Sam Whipple, Tim Kawakami, Brian Setzer (*himself*), Method Man (*himself*), Deezer D, Art Evans.

Dir: Reginald Hudlin. Pro: Fred Berner and Joshua Donen. Screenplay: Tony Hendra and Ron Shelton. Ph: Ron Garcia. Pro Des: Charles Rosen. Ed: Earl Watson. M: Marcus Miller; numbers performed by DJ U-Neek and Nyt Owl, Bone Thugs-N-Harmony, Method Man, Jamie Foxx, Brian Setzer, Lou Rawls, etc. Costumes: Ruth

Carter. (Atman Entertainment–Fox.) Rel: 20 September 1996. 91 mins. Cert 15. USA. 1996.

Gridlock'd

Detroit; now. When two junkie musicians decide to kick their drug habit, they find a few unexpected obstacles. It's not that their companion and meal ticket, Cookie, has OD'd; it's not that their dealer and friend has been shot dead; and it's not even the fact that they are being chased by a couple of trigger-happy crooks. Nope, the reason they can't get into rehab is because of the senseless bureaucracy tied up in forms, queues, blood tests, more forms and incompetent clerks. Doesn't anybody want these guys to go straight before they get killed? The actor Vondie Curtis Hall, who made such a memorable impression as Alfre Woodard's suitor in *Passion Fish* and played Dr Dennis Hancock in TV's *Chicago Hope*, decided to draw on his own experience growing up in Detroit for his writing-directing debut. The result is a quirky, street-wise and stylish comedy-drama with a peculiar charm all its own. As the jazz guitarist who takes the initiative, gangsta rap artist Tupac Shakur (who was shot dead in a drive-by shooting in 1996) brings a new gravity and warmth to his screen persona, making a beguiling, unlikely ally for Tim Roth's traditional low-life skunk.

Tim Roth (*Alexander 'Stretch' Rome*), Tupac Shakur (*'Spoon'*), Thandie Newton (*Barbara 'Cookie' Cook*), Lucy Alexis Liu (*Cee-Cee*), Vondie Curtis Hall (*D-Reper*), Charles Fleischer, Howard Hesseman, James Pickens Jr, John Sayles, Eric Payne, Tom Towles, Tom Wright, Debbie Zaricor, Richmond Arquette, Rusty Schwimmer, Elizabeth Anne Dickinson, Roslyn McKinney, Kasi Lemmons.
    Dir and Screenplay: Vondie Curtis Hall. Pro: Damian Jones, Paul Webster and Erica Huggins. Ex Pro: Ted Field, Russell Simmons and Scott Kroopf. Co-Ex Pro: Preston Holmes and Stan Lathan. Ph: Bill Pope. Pro Des: Dan Bishop. Ed: Christopher Koefoed. M: Stewart Copeland; numbers performed by The Angel, Critters Buggin', 2Pac, Barefoot, Danny Boy, Eight Mile Road, The Lady of Rage, etc. Costumes: Marie France. Animal trainer: Joe Camp. (PolyGram/Interscope/DEF Pictures/Webster and Dragon–PolyGram.) Rel: 30 May 1997. 91 mins. Cert 18. USA/UK. 1996.

Guantanamera

Cuba; the present. Blessed by an idyllic coastline and interior (and an absence of McDonald's), Cuba – one of the last bastions of Marxist-Leninism in the world – presents a stunning backdrop for filmmakers. Unfortunately, *Guantanamera* is a somewhat convoluted film, featuring the bizarre chance encounters between the occupants of a funeral cortege and a truck that follows the same route for very different reasons. Ultimately, then, the star of what is basically a glorified road movie is the ever-changing landscape. From the directors of *Strawberry and Chocolate*. [Nigel Mulock]

Carlos Cruz (*Adolfo*), Mirtha Ibarra (*Georgina*), Raul Eguren (*Candido*), Jorge Perugorria (*Mariano*), Pedro Fernandez, Luis Alberto Garcia, Conchita Brando.
    Dir: Tomas Gutierrez Alea and Juan Carlos Tabio. Pro: Gerardo Herrero. Ex Pro: Camilo Vives and Ulrich Felsberg. Screenplay: Alea, Tabio and Eliseo Alberto Diego. Ph: Hans Burmann. Pro Des: Onelio Larralde. Ed: Carmen Frias. M: Jose Nieto. Costumes: Nancy Gonzalez. (Tornasol Films/Alta Films/Road Movies/Canal Plus–Film Four.) Rel: 20 September 1996. 102 mins. Cert 15. Spain/Cuba/ Germany. 1995.

Hamlet

Hamlet (aka the Melancholy Dane) plots revenge on his uncle when he discovers that the latter has murdered his father in order to take over the throne of Denmark and the bed of Hamlet's mother... Arguably the most ambitious and daring talent working in the British cinema, Kenneth Branagh really has his hands full here. Not only has he resolved to present the entire uncut text of Shakespeare's most famous play (running at four hours), but he has shouldered the title role himself, introduced epic scenes of battle, taken on courageous shifts in narrative emphasis, employed a cast of international stars and shot the whole thing in 70mm. However, while some scenes fall flat (the melodramatic appearance of the dead king, Gerard Depardieu's distracting cameo as Reynaldo), others work extraordinarily well – particularly Branagh's cunning delivery of 'to be or not to be' to a two-way mirror (concealing Claudius), his dramatic 'how all occasions do inform against me' speech addressed in front of Fortinbras' encroaching, snowbound army and Ophelia's mad scene (hauntingly realised by Kate Winslet). In all, an intelligent, intrepid and inspired (if frequently heavy-going) accomplishment. P.S. Blenheim Palace stands in for the Castle of Elsinore.

Kenneth Branagh (*Hamlet, Prince of Denmark*), Julie Christie (*Gertrude*), Billy Crystal (*first gravedigger*), Gerard Depardieu (*Reynaldo*), Charlton Heston (*Player King*), Derek Jacobi (*Claudius*), Jack Lemmon (*Marcellus*), Rufus Sewell (*Fortinbras*), Robin Williams (*Osric*), Kate Winslet (*Ophelia*), Brian Blessed (*ghost*), Richard Briers (*Polonius*), Reece Dinsdale (*Guildenstern*), Ken Dodd (*Yorick*), Nicholas Farrell (*Horatio*), Rosemary Harris (*Player Queen*), Ian McElhinney (*Barnardo*), Michael Maloney (*Laertes*), Duke of Marlborough (*Fortinbras' general*), Simon Russell Beale (*second gravedigger*), Timothy Spall (*Rosencrantz*), Richard Attenborough, Michael Bryant, Judi Dench, Angela Douglas, Rob Edwards, Ray Fearon, John Gielgud, Ravil Isyanov, Rowena King, Jeffery Kissoon, Sarah Lam, John Mills, Andrew Schofield, Don Warrington, David Yip.
    Dir and Screenplay: Kenneth Branagh. Pro: David Barron. Ph: Alex Thomson. Pro Des: Tim Harvey. Ed: Neil Farrell. M: Patrick Doyle; 'In Pace' performed by Placido Domingo. Costumes: Alexandra Byrne. (Castle Rock–Rank–Castle Rock/Turner.) Rel: 14 February 1997. 242 mins. Cert PG. USA. 1996.

Happy Gilmore

Continuing to explore the permutations of his gormless loser, Adam Sandler plays Gilmore, the world's worst ice hockey player who discovers he has a gift for

Waiting to exhale: Tupac Shakur and Tim Roth try to kick the habit in Vondie Curtis Hall's quirky, stylish Gridlock'd *(from PolyGram)*

'Oh shame, where is thy blush?': Julie Christie and Kenneth Branagh in the latter's daring and intelligent Hamlet *(from Rank–Castle Rock/Turner)*

professional golf. At first dismissive of his new talent – 'I am a hockey player' – Gilmore then realises he can raise enough money to buy back his beloved grandmother's house (which is up for repossession). But can Happy Gilmore rein in his mad antics long enough to fit in with the gentleman's sport? Scripted by Sandler in collaboration with Tim Herlihy (*Billy Madison*), *Happy Gilmore* dumps enough off-the-wall jokes into the stew to keep the story bubbling along nicely. Furthermore, some unexpected shards of black humour help to cut through the predictable plot strings. It's certainly an improvement on *Billy Madison*.

Adam Sandler (*Happy Gilmore*), Christopher McDonald (*Shooter McGavin*), Julie Bowen (*Virginia Venit*), Frances Bay (*Grandma*), Carl Weathers (*Chubbs Peterson*), Dennis Dugan (*Doug Thompson*), Alan Covert, Robert Smigel, Bob Barker (*himself*), Richard Kiel, Joe Flaherty, Lee Trevino, Verne Lundquist, Jared Van Snellenberg, Nancy McClure, Mark Lye, Michelle Holdsworth.

Dir: Dennis Dugan. Pro: Robert Simonds. Ex Pro: Brad Grey, Bernie Brillstein and Sandy Wernick. Screenplay: Tim Herlihy and Adam Sandler. Ph: Arthur Albert. Pro Des: Perry Andelin Blake. Ed: Jeff Gourson. M: Mark Mothersbaugh; numbers performed by Exile, Pilot, Diana Ross, Kansas, House of Pain, Lynyrd Skynyrd, Gary Glitter, etc. Costumes: Tish Monoghan. (Universal–UIP.) Rel: 19 July 1996. 92 mins. Cert 12. USA. 1996.

Hard Men

Tone, Bear and Speed work for gangland boss Pops Den (played by real-life mobster 'Mad' Frankie Fraser) and enjoy the adrenalin that goes with the job. Then, slap in the middle of a showdown with three gun-toting hoods, Tone gets a call on his mobile. It transpires that he has fathered a baby girl by his ex-girlfriend. After blowing away the hoods, Tone decides that fatherhood must take precedence over killing and he announces his retirement. Strangely, he also becomes an instant expert on babies. Of course, nobody leaves the employ of Pops Den alive and the latter recruits Bear and Speed to have Tone terminated... Blatantly inspired by *Reservoir Dogs*, this

audacious, testosterone-driven celebration of all things laddish and criminal will entertain and shock in equal measure. Crass maybe, sick definitely, but *Hard Men* possesses a vigour, edge and self-deprecatory humour that cannot be ignored.

Vincent Regan (*Tone*), Ross Boatman (*Bear*), Lee Ross (*Speed*), 'Mad' Frankie Fraser (*Pops Den*), Ken Campbell (*Mr Ross*), Mirella D'Angelo (*Chantal*), Irene Ng, Robyn Lewis, Andrew Weatherall, Roger Griffiths, Stuart Jason Cole, Vic Tablian, Abigail Olek, Michael Riley.

Dir and Screenplay: J.K. Amalou. Pro: Amalou and Georges Benayoun. Ex Pro: Marina Gefter. Line Pro: Michael Riley. Ph: Nick Sawyer. Pro Des: Simon Elliott. Ed: Victoria Boydell. M: Nicola Fletcher; numbers performed by The Routers, Hurle, Lunaseed, Blowfly, Hoop, The StripKings, etc. Costumes: Mike O'Neill and Samantha Horn. (Dacia Films/ Venture Movies–Entertainment.) Rel: 4 April 1997. 87 mins. Cert 18. UK/France. 1996.

Harriet the Spy

'You know, there are as many ways to live as there are people in the world. And each one deserves a closer look.' It is this sort of advice, doled out by the worldly Ole Golly, that sets Harriet M. Welsch, 11, on the road to become a great novelist. Constantly taking notes in her omnipresent and very private journal, Harriet writes it as she sees it. However, when her book is exposed by the class prefect, Harriet's candid insights on her classmates are taken none too kindly. Instantly ostracised, Harriet becomes the butt of her friends, forcing her to resort to exceptionally cruel and personal acts of revenge... The concept of Louise Fitzhugh's enduring novel of 1964 was both amusing and perceptive, and while the moral of her story still wields a sting, it is diluted here by lack-lustre direction and lazy diction (particularly Michelle Trachtenberg's voice-over).

Michelle Trachtenberg (*Harriet M. Welsch*), Rosie O'Donnell (*Ole Golly*), Vanessa Lee Chester (*Janie Gibbs*), Gregory Smith (*Sport*), J. Smith-Cameron (*Mrs Welsch*), Robert Joy (*Mr Welsch*), Eugene Lipinski (*George Waldenstein*), Charlotte Sullivan (*Marion Hawthorne*), Nancy Beatty (*Miss Elson*), Eartha Kitt, Don Francks, Teisha Kim, Cecilley Carroll, Dov Tiefenbach, Gerry Quigley, Jackie Richardson, Mercedes Enriquez, Maury Chaykin (uncredited).
   Dir: Bronwen Hughes. Pro: Marykay Powell. Ex Pro: Debby Beece. Co-Pro: Nava Levin. Screenplay: Douglas Petrie and Theresa Rebeck, from the adaptation by Greg Taylor and Julie Talen. Ph: Francis Kenny. Pro Des: Lester Cohen. Ed: Debra

The custody of strangers: Sam Bould and Jason Flemyng in Angela Pope's implausible Hollow Reed *(from Film Four)*

Chiate. M: Jamshied Sharifi; numbers performed by Young-Holt Unlimited, Los Straitjackets, Eartha Kitt, Tito Puente, James Brown, Jill Sobule, etc. Costumes: Donna Zakowska. (Paramount/ Nickelodean Movies/Rastar–UIP.) Rel: 14 February 1997. 101 mins. Cert PG. USA. 1996.

High School High

Unceasingly quashed by his domineering father, a snooty headmaster, 39-year-old virgin Richard Clark decides to go his own way by opting to teach at the worst school in the world. And, true enough, with its own cemetery and parking lot reserved for the local SWAT team, the Marion Barry High School makes Bosnia look user-friendly. So, how on earth can this overweight clown make a difference against such insurmountable odds? In the tradition of such spoofs as *Airplane!*, *Hot Shots!* and (heaven forbid) *Silence of the Hams*, this blatant take-off of *Dangerous Minds* starts promisingly and then quickly loses steam. Yet, while not quite as numbingly awful as others of this ilk, it's still pretty painful. [*Charles Bacon*]

Jon Lovitz (*Richard Clark*), Tia Carrere (*Victoria Chappell*), Mekhi Phifer (*Griff McReynolds*), Louise Fletcher (*Mrs Evelyn Doyle*), Guillermo Diaz (*Paco*), John Neville (*Thaddeus Clark*), Malinda Williams (*Natalie*), Natasha Gregson Wagner (*Julie*), Brian Hooks, Marco Rodriguez, Nicholas Worth, Lexi Bigham, Gil Espinoza, Charlotte Zucker, Colleen Fitzpatrick.
   Dir: Hart Bochner. Pro: David Zucker, Robert LoCash and Gil Netter. Ex Pro:

Sasha Harari. Co-Pro: Patricia Whitcher. Screenplay: Zucker & LoCash and Pat Proft. Ph: Vernon Layton. Pro Des: Dennis Washington. Ed: James R. Symons. M: Ira Newborn; numbers performed by The Carpenters, Scarface, Glen Campbell, Nuttin' Nyce, The Braxtons, KRS-ONE, Ricky Jones, The Braids, etc. Costumes: Mona May. (TriStar–Columbia TriStar.) Rel: 16 May 1997. 89 mins. Cert 15. USA. 1996.

Hollow Reed

Bath, Avon; today. Although Martyn Wyatt, a doctor, has come to acknowledge his homosexual feelings and is living with a man, he is still deeply concerned for the welfare of his nine-year-old son, Oliver. When the latter incurs a number of mysterious injuries, but is unable to convincingly reveal their cause, Martyn renews his fight for custody... By dint of its morally sensitive subject matter, *Hollow Reed* strikes a number of resonant chords, pulling the heart this way and the mind that. Yet there are moments of gaping implausibility, as if the actors cannot believe the lines they are being fed. This, however, is no fault of the cast, but of the parts they are forced to wear, like ill-fitting jackets. Martin Donovan, the Californian actor best known for the quirky films of Hal Hartley, seems totally wrong for the role of a homosexual father and doctor living in Bath. Strangely, it is only when Anne Dudley's lush music is allowed to well and the film permits itself a modicum of cinematic gloss that the story's dramatic moves fall into place.

Martin Donovan (*Martyn Wyatt*), Joely Richardson (*Hannah Wyatt*), Ian Hart (*Tom Dixon*), Jason Flemyng (*Frank Donally*), Sam Bould (*Oliver Wyatt*), Annette Badland (*Martyn's barrister*), Shaheen Khan, Kelly Hunter, Simon Chandler, Dilys Hamlett, David Calder, Maeve Murphy, Roger Lloyd Pack, Douglas Hodge, Edward Hardwicke.
   Dir: Angela Pope. Pro: Elizabeth Karlsen. Ex Pro: Nik Powell and Stephen Woolley. Co-Ex Pro: Andres Vincente Gomez, Finola Dwyer, Neville Bolt and Hanno Huth. Screenplay: Paula Milne, based on an original story by Bolt. Ph: Remi Adefarasin. Pro Des: Stuart Walker. Ed: Sye Wyatt. M: Anne Dudley; numbers performed by Booker T and the MGs, Bob Dylan, Elvis Costello, Annie Lennox, Mike Batt, and Paul Weller. Costumes: Pam Downe. (Scala/Channel Four/Senator

Film–Film Four.) Rel: 6 September 1996. 104 mins. Cert 15. UK/Germany. 1995.

Home For the Holidays

Baltimore/Chicago; Thanksgiving weekend. Art restorer Claudia Larson has just lost her job, her cool and her coat – and with the prospect of a weekend with her very weird family she is about to lose her mind... A constant stream of character-driven gags keeps this classy ensemble comedy bubbling, interspersed with canny insights into the wayward cogs of the domestic machine. A superb cast hits its marks with accomplished élan, although Geraldine Chaplin's dotty aunt is a highlight in the actress's career. High marks, too, to Jodie Foster's slick, affectionate direction, which never lets a joke outstay its welcome. If nothing else, *Home For the Holidays* should act as an invaluable survival guide to family gatherings and how to overcome the trauma with a sense of humour and perspective. One of the year's funniest movies.

Holly Hunter (*Claudia Larson*), Robert Downey Jr (*Tommy Larson*), Anne Bancroft (*Adele Larson*), Charles Durning (*Henry Larson*), Dylan McDermott (*Leo Fish*), Geraldine Chaplin (*Aunt Glady*), Steve Guttenberg (*Walter Wedman*), Cynthia Stevenson (*Joanne Wedman*), Claire Danes (*Kitt*), Austin Pendleton (*Peter Arnold*), David Strathairn (*Russell Terziak*), Sam Slovick (*Jack Gordon*), Zachary Duhame, Emily Ann Lloyd, Angela Paton, Shawn Wayne Hatosy, Amy Yasbeck.
   Dir: Jodie Foster. Pro: Foster and Peggy Rajski. Ex Pro: Stuart Kleinman. Screenplay: W.D.Richter, based on a short story by Chris Radant. Ph: Lajos Koltai. Pro Des: Andrew McAlpine. Ed: Lynzee Klingman. M: Mark Isham; numbers performed by Rusted Root, The Beastie Boys, Nat King Cole, Tom Jones, Dinah Washington, and Janis Joplin. Costumes: Susan Lyall. (PolyGram/Egg Pictures–PolyGram.) Rel: 6 December 1996. 102 mins. Cert 15. USA. 1995.

Howard Stern's Private Parts

See *Private Parts*.

The Hunchback of Notre Dame

The world première for Disney's '34th animated feature' (which strangely excludes *Toy Story*) was supposed to have taken place in

Paris. However, the civic authorities were so outraged by the film's treatment of the Great French Novel that the première was shifted to New Orleans, the closest thing to Paris that the Americans can call their own. But what did the French expect? A graphic recreation of Victor Hugo's bleak depiction of medieval Paris and its underworld?

Beauty and the beast: Esmeralda admires Quasimodo's carvings as Hugo, Victor and Laverne, the companionable gargoyles, look on – in Disney's The Hunchback of Notre Dame *(from Buena Vista)*

Family vacation: Robert Downey Jr and Holly Hunter look on the bright side in Jodie Foster's very funny Home For the Holidays *(from PolyGram)*

I don't think so. No, this Quasimodo is the cutest freak to grace our screens since Sneezy, Bashful & co. and is a perfect endorsement for a McDonald's Happy Meal. The film itself, yet another illustration of why Disney is the finest animation studio in the world, is the stuff of a classic Broadway musical, complete with a terrific story, wonderful songs, wells of emotion and plenty of jokes. Kevin Kline, voicing the gallant Phoebus, has all the best lines (no surprises there), including the throwaway command to his horse, 'Come on boy, Achilles, heel!' And Demi Moore as Esmeralda has never looked sexier. The sceptics may mutter under their breath, but Disney have created another instant classic.

Voices: Tom Hulce (*Quasimodo*), Demi Moore (*Esmeralda*), Heidi Mollenhauer (*singing voice of Esmeralda*), Tony Jay (*Frollo*), Kevin Kline (*Phoebus*), Paul Kandel (*Clopin*), Jason Alexander (*Hugo*), Charles Kimbrough (*Victor*), Mary Wickes (*Laverne*), David Ogden Stiers (*Archdeacon*), Mary Kay Bergman, Corey Burton, Jim Cummings, Gary Trousdale, Frank Welker, Jane Withers.
    Dir: Gary Trousdale and Kirk Wise. Pro: Don Hahn. Co-Pro: Roy Conli. Assoc Pro:

Perfect for each other: Nicole Parker and Laurel Hollomon combine forces in Maria Maggenti's disarming The Incredibly True Adventure of 2 Girls In Love *(from Feature Film Company)*

Phil Lofaro. Screenplay: Tab Murphy, Irene Mecchi, Bob Tzudiker, Noni White and Jonathan Roberts. Art: David Goetz. Ed: Ellen Keneshea. M: Alan Menken; songs: Menken (music) and Stephen Schwartz (lyrics); 'Someday' performed by All 4 One. (Walt Disney–Buena Vista.) Rel: 12 July 1996. 90 mins. Cert U. USA. 1996.

Hustler White

Male hustlers in LA feature prominently in this cinematically knowing tale which, ultimately, concentrates on the love of a writer (Bruce LaBruce who, with Rick Castro, co-directs) for one of the hustlers (Tony Ward). Although some regard LaBruce as an artist, the film's graphic gay sex offers porn appeal rather than art, and few will see this as the romantic comedy promised by the publicity. But if LaBruce knows more about sex than romance, the scenes of sex with an amputee and consensual sado-masochism do mean that the filmmaker can validly claim to be breaking cinematic taboos. As to whether this is good or bad, opinions will inevitably differ. [*Mansel Stimpson*]

Tony Ward (*Montgomery 'Monti' Ward*), Bruce LaBruce (*Jurgen Anger*), Kevin Kramer (*himself*), Ron Athey (*Seymour Kasabian*), Alex Austin (*himself*), Kevin P. Scott (*Eigil Vesti*), Glen Meadmore, Graham David Smith, Ivar Johnson (*Piglet*), Miles H. Wildecock II, Bud Cockerham, Vaginal Davis, Joaquin Martinez, Tony Powers, Rick Castro.
    Dir, Screenplay and Pro Des: Bruce LaBruce and Rick Castro. Pro: Jurgen Bruning and Bruce LaBruce. Ph: James Carman. Ed and Sound: Rider Siphron. M: numbers performed by Glen Meadmore, Goo Goo Dolls, Coil, Smoke, The Boredoms, Rusty, The Dandy Warhols, etc. (Strand Releasing/Stance Co./Dangerous To Know/Swell Co.–ICA Projects.) Rel: 19 July 1996. 78 mins. Cert 18. USA/Germany/UK. 1996.

The Incredibly True Adventure of 2 Girls in Love

New Jersey; today. Following a tiff with her married lover, lesbian schoolgirl Randy Dean turns her attentions towards an affluent Afro-American classmate in the throes of breaking up from her boyfriend. A mutual interest quickly ensues, but

not without considerable personal cost to both girls... With a dedication reading 'To my first girlfriend – may our relationship finally rest in peace,' Maria Maggenti's debut feature is strong on charm and good intentions but weak on plot and wit. The writer-director has yet to learn how to set up an interesting situation and extract credible performances from her cast, but she has a lightness of touch that is admirable. Indeed, of the recent spate of lesbian films this is eminently the most palatable.

Laurel Hollomon (*Randy Dean*), Nicole Parker (*Evie Roy*), Maggie Moore (*Wendy*), Dale Dickey (*Regina*), Stephanie Berry (*Evelyn Roy*), Kate Stafford, Sabrina Artel, Toby Poser, Nelson Rodriguez, Andrew Wright, John Elson.
    Dir and Screenplay: Maria Maggenti. Pro: Dolly Hall. Assoc Pro: Zoe Oka Edwards, Mark Huisman and Melissa Painter. Ph: Tami Reiker. Pro Des: Ginger Thougas. Ed: Susan Graef. M: Terry Dame; Mozart; numbers performed by Scream, Lois, BETTY, Velocity, and Bikini Kill. Costumes: Cheryl Hurwitz. Sound: Steven Bourn. (Smash Pictures–Feature Film Company.) Rel: 20 September 1996. 98 mins. Cert 15. USA. 1995.

Independence Day

Two days before Independence Day, a number of giant spaceships hover over the world's major cities. It's hard to believe that an intelligent life form would travel several billion light years just to destroy us, even if the blind panic that their appearance produces does just that. But then these alien mothers haven't even started... Extracting the key elements of *Close Encounters of the Third Kind, Top Gun, Star Wars, Alien* and *The War of the Worlds, Independence Day* takes the Ultimate Story – mankind pulling together to defend its planet from outsiders – and gilds it with the best special effects money can buy. The destruction of the cities of New York, Washington DC and Los Angeles is some of the most amazing footage ever created on celluloid, the horror of which is tempered by the level-headed awe and irony of Jeff Goldblum's computer wizard, a man whose meticulous quest to 'save the planet' suddenly takes on epic dimensions. Indeed, it is the casting of recognisable, reliable and (relatively) inexpensive actors like Goldblum that enabled the producers

A beast of July: A city block is scratched off the map in Roland Emmerich's phenomenal Independence Day *(from Fox)*

to put their money where it counts: on the screen. Everything a film should be: audacious, scary, thrilling, funny, awe-inspiring, horrific, thought-provoking, sexy and mind-boggling.

Will Smith (*Captain Steven Hiller*), Bill Pullman (*President Thomas J. Whitmore*), Jeff Goldblum (*David Levinson*), Mary McDonnell (*Marilyn Whitmore*), Judd Hirsch (*Julius Levinson*), Margaret Colin (*Constance Spano*), Randy Quaid (*Russell Casse*), Robert Loggia (*General William Grey*), James Rebhorn (*Secretary Albert Nimziki*), Harvey Fierstein (*Marty Gilbert*), Adam Baldwin (*Major Mitchell*), Brent Spiner (*Dr Okun*), James Duval (*Miguel*), Vivica Fox (*Jasmine*), Lisa Jakub (*Alicia*), Ross Bagley (*Dylan*), Mae Whitman (*Patricia Whitmore*), Bill Smitrovich (*Captain Watson*), Kiersten Warren (*Tiffany*), Harry Connick Jr (*Jimmy*), Guiseppe Andrews, John Storey, Frank Novak, Jay Acovone, James Wong, John Capodice, Lyman Ward, Barbara Beck, Rance Howard, Adam Tomei, Kimberly Beck, Thomas F. Duffy, Lisa Star, Malcom Danare. Vocal effects: Frank Welker.

Dir: Roland Emmerich. Pro: Dean Devlin. Ex Pro: Roland Emmerich, Ute Emmerich (Roland's sister) and William Fay. Screenplay: Devlin and Roland Emmerich. Ph: Karl Walter Lindenlaub.

Pro Des: Oliver Scholl and Patrick Tatopoulos. Ed: David Brenner. M: David Arnold; numbers performed by Bill Elliott, Greta, Link Wray, etc; 'It's The End Of The World As We Know It' written and performed by REM. Costumes: Joseph Porro. Visual effects: Volker Engel and Douglas Smith. Creature effects: Tatopoulos. (Fox/Centropolis Entertainment–Fox.) Rel: 9 August 1996. 140 mins. Cert 12. USA. 1996.

Indian Summer
See *Alive and Kicking*.

In Love and War
1918; Northern Italy. When, during the First World War, the 19-year-old Ernest Hemingway volunteers to distribute cigarettes and sympathy on the frontline, he ends up in a makeshift hospital. There, he falls for

Resting Ernest Hemingway: Sandra Bullock brings succour to Chris O'Donnell in Richard Attenborough's sweeping romance, In Love and War *(from Entertainment)*

Terror in the terrace: Laura Sadler, Rupert Graves and Julie Walters cosy up in Philip Goodhew's Intimate Relations *(from Fox)*

his attendant nurse, who is seven years his senior and professionally forbidden to fraternise with her patients. But Hemingway is no ordinary convalescent... It's easy to be cynical when reviewing what is essentially an old-fashioned love story, but then romances aren't made for cynics. *In Love and War* is based on real events and is, even by today's liberal standards, a remarkable tale. However, any love story can only be as potent as the chemistry of its protagonists. Here, Chris O'Donnell cannot quite convey the sexual danger that the part demands, although Sandra Bullock gives him every reason to fall in love. After a few earnest glances from Hemingway, the girl is hooked and George Fenton's impassioned music soars. What actually carries the romance to its bitter-sweet conclusion is the tumult of extraordinary times the barbarism of war played out against the breathtaking, sun-dappled country-side of Italy. It's enough to make you swoon. FYI: Bullock's other suitor, played by Mackenzie Astin, is actually the real-life father of the film's producer Dimitri Villard.

Sandra Bullock (*Agnes Von Kurowsky*), Chris O'Donnell (*Ernest Hemingway*),

Mackenzie Astin (*Henry Villard*), Emilio Bonucci (*Domenico Caracciolo*), Ingrid Lacey (*Mac*), Margot Steinberg (*Rosie*), Tara Hugo (*Miss De Long*), Ian Kelly (*McBride*), Colin Stinton, Rocco Quarzell, Vincenzo Nicoli, Rebecca Craig, Matthew Sharp, Doreen Mantle, Colin Fox (*Dr Hemingway*), Kay Hawtrey, Avery Saltzman, Philippe Leroy, Laura Martelli. Dir: Richard Attenborough. Pro: Attenborough and Dimitri Villard. Ex Pro: Sara Risher. Supervising Pro: Chris Kenny. Co-Pro: Diana Hawkins. Screenplay: Allan Scott, Clancy Sigal and Anna Hamilton Phelan, from a story by Scott and Dimitri Villard, based on the book *Hemingway In Love and War* by Henry Serrano Villard and James Nagel. Ph: Roger Pratt. Pro Des: Stuart Craig. Ed: Lesley Walker. M: George Fenton. Costumes: Penny Rose. (New Line/Dimitri Villard Prods–Entertainment.) Rel: 14 February 1997. 116 mins. Cert 15. USA. 1996.

Intimate Relations

1954; suburbia, England. Returning from the Navy, young Harold Guppy seeks out his brother in a last-ditch attempt to mend fences with his family. However, when he is cold-shouldered by his sister-in-law, Guppy rents a room at a nearby semi. There, he is taken into the bosom of the Beasley clan, quickly winning the profound affections of mother, father and 13-year-old daughter. At last, it seems, Guppy has found his family, albeit one that is bent on sharing his bed... An uneasy mix of caricature, farce and thriller, *Intimate Relations* actually starts very promisingly. Playing on

the innate ordinariness of its working-class milieu, the film (which is inspired by real events) kicks off as a sharply observed comedy, with Julie Walters on splendid form as a sex-starved, hypocritical grandmother who makes a grand cup of post-coital cocoa. It is the considerable middle section – the bridge between the initial comedy and the horror of what is to come – that fails to hold our interest or solicit much compassion. These are ugly little people trapped in the claustrophobia of their own ugly little world – and there are not enough jokes or murders to go round.

Julie Walters (*Marjorie Beasley*), Rupert Graves (*Harold Guppy*), Laura Sadler (*Joyce Beasley*), Matthew Walker (*Stanley Beasley*), Holly Aird (*Deirdre*), Les Dennis (*Maurice Guppy*), Elizabeth McKechnie (*Iris Guppy*), James Aiden, Michael Bertenshaw, Judy Clifton, Candace Hallinan, Amanda Holden, Sarah-Jane McKechnie. Dir and Screenplay: Philip Goodhew. Pro: Angela Hart, Lisa Hope and Jon Slan. Ex Pro: Gareth Jones. Line Pro: Simon Hardy and Simon Scotland. Ph: Andres Garreton. Pro Des: Caroline Greville-Morris. Ed: Pia Di Ciaula. M: Lawrence Shragge; numbers performed by Rosemary Clooney, etc. Costumes: John Hibbs. (Handmade Films/Boxer Films/ Paragon Entertainment–Fox.) Rel: 20 June 1997. 99 mins. Cert 15. Canada/UK. 1995.

Irma Vep

Paris; today. Hong Kong movie star Maggie Cheung (playing herself) arrives in Paris to take the lead in a TV remake of the classic black and white serial *Les Vampires*. But when she adopts the screen persona of her character, her wardrobe mistress becomes infatuated. Then, when the director – a wonderfully calibrated performance by Jean-Pierre Leaud – has a chronic nervous breakdown, the whole project seems doomed. Angst, humour and sexiness pervade the chaos for ninety minutes of viewing time: the final six or so are a revelation. A gem of a movie. [*Nigel Mulock*]

Maggie Cheung (*Maggie Cheung/Irma Vep*), Jean-Pierre Leaud (*Rene Vidal*), Nathalie Richard (*Zoe*), Bulle Ogier (*Mireille*), Antoine Basler, Nathalie Boutefeu, Alex Descas, Lou Castel, Arsinee Khanjian, Jessica Doyle. Dir and Screenplay: Olivier Assayas.

Pro: Georges Benayoun. Ex Pro: Francoise Gugliemi. Ph: Eric Gautier. Art: Francois-Renaud Labarthe. Ed: Luc Barnier, Tina Baz and Marie Lecoeur. M: numbers performed by Luna, Sonic Youth, and Ry Cooder. Costumes: Francoise Clavel and Jessica Doyle. (Dacia Films–ICA.) Rel: 7 March 1997. 98 mins. No Cert. France. 1996.

I Shot Andy Warhol

Valerie Solanas was abused by her father, became sexually active at 11, had her first homosexual experience at 14 and majored in psychology at the University of Maryland, supporting herself by prostitution. A radical feminist (to say the least), she advocated genocide of the male sex, founded the revolutionary movement SCUM (Society for Cutting Up Men) – of which she was the sole member – wrote a play, *Up Your Ass*, and appeared in Andy Warhol's 1967 film *I, A Man* (an ironic title under the circumstances). Then, at 4.15pm on 3 June, 1968, she shot Andy Warhol, puncturing his lungs, spleen, stomach, liver and oesophagus. A truly fascinating character, played with unsparing conviction by Lili Taylor, Valerie Solanas is also a hard one to spend much time with. Strident, irrational and hysterical, she was, as she proclaimed to one individual, 'the incubation of your mother's nightmare.' But the main problem with the film is that it plays its trump card in its first few minutes (as reinforced by the title), thus robbing the remaining 100 minutes of any sense of expectation or suspense. Furthermore, watching it raises the curious dichotomy of wanting to know more about the subject but wishing it would all end very soon.

Lili Taylor (*Valerie Solanas*), Jared Harris (*Andy Warhol*), Martha Plimpton (*Stevie*), Stephen Dorff (*Candy Darling*), Danny Morgenstern (*Jeremiah*), Lothaire Bluteau (*Maurice Girodias*), Michael Imperioli (*Ondine*), Reg Rogers (*Paul Morrissey*), Tahnee Welch (*Viva*), Myriam Cyr (*Ultra Violet*), Peter Friedman, Jamie Harrold, Donovan Leitch, Bill Sage, Jill Hennessy, Coco McPherson, Craig Chester, James Lyons, Anna Thomson, Isabel Gillies.
Dir: Mary Harron. Pro: Tom Kalin and Christine Vachon. Ex Pro: Lindsay Law and Anthony Wall. Screenplay: Harron and Daniel Minahan. Ph: Ellen Kuras. Pro Des: Therese Deprez. Ed: Keith Reamer. M: John Cale; numbers performed by Wilco, Dionne Warwick, Jewel, REM, Luna, Hugh Masekela, The Lovin' Spoonful, Love, Pavement, Bob Dylan, Yo Lo Tengo, etc. Costumes: David Robinson. (Playhouse International/Samuel Goldwyn/BBC Arena/Orion Pictures–Electric.) Rel: 29 November 1996. 106 mins. Cert 18. USA/UK. 1996.

The Island of Dr Moreau

When his plane crashes in the Java Sea, United Nations envoy Edward Douglas becomes a reluctant guest on a remote island run by an enigmatic, Nobel Prize-winning recluse. Officially noted for his invention of Velcro, Dr Moreau is now on a quest to 'turn animals into humans and humans into gods'. But no sooner has Douglas witnessed some hideous mutations than Moreau's experiments in genetic engineering backfire dreadfully... Celebrating the centenary of H.G. Wells' disturbingly prophetic novel, the third screen incarnation of *The Island of Dr Moreau* was a lifelong dream for writer-director Richard Stanley (*Hardware*, *Dust Devil*). However, when his star – Val Kilmer – demanded that his leading role be cut by 40 per cent, Stanley was forced to re-cast him in the supporting character of Moreau's assistant. David Thewlis was hurriedly brought in to play Douglas, Kilmer failed to show up for the first two days of shooting and the resultant rushes got Stanley fired. Enter John Frankenheimer – director of *The Manchurian Candidate* and *Birdman of Alcatraz* – and the outcome is a slapdash, embarrassing shambles punctuated by some extraordinarily arresting images. N.B. The Swiss aristocrat George de Mestral is the real inventor of Velcro.

Marlon Brando (*Dr Moreau*), Val Kilmer (*Montgomery*), David Thewlis (*Edward Douglas*), Fairuza Balk (*Aissa Moreau*), Ron Perlman (*Sayer of the Law*), Marco Hofschneider (*M'Ling*), Temuera Morrison (*Azazello*), William Hootkins (*Kiril*), Mark Dacascos (*Lo-Mai*), Nelson De La Rosa.
Dir: John Frankenheimer. Pro: Edward R. Pressman. Ex Pro: Tim Zinnemann and Claire Rudnick-Polstein. Screenplay: Richard Stanley and Ron Hutchinson. Ph: William A. Fraker. Pro Des: Graham 'Grace' Walker. Ed: Paul Rubell. M: Gary Chang; numbers performed by Monk & Canatella Band, Val Kilmer, Deep Forest, and Salt. Costumes: Norma Moriceau. Creature and make-up effects: Stan Winston. (New Line Cinema– Entertainment.) Rel: 15 November 1996. 95 mins. Cert 12. USA. 1996.

It Takes Two

A streetwise orphan beloved by a New York case worker (Kirstie Alley) and the motherless daughter of a preoccupied billionaire (Steve Guttenberg) turn out to be physically identical and plot to entwine the hearts of their respective guardians... A painfully contrived family outing with all the subtlety of a Big Mac, *It Takes Two* is rescued from total banality by the winning performances of real-life twins Mary-Kate and Ashley Olsen. Aka *Me and My Shadow*. [*Charles Bacon*]

Kirstie Alley (*Diane Barrows*), Steve Guttenberg (*Roger Callaway*), Mary-Kate Olsen (*Amanda Lemmon*), Ashley Olsen (*Alyssa Callaway*), Philip Bosco (*Vincenzo*), Jane Sibbett (*Clarice Kensington*), Michelle Grisom (*Carmen*), Desmond Roberts, Tiny Mills, Shanelle Henry, Anthony Aiello, Lawrence Dane.
Dir: Andy Tennant. Pro: James Orr and Jim Cruickshank. Ex Pro: Keith Samples. Screenplay: Tennant, Deborah Dean Davis, Jeff Schechter and Rick Parks. Ph: Kenneth D. Zunder. Pro Des: Edward Pisoni. Ed: Roger Bondelli. M: Sherman Foote and Ray Foote. Costumes: Molly McGuiness. (Rysher Entertainment/Dualstar Prods–Entertainment.) Rel: 2 May 1997. 97 mins. Cert PG. USA. 1995.

Jack

Just two months pregnant, Karen Powell delivers a perfectly healthy baby boy, Jack. Jack, it transpires, is born with a rare ageing disease which causes his cells to multiply four times the normal rate. By the age of ten he looks like a 40-year-old man, and must confront the ordeal of school for the first time. But how are the other kids going to respond to a classmate who looks older than their teacher, albeit sharing their own mental and emotional age? All Jack wants is a normal life, although the advant- ages of looking 40 are not be squandered... Bravely leaping into the treadmarks left by *Big*, *Vice Versa* and *Like Father Like Son*, *Jack* proves to be a perfect vehicle for the enormous talent of Robin Williams: outrageous physical comedy laced with pathos and an overpowering

Jack *of all grades: Robin Williams (centre) joins his parents (Brian Kerwin, Diane Lane) in bed before facing the terrors of fifth grade – from Buena Vista*

message, i.e. seize the day. Williams is constantly reminding us of the value of our fleeting time on earth (cf. *Dead Poet's Society*, the TV movie *Seize the Day*), a sentiment that gains considerable weight when the comic shows us what life can be. Some may carp at the film's overt symbolism (Jack's spiritual link with a butterfly), and others barf at the scatological content, but *Jack* provides healthy entertainment with a big heart.

Robin Williams (*Jack Powell*), Diane Lane (*Karen Powell*), Brian Kerwin (*Brian Powell*), Jennifer Lopez (*Miss Marquez*), Bill Cosby (*Lawrence Woodruff*), Fran Drescher (*Dolores Durante*), Adam Zolotin (*Louis Durante*), Todd Bosley (*Edward*), Allan Rich (*Dr Benfante*), Seth Smith, Mario Yedidia, Jeremy Elliott, Jurnee Smollett, Dani Faith, Michael McKean, Edward Lynch, Don Novello, Keone Young, Irwin Corey, Dwight Hicks, Kendra Sutherland.
   Dir: Francis Ford Coppola. Pro: Coppola, Ricardo Mestres and Fred Fuchs. Ex Pro: Doug Claybourne. Screenplay: James DeMonaco and Gary Nadeau. Ph: John Toll. Pro Des: Dean Tavoularis. Ed: Barry Malkin. M: Michael Kamen; numbers performed by Bryan Adams, The Five Satins, Peaches and Herb, Texas Tornadoes, Blue Gill, and Santo & Johnny. Costumes: Aggie Guerard Rodgers. (Hollywood Pictures/American

Zoetrope/Great Oaks–Buena Vista.) Rel: 11 October 1996. 113 mins. Cert PG. USA. 1996.

James and the Giant Peach

Tormented by his cruel and ugly aunts, Spiker and Sponge, a nine-year-old English boy dreams of visiting New York, a city his late father (who was killed by a rhinoceros) described as a place

Seeing with new eyes: Grasshopper lends James a helping view in Henry Selick's James and the Giant Peach *(from Guild)*

where dreams come true. Then a chance meeting with Pete Postlethwaite introduces the boy to some magic crocodile tongues which rouse a dead peach tree to produce a luscious fruit 20 feet in diameter. Inside the giant peach James discovers a coterie of human-sized insects (and a spider) who assist him in his quest to discover the Big Apple... Who better to translate the grotesque, bizarre world of Roald Dahl to the big screen than Tim Burton and Henry Selick, producer and director of *Tim Burton's The Nightmare Before Christmas*? Dahl himself resisted temptations to bring his first published children's novel to the screen, but then he presumably failed to catch Burton's *Beetlejuice*, *Batman* or *Edward Scissorhands* before his death (in 1990). His widow, Liccy, was approached by Selick and duly capitulated. However, the subsequent compound of candyfloss fantasy, nightmarish demons and wise-cracking insects can only appeal to the most eclectic of tastes. Fitfully amusing, sporadically inventive and occasionally horrific, the film attempts to embrace a number of styles and themes, but fails to work as a satisfying whole. FYI: Dennis Potter penned the original screenplay, but it was rejected on the grounds of veering too far from the source material.

Paul Terry (*James Henry Trotter*), Joanna Lumley (*Aunt Spiker*), Miriam Margolyes (*Aunt Sponge*), Pete Postlethwaite (*old man*), Steven Culp, Mike Starr, Susan Turner-Gray. Voices: Simon Callow (*Grasshopper*), Richard Dreyfuss (*Centipede*), Jane Leeves (*Ladybug*), Miriam Margolyes (*Glowworm*), Susan Sarandon (*Spider*), David Thewlis (*Earthworm*).

Dir and Co-Pro: Henry Selick. Pro: Denise Di Novi and Tim Burton. Ex Pro: Jake Eberts. Screenplay: Karey Kirkpatrick, Jonathan Roberts and Steve Bloom. Ph: Pete Kozachik and Hiro Narita. Pro Des: Harley Jessup. Ed: Stan Webb. M: Randy Newman. Songs: Newman. Costumes: Julie Singer. Sound: Gary Rydstrom. Animation supervision: Paul Berry. Spider wrangler: Steven R. Kutcher. (Disney/ Allied Filmmakers–Guild.) Rel: 2 August 1996. 79 mins. Cert U. USA. 1996.

Jane Eyre

Condemned for her 'wilful, obstinate nature', the orphaned Jane Eyre is farmed off by her aunt to the grim Lowood Charity School, presided over by the Draconian Mr Brocklehurst. There, Jane spends the rest of her childhood in unmitigated misery before being engaged as governess to Thornfield Hall. While the new post augurs a break from Jane's travails, Thornfield's enigmatic owner, Mr Rochester, proves to be a difficult, troubled man, whose treatment of his new employee is brusque and ambiguous. But Jane's steely resolve and honesty has an unsettling effect on her master... On paper, this twelfth cinematic edition of *Jane Eyre* promised to be every bit as laughable as Franco Zeffirelli's last film,

Window of opportunity: Charlotte Gainsbourg in Franco Zeffirelli's poignant Jane Eyre *(from Guild)*

Sparrow. With the Washington-born William Hurt following the tradition of American actors playing Rochester (Irving Cummings, Alan Hale, Orson Welles, George C. Scott), the French actress Charlotte Gainsbourg cast as the adult Jane, New Zealand's Anna Paquin as the young Jane, the Australian Elle Macpherson as Blanche Ingram and Germany's Maria Schneider as Bertha, the film hardly strains for authenticity. None the less, the power of Charlotte Bronte's story remains undiminished and is well served here by a commanding reading from Hurt and an unflinching one from Mlle Gainsbourg (and won't her mother, Jane Birkin, be proud!). Furthermore, Hugh Whitemore's elegant adaptation, the austere production design, the crisp lensing of David Watkin and the sumptuous score from Alessio Vlad and Claudio

Capponi collaborate to make this a handsome, affecting version of a classic tale. Filmed on location in Derbyshire and Yorkshire.

William Hurt (*Edward Fairfax Rochester*), Charlotte Gainsbourg (*Jane Eyre*), Joan Plowright (*Mrs Fairfax*), Anna Paquin (*young Jane Eyre*), Billie Whitelaw (*Grace Poole*), Elle Macpherson (*Blanche Ingram*), Maria Schneider (*Bertha Antoinetta Mason*), John Wood (*Mr Brocklehurst*), Fiona Shaw (*Mrs Reed*), Samuel West (*St John Rivers*), Geraldine Chaplin (*Miss Scatcherd*), Amanda Root (*Miss Temple*), Josephine Serre (*Adele Varens*), Leanne Rowe (*Helen Burns*), Peter Woodthorpe (*Briggs*), Ralph Nossek (*Rev. Wood*), Charlotte Attenborough, Nic Knight, Miranda Forbes, Ann Queensbury, Edward de Souza, Chris Larkin, Richard Warwick, Sophie Revell, Sheila Burrell, Julian Fellowes.

Dir: Franco Zeffirelli. Pro: Dyson Lovell. Ex Pro: Riccardo Tozzi and Guy East. Co-Ex Pro: Bon Weinstein and Harvey Weinstein. Assoc Pro: Joyce Herlihy. Screenplay: Zeffirelli and Hugh Whitemore. Ph: David Watkin. Pro Des: Roger Hall. Ed: Richard Marden. M: Alessio Vlad and Claudio Capponi.

Tom as Jerry: Tom Cruise with the smashing Renee Zellweger in Cameron Crowe's heartfelt Jerry Maguire *(from Columbia TriStar)*

Costumes: Jenny Beavan. William Hurt's dialogue coach: Joan Washington. Charlotte Gainsbourg's dialogue coach: Sally Grace. (Rochester Films/Mediaset/ Flach Films SA/RCS Films & TV/Majestic Films/Miramax–Guild.) Rel: 27 September 1996. 108 mins. Cert PG. UK/Italy/ France/USA. 1995.

Jerry Maguire

When sports agent and self-confessed 'shark in a suit' Jerry Maguire wakes up to realise that he is no longer his father's son, he knocks out a 'mission statement' stressing the emotional need for fewer clients and less money. His memo gets him fired, activating a struggle to climb back into the game, an objective which clouds the sentiment that got Maguire into this trouble in the first place. Only his sole client, the opinionated footballer Rod Tidwell, and his personal assistant, Dorothy Boyd, still support the man that Jerry Maguire once tried to be... Juggling priceless dialogue; great songs, a well shaded supporting cast and a terrific

turn from Renee Zellweger (Empire Records), Jerry Maguire punches home its wholesome message with pizzazz. While the sports milieu may turn off some viewers, this is basically a romantic comedy brimming with heart that should appeal to anybody who fell for somebody for all the wrong reasons. Tom Cruise – as the smug, confused achiever on a losing streak – works hard to dispel his image as the clean-cut hero, receiving both an Oscar nomination and the best actor prize from The National Board of Review. Favourite line: 'Shut up. Just shut up! You had me at "hello"' (Zellweger, stopping short Jerry's penitent courtship speech).

Tom Cruise (*Jerry Maguire*), Cuba Gooding Jr (*Rod Tidwell*), Renee Zellweger (*Dorothy Boyd*), Kelly Preston (*Avery Bishop*), Jerry O'Connell (*Frank Cushman*), Jay Mohr (*Bob Sugar*), Regina King (*Marcee Tidwell*), Bonnie Hunt (*Laurel Boyd*), Jonathan Lipnicky (*Ray Boyd*), Todd Louiso (*Chad, the child technician*), Jared Jussim (*Dicky Fox*), Glenn Frey (*Dennis Wilburn*), Mark Pellington, Jeremy Suarez, Benjamin Kimball Smith, Ingrid Beer, Jann Wenner, Nada Despotovich, Alice Crowe, Donal Logue, Eric Stoltz (*Ethan Valhere*), Lamont Johnson, Beau Bridges.
  Dir and Screenplay: Cameron Crowe. Pro: Crowe, James L. Brooks, Laurence

Mark and Richard Sakai. Co-Pro: Bruce S. Pustin and John D. Schofield. Ph: Janusz Kaminski. Pro Des: Stephen Lineweaver. Ed: Joe Hutshing. M: numbers performed by The Who, His Name Is Alive, Enuff, The Replacements, Elvis Presley, Fleetwood Mac, Neil Young, The Rolling Stones, Gram Parsons, Tom Petty, Rickie Lee Jones, JB'S, Paul McCartney, AC/DC, Bad Company, Bob Dylan, Aimee Mann, etc. Costumes: Betsy Heimann. (TriStar/ Gracie Films–Columbia TriStar.) Rel: 7 March 1997. 139 mins. Cert 15. USA. 1996.

Jingle All the Way

Minneapolis, Minnesota; Christmas Eve. For high-powered businessman Howard Langston, Christmas means less time to cram in last-minute sales and absolutely no time for his only son, Jamie. When a traditional Yuletide traffic jam forces him to miss his son's karate awards ceremony – again – Langston promises Jamie the ultimate Christmas toy: TurboMan. But the heavily marketed action figure (whose popularity equals the frenzy that surrounded the Cabbage Patch dolls of the early eighties) has been off the shelves for days... Not only is Arnold Schwarzenegger wildly miscast as a married businessman from Minneapolis – nobody asks him why he's built like a Gladiator and sounds Austrian – but his eye-bulging reaction shots and mugging at the camera are truly embarrassing. Still, even these flights of over-acting are nowhere near as excruciating as the film's emetic sentimentality and the notion that the quality of Christmas is measured by the size of your shopping trolley. So skip the movie and buy the merchandising.

Arnold Schwarzenegger (*Howard Langston*), Sinbad (*Myron Larabee*), Phil Hartman (*Ted Martin*), Rita Wilson (*Liz Langston*), Robert Conrad (*Officer Hummell*), James Belushi (*Mall Santa*), Martin Mull (*DJ*), Jake Lloyd (*Jamie Langston*), E.J. De La Pena (*Johnny*), Laraine Newman, Justin Chapman, Harvey Korman, Richard Moll, Daniel Riordan, Kate McGregor-Stewart, Alan Blumenfeld, Marianne Muellerleile, Phil Morris, Amy Pietz, Curtis Armstrong, Vern Troyer.
  Dir: Brian Levant. Pro: Chris Columbus, Mark Radcliffe and Michael Barnathan. Ex Pro: Richard Vane. Co-Pro: Jennifer Blum and James Mulay. Assoc Pro: Paula DuPré Pesmen. Screenplay: Randy Kornfield. Ph: Victor J. Kemper. Pro Des: Leslie McDonald. Ed: Kent Beyda and Wilton

Henderson. M: David Newman; numbers performed by Ronnie Spector and Darlene Love, Chuck Berry, Nat King Cole, Tom Petty, Johnny Mathis, Clarence Carter, Frank Sinatra, Charles Brown, Lou Rawls, etc. Costumes: Jay Hurley. Data wrangler: Mark Buschbacher. (Fox/1492–Fox.) Rel: 6 December 1996. 89 mins. Cert PG. USA. 1996.

John Carpenter's Escape From L.A.

Los Angeles; 2013. Having escaped the maximum-security confines of Gotham in John Carpenter's *Escape From New York* (not to mention 'that thing' in Cleveland), indestructible anti-hero Snake Plissken finds himself in the City of Angels. Following the Big Quake, LA has broken off from the US mainland and is now used as a dumping ground for psychopaths, prostitutes and those who eat red meat. Injected with a lethal, time-coded virus, Snake has no choice but to enter LA to retrieve a vital, satellite-destroying gizmo that has fallen into seditious hands, return it to the US President and receive his antidote... Co-produced and co-scripted by Kurt Russell (who received $10m for his services), *Escape From L.A.* retains the bleak, tongue-in-cheek humour of its predecessor, augmented by some neat ideas and terrific sets. However, the film's total disrespect for any kind of logic, not to mention a preponderance of heavy metal music, weirdoes and nocturnal locations, ultimately gets rather tiresome.

Kurt Russell (*Snake Plissken*), Stacy Keach (*Malloy*), Steve Buscemi ('*Map To the Stars' Eddie*), Peter Fonda (*Pipeline*), George Corraface (*Cuervo Jones*), Cliff Robertson (*The President*), Bruce Campbell (*Surgeon General of Beverly Hills*), Valeria Golino (*Taslima*), Pam Grier (*Hershe*), A.J. Langer (*Utopia*), Michelle Forbes (*Brazen*), Robert Carradine (*skinhead*), Jordan Baker, Caroleen Feeney, Paul Bartel, Tom McNulty.
    Dir: John Carpenter. Pro: Debra Hill and Kurt Russell. Screenplay: Carpenter, Hill and Russell, based on characters created by Carpenter and Nick Castle. Ph: Gary B. Kibbe. Pro Des: Lawrence G. Paull. Ed: Edward A. Warschilka. M: Carpenter and Shirley Walker; numbers performed by Sugar Ray, Tool, Stabbing Westward, Gravity Kills, Randy Newman, Butthole Surfers, White Zombie, Tori Amos, and Dick Dale. Costumes: Robin Michel Bush. Make-up effects: Rick Baker. (Paramount/

Rysher Entertainment–UIP.) Rel: 20 September 1996. 101 mins. Cert 15. USA. 1996.

johns

While the film features a number of characters called John, the title actually refers to the homosexual term for a 'rent boy'. Inspired by his own experiences on his first visit to Los Angeles, Scott Silver's debut feature chronicles one day – Christmas Eve – in and around the byways of Santa Monica Boulevard. A male prostitute, John has his 'lucky' sneakers stolen from him in the park, along with all his money. Having planned to spend Christmas

Christmas turkey: Arnold Schwarzenegger finds himself dwarfed by a pesky Santa (Vern Troyer) and the materialism of the season, in Brian Levant's risible Jingle All the Way *(from Fox)*

(and, as it happens, his birthday) in the plush Park Plaza hotel, John is left to salvage the best out of an increasingly awful day... Utilising an edgy, naturalistic style, Silver brings a voyeuristic feel to the streets of Hollywood, using stories he bought for $20 a piece from real hustlers. Fascinating, maybe, but also morally questionable. [*Ewen Brownrigg*]

Lukas Haas (*Donner*), David Arquette (*John*), Arliss Howard (*John Cardoza*), Keith

Happy daze: Kate Winslet and Christopher Eccleston share a rare moment of elation in Michael Winterbottom's bleak, episodic Jude *(from PolyGram)*

David (*Homeless John*), Christopher Gartin (*Eli*), Elliott Gould, John C. McGinley, Josh Schaefer, Wilson Cruz, Terrence Dashon Howard, Nicky Katt, Alanna Ubach, Richard Kind, Nina Siemaszko, Craig Bierko.

Dir and Screenplay: Scott Silver. Pro: Beau Flynn and Stefan Simchowitz. Ex Pro: P. Holt Gardiner. Co-Ex Pro: Dolly Hall. Ph: Tom Richmond. Pro Des: Amy Beth Silver. Ed: Dorian Harris. M: Charles Brown and Danny Caron; numbers performed by Charles Brown and Danny Caron, Lucky Me, Gene Autry, Jude, and Keith David. Costumes: Sara Jane Slotnick. (Bandeira Entertainment–Metrodome.) Rel: 13 June 1997. 95 mins. Cert 18. USA. 1995.

Jude

Late 19th-century England. Determined to fight free from his working-class roots, Jude Fawley ploughs all his free time into studying Latin and Greek. However, the aspiring scholar fails to find work other than stonemasonry.

Meanwhile, his marriage to the lusty Arabella breaks down, and he finds himself increasingly drawn to his feisty, volatile cousin, Sue Bridehead... Previously filmed as a TV series starring Robert Powell, Thomas Hardy's 1895 novel is as relevant today as it has ever been. But that does not make it cinematic. It is the complex, modern characters that bring the material alive, yet due to the story's epic time span the protagonists have little opportunity to develop in just two hours. Some judicious editing of the plot – in favour of establishing the rapport between Jude and Sue – could have turned this adaptation into a powerful film. As it is, this *Jude* is a series of explanatory captions punctuated by trains steaming out of fog banks heralding yet another unwanted pregnancy. Christopher Eccleston (*Let Him Have It*, *Shallow Grave*) is a suitably gaunt, passionate and tortured Jude, but Kate Winslet lacks the fire and maturity to bring Sue to life. Notwithstanding, the production is technically magnificent (filmed in North Yorkshire, Northumberland, Durham, Edinburgh, London and New Zealand).

Christopher Eccleston (*Jude Fawley*), Kate Winslet (*Sue Bridehead*), Liam Cunningham (*Richard Phillotson*), Rachel Griffiths (*Arabella Donn*), June Whitfield (*Aunt Drusilla*), Ross Colvin Turnbull (*young Jude*), James Daley, Berwick Kaler, Sean McKenzie, Richard Albrecht, James Nesbitt, Mark Lambert, Paul Bown, Vernon Dobtcheff, Paul Copley, Ken Jones, Roger Ashton Griffiths, Freda Dowie, Dexter Fletcher, Kerry Shale.

Dir: Michael Winterbottom. Pro: Andrew Eaton. Assoc Pro: Sheila Fraser Milne. Ex Pro: Stewart Till and Mark Shivas. Screenplay: Hossein Amini. Ph: Eduardo Serra. Pro Des: Joseph Bennett. Ed: Trevor Waite. M: Adrian Johnston. Costumes: Janty Yates. (BBC Films/ Revolution Films–PolyGram.) Rel: 4 October 1996. 122 mins. Cert 15. UK. 1996.

Jungle 2 Jungle

When New York commodities trader Michael Cromwell slips down to Venezuela to tie up the loose ends of his divorce, he discovers that he has a 13-year-old son. The latter, raised by South American Indians, now wants to see the concrete jungle of his father's world and so Cromwell reluctantly agrees to escort him to the Big Apple. Sporting nothing but war paint and a loincloth, Cromwell Jr – Mimi-Siku – effortlessly triumphs over the intricacies of immigration, but finds Manhattan etiquette another thing entirely. Yet in spite of cooking Martin Short's irreplaceable tropical fish for dinner and peeing in pot plants, Mimi-Siku is obviously a far better man than his Gucci-suited brethren... Defying logic at every turn, this bland, mawkish re-make of the 1994 French film *An Indian In the City* is an assault on Franco-American relations. While Tim Allen, as Cromwell, displays the comic timing of a potato, the film itself is content to re-heat old gags and boil dry any new ones. It's like haute cuisine that's been put through a blender, microwaved and then vacuum-packed.

Tim Allen (*Michael Cromwell*), Martin Short (*Richard Kempster*), Lolita Davidovich (*Charlotte*), David Ogden Stiers (*Alexei Jovanovic*), JoBeth Williams (*Dr Patricia Cromwell*), Sam Huntington (*Mimi-Siku aka 'Cat Piss'*), Valerie Mahaffey (*Jan Kempster*), LeeLee Sobiesky (*Karen Kempster*), Dominic Keating (*Ian*), Frankie Galasso, Luis Avalos, Bob Dishy, Carole Shelley, Joan Copeland, Jack McGee, Adam LeFevre, John Pasquin (*bearded man in Times Square*).

Dir: John Pasquin. Pro: Brian Reilly. Ex Pro: Richard Baker, Rick Messina and Brad Krevoy. Co-Pro: William W. Wilson III. Screenplay: Bruce A. Evans and Raynold Gideon. Ph: Tony Pierce-Roberts. Pro Des: Stuart Wurtzel. Ed: Michael A. Stevenson. M: Michael Convertino; Vivaldi; numbers performed by Maxi Priest, Peter Gabriel and Youssou N'Dour with Shaggy, The Sha-Shees, etc. Costumes: Carol Ramsey. (Disney/TF1 International–Buena Vista.) Rel: 23 May 1997. 105 mins. Cert PG. USA. 1997.

Indian summer: Tim Allen (right) checks Sam Huntington for underarm odour in John Pasquin's vacuum-packed Jungle 2 Jungle *(from Buena Vista)*

privileged teachings of the *Kama Sutra* (including the naughty bits), while Maya is left to draw on her natural grace and sensuality. Then, on Tara's wedding night, Maya sees a way to settle the score... Attempting to embrace all the manifestations of love – affection, infatuation, passion, obsession, jealousy and a little bit of sex – *Kama Sutra* takes four principal characters and shakes them into a semblance of a story. Unfortunately, by merely serving as ciphers for an idea, the characters have no emotional resonance of their own, and it's hard to side with – or care about – any of them.

Love Position No. 9? A scene from Mira Nair's misconceived Kama Sutra *(from Film Four)*

Kama Sutra

Commonly misinterpreted as a Sanskrit *Joy of Sex*, the *Kama Sutra* is in fact a guide to social conduct and marriage compiled at some point in the first five centuries after the birth of Christ. Writer-director Mira Nair (*Mississippi Masala*, *The Perez Family*) returns to her native India (where she made *Salaam Bombay!*) to shed a fresh perspective on 'the greatest book of love ever written'. Set in 16th-century India, the film details the rivalry between Tara and Maya who, in spite of their social disparity, have been best friends since childhood. Because of her royal standing, Tara is privy to the

The great riff: Jennifer Jason Leigh keeps an eye on Miranda Richardson in Robert Altman's evocative Kansas City *(from Electric)*

Naveen Andrews (*Raj Singh*), Sarita Choudhury (*Tara*), Ramon Tikaram (*Jai Kumar*), Indira Varma (*Maya*), Rekha (*Rasa Devi*), Khalik Tyabji (*Biki*), Arundhati Rao, Surabhi Bhansali, Garima Dhup, Harish Patel, Ranjit Chowdhry, Debi Basu, Urvashi Nair.

Dir: Mira Nair. Pro: Nair and Lydia Dean Pilcher. Ex Pro: Michiyo Yoshizaki. Co-Pro: Caroline Baron. Screenplay: Nair and Helena Kriel. Ph: Declan Quinn. Pro Des: Mark Friedberg. Ed: Kristina Boden. M: Mychael Danna. Costumes: Eduardo Castro. Choreography: Debi Basu and Maya Krishna Rao. (NDF International/Pony Canyon/Pandora Film/Channel Four/Mirabai Films–Film Four.) Rel: 20 June 1997. 114 mins. Cert 18. India/UK. 1996.

Kansas City

Kansas City, mainly the '18th and Vine' district; 1934. At its peak during the Depression, Kansas City boasted between 50 and 100 night spots where jazz and gambling flourished in a confusion of dance halls, honky-tonks and illicit drinking establishments. It was also the home of Jean Harlow, Charlie Parker and Robert Altman. Here Altman pays a bitter yet affectionate tribute to his hometown by introducing a Jean Harlow wannabe who crosses paths with a 14-year-old Parker. However, the film, composed like a series of jazz riffs, just uses this as its starting-off point for the story of a hard-boiled telegraph operator who kidnaps the wife of a prominent politician in order to secure the release of her felonious husband... Stephen Altman's sublime production design, Oliver Stapleton's evocative cinematography and above all the constant swing of jazz autographs the film with its singular mood, although occasional outbursts of violence and a trickle of unexpected humour toughens the brew. As the kidnapper, Jennifer Jason Leigh, giving an uncharacteristically parodic performance, seems at loggerheads with her subject, allowing Miranda Richardson as the dopey socialite and Harry Belafonte as a charismatic gangster to abduct the acting honours.

Jennifer Jason Leigh (*Blondie O'Hara*), Miranda Richardson (*Carolyn Stilton*), Harry Belafonte (*Seldom Seen*), Michael Murphy (*Henry Stilton*), Dermot Mulroney (*Johnny O'Hara*), Steve Buscemi (*Johnny Flynn*), Brooke Smith (*Babe Flynn*), Jeff Ferigna (*Addie Parker*), A.C. Smith (*Sheepshan Red*), Albert J. Burnes (*Charlie Parker*), Ajia Mignon Johnson (*Pearl Cummings*), Jerry Fornelli (*Tom Pendergast*), Joe Digirolamo (*John Lazia*), Martin Martin, Tim Snay, Tawanna Benbow, Cal Pritner, Michael Ornstein, Michael Garozzo, John Durbin, Gina Belafonte.

Dir and Pro: Robert Altman. Ex Pro: Scott Bushnell. Screenplay: Altman and Frank Barhydt. Ph: Oliver Stapleton. Pro Des: Stephen Altman. Ed: Geraldine Peroni. M Pro: Hal Willner; all music performed and recorded live in Kansas City. Costumes: Dona Granata. (CiBy 2000/Sandcastle 5–Electric.) Rel: 22 November 1996. 118 mins. Cert 15. USA. 1995.

Kids in the Hall Brain Candy

Roritor is a major pharmaceutical corporation desperately in need of a miracle drug – or a lot of heads are due to roll. One Dr Chris Cooper is working on an antidepressant that chemically seeks out and locates one's happiest memory, but the drug is still relatively untested. Notwithstanding, Roritor goes ahead and releases it on the open market – to devastating results... Toronto's answer to *Monty Python*, Kids in the Hall are an anarchic, satirical writing-acting quintet composed of David Foley, Bruce McCulloch, Kevin McDonald, Mark McKinney and Scott Thompson. Here, the Kids try for the big time with their first movie, which thematically resembles *The Hudsucker Proxy*. Tackling all 32 major roles themselves, the team illustrate their thespian versatility but fail to find a comic momentum. Indeed, only the troupe's most devoted followers could find anything to laugh at in this tasteless, hopelessly inept shambles.

David Foley (*Marv/New Guy, etc.*), Bruce McCulloch (*Alice/Cancer Boy, etc.*), Kevin McDonald (*Dr Chris Cooper, etc.*), Mark McKinney (*Simon/Don Roritor/cabbie/ Nina Bedford, etc.*), Scott Thompson (*Mrs Hurdicure, etc.*), Kathryn Greenwood, Janeanne Garofalo, Brendan Fraser.

Dir: Kelly Makin. Pro: Lorne Michaels. Ex Pro: Tom Rosenberg, Sigurjon Sighvatsson and David Steinberg. Co-Pro: Barnaby Thompson and Richard S. Wright. Screenplay: Norm Hiscock, Bruce McCulloch, Kevin McDonald, Mark McKinney and Scott Thompson. Ph: David

A. Makin. Pro Des: Gregory P. Keen. Ed: Christopher Cooper. M: Craig Northey; numbers performed by Death Lurks, The Tragically Hip, The Art of Noise and Tom Jones, They Might Be Giants, Pavement, Matthew Sweet, Yo La Tengo, Liz Phair, etc. Costumes: Delphine White. (Paramount/Lakeshore Entertainment– UIP.) Rel: 8 November 1996. 90 mins. Cert 15. USA. 1996.

Killer: A Journal of Murder

Newly appointed to Fort Leavenworth Prison as a guard, young Henry Lesser takes pity on and befriends an inmate there, one Carl Panzram. Showing Panzram the first human kindness that he has ever encountered on the inside, Lesser agrees to smuggle in pencil and paper so that the convict can write his memoirs. It is then, page by page, that Lesser realises the full extent of Panzram's evil... Arriving belatedly in the slipstream of *Dead Man Walking*, *Last Dance* and *The Chamber*, *Killer* fails to shed much fresh light on the condemned prisoner scenario, in spite of its root in truth. If anything, the film soft pedals the atrocities of Panzram (who in reality confessed to over one thousand acts of forced sodomy) and does little justice to Lesser, who is presented as a bland, one-dimensional wimp (Chris O'Donnellite). Ultimately, then, this is a fascinating subject diluted by pedestrian direction and hackneyed cinematic devices, reduced to the level of an anodyne TV movie.

James Woods (*Carl Panzram*), Robert Sean Leonard (*Henry Lesser*), Ellen Greene (*Elizabeth Wyatt*), Cara Buono (*Esther Lesser*), Robert John Burke (*Robert Gregory Greiser*), Steve Forrest (*Warden Charles Casey*), Harold Gould (*Old Henry Lesser*), Seth Romitelli (*teenage Carl Panzram*), John Bedford Lloyd (*Karl Menninger*), Jeffrey DeMunn, Richard Riehle, Michael Jeffrey Woods, Raynor Scheine, Stephen Mendillo, Martha A. Woods, Lili Taylor (*uncredited, as Sally*).

Dir and Screenplay: Tim Metcalfe, from the book by Thomas E. Gaddis and James O. Long. Pro: Janet Yang and Mark Levinson. Ex Pro: Oliver Stone and Melinda Jason. Ph: Ken Kelsch. Pro Des: Sherman Williams. Ed: Harvey Rosenstock and Richard Gentner. M: Graeme Revell; numbers performed by Frederick Hodges, Jeff Gilbert, and Nicole Sill. Costumes: Kathryn Morrison. Sound: Dessie Markovsky and Emile Razpopov. (Spelling Films/Ixtlan/Breakheart Films–First

Independent.) Rel: 16 May 1997. 91 mins. Cert 18. USA. 1995.

Kingpin

Roy Munson is the state bowling champion of Iowa. He's got a great future ahead of him, but when a scam turns sour he loses his right hand and resorts to the bottle. Seventeen years later he spots Amish *wunderkind* Randy Quaid and takes him on as his protégé... From the team 'what brung us *Dumb and Dumber*', *Kingpin* is not as retarded as most entries in the current morons' cycle – and the laugh quotient is higher. Having said that, the film is all over the place, derivative and likely to offend many by its surprisingly cruel streak. But to give it its due, it never misses a chance to scramble for laughs: at the dramatic finale, the hair styles of Harrelson and Murray take on a life of their own – a great visual gag. FYI: Harrelson once shared an apartment with director Peter Farrelly.

Woody Harrelson (*Roy Munson*), Randy Quaid (*Ishmael*), Vanessa Angel (*Claudia*), Bill Murray (*Ernie McCracken*), Chris Elliott (*the gambler*), William Jordan (*Mr Boorg*),

Tugging the heart strings: Andrej Chalimon as Kolya (from Buena Vista)

Richard Tyson (*owner of Stiffy's*), Lin Shaye (*Mrs Dumars*), Rob Moran (*Stanley Osmanski*), Zen Gesner, Prudence Wright Holmes, Danny Green, Sayed Badreya, Googie Gress, Willie Garson, Nancy Frey-Jarecki, Kathy Farrelly, Steve Tyler, The Artist Formerly Known as Docky, Cynthia Farrelly Gesner, Nancy Farrelly, Mariann Farrelly, Jon Dennis (*himself*), Chris Schenkel (*himself*), Chris Berman (*himself*), Urge Overkill, Morganna (*herself*), Joe Lewis, Blues Traveler.

Dir: Peter Farrelly and Bobby Farrelly. Pro: Brad Kevroy, Steve Stabler and Bradley Thomas. Ex Pro: Keith Samples. Screenplay: Mort Nathan and Barry Fanaro. Ph: Mark Irwin. Pro Des: Sidney Jackson Bartholomew Jr. Ed: Christopher Greenbury. M: Freedy Johnston; numbers performed by Cat Stevens, The Tramps, The Go-Betweens, The Rascals, Simon & Garfunkel, Freedy Johnston, English Beat, Goldfinger, Jonathan Richman, The Strangeloves, Todd Rundgren, Thunderclap Newman, Zuba, Urge Overkill, Electric Light Orchestra, Gary Glitter, Blues Traveler, Peacefield, etc. Costumes: Mary Zophres. (Rysher Entertainment/ Motion Picture Corporation of America–Entertainment.) Rel: 12 July 1996. 114 mins. Cert 12. USA. 1996.

Kolya

Prague; 1988. Barred from playing with the Czech Philharmonic Orchestra (following an ill-advised anti-Communist remark), virtuoso

Dumbo & dumber: Tai and Bill Murray swap gags in Howard Franklin's lumbering Larger Than Life *(from Guild)*

cellist Frantisek Louka is reduced to playing at funerals and, to make ends meet, renovates inscriptions on tombstones. Falling deeper and deeper into debt, he reluctantly agrees – for a price – to marry a Russian woman so that she can acquire Czech residency. But when she flees to Germany, he is left to fend off inevitable persecution by the Czech police and to babysit her five-year-old son... Flush with telling detail and droll humour, *Kolya* manages to touch the heart while nimbly bypassing the gushing self-conscious sentimentality of a film like *Cinema Paradiso*. As the granite-hearted cellist, Zdenek Sverak is simply wonderful, establishing a believable mask of stoicism, under-neath which sparkles a genuine warmth. Incidentally, Sverak – the father of the director – also wrote the screenplay, adding to a distinguished list of screenwriting credits that includes such recent Czech classics as *My Sweet Little Village*, *The Elementary School* and *The Life and Extraordinary Adventures of Private Ivan Chonkin*. A minor masterpiece and winner of the Oscar for best foreign language film.

Zdenek Sverak (*Frantisek Louka*), Andrej Chalimon (*Kolya*), Libuse Safrankova (*Klara*), Ondrez Vetchy (*Mr Broz*), Stella Zazvorkova (*Maminka, Frantisek's mother*), Ladislav Smoljak (*Mr Houdek*), Irena Livanova (*Nadezda*), Sylvia Suvadova (*Blanka*), Lilian Mankina, Petra Spalova, Nella Boudova.

Dir: Jan Sverak. Pro: Jan Sverak and Eric Abraham. Assoc Pro: Ernst Goldschmidt. Screenplay: Zdenek Sverak, based on a story by Pavel Taussig. Ph: Vladimir Smutny. Pro Des: Milos Kohout. Ed: Alois Fisarek. M: Ondrej Soukup; Dvorak, Tchaikovsky. Costumes: Katerina Holla. (Biograf Jan Sverak/Portobello Pictures/Ceska Televize/Pandora Cinema, etc.–Buena Vista.) Rel: 9 May 1997. 105 mins. Cert 12. Czech Republic/UK/France. 1996.

Larger Than Life

Jack Corcoran is a successful motivational speaker hired by companies to introduce emotional incentive into the lives of their employees. Basing his entire pitch on the fact that his father perished saving a drowning child before he was even born, Corcoran is some-what nonplussed to discover that his old man has only just died. Odder still, it transpires that Corcoran Snr was a circus clown and has bequeathed his son a debt of $35,000 and an elephant called Vera... Basically a one-joke film – Bill Murray gets stuck with an elephant – *Larger Than Life* neither works as a vehicle for the caustic comic nor as a family comedy. Indeed, 'a Bill Murray family picture' is a contradiction in terms. Furthermore, the actor is (for once) truly upstaged by his pachydermous co-star (who remains sublimely deadpan throughout), while the likes of Matthew McConaughey and Keith David are allowed to mug tiresomely. Previously known as *Nickel and Dime*. FYI: Tai the Elephant hitherto starred in Disney's *Operation Dumbo Drop*.

Bill Murray (*Jack Corcoran*), Janeane Garofalo (*Mo*), Pat Hingle (*Vernon 'The Human Blockhead' Sawitsky*), Keith David (*Hurst*), Jeremy Piven (*Walter*), Matthew McConaughey (*Tip Tucker*), Lois Smith (*Luluna Sawitsky*), Anita Gillette (*Vera Corcoran, Jack's mother*), Maureen Mueller (*Celeste*), Linda Fiorentino (*Terry Venura*), Tai (*Vera the elephant*), Harve Presnell, Tracey Walter, Jerry Adler, Roy Blount Jr, Dirk Blocker.

Dir: Howard Franklin. Pro: Richard Lewis, John Watson and Pen Densham. Ex Pro: Wolfgang Glattes, Guy East and Sue Baden-Powell. Screenplay: Roy Blount Jr. Ph: Elliot Davis. Pro Des: Marcia Hinds-Johnson. Ed: Sidney Levin. M: Miles Goodman; Johann Strauss Jr; numbers performed by Los Lobos, Charles Brown, The Band, The Staple Singers, etc. Costumes: Jane Robinson. (United Artists/Trilogy/RCS/Majestic Pictures–Guild.) Rel: 28 March 1997. 93 mins. Cert PG. USA. 1996.

Last Dance

In an effort to win black votes, the governor of a southern state commutes the death sentence of a renowned Afro-American murderer (with a book on *The New York Times'* bestseller list, no less). Then, to show that he is in touch with the women's movement for equal rights, he decides that the hasty demise of one Cindy Liggett would further polish his profile. However, Cindy, a talented drawer and art-lover, was convicted under suspicious circumstances and is now a changed woman. Rookie appeals attorney and former playboy Rick Hayes is determined to ameliorate her sentence – and prove to himself that he can make a difference... It's unfortunate that *Last Dance* arrived so promptly in the wake of *Dead Man Walking* as it tackles the same argu-ments with equal conviction and effect. However, by casting Sharon Stone as the white-trash convict-made-good, the film stacks its cards a little unfairly as even an actress as steely as Ms Stone cannot compete with the frightening machismo and ambiguity of Sean Penn. Neverthe-less, this could be the actress's best performance to date (far more measured and controlled than her shrill exhibition in *Casino*), while Bruce Beresford has turned in a handsome piece of craftsmanship. Ron Koslow's script itself never resorts to melodrama, although, occasionally, the strings of manipulation do show through.

Sharon Stone (*Cindy Liggett*), Rob Morrow (*Rick Hayes*), Randy Quaid (*Sam Burns*), Peter Gallagher (*John Hayes*), Jack Thompson (*The Governor*), Jayne Brook (*Jill*), Pamela Tyson (*legal aid attorney*), Skeet Ulrich (*Billy*), Don Harvey (*Doug*), Jeffery Ford (*John Henry Rusk*), Diane Sellers, Patricia French, Dave Hager, Christine Cattell, Mimi Craven, John Cunningham, Ralph Wilcox, Ken Jenkins.

Dir: Bruce Beresford. Pro: Steven Haft. Ex Pro: Richard Luke Rothschild. Co-Pro: Chuck Binder. Screenplay: Ron Koslow, from a story by Haft and Koslow. Ph: Peter James. Pro Des: John Stoddart. Ed: John Bloom. M: Mark Isham; numbers performed by BoDeans, Texas, Jennifer Brown, Annie Lennox, etc. Costumes: Colleen Kelsall. (Touchstone Pictures–Buena Vista.) Rel: 16 August 1996. 105 mins. Cert 18. USA. 1995.

Last Man Standing

Jericho, West Texas; 1931. Jericho is a dead-end town torn apart by rival gangs cashing in on the Prohibition. John Smith is a lone mercenary up for the highest bidder. Either way, he is going to make a killing... Like a bad western trying to ape a Wrangler commercial, *Last Man Standing* starts like a dream sequence and refuses to wake up. All the old trademarks of Walter Hill are here – infinite close-ups of feet, filtered sunlight, lots and lots of dust and comic-book violence doused in sadism. During all this Bruce Willis acts very hard not to look like he's acting, while he's really preoccupied with his awful haircut. Label this the cinematic equivalent of a cheap dime novel. And by the way, the film is a remake of Akira Kurosawa's 1961 classic *Yojimbo* (!). Previously known as *Gundown*.

Bruce Willis (*John Smith*), Christopher Walken (*Hickey*), Alexandra Powers (*Lucy Kolinski*), David Patrick Kelly (*Doyle*), William Sanderson (*Joe Monday*), Karina Lombard (*Felina*), Ned Eisenberg (*Fredo Strozzi*), Michael Imperioli (*Giorgio Carmonte*), Ken Jenkins (*Captain Tom Pickett*), R.D. Call (*Jack McCool*), Leslie Mann (*Wanda*), Bruce Dern (*Sheriff Ed*

Galt), Ted Markland, Patrick Kilpatrick, Luis Contreras, Raynor Scheine, Tiny Ron, John Paxton, Lin Shaye.

Dir and Screenplay: Walter Hill, based on a story by Ryuzo Kikushima and Akira Kurosawa. Pro: Hill and Arthur Sarkissian. Ex Pro: Sara Risher and Michael De Luca. Co-Pro: Ralph Singleton. Assoc Pro: Paula Heller. Ph: Lloyd Ahern. Pro Des: Gary Wissner. Ed: Freeman Davies. M: Ry Cooder; 'Boogaboo' performed by Jelly Roll Morton. Costumes: Dan Moore. (New Line Cinema/Lone Wolf–Entertainment.) Rel: 27 September 1996. 101 mins. Cert 18. USA. 1996.

The Last of the High Kings

30 June-17 August 1977; Howth, County Dublin. While his fanatical mother declares that he is the last descendant of the ancient High Kings of Ireland – and that he should avoid all Protestant bastards – Frankie Griffin, 17, has other things on his mind. He'd rather talk about The Stranglers and Ernest Hemingway than Irish politics and, besides, his hormones are on overdrive and he's worried senseless about his exam results... Based on the semi-autobiographical novel by Ferdia MacAnna, *The Last of the High Kings* is brimming with eccentric detail but cannot escape the anecdotal nature of its narrative. Furthermore, David Keating's heavy-handed direction robs us of the opportunity of really caring for Frankie's various dilemmas as every situation is so

The unenlightened guest: Bill Paxton bites the hand that feeds him (Ron Eldard's) in Stacy Title's chilling The Last Supper *(from Electric)*

knowingly set up. Notwithstanding, there are many fleeting pleasures (not least some delicious dialogue, Stephen Rea's lugubrious taxi driver and a delightful turn from Emily Mortimer), although Catherine O'Hara, as Frankie's ma, flounders in tiresome caricature.

Catherine O'Hara (*Cathleen Griffin*), Jared Leto (*Frankie Griffin*), Christina Ricci (*Erin*), Gabriel Byrne (*Jack Griffin*), Colm Meaney (*Jim Davern*), Stephen Rea (*taxi driver*), Lorraine Pilkington (*Jayne Wayne*), Emily Mortimer (*Romy Thomas*), Jason Barry (*Nelson Fitzgerald*), Peter Keating (*Ray Griffin*), Renee Weldon (*Maggie Griffin*), Mark O'Regan (*Father Michael*), Murphy (*Parnell the dog*), Karl Hayden, Ciaran Fitzgerald, Darren Monks, Alexandra Haughey, Vincent Walsh, Amanda Shun.

Dir: David Keating. Pro: Tim Palmer. Ex Pro: John Wolstenholme and Keith Northrop. Co-Ex Pro: Bob Weinstein, Harvey Weinstein, Paul Feldsher and Gabriel Byrne. Screenplay: Keating and Byrne. Ph: Bernd Heinl. Pro Des: Frank Conway. Ed: Ray Lovejoy. M: Michale Convertino; numbers performed by Elvis Presley, Thin Lizzy, Mink de Ville, Elvis Costello, Gallagher & Lyle, Mott the Hoople, etc. Costumes: Mary Zophres. (Parallel Films/Northolme Entertainment/Nordisk Film/Irish Film Board–First Independent.) Rel: 6 December 1996. 104 mins. Cert 15. Ireland/UK/Denmark 1996.

The Last Supper

Iowa, like Scotland, is pretty much off the pop cultural map. Crazy things can happen there without attracting the Home Guard. Five grad students meet up regularly for dinner to quaff red wine and thrash out theoretical arguments. The

Pants on fire: Jim Carrey entertains Justin Cooper in a brief flurry of domestic harmony in Tom Shadyac's phenomenally successful Liar Liar *(from UIP)*

opening scene is terrific, with first-time director Stacy Title deftly establishing the tilt of her drama and the agenda of her five characters – three guys, two girls, one black, one Jew, and so on. Enter Bill Paxton as a solemn, deranged Marine who's invited to supper out of courtesy (he's given Ron Eldard a lift), and who then scatters the cat among the proverbial pigeons ('you people make me puke'). Paxton is trying to prove a point – in a crude way – but in the ensuing scuffle ends up with a hunting knife in his back. Unfortunately, this chilling compound of *The Big Chill* and *Shallow Grave* goes on to repeat itself relentlessly, diminishing the credibility of its characters and draining the barrel dry of wit and suspense. None the less, there is much to savour, if even more to regret.

Cameron Diaz (*Jude*), Ron Eldard (*Pete*), Annabeth Gish (*Paulie*), Jonathan Penner (*Marc*), Courtney B. Vance (*Luke*), Nora Dunn (*Sheriff Stanley*), Bill Paxton (*Zac*), Ron Perlman (*Norman Arbuthnot*), Jason Alexander, Charles Durning, Mark Harmon, Bryn Erin, Dan Rosen, Matt Cooper, Larry Weinberg.

Dir: Stacy Title. Pro: Matt Cooper and Larry Weinberg. Ex Pro: David Cooper. Co-Ex Pro: Stacy Title and Jonathan Penner. Co-Pro: Lori Miller and Dan Rosen. Ph: Paul Cameron. Pro Des: Linda Burton. Ed: Luis Colina. M: Mark Mothersbaugh and Mick Jones; numbers performed by KC & The Sunshine Band, Ten Years After, Sam Phillips, Los Lobos, Wild Colonials, Mick Jones, The Toys, Shonen Knife, and UB40. Costumes: Leesa Evans. Title Paintings: David Ivie. (Vault Inc.–Electric.) Rel: 23 August 1996. 92 mins. Cert 15. USA. 1995.

Leo Tolstoy's Anna Karenina
See *Anna Karenina*.

Liar Liar
For slick attorney Fletcher Reede, truth is as flexible as his rubber features. But when his son's birthday wish comes true – that his father will be unable to tell a lie for 24 hours – Reede finds his career in a nose dive. How can a lawyer conduct his business when everything that comes out of his mouth is true? Edging into Michael Keaton/early Tom Hanks territory, Jim Carrey thrusts his ballistic persona into situation comedy, playing the semblance of a human being for the first time since before *Ace Ventura: Pet Detective*. However, Carrey doesn't let the story's sentimental digressions impede his flights of physical excess and his fans shouldn't be disappointed. There are some moments of priceless comic invention here, spoon-fed by the concept of a man who cannot lie: such as when Carrey gleefully insults the entire staff of a boardroom conference, or, when asked, 'How's it hanging?,' he inadvertently replies: 'Short, shrivelled and slightly to the left.' Love him or hate him, whatever you throw at this comic original, he's going to snatch the ball and run with it. FYI: The role of Reede was originally earmarked for Hugh Grant.

Jim Carrey (*Fletcher Reede*), Maura Tierney (*Audrey Reede*), Jennifer Tilly (*Samantha Cole*), Swoosie Kurtz (*Dana Appleton*), Amanda Donohoe (*Miranda*), Cary Elwes (*Jerry*), Justin Cooper (*Max Reede*), Anne

Haney (*Greta*), Jason Bernard (*Judge Marshall Stevens*), Mitchell Ryan (*Mr Allan*), Chip Mayer, Eric Pierpoint, Randall 'Tex' Cobb, Cheri Oteri, Marianne Muellerleile, Krista Allen, Paul Roache.

Dir: Tom Shadyac. Pro: Brian Grazer. Ex Pro: James D. Brubaker and Michael Bostick. Screenplay: Paul Guay and Stephen Mazur. Ph: Russell Boyd. Pro Des: Linda DeScenna. Ed: Don Zimmerman. M: John Debney. Costumes: Judy L. Ruskin. Jim Carrey's massage therapist: Linaia Light. (Universal/Imagine–UIP.) Rel: 2 May 1997. 86 mins. Cert 12. USA. 1996.

Like Grains of Sand – Nagisa No Sindbad

On the cusp of manhood, Shuji Ito is becoming increasingly aware of his sexual attraction to his best friend, Hiroyuki Yoshida. With his father seeking medical help to cure his own homosexuality, Ito is determined to face the consequences of his burgeoning sexual orientation. Yoshida, on the other hand, exhibits some cowardice by refusing to acknowledge his obvious discomfort for Ito's affections and starts to fall for Kasane Aihara, Ito's only sympathetic ally in his psychological confusion. As a gift to his romantic object, Ito leads Yoshida to Aihara so that he can see how Yoshida loves, activating a bizarre clash of needs... Eschewing the forced humour and contrived devices of most films

Digging out the foundations: Chris Cooper explores the past with Gordon Tootoosis in John Sayles' quietly observed Lone Star *(from Rank–Castle Rock/Turner)*

heading down this path, writer-director Ryosuke Hashiguchi distances his camera from his protagonists, allowing awkward silences to build a natural resonance. And so, ever compassionate and questioning, Hashiguchi has managed to forge a drama of uncommon sensitivity and intelligence.

Yoshinori Okada (*Shuji Ito*), Kota Kusano (*Hiroyuki Yoshida*), Ayumi Hamazaki (*Kasane Aihara*), Koji Yamaguchi (*Toru Kanbara*), Kumi Takada (*Ayako Shimizu*), Shizuka Isami (*Rika Matsuo*), Cho Bang-Ho (*teacher*), Yoshihiko Hakamada.

Dir and Screenplay: Ryosuke Hashiguchi. Pro: Yoshishige Shimatani, Kazuo Hayashi, Kiyomi Kanazawa and Yuuka Kakazawa. Ex Pro: Hideyuki Takai and Hiroshi Yanai. Ph: Shogo Ueno. Ed: Miho Yoneda. M: Kazuya Takahashi. Costumes: Junko Tsuchiya. (Toho/Pia Corporation/YES–ICA.) Rel: 24 January 1997. 129 mins. No cert. Japan. 1995.

Loaded

When a neophyte filmmaker invites six friends to a remote country house to knock out a horror video, paranoia erupts in a flurry of insecurity and rivalry. Determined to keep his cast under control, the director suggests they drop acid, a move which leads to more disharmony and a tragic accident... Severely self-indulgent, this talky, quirkily directed thriller aims to explore the malaise of the nineties but merely reveals the shortcomings of the MTV school of filmmaking. FYI: The director is the older sister of New Zealand

filmmaker Jane Campion (*The Piano, The Portrait of a Lady*). [*Charles Bacon*]

Oliver Milburn (*Neil*), Nick Patrick (*Giles*), Catherine McCormack (*Rose*), Thandie Newton (*Zita*), Matthew Eggleton (*Lionel*), Danny Cunningham (*Lance*), Biddy Hodson (*Charlotte*), Dearbhla Molloy (*Ava*), Caleb Lloyd, Joe Gecks, Bridget Brammall, Tom Welsh.

Dir: Anna Campion. Pro: Caroline Hewitt, David Hazlett, John Maynard and Bridget Ikin. Ex Pro: Ben Gibson. Ph: Alan Almond. Pro Des: Alistair Kay. Ed: John Gilbert. M: Simon Fisher Turner. Costumes: Stewart Meacham. (The National Film Trustee Co./British Screen/New Zealand Film Commission/BFI/Channel Four/Geissendorfer/Strawberry Vale/Movie Partners–Blue Dolphin.) Rel: 1 November 1996. 92 mins. Cert 15. UK/New Zealand. 1994.

Lone Star

When a Masonic ring, sheriff's badge and human skull are unearthed in the desert, Sam Deeds – the sheriff of Frontera, a southern Texas town bordering Mexico – embarks on a 40-year-old murder inquiry. He believes that the skull belongs to Charlie Wade, a notorious lawman that his own father, the legendary Buddy Deeds, succeeded. As his investigation progresses, Sam uncovers a hornet's nest of lies and deceit that is about to transform the legend of his father and alter his own views of the past... John Sayles, whose best films include *Matewan, City of Hope* and *Passion Fish*, is a masterful filmmaker, for whom credibility, emotional honesty and subtext is everything. No flashy histrionics, flamboyant acting or gratuitous wish fulfilment for him. Here he leisurely weaves a number of concepts through a multi-layered story punctuated by socio-political detail and clunky flashbacks. Worthy sentiments abound, but without a strong narrative to hold on to they drift off into the desert like dehydrated tumbleweed.

Ron Canada (*Otis 'Big O' Payne*), Chris Cooper (*Sam Deeds*), Clifton James (*Hollis Pogue*), Kris Kristofferson (*Charlie Wade*), Frances McDormand (*Bunny*), Joe Morton (*Col Del Payne*), Elizabeth Pena (*Pilar Cruz*), Matthew McConaughey (*Buddy Deeds*), Miriam Colon (*Mercedes Cruz*), Jeff Monahan (*young Hollis Pogue*), Beatrice Winde (*Minnie Bledsoe*), Stephen Mendillo, Stephen J. Lang, Oni Faida Lampley,

The ultimate snub: Samuel L. Jackson gets a wake-up call in Renny Harlin's slick-and-mean The Long Kiss Goodnight *(from Entertainment)*

Eleese Lester, Joe Stevens, Richard Coca, LaTanya Richardson, Eddie Robinson, Jesse Borrego, Tony Plana, Richard A. Jones, Leo Burmester, Carmen de Lavallade, James Borrego, Gordon Tootoosis.
   Dir, Screenplay and Ed: John Sayles. Pro: R. Paul Miller and Maggie Renzi. Ex Pro: John Sloss. Ph: Stuart Dryburgh. Pro Des: Dan Bishop. M: Mason Daring; numbers performed by Conjunto Bernal, Fito Olivares, Little Walter, Little Willie John, Lucinda Williams, Ivory Joe Hunter, Duke Levine, Freddie Fender, etc. Costumes: Shay Cunliffe. (Castle Rock/ Rio Dulce–Rank–Castle Rock/Turner.) Rel: 11 October 1996. 135 mins. Cert 15. USA. 1995.

The Long Kiss Goodnight

Eight years ago Samantha Caine woke up two months pregnant with focal retrograde amnesia. Since then she's married and settled down to domestic bliss, but she still wonders about the identity of her daughter's father. Then, following a car accident, her former personality begins to re-surface. In fact, Samantha Caine was never designed to be a loving wife and mother, and an army of terrorists are out to prove it – before her memory returns... Shane Black, who penned the original *Lethal Weapon* and *The Last Boy Scout*, was paid a record $4 million for this, his latest script – and it's easy to see why. A terrific story is jacked up with a stream of great lines and a new genre

is dragged from the pages by the scruff of the neck: the domestic action-comedy-thriller. Slick, fast, mean, stylish and very, very funny, *The Long Kiss Goodnight* blends *Pulp Fiction*, *True Lies*, *Nikita* and *The Good Mother* to enormous effect. Yet the most astonishing thing about the film is that in spite of all the mayhem and pyrotechnics it still makes one care for its leading characters. In fact, preview audiences had become so attached to Samuel L. Jackson's wry, down-to-earth side-kick that his death scene had to be axed and a new scene added.

Geena Davis (*Samantha Caine/Charly Elizabeth Baltimore*), Samuel L. Jackson (*Mitch Henessey*), Patrick Malahide (*Perkins*), Craig Bierko (*Timothy*), Brian Cox (*Nathan*), David Morse (*Luke/ Daedalus*), Tom Amandes (*Hal*), Yvonne Zima (*Caitlin Caine*), Joseph McKenna (*One-Eyed Jack*), G.D. Spradlin, Melina Kanakaredes, Dan

Warry-Smith, Rex Linn, Edwin Hodge, Alan North, Sharon Washington, Larry King.
   Dir: Renny Harlin. Pro: Harlin, Stephanie Austin and Shane Black. Ex Pro: Steve Tisch, Richard Saperstein and Michael De Luca. Co-Pro: Carla Fry. Screenplay: Black. Ph: Guillermo Navarro. Pro Des: Howard Cummings. Ed: William C. Goldenberg. M: Alan Silvestri; numbers performed by Elvis Presley, US, Ronnie Spector and Darlene Love, Jr Parker, Dean Martin, Marvin Gaye and Tammi Terrell, Jimmy Cliff, Muddy Waters, Santana, Labelle, Gus, Neneh Cherry, Patty Labelle and Dr Dre, Jingle Dogs, John Williams, etc. Costumes: Michael Kaplan. Visual effects: Jeffrey A. Okun. (New Line Cinema/Forge–Entertainment.) Rel: 29 November 1996. 120 mins. Cert 18. USA. 1996.

Looking For Richard

Al Pacino's passionate, loose-limbed documentary is as much about the process of struggling to understand Shakespeare as it is about the universal ignorance of the theatre. Taking to the streets of New York, Pacino interviews passers-by who don't seem to know Richard III from Richard Branson. Admitting to his own insecurities about the text of Shakespeare's historical play, Pacino jumps in with both feet, goading friends, colleagues and even a handful of Hollywood stars to tackle a full-blown screen version of *Richard III*, complete with costumes, armour and battle scene. Gradually, in

The play's the thing: Al Pacino and Winona Ryder rehearse Richard III *in Pacino's fascinating documentary,* Looking For Richard *(from Fox)*

between casting sessions, discussions with theatrical experts (Gielgud, Kenneth Branagh) and a visit to Stratford-upon-Avon, a powerful historical thriller emerges from the engaging shambles. A labour of love which has taken Pacino years to realise, *Looking For Richard* is blessed by its maker's refusal to succumb to pomposity, allowing the poetry and passion of the verse to forge its magic.

Alec Baldwin (*Clarence*), Al Pacino (*Richard III*), Aidan Quinn (*Richmond*), Winona Ryder (*Lady Anne*), Kevin Spacey (*Buckingham*), Penelope Allen (*Queen Elizabeth*), Harris Yulin (*King Edward*), Kevin Conway (*Hastings*), Estelle Parsons (*Margaret*), Frederic Kimball (*Bishop of Ely*), Larry Bryggman, Bruce MacVittie, Paul Guilfoyle, Richard Cox, Julie Moret, Daniel Von Bargen, F. Murray Abraham, Gil Bellows, Kate Burton, Paul Gleason, Clare Holman, Viveca Lindfors, Judith Malina, Michael Maloney, Jaime Sanchez, Heathcote Williams (*irate Irishman*), Jeremy Irons (*narrator*). Interviewees: Kenneth Branagh, Kevin Kline, James Earl Jones, Rosemary Harris, Emrys Jones, Peter Brook, Barbara Everett, Derek Jacobi, John Gielgud, Vanessa Redgrave.

Dir: Al Pacino. Pro: Pacino and Michael Hadge. Ex Pro: William Teitler. Ph: Robert Leacock. Art: Kevin Ritter. Ed: Pasquale Buba, William A. Anderson and Ned Bastille. M: Howard Shore. Costumes: Aude Bronson Howard. (Fox–Fox.) Rel: 31 January 1997. 112 mins. Cert 12. USA. 1996.

Love and Other Catastrophes

Melbourne; today. Alice is a film student who has spent four years working on her thesis *Doris Day as a Feminist Warrior*. Her flatmate, Mia, is a lesbian who has one day to pay her mysterious library fine of $A663. Mia's lover, Danni, wants to take up the vacancy in the girls' new apartment, but Mia is afraid of commitment. Meanwhile, Danni makes friends with the apparently mute Savita. Michael, a timid medical student, is also looking for a place to stay and meets up with Ari, a pretentious classics student and part-time gigolo, who leads Michael to Alice and Mia... A day-in-the-life of five university students, *Love and Other Catastrophes* is a breezy, witty and irresistible concoction from the low-budget school of Australian filmmaking (budget: $A30,000). While citing such American 'indies'

Chicago Jones and the Slow Girl: Nia Long and Larenz Tate find themselves irresistible in Theodore Witcher's smart, slick love jones *(from Entertainment)*

as *Clerks* and *El Mariachi* as her inspiration, 23-year-old first-time writer-director Emma-Kate Croghan does herself an injustice. Her natural narrative flair and skill for eliciting lively, credible performances from her radiant cast elevates her well above the likes of Kevin Smith and Robert Rodriguez. Croghan not only exhibits cinematic style and daring, but reveals a dynamic passion and love for humanity.

Alice Garner (*Alice*), Frances O'Conner (*Mia*), Matthew Dyktynski (*Ari*), Matt Day

A Strine Romance: Frances O'Conner contemplates her future in Emma-Kate Croghan's blissful Love and Other Catastrophes *(from Fox)*

(*Michael*), Radha Mitchell (*Danni*), Suzi Dougherty (*Savita*), Kim Gyngell (*Professor Richard Leach*), Suzanne Dowling, Torquil Neilson, Christine Stephen-Daly, Adrian Martin (*himself*).

Dir: Emma-Kate Croghan. Pro: Stavros Andonis Efthymiou. Co-Pro: Helen Bandis and Yael Bergman. Line Pro: Anastasia Sideris. Screenplay: Bergman, Croghan and Bandis, from a story by Efthy-miou. Ph: Justin Brickle. Pro Des and Costumes: Lisa Collins. Ed: Ken Sallows. M: Oleh Witer and (opening credits) Daryl McKenzie; numbers performed by Bellydance, Smog, Aibara, Tumbleweed, Cardi-gans, Godstar, Frances O'Conner, Velvet Underground, The Cruel Sea, Blue Mink, Died Pretty, etc. (Screwball Five/Beyond Films/Australian Film Commission–Fox.) Rel: 23 May 1997. 78 mins. Cert 15. Australia. 1996.

love jones

Chicago; today. Having expressed his view that 'romance is about the

Teacher's petting: Marika Lagercrantz and Johan Widerberg in the late Bo Widerberg's erotic Love Lessons *(from Gala)*

possibility of the thing', confirmed Romeo and struggling novelist Darius Lovehall blows his first overture by serenading his object of desire with a poem about sex. However, his persistence and self-deprecatory grin eventually wins the heart of aspiring photographer Nina Mosley, although the path of true love never runs smoothly... Venturing into an area seldom explored by Afro-American film-makers – the lives of cultured, middle-class blacks – *love jones* is smart, slick and smoky, the cinematic equivalent of dinner jazz. Notwith-standing, it's hard to swallow any creed of lovebirds swapping quotes by GBS and Mozart and one can never entirely believe in the humanity of these smart movers. Still, *love jones* is a hard film to dislike, and is distinguished by charismatic performances from Tate and Long, arresting photography and rich, flavourful dialogue.

Larenz Tate (*Darius Lovehall*), Nia Long (*Nina Mosley*), Isaiah Washington (*Savon Garrison*), Lisa Nicole Carson (*Josie Nichols*), Khalil Kain (*Marvin Cox*), Bill Bellamy (*Hollywood*), Bernadette L. Clarke (*Sheila Downes*), Leonard Roberts, Cerall Duncan, David Nisbet, Simon James, Marie-Francoise Theodore, Reginald Gibson (*himself*), Malik Yosef (*himself*).

Dir and Screenplay: Theodore Witcher. Pro: Nick Wechsler and Jeremiah Samuels. Ex Pro: Julia Chasman, Jay Stern, Amy Henkels and Helena Echegoyen. Ph: Ernest Holzman. Pro Des: Roger Fortune. Ed: Maysie Hoy. M: Darryl Jones; numbers performed by Dionne Farris, Cameo, Charlie Parker, Maxwell, Charles Cameron and Sunshine Festival, Al Green, Buddy Guy, Jamiroquai, The Brand New Heavies, James Brown, John Coltrane and Duke Ellington, Cassandra Wilson, Curtis Mayfield, Lauryn Hill, etc. Costumes: Shawn Barton. Photographs: Melodie McDaniel. (New Line–Entertainment.) Rel: 27 June 1997. 108 mins. Cert 15. USA. 1997.

Love Lessons - Lust och Fagring Stor - Laererinden

Malmo, southern Sweden; 1943. Starting out in much the same vein as other wartime childhood dramas, Bo Widerberg's *Love Lessons* swiftly switches to its own agenda. Boys exchange esoteric snatches of sexual information during class and compare the length of their pubic hair in the school break. However, 15-year-old Stig Santesson (played by the director's son, Johan) is into bigger things as he ogles his new teacher, Viola, who, although 22 years his senior, is still a singularly good-looking woman. Married to a hard-drinking adulterer, Viola eagerly returns Stig's sexual advances and soon the pair are breaking every scholastic, marital and moral rule in the book... Thanks to the remarkable performances of Johan Widerberg and Marika Lagercrantz, Widerberg's first film in nine years delivers a powerful erotic charge. There are also some delightful moments of poignant humour between Stig and Viola's pathetic but endearing husband, from whom the former learns to appreciate and love classical music. Only the film's later, more dramatic passages fail to ring true, while the repeated use of Handel's 'Lascia ch'io pianga' veers from the inspiring to the irritating. Nominated for an Oscar for best foreign film. US title: *All Things Fair.*

Johan Widerberg (*Stig Santesson*), Marika Lagercrantz (*Viola*), Tomas von Bromssen (*Frank/Kjell*), Karin Huldt (*Lisbet*), Nina Gunke (*Stig's mother*), Bjorn Kjellman (*Sigge*), Kenneth Milldoff, Frida Lindholm.
Dir, Screenplay and Ed: Bo Widerberg. Pro: Per Holst. Line Pro: Anne Ingvar. Ph: Morten Bruus. Pro Des: Palle Arestrup. M: mainly Handel's 'Lascia ch'io pianga'; also Bach, Beethoven, Mahler, Tchaikovsky; numbers performed by Ulla Billquist, and The Andrews Sisters. Costumes: Lotta Petersson. (Per Holst Film/Danish Filminstitute, etc.–Gala.) Rel: 28 March 1997. 130 mins. Cert 15. Sweden/Denmark. 1995.

Lush Life

New York; the present. Al Gorky, a saxophonist, and Buddy Chester, a trumpeter, are session musicians and best friends who revel in their free-wheeling lifestyle, whether they're playing on Broadway or at bar mitzvahs. However, Gorky's wife, an assistant school principal, is ready to settle down to a 'normal' life, while Chester discovers that his own life is fast coming to an end. Faced with his wife's imminent departure and his friend's inoperable tumour, Gorky is forced to reappraise his own self-serving 'lush life'... Displaying a genuine affection for each other and their music, Jeff Goldblum and Forest Whitaker bring this atmospheric character piece resoundingly to life, aided by Michael Elias's carefree direction, which provides just the right improvised feel for the material. However, it would be easy to overlook the quality of Elias's insightful script – although Leslie Niehaus's gloriously jazzy score riffs for itself. A celebration of jazz and friendship, *Lush Life* doesn't sound a false note.

Jeff Goldblum (*Al Gorky*), Forest Whitaker (*Buddy Chester*), Kathy Baker (*Janice Oliver*), Tracey Needham (*Sarah*), Lois Chiles (*Lucy*), Don Cheadle (*Jack*), Zack Norman (*Beanstrom*), Alex Desert (*Lester*), Perry Moore, Jack Sheldon, 'Nita Whitaker.
Dir and Screenplay: Michael Elias. Pro: Thom Colwell. Ex Pro: Jana Sue Memel and Jonathan Sanger. Co-Pro: Hillary Anne Ripps and Ron Colby. Ph: Nancy Schreiber. Pro Des: John Jay Moore. Ed: Bill Yahraus. M: Lennie Niehaus. Costumes: Mary Kay Stolz. (Showtime/Chanticleer Film–NFT.) Rel: 16 May 1997. 104 mins. No Cert. USA. 1993.

Madame Butterfly

Frederic Mitterand's film version of Puccini's ever-popular opera may lack the weight and experience which Zeffirelli brought to *La Traviata*, but it captures wonderfully the emotional charge of this tragic love story. The period tale of a Japanese girl betrayed by the American she marries in turn-of-the-century Nagasaki may have wider social and historical implications, but it is as a portrayal of emotional disillusionment that the piece touches the hearts of its audience. Here, admirably supported by the conducting of James Conlon, the young Shanghai soprano Ying Huang proves ideal for the title role, so much so that even those dubious about opera would be advised to see this film. [*Mansel Stimpson*]

Ying Huang (*Sho-Sho-San*), Ning Liang (*Suzuki*), Richard Troxell (*Pinkerton*), Richard Cowan (*Sharpless*), Jing-Ma Fan (*Goro*), Constance Hauman (*Kate Pinkerton*), Christopheren Nomura (*Prince Yamadori*).
　　Dir and Screenplay: Frederic Mitterand. Pro: Daniel Toscan du Plantier and Pierre-Olivier Bardet. Ph: Philippe Welt. Ed: Luc Barnier. Art: Michel Glozz and Daniel Zalay. M: Giacomo Puccini. Libretto: Giuseppe Giacosa and Luigi Illica. Costumes: Christian Gasc. (Erato Films/Ideale Audience/France 3 Cinema/Imalyre/VTCOM France Telecom/Sony Classical/Canal Plus/BBC/ZDF/S4C/France Telecom Fondation/European Script Fund–Blue Dolphin.) Rel: 20 June 1997. 134 mins. Cert PG. France/Japan/Germany/UK. 1995.

Mad Dog Time
See *Trigger Happy*.

Malina
Vienna; the present. Tormented by the memories of her abusive father, a writer struggles to hold on to her sanity as she is emotionally torn between her mentor, Malina, and a new lover, Ivan... Apparently an exercise in 'camp excess and artifice', *Malina* is the sort of film in which characters would never put a glass down if, instead, they could throw it across the room. An incomprehensible and pretentious mess, it lurches from 'reality' to fantasy and from the present to the past with little narrative indication. Worse, the love scenes are devoid of credibility and passion and the dialogue is laughable (Isabelle Huppert: 'I'm not who you think I am. I am double. Double.'). Huh? Based on the novel by Ingeborg Bachman.

Isabelle Huppert (*the woman*), Mathieu Carriere (*Malina*), Can Togay (*Ivan*), Fritz Schediwyiwy (*the father*), Isolde Barth (*mother*), Libcart Schwarz (*Ms Jellinek*).
　　Dir: Werner Schroeter. Pro: Thomas and Steffen Kuckenreuther. Screenplay: Elfriede Jelinek. Ph: Elfi Mikesch. Pro Des and Costumes: Alberte Barsack. Ed: Juliane Lorenz. M: Giacomo Manzoni. (Independent/Public Theatre–ICA.) Rel: 8 April 1997. 125 mins. No Cert. Germany/Austria. 1990.

Margaret's Museum
Cape Breton; the 1940s. For the citizens of Glace Bay in Nova Scotia, the local coal mines offer the only regular employment. But the toll is high, the eerie wail of a siren regularly announcing another fatal accident. Margaret MacNeil has already lost her father and brother to the pits and she is not about to marry a miner. Just then the 6'6" bagpipe-playing Neil Currie enters her life, a man every bit as unusual as herself... While visually and musically seductive, *Margaret's Museum* chugs along more or less aimlessly until hitting its mark in the final 20 minutes. There are some nice elements – Kate Nelligan's unceasingly bitter malcontent, some flashes of dark, unforced humour – but there's not enough here to sustain or warrant a movie. Furthermore, Helena Bonham Carter never entirely convinces as the mercurial misfit, not helped by an erratic accent that lurches between Belfast and the Bible Belt.

President Jack Nicholson confers with an envoy of foreign affairs, in Tim Burton's gleefully sadistic Mars Attacks! *(from Warner)*

Helena Bonham Carter (*Margaret MacNeil*), Kate Nelligan (*Catherine MacNeil*), Clive Russell (*Neil Currie*), Kenneth Welsh (*Angus MacNeil*), Craig Olejnik (*Jimmy MacNeil*), Andrea Morris (*Marilyn Campbell*), Peter Boretski (*grandfather*), Barry Dunn, Norma Dell'Agnese, Glenn Wadman, Ida Donovan, Emma Fahey, Paul Young.
　　Dir: Mort Ransen. Pro: Ransen, Christopher Zimmer, Claudio Luca and Steve Clark-Hall. Ex Pro: Marilyn A. Belec. Assoc Pro: Brian Donovan. Screenplay: Ransen and Gerald Wexler, based on *The Glace Bay Miner's Museum (and other stories)* by Sheldon Currie. Ph: Vic Sarin. Pro Des: William Flemming and David McHenry. Ed: Rita Roy. M: Milan Kymlicka; numbers performed by The Rankin Family, Barry Shears, Kyle MacNeil & Sheumas MacNeil, Clive Russell, etc. Costumes: Nicoletta Massone. (Glace Bay Pictures/Tele-Action Ranfilm/Imagex/Skyline/Telefilm Canada/British Screen/National Film Board of Canada/Nova Scotia Film Development, etc.–Metrodome.) Rel: 2 May 1997. 99 mins. Cert 15. Canada/United Kingdom. 1995.

Mars Attacks!
Kansas/Las Vegas/Washington DC; May. Deviously proffering messages of peace, an army of little green Martians descend on earth to blow it to smithereens... The first film to be based on a trading card series, *Mars Attacks!* aims to reproduce the tacky allure of such fifties' B-movies as *The Day the Earth Stood Still* and *Invaders From Mars*, while director Tim Burton admits that his project is nothing more than a 'cheesy science-fiction movie'. Nevertheless, with such a stellar cast, enormous budget ($80 million) and epic sweep (See the Eiffel Tower topple! Watch the Taj Mahal explode!), the film sets up other expectations. Yet from the

spectacular opening, in which a mass of pewter flying saucers shimmer like an ocean of eyeballs, the film (accompanied by Danny Elfman's tongue-in-cheek score) quickly dispenses with our preconceptions. So, falling between the stools of the heroic spectacle of *Independence Day* and the arch self-consciousness of *Attack of the Killer Tomatoes*, Burton's odyssey collapses into a cinematic black hole. Sci-fi junkies may get off on the comic carnage (surely no other film has featured the grisly death of so many major stars); others will find the exercise the summation of their worst nightmare. Tim Burton is one sick puppy – and his fans love him for it.

Jack Nicholson (*President James Dale/Art Land*), Glenn Close (*First Lady Marsha Dale*), Annette Bening (*Barbara Land*), Pierce Brosnan (*Professor Donald Kessler*), Danny DeVito (*Rude Gambler*), Martin Short (*Jerry Ross*), Sarah Jessica Parker (*Nathalie Lake*), Michael J. Fox (*Jason Stone*), Rod Steiger (*General Decker*), Tom Jones (*Tom Jones*), Lukas Haas (*Richie Norris*), Natalie Portman (*Taffy Dale*), Jim Brown (*Byron Williams*), Lisa Marie (*Martian Girl*), Sylvia Sidney (*Grandma Norris*), Paul Winfield (*General Casey*), Pam Grier (*Louise Williams*), Jack Black (*Billy Glenn Norris*), Janice Rivera (*Cindy*), Joe Don Baker (*Glenn Norris*), Christina Applegate (*Sharona*), Brian Haley (*Mitch*), O-Lan Jones, Jerzy Skolimowski, Barbet Schroeder (French President), Ray J, Brandon Hammond, Joseph Maher, Willie Garson, Rebecca Broussard, Enrique

Room for improvement: Diane Keaton and Meryl Streep confront their ghosts in Jerry Zaks' sharp, intelligent Marvin's Room *(from Buena Vista)*

Castillo, John Gray, Gregg Daniel, J. Kenneth Campbell, Rance Howard, Frank Welker (*various Martian voices*).

Dir: Tim Burton. Pro: Burton and Larry Franco. Screenplay: Jonathan Gems. Ph: Peter Suschitzky. Pro Des: Wynn Thomas. Ed: Chris Lebenzon. M: Danny Elfman; numbers performed by Rupert Holmes, Elisabeth Troy-Antwi, Slim Whitman, The Bee Gees, with 'It's Not Unusual' sung by Tom Jones. Costumes: Colleen Atwood. Martian effects: Industrial Light & Magic. (Warner–Warner.) Rel: 28 February 1997. 106 mins. Cert 12. USA. 1996.

Marvin's Room

Orlando, Florida; now. Bessie has been nursing her sick father, Marvin, for 20 years when she discovers that she has leukaemia. For any hope of survival she must find a relative whose bone marrow matches her own. So, for the first time in two decades, she calls her estranged sister, Lee, in Ohio. With both sisters nursing years of resentment – Bessie, for being abandoned; Lee, for being ostracised – the family takes a tenuous step towards reconciliation... One year before his death from Aids in 1992, Scott McPherson saw his semi-autobiographical play, *Marvin's Room*, open to rave reviews in New York. A funny, painful story of love, death and family, the film version – which McPherson scripted himself – is enlivened by superlative performances from a powerhouse cast. Refreshingly free from over-explanation, the script goes boldly and lovingly where few have gone before. Only Rachel Portman's suffocating score, which telegraphs every emotional nuance, is at

loggerheads with the sharp, intelligent (and above all heartfelt) material.

Meryl Streep (*Lee*), Leonardo DiCaprio (*Hank*), Diane Keaton (*Bessie*), Robert De Niro (*Dr Wally*), Hume Cronyn (*Marvin*), Gwen Verdon (*Ruth*), Hal Scardino (*Charlie*), Dan Hedaya (*Bob*), Margo Martindale, Cynthia Nixon, Bitty Schramm, Victor Schramm.

Dir: Jerry Zaks. Pro: Scott Rudin, Jane Rosenthal and Robert De Niro. Ex Pro: Tod Scott Brody and Lori Steinberg. Co-Pro: David Wisnievitz and Adam Schroeder. Screenplay: Scott McPherson. Ph: Piotr Sobocinski. Pro Des: David Gropman. Ed: Jim Clark. M: Rachel Portman; Vivaldi; 'Two Little Sisters' sung by Carly Simon and Meryl Streep. Costumes: Julie Weiss. (Miramax/Tribeca–Buena Vista.) Rel: 20 June 1997. 98 mins. Cert 12. USA. 1996.

Matilda

See *Roald Dahl's Matilda*

Men Women: A User's Manual - Hommes Femmes: Mode d'Emploi

Two men, arriving at the clinic of Dr Nitez from different directions in life, are grounded by a common predicament: they fear that the pain in their stomachs could be life threatening. They weren't meant to meet, but their encounter changes their lives for ever. As does the questionable prognosis of their ailment... Picking at a thread of narrative here and a motif there, writer-director Claude Lelouch playfully weaves his provocative, vastly entertaining tapestry like a composer shaping a symphony. And, with his camera constantly on the move (but never intrusively so), Lelouch fills every second with observant detail, whether building up the background atmosphere (some marvellous shots of Paris in winter) or unravelling the psychological layers of his characters. An extraordinarily rich film, photographically, musically and philosophically. P.S. The part of Benoit is played by real-life entrepreneur and politician Bernard Tapie (in his film debut), who was later imprisoned for corruption. P.P.S. The role of the female doctor is played by Claude Lelouch's wife,

Alessandra Martines, and Lola by the filmmaker's daughter, Salome. P.P.P.S. The homeless soprano is portrayed by a gardener Lelouch spotted on a local TV variety show.

Fabrice Luchini (*Fabio Lini*), Bernard Tapie (*Benoit Blanc*), Alessandra Martines (*Dr Nitez*), Pierre Arditi (*Dr Pierre Lerner*), Salomé Lelouch (*Lola*), Christophe Hémon (*Loulou, boy from train*), Ticky Holgado (*Toc Toc, Loulou's father*), Caroline Céllier (*Jeanne Blanc*), Gisèle Casadesus (*Clara Blanc*), Anouk Aimée (*the widow*), Patrick Husson (*falsetto singer*), Ophélie Winter, William Leymergie, Daniel Gélin, Agnes Soral, Daniel Olbrychski, Nadia Farès, Claude Lelouch.

Dir and Pro: Claude Lelouch. Ex Pro: Tania Zazulinsky. Screenplay: Lelouch, Rene Bonnell and Jean-Philippe Chatrier. Ph: Lelouch and Philippe Pavans de Ceccatty. Pro Des: Jacques Buf-noir. Ed: Hélène de Luze. M: Francis Lai; Johann Strauss, Puccini. Costumes: Dominique Borg. (Les Films 13/TF1 Films/Canal Plus–Gala.) Rel: 6 June 1997. 123 mins. Cert 12. France. 1996.

Metro
When you're a hostage negotiator for the San Francisco Police Department, talk is anything but cheap. For top arbitrator Scott Roper, words are his stock in trade, although his sixth sense, split-second timing and marksman's eye are not to be dismissed lightly. Then he gets personally involved in a case in which his friend and mentor has his throat slashed by a merciless jewel thief. The latter proves to be every bit Roper's equal, the toughest adversary he's ever had the displeasure to track down... Bringing a new weight and gravity to the braying, wisecracking character he perfected in *Beverly Hills Cop*, Eddie Murphy holds his own against some seat-wetting stunts and ear-rocking explosions – not to mention the obligatory San Francisco car chase (in this instance featuring a runaway tram). Of course, *Metro* is nothing more than a conventional action-thriller spiced with humour and romance, but thanks to a perfectly despicable villain from Michael Wincott (the next James Woods?), a spunky, attractive leading lady (England's Carmen Ejogo), some rapid-fire editing and a splendidly mischievous score, it is top-of-the-range escapism.

Eddie Murphy (*Scott Roper*), Michael Rapaport (*Kevin McCall*), Michael Wincott (*Michael Korda*), Carmen Ejogo (*Veronica 'Ronnie' Tate*), Denis Arndt (*Captain Frank Solis*), Art Evans (*Lt Sam Baffert*), Donal Logue (*Earl*), Paul Ben-Victor (*Clarence Teal*), Kim Miyori (*Det. Kimura*), Jeni Chua, Charleston Pierce, Jeff Mosley.

Dir: Thomas Carter. Pro: Roger Birnbaum. Ex Pro: Mark Lipsky and Riley Kathryn Ellis. Co-Pro: George W. Perkins, Ray Murphy Jr and Randy Feldman. Screenplay: Feldman. Ph: Fred Murphy. Pro Des: William Elliott. Ed: Peter E. Berger. M: Steve Porcaro; numbers performed by New Edition, Duke Ellington, Sonny Rollins, and James Brown. Costumes: Ha Nguyen. (Touchstone Pictures/Caravan Pictures–Buena Vista.) Rel: 18 April 1997. 117 mins. Cert 18. USA. 1997.

Michael
When tabloid reporter Frank Quinlan hears of an angel in Iowa, he smells a front-page scoop for the Christmas edition of Chicago's *National Mirror*. Accompanied by fellow hack Huey Driscoll and 'angel expert' Dorothy Winters, Quinlan drives down to the Midwest and is astonished to find

San Francisco Cop: Eddie Murphy stalking Stallone territory in Thomas Carter's slick, fast-moving Metro *(from Buena Vista)*

that the divine messenger is an overweight, chain-smoking, foul-mouthed slob. Be that as it may, wherever archangel Michael goes girls follow, as does the occasional miracle... Highly conceptual and contrived, Nora Ephron's stodgy fantasy aims to capture the magic of *Sleepless in Seattle* (which she also directed), but lacks both chemistry and narrative momentum. Although

Taking the Michael: *John Travolta wings it in Nora Ephron's stodgy, misconceived fantasy (from Rank–Castle Rock/Turner)*

Playing by their own rules: Alan Rickman, Liam Neeson and Aidan Quinn line up for the British in Neil Jordan's passionate and eloquent Michael Collins *(from Warner)*

John Travolta has a whale of a time as the fun-loving angel, there's little evidence to suggest that his cohorts believe in him. William Hurt and Andie MacDowell look like they've been dragged in from another movie and can't wait to get back to it. There are, however, some choice moments, notably Travolta's first appearance and the sublime last five minutes.

John Travolta (*Michael*), Andie MacDowell (*Dorothy Winters*), William Hurt (*Frank Quinlan*), Bob Hoskins (*Vartan Malt*), Robert Pastorelli (*Huey Driscoll*), Jean Stapleton (*Pansy Milbank*), Teri Garr, Wallace Langham, Joey Lauren Adams, Carla Gugino, Tom Hodges, Catherine Lloyd Burns, Richard Schiff, Joann Jansen, Jane Lanier, Margaret Travolta, Dianne Dreyer.
   Dir: Nora Ephron. Pro: Sean Daniel, Nora Ephron and James Jacks. Ex Pro: Delia Ephron and Jonathan D. Krane. Co-Pro: G. Mac Brown. Screenplay: Nora Ephron & Delia Ephron and Pete Dexter and Jim Quinlan, from a story by Dexter,

Quinlan, Daniel, Nora Ephron and Jacks. Ph: John Lindley. Pro Des: Dan Davis. Ed: Geraldine Peroni. M: Randy Newman; 'Heaven Is My Home' performed by Randy Newman and Valerie Carter; other numbers performed by Dion, Chet Atkins, Erik and the Offbeats, Creedence Clearwater Revival, The Mavericks, Aretha Franklin, Mark Knopfler, Andie MacDowell ('Sittin' By The Side Of The Road'), George Benson, Bonnie Raitt, Willie Nelson, Frank Sinatra, Van Morrison, Don Henley, Al Green, Norman Greenbaum, etc. Costumes: Elizabeth McBride. (Turner Pictures/Alphaville Prods–Rank–Castle Rock/Turner.) Rel: 21 February 1997. 105 mins. Cert PG. USA. 1996.

Michael Collins

Ireland; 1916-22. Following his release from prison for his part in the Easter Uprising of 1916, Michael Collins was more determined than ever to end Britain's 700-year rule of tyranny. Furthermore, the summary execution by firing squad of many of his colleagues made Collins realise that the Irish Republican Army had to take a fresh approach to secure Ireland's freedom ('We won't play by their rules, Harry, we'll invent our

own'). But the harder Collins hit back at the English, the more brutal was their retort, culminating in the mobilisation of a paramilitary force (known as 'the Black and Tans') not above torture and, in one infamous case, the unprovoked slaughter of an innocent crowd of football spectators. Reduced to fighting violence with violence, Collins complained, 'I hate them for making hate necessary,' and went on to become the hero of the Irish revolution... Doing for the IRA what *The Godfather* did for the Mafia, Neil Jordan's realisation of his 13-year-old dream bestows a dignity and compassion on an organisation till now daubed in the dirty colours of propaganda. Depicting with passionate clarity the tragic escalation of violence that clouded Ireland's struggle for liberation, Jordan has accomplished a nigh-impossible objective. Liam Neeson heads a magnificent cast with a commanding, powerful reading as Collins, while the impressive battle scenes, rousing score and fluid editing help make this an eloquent, stirring history lesson. Only the ill-advised introduction of a romantic subplot – with Julia Roberts in the thankless part of Collins' love interest – slows matters down. FYI: Kevin Costner had been planning to mount a film biography of Collins for some time. Having previously lost the role of Oskar Schindler to Liam Neeson, Costner must now be really mad.

Liam Neeson (*Michael Collins*), Aidan Quinn (*Harry Boland*), Stephen Rea (*Ned Broy*), Alan Rickman (*Eamon De Valera*), Julia Roberts (*Kitty Kiernan*), Charles Dance (*Soames*), Ian Hart (*Joe O'Reilly*), Ger O'Leary (*Thomas Clarke*), Sean McGinley (*Smith*), Gary Whelan (*Hoey*), Brendan Gleeson (*Liam Tobin*), Gerard McSorley (*Cathal Brugha*), Jonathan Rhys Myers (*Collins' assassin*), Richard Ingram, John Kenny, Roman McCairbe, Aiden Grennell, Laura Brennan, Mike McCabe, Jean Kennedy Smith.

Dir and Screenplay: Neil Jordan. Pro: Stephen Woolley. Co-Pro: Redmond Morris. Ph: Chris Menges. Pro Des: Anthony Pratt. Ed: J. Patrick Lawson and Tony Lawson. M: Elliot Goldenthal; 'She Moved Through the Air' performed by Sinead O'Connor. Costumes: Sandy Powell. (The Geffen Company–Warner.) Rel: 8 November 1996. 132 mins. Cert 15. UK/USA. 1996.

Microcosmos - Microcosmos Le Peuple de l'Herbe

Following the most spectacular shot of a bank of clouds ever filmed, *Microcosmos* dives earthward in search of its true story. A virtually wordless tribute to nature in all its mystery, humour and tragedy, this award-winning French film is neither documentary nor fiction, but an awe-inspiring salute to the world beneath our feet. Utilising staggeringly detailed, crystal-clear camera-work matched to a subtle, witty soundtrack (the patter of tiny feet, an operatic aria accompanying the lovemaking of two Burgundy snails), *Microcosmos* avoids both the cruelty of many nature films and the cloying sentimentality of a Disney 'True-Life Adventure'. Highlights include the confused march of a column of caterpillars, a sacred beetle grappling with a ball of dung and the ruthless attack of an Argiope spider. Both a sensual celebration of our earth and the potential of cinema. But how did they film it?

Argiope spider, Argyronet spider, bee, climbing caterpillars, dragonflies, drosera carnivorous plant, great peacock moth, ladybird (with seven spots), mosquito, pheasant, polist wasps, red ants, rhinoceros beetle, stag beetles, swallow-tail butterfly, water spiders, etc, etc. Narrator: Kristin Scott-Thomas.

Dir: Claude Nuridsany and Marie Perennou. Pro: Jacques Perrin, Christophe Barratier and Yvette Mallet. Ex Pro: Michel Faure, Philippe Gautier, Andre Lazare and Patrick Lancelot. Ph: Nuridsany, Perennou, Hughes Ryffel and Thierry Machado. Ed: Marie-Josephe Yoyotte and Florence Ricard. M: Bruno Coulais; aria sung by Mari Kobayashi. Sound: Laurent Quaglio. (Galatee Films/France 2 Cinema/Bac Films/Delta Images/Canal Plus, etc.–Guild.) Rel: 16 May 1997. 75 mins. Cert U. France/Switzerland/Italy. 1996.

A Midsummer Night's Dream

A variation of his critically acclaimed production for The Royal Shakespeare Company, Adrian Noble's studio-bound adaptation jettisons the pastoral lyricism of the Bard's magical play in favour of gimmicky tricks. Seen through the eyes of an impressionable young boy (the irresistibly photogenic Osheen Jones), the events unfold in a digital

'All right, Mr De Mille, I'm ready for my close up': A dragonfly faces the camera in Claude Nuridsany and Marie Perennou's awe-inspiring Microcosmos *(from Guild)*

dimension more in keeping with a video arcade than the sylvan habitat of fairies. The largely unknown cast keeps the sense vivid, although Alex Jennings' Oberon borders on an impression of Lionel Blair and Barry Lynch's Puck is more creepy than mischievous. Still, Desmond Barrit's Bottom is a wonderful comic invention and the rest of the actors barely swallow a syllable. Fast paced and brightly lit, this *Dream* should appeal more to schools than Shakespearean purists. It does, how-ever, whet the appetite for a future production, preferably directed by Kenneth Branagh. If any play of Shakespeare's deserves the Great Outdoors, it is his *Dream*.

Lindsay Duncan (*Hippolyta/Titania*), Alex Jennings (*Theseus/Oberon*), Desmond Barrit (*Nick/Bottom*), Barry Lynch (*Puck/ Philostrate*), Monica Dolan (*Hermia*), Kevin Doyle (*Demetrius*), Daniel Evans (*Lysander*), Emily Raymond (*Helena*), Alfred Burke (*Egeus*), Howard Crossley (*Tom Snout*), Robert Gillespie (*Robin Starvelling*), John Kane (*Peter Quince*), Mark Letheren (*Francis Flute*), Kenn Sabberton (*Snug*), Ann Hasson (*First Fairy*), Osheen Jones (*the boy*), Emily Button, Tim Griggs, Joseph Morton.

Dir and Adaptation: Adrian Noble. Pro: Paul Arnott. Line Pro: Ian Scaife. Ph: Ian Wilson. Pro Des and Costumes: Anthony Ward. Ed: Paul Hodgson and Peter Holly-wood. M: Howard Blake. (Channel Four/ Arts Council England/Capitol Films/Eden-wood Prods–Film Four.) Rel: 29 November 1996. 105 mins. Cert PG. UK. 1996.

When Harry Met the Ugly Duckling: Jeff Bridges (centre) is entertained by Lauren Bacall and Barbra Streisand in the latter's overwhelming The Mirror Has Two Faces *(from Columbia TriStar)*

The Mirror Has Two Faces

Gregory Larkin works in the math department at Columbia University, treats each lesson like a private math party and has taken 14 years to write his first book. One of the world's most boring men, he blames his string of failed relationships on the fatal love potion of romance – sex. Rose Morgan teaches romantic literature at the same university and readily admits that in the Holy Trinity of womanhood she is neither divine whore nor Medusa – she is the bridesmaid. Gregory loves Rose for her mind, her passion and her humour. Rose loves Gregory for his mind, his passion and his body. So when Gregory suggests that they endorse their partnership with a wedding contract, Rose believes that her romantic dreams have finally come true. Even if, for the time being, sex is left out of the equation... A big, gushing musical without the songs,

The Mirror Has Two Faces is the year's most hopelessly romantic, over-produced, old-fashioned love story. And yet, perhaps conversely, it is also a brave, highly personal vanity project from one of the last great entertainers of Hollywood. Obviously a subject close to Streisand's heart – the stigmatisation of the non-beautiful – the theme is given a powerful voice in Richard LaGravenese's skilfully crafted, articulate screenplay, entertainingly realised by a colourful cast. It's good to see Jeff Bridges in such madcap good humour, although everybody is on top form under Streisand's breezy direction.

Barbra Streisand (*Rose Morgan*), Jeff Bridges (*Gregory Larkin*), Pierce Brosnan (*Alex*), George Segal (*Henry Fine*), Mimi Rogers (*Claire*), Brenda Vaccaro (*Doris*), Lauren Bacall (*Hannah Morgan*), Austin Pendleton (*Barry*), Elle Macpherson (*Candace*), Ali Marsh, Leslie Stefanson, Taina Elg, Lucy Avery Brooks, Jimmy Baio, Emma Fann, Laura Bailey, Anne O'Sullivan, Adam LeFevre, Carlo Scibelli.
    Dir: Barbra Streisand. Pro: Streisand and Arnon Milchan. Ex Pro: Cis Corman. Co-Ex Pro: Ronald Schwary. Screenplay: Richard LaGravenese, from the 1959 French film *Le Miroir à Deux Faces*. Ph:

Dante Spinotti and Andrzej Bartkowiak. Pro Des: Tom John. Ed: Jeff Werner. M: Marvin Hamlisch; Streisand; numbers performed by Streisand and Bryan Adams ('I Finally Found Someone'), Richard Marx, Earth, Wind & Fire, Tony Scott, David Sanborn, David Foster, Lesley Garrett, Luciano Pavarotti, etc. Costumes: Theoni V. Aldredge. (TriStar/Phoenix Pictures–Columbia.) Rel: 10 January 1997. 125 mins. Cert 15. USA. 1996.

Mission: Impossible

Kiev/Prague/Washington DC/London; today. The agents of IMF (Impossible Missions Force) are on a routine assignment in Prague when a startling double-cross scatters their ranks. Master-of-disguise Ethan Hunt finds himself running for his life and forced to bargain with a covert agency in order to save his skin. Then the plot gets really baffling... Unlike other big-screen adaptations of TV fodder, Brian De Palma's high-octane express ride lunges from affectionate pastiche to downright adulteration. Devotees of the show will delight at the familiarity of old touches – the gadgets, the self-destructing instruction tape, Lalo Schifrin's

Jean Reno admires Tom Cruise's right bicep in Brian De Palma's impossibly confused, flashy treatment of TV's Mission: Impossible *(from UIP)*

pounding theme tune – but will then be outraged as the film steamrolls over the memory of the old team as led by Jim Phelps (Jon Voight replacing Peter Graves). Still, despite De Palma's irritating and distracting camera angles, the action sequences work a treat, not least the near-silent break-in of a high-security vault and the fight on top of a high-speed train.

Tom Cruise (*Ethan Hunt*), Jon Voight (*Jim Phelps*), Henry Czerny (*Kittridge*), Emmanuelle Beart (*Claire*), Jean Reno (*Krieger*), Ving Rhames (*Luther*), Kristin Scott Thomas (*Sarah*), Vanessa Redgrave (*Max*), Ingeborga Dapkunaite (*Hannah*), Rolf Saxon (*CIA Analyst William Donloe*), Emilio Estevez (*Jack*), Dale Dye, Ion Caramitru, John McLaughlin, Andreas Wisniewski, Bob Friend, David Schneider, Helen Lindsay, Pat Starr, Tony Vogel.
  Dir: Brian De Palma. Pro: Tom Cruise and Paula Wagner. Ex Pro: Paul Hitchcock. Screenplay: David Koepp and Robert Towne, based on a story by Koepp and Steven Zaillian. Ph: Stephen H. Burum. Pro Des: Norman Reynolds. Ed:

Paul Hirsch. M: Danny Elfman; Lalo Schifrin, Mozart; numbers performed by Larry Mullen and Adam Clayton, and The Cranberries. Costumes: Penny Rose. Make-Up Effects: Rob Bottin. Visual Effects: John Knoll. (Paramount–UIP.) Rel: 5 July 1996. 110 mins. Cert PG. USA. 1996.

Moll Flanders

London; the early 1700s. Having found the ten-year-old daughter of Moll Flanders in a forbidding orphanage, a stately black stranger resolves to tell the girl of her mother's troubled life. Reading from the pages of the latter's memoirs, the stranger relates how Moll escaped from a cruel orphanage herself and went on to stand up for her rights in a world dominated by greed, prejudice and injustice... Having made a mockery of the legend of Robin Hood with his script for *Robin Hood: Prince of Thieves*, producer Pen Densham (*Tank Girl*) makes his directorial debut with this historical romp 'based on the character created by Daniel Defoe'. Adopting an uneasy flashback format, Densham casts three Americans in principal roles and, in her film debut, the

highly unappealing Aisling Corcoran as Moll's daughter, Flora. While Robin Wright yet again displays her lingual mastery with an impeccable lower-class English accent, she never

Period pains: Texas-born Robin Wright teams up with Tennessee-born Morgan Freeman in Pen Densham's laborious Moll Flanders *(from Fox)*

entirely brings the eponymous fire-brand to life – inspired not only be Defoe's heroine but by various women depicted in Fielding, Voltaire and others. Both episodic and heavy-handed, the film lumbers along for most of its considerable running time until collapsing into soap opera in its final hurried minutes.

Robin Wright (*Moll Flanders*), Morgan Freeman (*Hibble*), Stockard Channing (*Mrs Allworthy*), John Lynch (*Fielding, the artist*), Brenda Fricker (*Mrs Mazzawatti*), Geraldine James (*Edna*), Aisling Corcoran (*Flora*), Jim Sheridan (*priest*), Jeremy Brett, Britta Smith, Cathy Murphy, Emma McIvor, Maria Doyle Kennedy, Ger Ryan, Harry Towb, Alan Stanford, Gary Whelan.
   Dir and Screenplay: Pen Densham. Pro: Denshamn, John Watson and Richard B. Lewis. Ex Pro: Morgan O'Sullivan. Ph: David Tattersall. Pro Des: Caroline Hanania. Ed: Neil Travis and James R. Symons. M: Mark Mancina; 'Full of Grace' sung by Sarah McLachlan. Costumes: Consolata Boyle. (Spelling Films/MGM/Trilogy Entertainment/Irish Film

Shotgun honeymoon: Colin Friels, Jacqueline McKenzie and a kid called Kenny battle the limelight in Nadia Tass's incredible Mr Reliable *(from PolyGram)*

Industry–Fox.) Rel: 9 May 1997. 122 mins. Cert 12. USA. 1995.

Mon Homme

Marie Arbath, a Parisian prostitute, loves men, money and 'bringing dreams alive'. She is the quint-essential hooker with a heart of gold. Then, when she finds a tramp sleeping in her doorway, she takes pity on him and offers him food, wine and lodging for the night. And, as if unwrapping the sheets of a surprise package, she digs beneath the layers of dirty clothing to find the man inside. But what does she unearth? Like any project from the 57-year-old writer-director Bertrand Blier (*Beau-Pere, Notre Histoire, Trop Belle Pour Toi*), the premise is fascinating, the story unpredictable and the acting shockingly committed. Here, Blier has elicited one of the most naked performances (both emotionally and literally) that I have ever seen committed to screen by an actress. 'Discovered' by Blier himself in his 1991 *Mercie la Vie*, the once-gawky Anouk Grinberg has blossomed into a sensuous, commanding actress, not unlike Juliette Binoche in appearance. Unfortunately, the film itself flies off at a tangent near the end (as if in a frantic search for some neat narrative conclusion), upsetting the balance of a compelling, provocative and frequently amusing diversion.

Anouk Grinberg (*Marie Arbath*), Gerard Lanvin (*Jeannot Bourdelle*), Valeria Bruni-Tedeschi (*Sarah Sanguine Veziain*), Olivier Martinez (*Jean-Francois*), Dominique Valadie (*Gilberte*), Dominique Lollia (*Melissa*), Sabine Azema, Mathieu Kassovitz, Jean-Philipe Ecoffey, Jacques Francois, Michel Galabru, Bernard Lecoq, Bernard Fresson, Jean-Pierre Daroussin, Aurore Clement, Jean-Pierre Leaud.
   Dir and Screenplay: Bertrand Blier. Pro: Alaine Sarde. Line Pro: Claude Albouze. Ph: Pierre Lhomme. Pro Des: Willy Holt and Georges Glon. Ed: Claudine Merlin. M: Henryk Mikolaj Gorecki; numbers performed by Barry White. Costumes: Christian Gase. (Plateau A/Studio Images 2/Canal Plus–Artificial Eye.) Rel: 23 May 1997. 99 mins. Cert 18. France. 1996.

Mother Night

In 1961 Howard Campbell, an obscure American playwright, is transferred to prison in Israel, directly beneath a cell occupied by the monstrous war criminal Adolf Eichmann. Accused of broadcasting Nazi propaganda during the war, Campbell has little time – three weeks – to convince the authorities that he was, in fact, delivering top secret, coded messages to the West through his radio scripts... Based on the novel by Kurt Vonnegut Jr and directed by former actor Keith Gordon, *Mother Night* is a difficult work that has lost none of its subtle strength in this intelligent, superbly realised adaptation. Usually, literary endeavours this ideologically complex fail to find their voice in the cinema, but thanks to a stunning turn from Nick Nolte as the tragically misunderstood war hero and good support from Alan Arkin as his erstwhile New York neighbour, *Mother Night* exerts a powerful, uncompromising grip. [*Ewen Brownrigg*]

Nick Nolte (*Howard Campbell*), Sheryl Lee (*Helga Noth/Resi Noth*), Alan Arkin (*George Kraft*), John Goodman (*Major Frank Wirtanen*), Kirsten Dunst (*young Resi Noth*), Arye Gross (*Abraham Epstein*), Frankie R. Faison (*Black Fuhrer of Harlem*), David

Strathairn (*Bernard B. O'Hare*), Bernard Behrens (*Dr Lionel Jones*), Norman Rodway (*Werner Noth*), Anna Berger, Henry Gibson (*voice of Adolf Eichmann*), Anthony J. Robinow, Bill Corday, Bronwen Mantel, Brawley Nolte (*young Howard Campbell*), Kurt Vonnegut Jr.

Dir: Keith Gordon. Pro: Gordon and Robert B. Weide. Ex Pro: Ruth Vitale, Mark Ordesky and Linda Reisman. Screenplay: Weide. Ph: Tom Richmond. Pro Des: Francois Seguin. Ed: Jay Rabinowitz. M: Michael Convertino; Vivaldi, Beethoven; 'White Christmas' sung by Bing Crosby. Costumes: Renee April. Sound: Ann Scibelli. (New Line/Fine Line Features/ Whyaduck–Entertainment.) Rel: 14 March 1997. 114 mins. Cert 15. USA. 1996.

Mr Reliable

Glenfield, New South Wales; July, 1968. Having served nine months in prison for car theft, Wally Mellish abuses his parole to set up home 45 miles from the centre of Sydney. Putting his DIY skills to use, the ex-con quickly makes a ramshackle house habitable and christens the master bedroom with a local single mother, Beryl. Shortly afterwards he is paid a visit by two aggressive cops whom he chases off down the barrel of a shotgun. Then, due to a series of misunderstandings, Wally's predicament snowballs into a full-scale police operation. Crowds gather outside his house, refresh-ment stands spring up, barbecues are lit and the number of police increase by the hour. Described as 'Australia's first hostage drama', Wally's dilemma develops into a media event that could only have happened Down Under. Indeed, it is the local colour that shades this true story so effectively, bringing enormous charm and humour to an incredible story. Played for laughs, *Mr Reliable* takes enormous satisfaction in showing up the ineptitude of the police and exploiting the eccentricity of the Australian people. A delight.

Colin Friels (*Wally Mellish*), Jacqueline McKenzie (*Beryl Muddle*), Paul Sonkkila (*Norman Allan*), Frank Gallacher (*Don Fergusson*), Lisa Hensley (*Penny Wilberforce*), Aaron Blabey (*Bruce Morrison*), Barry Otto (*the premier*), Geoff Morrell, Neil Fitzpatrick, Ken Radley, Graham Rouse, Jonathon Hardy, Amanda Muggleton, Nathan Doekes, George Shevtsov, Russell Krouse.

Dir: Nadia Tass. Pro: Jim McElroy & Terry Hayes and Michael Hamlyn. Line

Underhand cops: Chazz Palminteri and Nick Nolte in Lee Tamahori's stylish Mulholland Falls *(from PolyGram)*

Pro: Dennis Kiely. Screenplay: Hayes and Don Catchlove. Ph: David Parker. Pro Des: Jon Dowding. Ed: Peter Carrodus. M: Philip Judd; numbers performed by The Lovin' Spoonful, Cream, The Muttonbirds, The Marbles, INXS, The Small Faces, Buffalo Springfield, Joe Cocker, and The Bee Gees. Costumes: Tess Schofield. (PolyGram/Australian Film Finance Corp/Hayes McElroy/Specific Films–PolyGram.) Rel: 22 November 1996. 113 mins. Cert 15. Australia. 1996.

Mulholland Falls

It is Mulholland Falls, a fictitious ravine in Los Angeles, where four real-life LA cops – the 'Hat Squad' – meter out their own variety of justice by hurling offending personnel off the eponymous cliff. Bestowed with special powers to break up organised crime in LA, Squad leader Max Hoover strides a thin line between right and wrong. When he encounters similar corruption in the US army, he is cautioned by his FBI namesake to let things be, but events have got too personal for Max to back off... Handsome, stylish and brimming with testosterone, *Mulholland Falls* recalls *Chinatown* with its lush photography, sumptuous production design,

labyrinthine plot twists and elegantly tailored protagonists. Nolte, heaving his excess bulk around like a permanent threat, is simply mesmerising, and is ably supported by a terrific cast, including Palminteri, Madsen, Malkovich, Bruce Dern and even Melanie Griffith, who brings a touching tenderness to her role as the cheated wife. All the more extraordinary is that *Mulholland Falls* is just the second film directed by the New Zealand native Lee Tamahori (*Once Were Warriors*).

Nick Nolte (*Max Hoover*), Melanie Griffith (*Katherine Hoover*), Chazz Palminteri (*Ellery Coolidge*), Michael Madsen (*Eddie Hall*), Chris Penn (*Arthur Relyea*), Treat Williams (*Col Nathan Fitzgerald*), Jennifer Connelly (*Allison Pond*), Daniel Baldwin (*FBI Special Agent McCafferty*), Andrew McCarthy (*Jimmy Fields*), John Malkovich (*General Thomas Timms*), William Petersen (*Jack*), Kyle Chandler, Ed Lauter, Larry Garrison, Chelsea Harrington, Ernie Lively, Richard Sylbert, Drew Pillsbury, Aaron Neville, Bruce Dern, Rob Lowe.

Dir: Lee Tamahori. Pro: Richard D. Zanuck and Lili Fini Zanuck. Ex Pro: Mario Iscovich. Screenplay: Pete Dexter, from a story by Dexter and Floyd Mutrux. Ph: Haskell Wexler. Pro Des: Richard Sylbert. Ed: Sally Menke. M: Dave Grusin; numbers performed by Aaron Neville, Ray Anthony, Dean Martin, etc. Costumes: Ellen Mirojnick. (MGM/Largo Entertain-ment–PolyGram.) Rel: 30 August 1996. 107 mins. Cert 18. USA. 1995.

Four's allowed: Michael Keaton, Michael Keaton, Michael Keaton and Michael Keaton in Harold Ramis's ingenious Multiplicity *(from Columbia)*

Multiplicity

Doug Kinney is running out of time. He's just been asked to put in more hours at the office, he's missed his daughter's 'campfire trail' graduation and he's got the water heater to fix. For relaxation he plays golf, but he's never had time to play. When a serene, unflappable professor offers him the chance to cope with his life by cloning him into two, the would-be renaissance man takes the bull by the horns. But even two Dougs cannot cope with the mounting workload, so a third is added to the roster (and then a fourth). The downside is that Doug and his clones have to carefully coordinate with each other. The last thing he/they want is for his/their wife to cotton on to the fact that her husband has multiplied. The upside is that each clone takes on a side of Doug's character to advantageous effect. Thus, Doug's aggressive nature is absorbed by clone 2, who does wonders at work. Then clone 3 takes on Doug's effeminate side and masters the domestic duties (while turning into a loving and compassionate companion to the missus). Doug himself decides to capitalise on all the selfish things he's never had time for – golf, sailing, sex – but discovers that he's missing out on the more meaningful things in life... Taking a conceit every bit as audacious as Harold Ramis's *Groundhog Day*, *Multiplicity* juggles the comic and psychological ramifications of its scenario with some skill. It's easy to see why Michael Keaton dropped out of *Kingpin* to play such a wonderful part (or parts) and does, indeed, rise magnificently to the occasion. However, Andie MacDowell – in an equally difficult role (all reaction shots) – is just as good. And the special effects are flawless.

Michael Keaton (*Doug Kinney x 4*), Andie MacDowell (*Laura Kinney*), Harris Yulin (*Dr Owen Leeds*), Richard Masur (*Del King*), Eugene Levy (*Vic*), Zack Duhame (*Zack Kinney*), Katie Schlossberg (*Jennifer Kinney*), Ann Cusack (*Noreen*), John DeLance (*Ted*), Brian Doyle-Murray (*Walt*), Julie Bowen (*Robin*), Judith Kahan, Obba Babatunde, Dawn Maxey, Kari Coleman, Steven Kampmann, James Piddock, Robin Duke, Glenn Shadix.

Dir: Harold Ramis. Pro: Ramis and Trevor Albert. Ex Pro: Lee R. Mayes. Screenplay: Chris Miller, Mary Hale, Lowell Ganz and Babaloo Mandel. Ph: Laszlo Kovacs. Pro Des: Jackson DeGovia. Ed: Pem Herring and Craig Herring. M: George Fenton; numbers performed by Grupo Niche, Jim Cummings, Montell Jordan, Stevie Ray Vaughan and Double Trouble, and The Specials. Costumes: Shay Cunliffe. Visual effects: Richard Edlund. (Columbia–Columbia.) Rel: 27 September 1996. 117 mins. Cert 12. USA. 1996.

Never Talk To Strangers

New York; now. 'If you never talk to strangers,' argues enigmatic Puerto Rican greaseball Tony Ramirez, 'you'll never make any friends.' Cutting through the resolve of criminal psychologist Sarah Taylor with his charm and smarm, Ramirez soon has the good doctor in his bed. Then the latter finds herself at the receiving end of threatening phone calls and dead flowers. Who could the aggressor be? A psychotic patient? Her neighbour? Her estranged father? A melodramatic whodunit pieced together from other movies (*Fatal Attraction*, *The Silence of the Lambs*), *Never Talk To Strangers* fails to struggles free from the coils of cliché and improbability, in spite of a reasonable performance from Rebecca De Mornay as the doctor plagued by Repressed Memory Syndrome and an over-zealous director. [*Charles Bacon*]

Rebecca De Mornay (*Dr Sarah Taylor*), Antonio Banderas (*Tony Ramirez*), Dennis Miller (*Cliff Raddison*), Len Cariou (*Henry Taylor*), Beau Starr (*Grogan*), Harry Dean Stanton (*Max Cheski*), Tim Kelleher, Eugene Lipinski, Philip Jarrett, Martha Burns.

Dir: Peter Hall. Pro: Andras Hamori and Jeffrey R. Neuman & Martin J. Wiley. Ex Pro: Rebecca De Mornay. Co-Pro: Jean Desormeaux and Ralph S. Dietrich. Screenplay: Lewis Green and Jordan Rush. Ph: Elemer Ragalyi. Pro Des: Linda Del Rosario and Richard Paris. Ed: Roberto Silvi. M: Pino Donaggio. Costumes: Terry Dresbach. (TriStar Pictures/Peter Hoffman/Alliance–Columbia TriStar.) Rel: 21 March 1997. 86 mins. Cert 18. Canada/USA. 1995.

Nick of Time

Union Station/Westin Bonaventure Hotel, Los Angeles; noon-13.30. Returning to LA with his six-year-old daughter after attending the funeral of his wife, timid accountant Gene Watson is stopped by two cops. Escorted into a van, he is informed that he has 90 minutes to assassinate a high-ranking governor or his daughter will be executed. The choice is his... Like *Speed*, this truly Hitchcockian thriller dispenses with background characterisation in favour of a one-line concept. Unlike *Speed*, the concept is shot through with improbabilities and there's no Sandra Bullock in sight. However, Johnny Depp conveys the anxiety of the accountant with accomplished unease, while John Badham (*Stakeout*, *Blue Thunder*) brings a documentary urgency to his pacing. As an added novelty, the film lasts just as long as Depp's traumatic countdown. Not the thriller of the year, but an engrossing Saturday night's entertainment. FYI: Scripted by Patrick Sheane Duncan, writer of *Mr Holland's Opus* and *Courage Under Fire*.

Johnny Depp (*Gene Watson*), Christopher Walken (*Mr Smith*), Charles S. Dutton

(*Huey*), Peter Strauss (*Brendan Grant*), Roma Maffia (*Ms Jones*), Gloria Reuben (*Krista Brooks*), Marsha Mason (*Governor Eleanor Grant*), Courtney Chase (*Lynn Watson*), Bill Smitrovich, G.D. Spradlin, Yul Vazquez, Edith Diaz, Lance August, Tom Bradley (*as himself*), Pamela Dunlap.

Dir and Pro: John Badham. Ex Pro: D.J. Caruso. Screenplay: Patrick Sheane Duncan. Ph: Roy H. Wagner. Pro Des: Philip Harrison. Ed: Frank Morriss. M: Arthur B. Rubinstein. Costumes: Mary E. Vogt. (Paramount–UIP.) Rel: 16 August 1996. 89 mins. Cert 15. USA. 1995.

Nico-Icon

This is a most eloquent and compelling testament to the drug-fuelled life of Christa Paffgen – aka Nico – the iconic German-born model, actress and singer. Using film clips, video, home movies, stills and interviews, the documentary brilliantly harnesses its material to convey Nico's tragic progression from a beautiful, statuesque 16-year-old *Vogue* model to the bizarre, burnt-out heroin-ravaged freak   96 who succumbed to a cerebral haemorrhage in 1988 at the age of 49. Peopled by an array of fantastic characters who touched Nico's life and survived to tell the tale, the film draws us like voyeurs into a heart of darkness. Fortunately, for fans like myself, the singer bequeathed an extensive discography featuring her

Everyday criminals: Luke Perry and Ashley Judd in John McNaughton's stark Normal Life *(from First Independent)*

deep, resonant and hauntingly beautiful vocals. [*Nigel Mulock*]

With Nico, Tina Aumont, Jackson Browne, Ari Boulogne, Edith Boulogne, John Cale, Nico Papatakis, Sterling Morrison, Paul Morrissey, Lutz Ulbrich, Viva, Helma Wolff, James Young, etc.

Dir and Screenplay: Susanne Ofteringer. Pro: Annette Pisacane and Thomas Mertens. Ph: Judith Kaufmann and Katarzyna Remin. Ed: Elfe Brandenburger and Guido Krajewski. Numbers performed by Nico, Nico & The Faction, The Velvet Underground, The Doors, and John Cale. (ZDF–ICA.) Rel: 25 October 1996. 72 mins. No Cert. Germany. 1995.

Normal Life

The Chicago suburbs; not long ago. Ostracised at work for his adherence to the rule book, rookie cop Chris Anderson ploughs his frustrations into a fling with a good-looking wildcat called Pam (soon to become Pam Anderson). Yet while Chris seeks a 'normal life' and a second-hand book shop, Pam is more into slashing her breasts and playing Russian roulette. Talk about the attraction of opposites... Returning to the social malaise and emotionally unstable characters of his first film (*Henry: Portrait of a Serial Killer*), director John McNaughton again displays his capacity for cutting his drama to the bone, dispensing with extraneous exposition, attention-grabbing camera moves and symphonic orchestra. As the buttoned-up, personality-impaired cop, Luke Perry is surprisingly convincing, while Ashley Judd gives her all as the pill-popping, hard-drinking and spliff-smoking psycho with a soft spot for Stephen Hawking. *Normal Life* is unlikely to appeal to the multiplex crowd, but its stark portrayal of the real world is refreshingly unsensational (and, apparently, inspired by a true story).

Luke Perry (*Chris Anderson*), Ashley Judd (*Pam Seaver Anderson*), Bruce Young (*Agent Parker*), Jim True (*Mike Anderson*), Dawn Maxey (*Eva*), Scott Cummins (*Officer Hank Chilton*), Kate Walsh (*Cindy Anderson*), Penelope Milford (*Adele Anderson*), Tom Towles (*Frank Anderson*), Michael Skewes, Edmund Wyson, Kevin Hurley.

Dir: John McNaughton. Pro: Richard Maynard. Ex Pro: John Saviano. Co-Pro: Steven A. Jones. Screenplay: Peg Haller and Bob Schneider. Ph: Jean De Segonzac. Pro Des: Rick Paul. Ed: Elena Maganini. M: Robert McNaughton and Ken Hale; numbers performed by Universal Honey, Urge Overkill, Pegboy, Positively Hard Core, D.O.P.E., Fix Your Wagon, etc. Costumes: Jacqueline Saint Anne. (Spelling Films/New Line–First Independent.) Rel: 7 March 1997. 102 mins. Cert 18. USA. 1995.

Nothing Personal

Belfast; 1975. Following the bombing of a Protestant pub, a street skirmish ends in pointless bloodshed, prompting the declaration of a temporary ceasefire between the Loyalist and Republican armies. But

For God and country: John Lynch faces up to the inevitable in Thaddeus O'Sullivan's uncompromising Nothing Personal *(from Film Four)*

for Loyalist 'foot soldiers' Kenny and Ginger, the war has become too much a part of their lives for them to stop their 'soldiering', and so they take personal steps to end the truce... As a man is doused in petrol and set alight, and another force-fed live bullets, one is prompted to wonder at the point of films like this. Yet with its unrelenting pessimism and brutality, *Nothing Personal* never purports to be entertainment. What it does do is show the terrible consequences of a war that nobody wants – a conflict in which homicidal psychopaths are given licence to carry out their monstrous crimes in the name of God and country. The message is loud and clear: Pray God it's over soon.

Ian Hart (*Ginger*), John Lynch (*Liam*), James Frain (*Kenny*), Michael Gambon (*Leonard*), Gary Lydon (*Eddie*), Ruaidhri Conroy (*Tommy*), Maria Doyle Kennedy (*Ann*), Jeni Courtney (*Kathleen*), Gerard McSorley (*Cecil*), Gareth O'Hare, Ciaran Fitzgerald, Anthony Brophy, B.J. Hogg, Jim Duran, Cathy White, Lynne James, Frankie McCafferty.

Dir: Thaddeus O'Sullivan. Pro: Jonathan Cavendish and Tracey Seaward. Ex Pro: James Mitchell. Screenplay: Daniel Mornin, from his book *All Our Fault*. Ph: Dick Pope. Pro Des: Mark Geraghty. Ed: Michael Parker. M: Philip Appleby; numbers performed by Vanity Fair, Barry White, The Stylistics, Bachman Turner Overdrive, Slade, Billy Preston, Jimmy Cliff, Mungo Jerry, Elton John, Free, Cathy White, and Billy Fury. Costumes: Consolata Boyle. (Channel Four Films/Irish Film Board/British Screen/Little Bird–Film Four.) Rel: 18 October 1996. 85 mins. Cert 15. UK/Ireland. 1995.

No Way Home

Staten Island, New York; now. Following his release from prison for the murder of a shopkeeper, Joey Larabito moves into the basement of his family home, now presided over by his volatile brother, the drug-dealing Tommy. This creates some friction between Joey and his sister-in-law, a stripper, until the fine line between Joey's criminal past and Tommy's current underground activities becomes increasingly blurred... Thanks to estimable performances from its three leads, *No Way Home* exerts a credible grip, further enhanced by Buddy Giovinazzo's atmospheric, detailed and leisurely direction. This is a character piece, and even though it explores familiar terrain it does so with compassion and authority. [*Ewen Brownrigg*]

Tim Roth (*Joey Larabito*), Deborah Kara Unger (*Lorrain Larabito*), James Russo (*Tommy Larabito*), Bernadette Penotti (*Ronnie*), Larry Romano (*Carter*), Mike Grief (*GasTank*), Brian Burke, James Starace, Saul Stein, Catherine Kellner, Huckleberry Fox, Carmine Giovinazzo, Joey Giovinazzo.

Dir and Screenplay: Buddy Giovinazzo. Pro: Lisa Bruce and Robert Nickson. Ex Pro: John Quested and Guy Collins. Co-Pro: Marcia Shulman. Ph: Claudia Raschke. Pro Des: Phyllis Cedar. Ed: Stan Warnow. M: Rick Giovinazzo, Robben Ford, Jeff Healey and Buddha Heads. Costumes: Anne Crabtree. (Goldcrest/Orenda Films/Back Alley Prods–Blue Dolphin.) Rel: 23 May 1997. 93 mins. Cert 18. USA. 1996.

The Nutty Professor

Severely obese, Professor Sherman Klump discovers a miraculous fat gene formula that reduces him to half his weight in seconds. The downside is that Klump's new, slim persona – adopting the brash monicker of Buddy Love – can only survive for a matter of hours. Worse, Buddy is the antithesis of the gentle and loveable professor and, in the tradition of Dr Jekyll and Mr Hyde, is determined to seize total control of his maker... Eddie Murphy's biggest hit for eight years, *The Nutty Professor* is a high-concept remake of Jerry Lewis's 1963 'masterpiece' and is executive produced by Lewis himself. Certainly, Murphy has never demonstrated his range to greater

Chocolate bars and barbells: Eddie Murphy (right – believe it or not) builds up fat to burn in Tom Shadyac's moral The Nutty Professor *(from UIP)*

effect (he also plays Sherman's mother, brother and both grand-parents), and the special effects are truly astounding. Yet the humour is so over the top, and the senti-mentality so thickly spread, that this moral farce fails to achieve the comedic heights of, say, *Tootsie,* or the dark brilliance of *Death Becomes Her.* From the director of *Ace Ventura: Pet Detective* (which says a lot).

Eddie Murphy (*Sherman Klump/Buddy Love/Lance Perkins/Papa Klump/Mama Klump/Grandma Klump/Ernie Klump*), Jada Pinkett (*Carla Purty*), James Coburn (*Harlan Hartley*), Larry Miller (*Dean Richmond*), Dave Chappelle (*Reggie Warrington*), John Ales (*Jason*), Patricia Wilson, Jamal Mixon, Alexia Robinson, Lisa Boyle, Athena Massey.
   Dir: Tom Shadyac. Pro: Brian Grazer and Russell Simmons. Ex Pro: Jerry Lewis, Karen Kehela and Mark Lipsky. Screenplay: Shadyac, David Sheffield, Barry W. Blaustein and Steve Oedekerk, based on the motion picture written by Lewis and Bill Richmond. Ph: Julio Macat.

Pro Des: William Elliott. Ed: Don Zimmerman. M: David Newman; numbers performed by The Village People, James Brown, Montell Jordan, Valerie George, Teddy Pendergrass, The Pointer Sisters, Back Street Boys, Danielle LoPresti, and

Spot the boss: Pongo and a hangdog Jeff Daniels pine for romance in Stephen Herek's entertaining 101 Dalmatians *(from Buena Vista)*

Clarence Carter. Costumes: Ha Nguyen. Visual effects: Jon Farhat. Make-up effects: Rick Baker. (Imagine Entertainment/Universal–UIP.) Rel: 4 October 1996. 95 mins. Cert 12. USA. 1996.

101 Dalmatians

London, England; the present. Perdy, a comely and intelligent Dalmatian, cares for Anita, a talented dress designer in the employ of the

eccentric couture tycoon Cruella DeVil. Pongo, a dashing and equally intelligent Dalmatian, looks after Roger, a designer of computer games. Then, one fateful day, Pongo and Perdy spot each other in Leicester Square and arrange for Roger and Anita to go on heat. Thus united, the love-struck Dalmatians produce a litter of adorable puppies that catches the eye of the zoologically insensitive Cruella... Broadly comic-strip in tone, this updated version of Dodie Smith's classic children's novel is hugely entertaining, aided by some ingenious slapstick and a high cute factor. Of course, one may be prompted to ask, 'Why bother to do it in the first place?', but it's hard to imagine a more accomplished live-action version of Disney's immortal 1961 cartoon. Yet while the human cast is singularly outstanding, it is the team of animal trainers who are the real stars – with a little help from Industrial Light & Magic and Jim Henson's Creature Shop. FYI: Joan Collins was the original choice for the role of Cruella.

Glenn Close (*Cruella DeVil*), Jeff Daniels (*Roger*), Joely Richardson (*Anita*), Joan Plowright (*Nanny*), Hugh Laurie (*Jasper*), Mark Williams (*Horace*), John Shrapnel (*Skinner*), Tim McInnerny (*Alonzo*), Zohren Weiss (*Herbert*), Hugh Fraser, Mark Haddigan, Michael Percival, Neville Phillips, John Benfield.
    Dir: Stephen Herek. Pro: John Hughes and Ricardo Mestres. Ex Pro: Edward S. Feldman. Assoc Pro: Rebekah Rudd. Screenplay: Hughes. Ph: Adrian Biddle. Pro Des: Assheton Gorton. Ed: Trudy Ship. M: Michael Kamen; numbers performed by Dr John, and Nat King Cole. Costumes: Anthony Powell and Rosemary Burrows. Special effects: Industrial Light & Magic. Animatronics: Jim Henson's Creature Shop. (Walt Disney Pictures/Great Oaks–Buena Vista.) Rel: 13 December 1996. 103 mins. Cert U. USA. 1996.

Original Gangstas

Gary, Indiana – the murder capital of the US; now. Back in the old days John Bookman and Jake Trevor started up a gang called The Rebels to help protect the hood. Now Bookman is a famous football coach in LA and Trevor a veteran of the boxing world. Meanwhile, The Rebels have continued to thrive but have turned to guns, drugs and

intimidation to rule the streets with terror. As the mother of one victim observes, 'They're more scared of living than of dying.' When they shoot Bookman's father down in cold blood, the football hero returns to his old stompin' ground to sort out the men from the boyz... Reuniting the icons of blaxploitation cinema of the seventies, producer and star Fred Williamson (*Hammer*, *Black Caesar*) has hit on a great idea to expand the boundaries of contemporary black cinema, pay homage to the old and give himself and his cronies a job. Crossing the formula of the former movies with more recent product like *Menace II Society*, *Original Gangstas* has fun mixing up a number of black motifs, from Paul Winfield's gospel choir to the hard-hitting rap soundtrack and even to a guest appearance from The Chi-Lites. However, the film's gratuitous violence and profane language does little to reform the genre. Previously known as *Hot City*.

Fred Williamson (*John Bookman*), Jim Brown (*Jake Trevor*), Pam Grier (*Laurie Thompson*), Paul Winfield (*Reverend Dorsey*), Isabel Sanford (*Gracie Bookman*), Ron O'Neal (*Bubba*), Robert Forster (*Detective Statten*), Charles Napier (*Mayor Ritter*), Wings Hauser (*Michael Casey*), Frank Pesce (*Detective Waits*), Richard Roundtree (*Slick*), Christopher B. Duncan (*Spyro*), Tim Rhoze (*Blood*), Eddie 'Bo' Smith (*Damian*), Godfrey C. Danchimah (*Marcus*), Oscar Brown Jr (*Melvin Bookman*), Dru Down (*Kayo*), Shyheim Franklin (*Dink*), Timothy Lewis (*Kenny Thompson*), Seraiah Carol, Dawn Stern, Lisa Marie Bright, Luniz, The Chi-Lites.
    Dir: Larry Cohen. Pro: Fred Williamson. Line Pro: Linda Williamson. Screenplay: Aubrey Rattan. Ph: Carlos Gonzalez. Pro Des: Elayne Barbara Ceder. Ed: David Kern and Peter B. Ellis. M: Vladimir Horunzhy; numbers performed by 3X Krazy, Ice-T, Scarface, Luniz, Ideal & The Chi-Lites, The Dramatics, etc. Costumes: Lisa Moffie. (Orion Pictures/Po' Boy Prods–First Independent.) Rel: 23 August 1996. 99 mins. Cert 18. USA. 1996.

La Passione

So many critic friends warned me against seeing this vanity project written and produced by the singer Chris Rea, that I took the unusual stance that life is too short – even to sit through 91 minutes of celluloid. The story of a Northern English lad who resists the temptation to follow

in his father's ice cream business in order to pursue his obsession with Ferraris, the film was described as 'strained and vacuous' by *The Sunday Times* and 'astonishingly awful' by *What's On In London*, while *The Mirror* opined 'this is possibly the most pretentious, tedious thing it has ever been my misfortune to sit through.' Meanwhile, *The Telegraph* suggested readers look up 'excrement' in *Roget's Thesaurus* for more detailed comment, whereas *The Independent on Sunday* described it as 'so awesomely ill-accomplished you could rent it out to Third World dictators as an instrument of torture'.

Paul Shane (*Papa Maldini*), Shirley Bassey (*herself*), Jan Ravens (*Mama Maldini*), Thomas Orange (*young Jo Maldini*), Carmen Silvera (*Grandmother*), Sean Gallagher (*Jo Maldini*), Keith Barron (*Roy*), Anna Pernicci (*Francesca*), Belinda Stewart-Wilson, Ruth Harford, Gavin Abbott, Freddie Davies, Gordon Milne, Stanley Lebor, Jack Smethurst, Stewart Harwood.
    Dir: John B. Hobbs. Pro, Screenplay and M: Chris Rea. Ex Pro: Jim Beach and Ray Still. Line Pro: Sarah-Jane Wright. Ph: Roger Bonnici. Pro Des: Garry Freeman. Ed: Paul Endacott. Costumes: Venetia Ercolani. (Warner Vision/Fugitive–Warner.) Rel: 16 May 1997. 91 mins. Cert 15. UK. 1996.

The People vs. Larry Flynt

Larry Flynt, the product of a redneck Kentucky upbringing, could not understand why it was legal to photograph war, murder and genocide, yet illegal to photograph nudity and sex, something people really wanted to see. The owner of a string of Ohio strip clubs and publisher of the obscene magazine *Hustler*, Flynt fought for the right for free expression, becoming a champion of the First Amendment... Taking the madness out of *One Flew Over the Cuckoo's Nest* and plunging it into the opulence of *Amadeus* and *Valmont*, Milos Forman (who took over megaphone duty from Oliver Stone) brings a fine satirical polish to the bizarre facts of Flynt's life. Woody Harrelson is a revelation as the dogged, visionary potentate of porn, backed up by committed performances from a first-rate cast. P.S. Larry Flynt himself plays Judge Morrissey, the man who sentences Larry Flynt to 25 years in prison.

Woody Harrelson (*Larry Flynt*), Courtney Love (*Althea Leasure*), Edward Norton (*Alan Isaacman*), Brett Harrelson (*Jimmy Flynt*), Donna Hanover (*Ruth Carter Stapleton*), James Cromwell (*Charles Keating*), James Carville (*Simon Leis*), Richard Paul (*Jerry Falwell*), Larry Flynt (*Judge Morrissey*), Crispin Glover, Vincent Schiavelli, Miles Chapin, Burt Neuborne, Jan Triska, Robert Davis, John Ryan, Rainbeau Mars, Nancy Lea Owen, John Fergus Ryan, Oliver Reed, Meresa T. Ferguson, Andrena Fisher, Janie Paris, Miss Ruby Wilson, D'Army Bailey, Jim Grimshaw.

Dir: Milos Forman. Pro: Oliver Stone, Janet Yang and Michael Hausman. Screenplay: Scott Alexander and Larry Karaszewski. Ph: Philippe Rousselot. Pro Des: Patrizia Von Brandenstein. Ed: Christopher Tellefsen. M: Thomas Newman; Richard Wagner, Chopin, Dvorak; numbers performed by Faron Young, Porter Wagoner, Average White Band, KC & The Sunshine Band, Gary Wright, etc. Costumes: Theodor Pistek and Arianne Phillips. (Columbia Pictures/ Phoenix Pictures/Ixtlan Prods–Columbia TriStar.) Rel: 11 April 1997. 130 mins. Cert 18. USA. 1996.

The Perez Family

Following twenty years in prison under the brutal regime of Castro's police state, sugar plantation owner Juan Raul Perez is granted political asylum to join his wife and daughter in Miami. For twenty years he has dreamed of his reunion with Carmela, but a lot of water has flown under the bridge since then. Then, as Carmela waits with baited breath for the return of her amour, Cupid starts to rearrange the rules... Having made her mark with the vivid, touching *Salaam Bombay!* and *Mississippi Masala*, the Indian filmmaker Mira Nair tackles an alternate ethnic scenario with this, her third film. Obviously intended as an earthy, romantic and magical tale of misplaced love, *The Perez Family* lumbers on to the screen as a painfully miscalculated, leaden and embarrassing curry. Besides the culturally insensitive casting (the Brooklyn-born Marisa Tomei, English Alfred Molina and Irish-American Anjelica Huston), the film is shoddily made and constantly rings untrue. The naturally steely Ms Huston has never been more out of her depth than as the coyly amorous Carmela, while Molina again proves

Courtney Love and Woody Harrelson share one of those Playboy moments in Milos Forman's The People vs. Larry Flynt *(from Columbia TriStar)*

that he is the most regularly miscast actor in the business.

Marisa Tomei (*Dottie*), Alfred Molina (*Juan Raul Perez*), Chazz Palminteri (*Officer Pirelli*), Anjelica Huston (*Carmela Perez*), Trini Alvarado (*Teresa Perez*), Celia Cruz (*Luz Paz*), Lazaro Perez (*Armando Perez*), Diego Wallraff (*Angel Diaz*), Bill Sage (*Steve*), Angela Lanza (*Flavia*), Jose Felipe Padron, Ranjit Chowdhry, Ellen Cleghorne, Billy Hopkins, Sarita Choudhury, Jody Wilson, Vincent Gallo, Mira Nair (*woman buying flowers*), Mel Gorham.

Dir: Mira Nair. Pro: Michael Nozik and Lydia Dean Pilcher. Ex Pro: Julia Chasman and Robin Swicord. Screenplay: Swicord, based on the novel by Christine Bell. Ph: Stuart Dryburgh. Pro Des: Mark Friedberg. Ed: Robert Estrin. M: Zbigniew Preisner and Arturo Sandoval. Music Supervisor: Jellybean Benitez. Costumes: Eduardo Castro. Sound: Skip Lievsay. (The Samuel Goldwyn Company–Film Four.) Rel: 23 August 1996. 113 mins. Cert 15. USA. 1995.

The Phantom

A hunk in a purple leotard finds himself up against phenomenal avarice and wickedness when a corrupt New York businessman attempts a bit of the old world domination. The latter, the sharply dressed Xander Drax, just needs three mystical skulls in order to acquire a power one thousand times greater than any energy source known to man... What the cinema needs is another superhero? A notion of fun was obviously intended, but the non-stop action, ludicrous plot and breathtaking lapses in logic (not to mention the occasional boom shot) quickly become terribly tiresome. The best one can say for the film is that the colourful cast tries hard, with Treat Williams and Catherine Zeta Jones scoring the highest points. Based on the comic strip by Lee Falk, *The Phantom* is produced by Robert

Brain charisma: John Travolta charms his way into academic circles in Jon Turteltaub's irresistible Phenomenon *(from Buena Vista)*

Evans (*The Godfather*, *Chinatown*) and Alan Ladd Jr (*Braveheart*, *Chariots of Fire*), executive produced by Joe Dante (director of *Gremlins*) and written by Jeffrey Boam (*Lethal Weapons 2 & 3*). So what happened? Filmed in Los Angeles, Queensland and Thailand.

Billy Zane (*Kit Walker/The Phantom aka The Ghost Who Walks*), Treat Williams (*Xander*

Photographic evidence: Youki Kudoh in Kayo Hatta's Picture Bride *(from Artificial Eye)*

Drax), Kristy Swanson (*Diana Palmer*), Catherine Zeta Jones (*Sala*), James Remar (*Quill*), Patrick McGoohan (*father of The Phantom*), Cary-Hiroyuki Tagawa (*Kabai Sengh*), Bill Smitrovich (*Uncle Dave*), Casey Siemaszko (*Morgan*), Samantha Eggar (*Lilly Palmer*), Jon Tenney (*Jimmy Wells*), David Proval, Joseph Ragno, Robert Coleby, Al Ruscio, Leon Russom, John Capodice, Bob Kane.

Dir: Simon Wincer. Pro: Robert Evans and Alan Ladd Jr. Ex Pro: Richard Vane, Joe Dante, Graham Burke, Greg Coote, Peter Sjoquist and Bruce Sherlock. Co-Pro and Screenplay: Jeffrey Boam. Assoc Pro: Bonnie Abaunza. Ph: David Burr. Pro Des: Paul Peters. Ed: O. Nicholas Brown. M: David Newman. Costumes: Marlene Stewart. Second unit director: Vic Armstrong. Special creature props design/creation: Chris Walas Inc. Visual effects supervisor: Wally Schaab. The Phantom's 'costume elements': Jim Henson's Creature Shop. (Paramount/The Ladd Company/Village Roadshow–UIP.) Rel: 21 February 1997. 100 mins. Cert 12. USA/Australia. 1996.

Phenomenon

George Malley, a simple car mechanic from a backwater town in Northern California, is having trouble with his vegetable patch, learning Spanish and attracting the attention of Lace Pennamin, a beautiful but stand-offish single mom. Then, on his 37th birthday, George sees a light in the night sky that knocks him off his feet. Shortly afterwards his Spanish dramatically improves, he develops a master's knack for chess and his grasp of the complexities of photosynthesis has to be heard to be believed. Then, when he predicts a minor earthquake and starts moving objects with his mind, his friends begin to fear and mistrust him. Only Lace Pennamin, it seems, is not impressed by the crank who 'thinks he saw a UFO'... As a piece of sheer 'feel-good' entertainment, *Phenomenon* is pretty hard to resist. John Travolta has never been more engaging than as the small-town charmer bestowed with extra-ordinary powers, and is well matched by a concept that nudges the heart as it stirs the imagination. When George tries to explain that 'everything is on its way to somewhere', you want to listen, not giggle. Wonderful support, too, from Kyra Sedgwick and Forest Whitaker.

John Travolta (*George Malley*), Kyra Sedgwick (*Lace Pennamin*), Forest Whitaker (*Nate Pope*), Robert Duvall (*Doc*), Jeffrey DeMunn (*Professor Ringold*), David Gallagher (*Al Pennamin*), Ashley Buccille (*Glory Pennamin*), Tony Genaro (*Tito*), Bruce Young (*Jack Hatch*), Michael Milhoan (*Jimmy*), Sean O'Bryan, Vyto Ruginis, Mark Valim, Troy Evans, Ellen Geer, James Keane, Susan Merson, James Cotton, Brent Spiner, Anni Long, Daniel Zacapa.

Dir: Jon Turteltaub. Pro: Barbara Boyle and Michael Taylor. Ex Pro: Charles Newirth and Jonathan Krane. Screenplay: Gerald DiPego. Ph: Phedon Papamichael. Pro Des: Garreth Stover. Ed: Bruce Green. M: Thomas Newman; numbers performed by Diana Ross & The Supremes, The Iguanas, The Impressions, Eric Clapton, Bryan Ferry, Aaron Neville and Robbie Robertson, Dorothy Moore, Taj Mahal, Peter Gabriel, J.J. Cale, and Marvin Gaye. Costumes: Betsy Cox. (Touchstone Pictures–Buena Vista.) Rel: 30 August 1996. 123 mins. Cert PG. USA. 1996.

Picture Bride

Drawing on historical reality, Kayo Hatta's film, set in 1918, epitomises the problems faced by many brides from the Far East who, arranging a marriage by exchange of photo-graphs, sought both a husband and greater prosperity in Hawaii. Here an 18-year-old Japanese orphan (Youki Kudoh) confronts a husband (Akira Takayama) much older than his photograph. This is clearly a committed project and well acted, too. Nevertheless, both the style and tone of this romanticised drama suggest a TV mini-series truncated for the cinema. Never achieving the emotional highs of a film like *The Joy Luck Club*, it offers no big-screen appeal to draw in an audience despite its sincerity. [*Mansel Stimpson*]

Youki Kudoh (*Riyo Nakamura*), Akira Takayama (*Matsuji Kimura*), Tamlyn Tomita (*Kana*), Cary-Hiroyuki Tagawa (*Kanzaki*), Toshiro Mifune (*Benshi*), Yoko Sugi (*Aunt Sode*), Peter Clark, Nobu McCarthy (*narrator*).

Dir: Kayo Hatta. Pro: Lisa Onodera. Ex Pro: Diana Mei Lin Mark. Screenplay: Kayo Hatta and Mari Hatta. Ph: Claudio Rocha. Pro Des: Paul Guncheon. Ed: Lynzee Klingman and Mallory Gottlieb. M: Mark Adler. Costumes: Ada Akaji. Sound: Jonathan Miller. (Thousand Cranes Filmworks/Miramax/Cecile Co–Artificial Eye.) Rel: 17 January 1997. 95 mins. Cert 12. USA. 1994.

Reading his writes: Ewan McGregor has a quick word with Vivian Wu in Peter Greenaway's visually daring The Pillow Book *(from Film Four)*

The Pillow Book

Kyoto, Japan; Hong Kong; 1997-99. A thousand years ago, Sei Shonagon, a female courtier of the Heian Dynasty, wrote a collection of reminiscences and lists that became known as the pillow book. Sharing her birthday with the great diarist, Nagiko Kiohara embarks on her own pillow book, but desires it to be written on her skin. In Japan, writing is as much an ornamental skill as it is a written one, where literature and art are united in the elegance of calligraphy. To fuse this skill with the pleasures of the flesh becomes the ultimate quest for Nagiko, who resorts to composing thirteen books on the naked bodies of as many men. For her it becomes the perfect union of text and sex, of art and literature; a metaphor for the meeting of worlds,

of East and West and image and the written word, like cinema itself... To appreciate the films of Peter Greenaway one really has to be in the right mood. His latest cinematic conundrum returns to the multi-visual tricks of *Prospero's Books* and further stretches the concept of what film can do and be. Yet for all its intellectual wile and pictorial splendour, the film cannot sustain itself either as an emotional or an arresting experience. Ultimately, it is an empty exercise, albeit a gift to scholars of medieval Japanese literature with a penchant for male nudity.

Vivian Wu (*Nagiko Kiohara*), Ken Ogata (*Nagiko's father*), Ewan McGregor (*Jerome*), Yoshi Oida (*the publisher*), Hideko Yoshida (*Nagiko's aunt and the maid*), Judy Ongg (*Nagiko's mother*), Ken Mitsuishi (*Nagiko's husband*), Barbara Lott (*Jerome's mother*), Yutaka Honda, Wichert Dromkert, Martin Tukker, Tom Kane, Ronald Guttman.
  Dir and Screenplay: Peter Greenaway. Pro: Kees Kasander. Ex Pro: Terry Glinwood, Jean Louis Piel and Denis

Wigman. Ph: Sacha Vierny. Pro Des (and Japanese costumes): Emi Wada. Ed: Greenaway and Chris Wyatt. M: 'Blonde,' performed by Guesch Patti. Costumes: Dien van Straalen, Koji Tatsuno, Martin Margiela and Paul Smith. Sound: Garth Marshall and Nigel Heath. Calligraphy: Brody Neuenschwander and Yukki Yaura. Lighting effects: Reinier van Brummelen. (Woodline Films/Alpha Films/Channel Four/Canal Plus/DeLux Prods–Film Four.) Rel: 8 November 1996. 126 mins. Cert 18. Netherlands/France/UK. 1995.

The Portrait of a Lady

A woman of independent spirit, if not means, Isabel Archer is an expatriate New Yorker living in England with her aunt. There, she finds herself courted left, right and centre, but resolves to experience more of the world before settling down to marriage. Having inherited a vast fortune from her uncle, Isabel visits Florence with her aunt, where she meets the intellectually powerful dilettante Gilbert Osmond. Won over by the latter's psychological

Still life: Nicole Kidman and John Malkovich frozen in transformation, in Jane Campion's lifeless, stilted The Portrait of a Lady *(from PolyGram)*

Otherwise, this Gothic opera of nuance left this critic cold (and yawning).

Nicole Kidman (*Isabel Archer*), John Malkovich (*Gilbert Osmond*), Barbara Hershey (*Madame Serena Merle*), Mary-Louise Parker (*Henrietta Stackpole*), Martin Donovan (*Ralph Touchett*), Shelley Winters (*Mrs Touchett*), Richard E. Grant (*Lord Warburton*), Shelley Duvall (*Countess Gemini*), Christian Bale (*Edward Rosier*), Viggo Mortensen (*Caspar Goodwood*), Valentina Cervi (*Pansy Osmond*), John Gielgud (*Mr Touchett*), Roger Ashton-Griffiths, Catherine Zago, Pat Roach.

Dir: Jane Campion. Pro: Monty Montgomery and Steve Golin. Co-Pro: Ann Wingate. Screenplay: Laura Jones. Ph: Stuart Dry burgh. Pro Des and Costumes: Janet Patterson. Ed: Veronika Jenet. M: Wojciech Kilar; Schubert, Johann Strauss II. Sound: Lee Smith. (Propaganda Films/PolyGram–PolyGram.) Rel: 28 February 1997. 144 mins. Cert 12. UK/USA. 1996.

superiority, she succumbs to his offer of marriage, unaware that he is merely after her inheritance... Regardless of whether or not it is faithful to the spirit of Henry James's 1881 masterpiece (which is a moot point), the film's primary allegiance must be to the cinema. Yet as such it is distant, tricksy and heavy-handed. It is also sexless, humourless and colourless, the natural hues of the English and Italian backdrops quite literally drained from the picture. On the plus side, the production design and score are magnificent. And so are the performances of Malkovich and Hershey, which recall the civilised brutality of the protagonists of *Dangerous Liaisons* (which, as it happens, also starred Malkovich).

Talcum tryst: Missy Crider and Sean Patrick Flanery in Victor Salva's heartfelt Powder *(from Buena Vista)*

Powder

Rural Texas; today. If someone had the power to express themselves without sarcasm, lies, deception or exaggeration, to feel the pain of others and read their fears, would they be embraced as an angel or cast out as a devil? Jeremy Reed, nicknamed Powder because of his albinic condition, becomes invested with supernatural powers due to a freak accident on the day of his birth. Disowned by his father and brought up by his grandparents in the seclusion of their remote farmhouse, Powder knows that, one day, he will have to face up to the outside world... An intriguing blend of *Rain Man*, *Mask* and *Carrie*, *Powder* is a heartfelt, passionate exploration of our loss of humanity as viewed from the perspective of an extraordinary soul. Enhanced by the presence of such old pros as Mary Steenburgen, Lance Henriksen and Jeff Goldblum, the film is never less than engaging. Unfortunately, the market for such oddball, well-meaning films is claustrophobically limited, but for those immune to immoderate glucose and looking for something a little different, *Powder* has much to offer. To be honest, I couldn't stop thinking about it.

Mary Steenburgen (*Jessie Caldwell*), Sean Patrick Flanery (*Jeremy 'Powder' Reed*), Lance Henriksen (*Sheriff Barnum*), Jeff Goldblum (*Donald Ripley*), Brandon Smith

(*Harley Duncan*), Bradford Tatum (*John Box*), Susan Tyrrell (*Maxine*), Missy Crider (*Lindsey Kelloway*), Esteban Louis Powell (*Stipler*), Tom Tarantini (*Steven Barnum*), Ray Wise, Reed Frerichs, Chad Cox, Joe Marchman, Philip Maurice Hayes, Woody Watson, Alex Allen Morris.

Dir and Screenplay: Victor Salva. Pro: Roger Birnbaum and Daniel Grodnik. Ex Pro: Riley Kathryn Ellis and Robert Snukal. Ph: Jerzy Zielinski. Pro Des: Waldemar Kalinowski. Ed: Dennis M. Hill. M: Jerry Goldsmith. Costumes: Betsy Cox. (Hollywood Pictures/Caravan Pictures–Buena Vista.) Rel: 14 February 1997. 112 mins. Cert 12. USA. 1995.

The Preacher's Wife

The otherwise competent helmer Penny Marshall (*Big*, *Awakenings*, *A League Of Their Own*) must have taken a holiday during the making of this banal Christmas comedy which had all the necessaries for a solid feel-good family film. Denzel Washington stars as an all-too-human angel who falls for the wife (Whitney Houston) of the inner-city preacher he is sent to help on earth. Despite a wholesome storyline (evil comes in the form of property developer Gregory Hines), a tasteful hint of ethereal romance and the prudent use of Whitney's thrilling vocals, *The Preacher's Wife* remains a flat, simple-minded morality tale with no vigour, soul or knowingness. Save for Washington's crisp grey suits, it leaves no impact whatsoever upon the mind, ears or soul. P.S. The film's original form, the 1947 comedy *The Bishop's Wife* (which starred an angelic Cary Grant alongside David Niven and Loretta Young), was a true godsend. [*Karen Krizanovich*]

Denzel Washington (*Dudley*), Whitney Houston (*Julia Biggs*), Courtney B. Vance (*Rev. Henry Biggs*), Gregory Hines (*Joe Hamilton*), Jenifer Lewis (*Marguerite Coleman*), Loretta Devine (*Beverly*), Justin Pierre Edmund (*Jeremiah Biggs*), Lionel Richie (*Britsloe*), Paul Bates, Lex Monson, Willie James Stiggers Jr, Marcella Lowery, Cissy Houston, Taral Hicks, Toukie Smith.

Dir: Penny Marshall. Pro: Samuel Goldwyn Jr. Ex Pro: Robert Greenhut and Elliot Abbott. Co-Pro: Debra Martin Chase, Amy Lemisch and Timothy M. Bourne. Screenplay: Nat Mauldin and Allan Scott. Ph: Miroslav Ondricek. Pro Des: Bill Groom. Ed: Stephen A. Rotter and George Bowers. M: Hans Zimmer; numbers performed by Whitney Houston and The Georgia Mass Choir, Loretta Devine, and

Reaching the parts... The very public Howard Stern in Betty Thomas's rib-aching Private Parts *(from Entertainment)*

Soul Tempo. Gospel Pro: Mervyn Warren and Whitney Houston. Costumes: Cynthia Flynt. (Touchstone Pictures/Samuel Goldwyn/Parkway Prods/Mundy Lane–Buena Vista.) Rel: 17 January 1997. 124 mins. Cert U. USA. 1996.

Private Parts

Howard Stern's private parts – as we are constantly informed – are not his biggest asset. His mouth, however, is another matter. Best described as Jeff Goldblum dressed up like Alice Cooper and then dubbed by Alan Alda, Stern happily plays on his ugliness and genital shortcomings in this hilarious film version of his 1993 memoirs. Playing himself alongside a number of his real-life colleagues, the shock jock has created a new genre of cinema: the cine-autobiography. A legend in the States for his outrageous, controversial antics on the radio, Stern eases effortlessly into the role of movie star, like a tall, scatological version of Woody Allen. Yet he is proud of his neuroses and his blatant honesty is deeply appealing. Scattering the screen with half-naked and amply bosomed women, he now completes the self-centred, hormonal paradise that he only half-realised on the airwaves.

Yet the 'offensive, obnoxious' Howard Stern that we have come to admire is only the persona he acts out for the microphone. Beneath this is a sweet, loving father and adoring husband whose first film is as much a love letter to his wife as it is a V-sign to the Establishment. FYI: Apparently, Stern would not commit to the film until at least 30 scripts had been drafted. Aka *Howard Stern's Private Parts*.

Howard Stern (*himself*), Robin Quivers (*herself*), Mary McCormack (*Alison Stern*), Fred Norris (*himself*), Paul Giamatti (*Kenny*), Gary Dell'Abate (*himself*), Jackie Martling (*himself*), Carol Alt (*Gloria*), Richard Portnow (*Ben Stern*), Kelly Bishop (*Ray Stern*), Reni Santoni (*Vin Vallesecca*), Melanie Good (*Brittany Murphy*), Matthew Friedman (*16-year-old Howard Stern*), Henry Goodman, Lee Wilkof, Jonathan Hadary, Paul Hecht, Allison Janney, Michael Murphy, Theresa Lynn (*woman having orgasm on loudspeaker*), Amber Smith, Althea Cassidy, Richard B. Shull, Jenna Jameson, Mia Farrow (*herself*).

Dir: Betty Thomas. Pro: Ivan Reitman. Ex Pro: Daniel Goldberg, Joe Medjuck and Keith Samples. Co-Pro: Celia Costas. Screenplay: Len Blum and Michael Kalesniko. Ph: Walt Lloyd. Pro Des: Charles Rosen. Ed: Peter Teschner. M: Van Dyke Parks; numbers performed by Nat King Cole, The Temptations, Doris Day, Average White Band, Deep Purple, ZZ Top, Cheap Trick, The Pretenders, The Ramones, Soft Cell, Devo, Ted Nugent, Van Halen, The Cars, David Bowie, Marilyn Mason, etc. Costumes: Joseph G.

Branson ransom: Mel Gibson as the Richard Bransonesque entrepreneur Tom Mullen – with Delroy Lindo – in Ron Howard's taut Ransom *(from Buena Vista)*

Aulisi. (Paramount/Rysher Entertainment–Entertainment.) Rel: 20 June 1997. 109 mins. Cert 18. USA. 1997.

The Promise - Das Versprechen

This is the story of how the Berlin Wall separates two lovers, only one of whom escapes to the West. By following their situation from 1961 to 1989, Margarethe von Trotta, director and co-writer, seeks to comment on history through a personal story with emotional appeal. But, despite a competent cast headed by Meret Becker, the effect is to trivialise a human tragedy by turning it into effective soap opera. Some may be content with that, even if the narrative sometimes feels disjointed, but it's difficult not to see it as a sad decline from the intellectual vigour of von Trotta's masterly *Rosa Luxemburg*. [*Mansel Stimpson*]

Meret Becker (*Sophie, as a young woman*), Corinna Harfouch (*Sophie*), Anian Zollner (*Konrad, as a young man*), August Zirner (*Konrad*), Jean-Yves Gaultier (*Gerard*), Eva Mattes (*Barbara*), Susanne Uge, Hans Kremer, Pierre Besson, Tina Engel, Otto Sander (*Professor Lorenz*), Hark Bohm, Dieter Mann.

Dir: Margarethe von Trotta. Pro: Eberhard Junkersdorf. Screenplay: von Trotta, Peter Schneider and Felice Laudadio, based on an idea by Francesco Laudadio. Ph: Franz Rath. Pro Des: Martin Dostal. Ed: Suzanne Baron. M: Juergen Knieper. Costumes: Petra Kray and Yoshio Yabara. (Bioskop-Film/Odessa Films–Artificial Eye.) Rel: 6 September 1996. 115 mins. Cert 15. Germany/France/Switzerland. 1995.

The Proprietor - La Proprietaire

New York/Paris/London/Cannes; 1943-1996. Needing to reclaim her roots, an ageing French-Jewish novelist living in New York returns to Paris to confront the chequered past she left three decades before... Directed by Ismail Merchant from his own screenplay, this is an uneven tale of remembrance of things past with a clashing cast of co-stars, including Sean Young and Christopher Cazenove. [*Marianne Gray*]

Jeanne Moreau (*Adrienne Mark*), Sean Young (*Virginia Kelly/Sally*), Sam Waterston (*Harry Bancroft*), Christopher Cazenove (*Elliott Spencer*), Nell Carter (*Milly*), Jean-Pierre Aumont (*Franz Legendre*), Austin Pendleton (*Willy Kunst*), Josh Hamilton (*William O'Hara*), Charlotte de Turckheim, Pierre Vaneck, Marc Tissot, Joanna Adler, James Naughton, J. Smith-Cameron, Jean-Yves Dubois, Sophie Camus.

Dir: Ismail Merchant. Pro: Humbert Balsan and Donald Rosenfeld. Ex Pro: Paul Bradley and Osman Eralp. Screenplay: Jean-Marie Besset and George Trow. Ph: Larry Pizer. Pro Des: Bruno Santini and Kevin Thompson. Ed: William Webb. M: Richard Robbins. Costumes: Anne de Laugardiere and Abigail Murray. (Merchant Ivory/Ognon Pictures & Fez Prods/Largo Entertainment/Canal Plus/Channel Four–Warner.) Rel: 7 February 1997. 113 mins. Cert 12. UK/France/Turkey/USA. 1996.

Rainbow

A rainbow's got to end somewhere, right? Well, Mike, a 10-year-old boy from Hudson Harbour, New Jersey, sees one actually land and cannot believe his eyes. When his best mates, Pete and Tissy, analyse the earth from the site – where a giant triangle has been cut into the ground

– they realise that Mike is telling the truth. But no sooner is the rainbow's secret revealed to the kids than the world's equilibrium takes a tumble for the worse. Remember, children, that without the colour green we would have no photosynthesis which provides us with our essential oxygen – and it is rainbows that bring colour to our life... Updating a number of plot elements from *The Wizard of Oz*, Bob Hoskins' second directorial effort attempts to conjure up a world of enchantment but cannot find the magic ingredient. Clumsily cross-breeding contemporary realism with fantasy, the film is further hamstrung by iffy special effects, poor lighting and an undernourished score.

Bob Hoskins (*Frank Bailey*), Dan Aykroyd (*Sheriff Wyatt Hampton*), Saul Rubinek (*Sam Cohen*), Terry Finn (*Jackie Bailey*), Jacob Tierney (*Steven Bailey*), Willy Lavendal (*Mike Bailey*), Jonathan Schuman (*Pete*), Eleanor Misrahi (*Tissy*), Eric Hansen (*Keefe Russel*), Sonny (*Mutt*), Jack Fisher, Norris Dominique, Babs Gadbois, Suzan Glover, Larry Day, Griffith Brewer, Gordon Masten, Daniel Brochu, Dana Williams, Richard Jutras, Susie Almgren, Mark Camacho.
   Dir: Bob Hoskins. Pro: Robert Sidaway and Nicolas Clermont. Ex Pro: Gary Smith. Line Pro: Stewart Harding. Screenplay: Ashley Sidaway and Robert Sidaway, based on the former's story. Ph: Freddie Francis. Pro Des: Claude Pare. Ed: Ashley Sidaway and Ray Lovejoy. M: Alan Reeves; Vivaldi; numbers performed by MN8, Collapsed Lung, Ragga Twins, Urban Species, Credit to the Nation, East 17, etc. Costumes: Janet Campbell. (Winchester/Filmline International/Screen Partners/Ealing Studios–First Independent.) Rel: 26 July 1996. 101 mins. Cert PG. Canada/UK. 1995.

Ransom

New York; today. A buccaneering entrepreneur dubbed 'Mr Risk' by the media, Tom Mullen has built a formidable business empire from the ground up. Now established as the head of America's fourth-largest airline, Mullen enjoys the fast lane, juggling high-powered deals with a charmed family life in his exclusive Fifth Avenue penthouse. Then his world collapses when his young son is kidnapped by ruthless terrorists who demand $2 million for the boy's release. But Mullen is not a man who follows other people's orders and his

Something nasty in the basement: Penelope Ann Miller does her Sigourney Weaver routine in Peter Hyams' routine The Relic *(from PolyGram)*

renegotiation of the kidnapping terms shocks even his most dedicated followers... On the downside, *Ransom* seldom strays from the constraints of Hollywood formula, Mel Gibson is far from believable as the Richard Bransonesque hero and James Horner's music overdoes the menacing chords. Yet the film's brutal premise – updated from the 1956 thriller starring Glenn Ford and Donna Reed – is so efficiently honed by Ron Howard's taut direction and Richard Price's intelligent screenplay that it should cut a nerve for anybody with a child and a bank account.

Mel Gibson (*Tom Mullen*), Rene Russo (*Kate Mullen*), Gary Sinise (*Jimmy Shaker*), Delroy Lindo (*Lonnie Hawkins*), Lili Taylor (*Maris Connor*), Brawley Nolte (*Sean Mullen*), Liev Schreiber (*Clark Barnes*), Donnie Wahlberg (*Cubby Barnes*), Evan Handler (*Miles Roberts*), Kevin Neil McCready (*Paul Rhodes*), Jose Zuniga (*David Torres*), Dan Hedaya (*Jackie Brown*), Nancy Ticotin, Michael Gaston, Paul Guilfoyle, Allen Bernstein, A.J. Benza, Todd Hallowell, Richard Price, Cheryl Howard.
   Dir: Ron Howard. Pro: Scott Rudin, Brian Grazer and B. Kipling Hagopian. Ex Pro: Todd Hallowell. Co-Pro: Adam Schroeder and Susan Merzbach. Screenplay: Richard Price and Alexander Ignon, from a story by Cyril Hume and Richard Maibaum. Ph: Piotr Sobocinski. Pro Des: Michael Corenblith. Ed: Dan Hanley and Mike Hill. M: James Horner. Costumes: Rita Ryack; Giorgio Armani. (Touchstone Pictures–Buena Vista.) Rel: 31 January 1997. 121 mins. Cert 15. USA. 1996.

The Relic

If a tadpole can transmogrify into a frog, who is to say what other extraordinary transformations are possible in nature? When what seem like empty packing cases turn up at

The wit to woo: Bernard Giraudeau borrows the ear of Fanny Ardant in Patrice Leconte's wickedly sublime Ridicule *(from Electric)*

the Natural History Museum in Chicago, a virus is released that forces new genetic material into foreign DNA, in turn activating a hormone that produces dramatic physical changes in its host. In this case the host is unknown, but

something nasty is growing in the basement of the museum and is hungry for the hypothalamus in the human brain. Pray God, then, that the damn thing is ectothermic.

When Carrie was little... Mara Wilson reads up on her potential in Danny DeVito's funny, scary Roald Dahl's Matilda *(from Columbia TriStar)*

Students of biology may get a kick out of the techno-jargon unleashed by this dressed-up monster flick, but less scientifically inclined viewers may see the film for what it is: a derivative, hysterically illogical and unevenly constructed hoot. Still, the set-up is fun and in spite of some repetition, this blatant blend of *Alien* and *Ghostbusters* sustains its momentum until the predictably OTT climax.

Penelope Ann Miller (*Dr Margo Green*), Tom Sizemore (*Lt Vincent D'Agosta*), Linda Hunt (*Dr Ann Cuthbert*), James Whitmore (*Dr Albert Frock*), Clayton Rohner (*Det. Hollingsworth*), Chi Muoi Lo (*Greg Lee*), Thomas Ryan (*Tom Parkinson*), Robert Lesser (*Mayor Owen*), Lewis Van Bergen (*John Whitney*), Audra Lindley (*Dr Zweizig*), Diane Robin, Constance Towers, Francis X. McCarthy, John Kapelos, Tico Wells, Mike Bacarella, Gene Davis, John Di Santi, David Proval, Don Harvey, Aaron Lustig.

Dir and Ph: Peter Hyams. Pro: Sam Mercer and Gale Anne Hurd. Ex Pro: Gary Levinsohn and Mark Gordon. Screenplay: Amy Jones and John Raffo, based on the novel by Douglas Preston and Lincoln Child. Pro Des: Philip Harrison. Ed: Steven Kemper. M: John Debney; Haydn. Costumes: Dan Lester. Visual effects: Gregory L. McMurry. Creature effects: Stan Winston. (Paramount/Cloud Nine/ PolyGram/Toho-Towa/Tele Munchen/ BBC/Marubeni/PacificWestern–Poly-Gram.) Rel: 16 May 1997. 109 mins. Cert 15. USA. 1996.

Ridicule

France; circa 1780. With the people under his protectorate suffering from deprivation and swamp fever, the noble Ponceludon de Malavoy draws up a series of ingenious designs to drain the swamp. To raise the requisite funds, however, he has to petition the royal household in Versailles, but in order to do so he must first worm his way into the social strata, using his wit to enter the inner sanctums of the elite... As Valmont in *Dangerous Liaisons* used flattery and ridicule as weapons to disarm his social rivals, so the predatory gentry in Patrice Leconte's eloquent and riveting film verbally disable their peers. Disadvantaged as a man of honour, Ponceludon perseveres with his quest, rapidly sharpening his tongue as a means to his end. Working from a superlative screenplay by Remi Waterhouse,

Leconte matches the latter's semantic athletics with a voluptuous visual style of which the French have recently become past masters. Both a fascinating insight into eighteenth-century social history and a compelling human story.

Fanny Ardant (*Madame de Blayac*), Charles Berling (*Gregoire Ponceludon de Malavoy*), Bernard Giraudeau (*Abbot de Vilecourt*), Judith Godreche (*Mathilde de Bellegarde*), Jean Rochefort (*Marquis de Bellegarde*), Bernard Dheran (*Monsieur de Montalieri*), Jacques Mathou (*Abbot de l'Epee*), Urbain Cancelier (*Louis XVI*), Carlo Brandt, Albert Delpy, Bruno Zanardi, Marie Pillet, Jacques Roman, Philippe Magnan, Mirabelle Kirkland, Didier Abot, Jose Fumanal.
   Dir: Patrice Leconte. Pro: Gilles Legrand, Frederic Brillion and Philippe Carcassonne. Screenplay: Remi Waterhouse. Ph: Thierry Arbogast. Pro Des: Ivan Maussion. Ed: Joelle Hache. M: Antoine Duhamel. Costumes: Christian Gasc. (Epithete/Cinea/France 3 Cinema/Canal Plus, etc.–Electric.) Rel: 7 February 1997. 102 mins. Cert 15. France. 1996.

Roald Dahl's Matilda

Matilda Wormwood is a rather special child, a girl with extra-ordinary gifts. By the time she's four she has read every magazine in the house and so turns to the library to extend her knowledge. But her parents, used car salesman Harry Wormwood and bingo zealot Zinnia Wormwood, are so wrapped up in themselves – and TV game shows – that they barely notice her. Indeed, Zinnia can't remember her daughter's age nor Harry her name ('Melinda, Matilda, whatever'). Left to her own devices, Matilda brushes up on her gifts, particularly her knack for telekinesis... Directed with enormous pizzazz by Danny DeVito (whose subversive nature perfectly mirrors Roald Dahl's), *Matilda* is everything a family picture should be: moving, scary, confrontational and very, very funny. But it's the little touches, visual flourish and constant refusal to kowtow to the conventions of children's cinema that mark this out as a classic of its kind.

Danny DeVito (*narrator/Harry Wormwood*), Rhea Perlman (*Zinnia Wormwood*), Embeth Davidtz (*Miss Honey*), Pam Ferris (*Agatha Trunchbull*), Mara Wilson (*Matilda Wormwood*), Kiami Davael (*Lavender*), Jimmy Karz (*Bruce Bogtrotter*), Jon Lovitz

Disguise surprise: Val Kilmer exercises his facial versatility (with Alun Armstrong) in Phillip Noyce's rollicking The Saint *(from UIP)*

(*game show host*), Paul Reubens, Tracey Walter, Brian Levinson, Jean Speegle Howard, R.D. Robb, Jacqueline Steiger, Kira Spencer Hesser.
   Dir: Danny DeVito. Pro: DeVito, Michael Shamberg, Stacey Sher and Liccy Dahl. Ex Pro: Michael Peyser and Martin Bregman. Co-Pro and Screenplay: Nicholas Kazan and Robin Swicord, based on the book by Roald Dahl. Ph: Stefan Czapsky. Pro Des: Bill Brzeski. Ed: Lynzee Klingman and Brent White. M: David Newman. Costumes: Jane Ruhm. Pam Ferris's trainer: Bill Green. (TriStar Pictures/Jersey Films–Columbia TriStar.) Rel: 20 December 1996. 98 mins. Cert PG. USA. 1996.

Romeo and Juliet

See *William Shakespeare's Romeo + Juliet*.

The Saint

When the absurdly pretty scientist Emma Russell completes the formula for cold fusion, she realises an energy source that can run a car for 50 million miles on one gallon of water. Enter international mercenary Simon Templar who's trying to knock his bank balance up to the $50 million mark. Agreeing a price with the · seditious leader of Russia's all-

powerful Tretiak Gas and Oil Industries, Templar travels to Oxford, England, to steal the formula from the absurdly pretty scientist... An amalgam of magician, lover, thief and all-round enigma, Simon Templar is arguably the most entertaining anti-hero of contemporary fiction. Thanks to state-of-the-art make-up and more accents than a Rory Bremner retrospective, Val Kilmer almost pulls off the showiest role of his career (however, charisma is not the actor's strong suit.) Still, this is more fun than James Bond and more suspenseful than *Mission: Impossible* (with which the film shares a number of comparisons), and what with the in-jokes, colourful location work and strong romantic thrust, this Saint's halo really does shine.

Val Kilmer (*The Saint/Simon Templar/John Rossi, etc.*), Elisabeth Shue (*Dr Emma Russell*), Rade Serbedzija (*Ivan Tretiak*), Valery Nikolaev (*Ilya Tretiak*), Henry Goodman (*Dr Lev Botvin*), Alun Armstrong (*Chief Inspector Teal*), Michael Byrne, Evgeny Lazarev, Irina Apeximova (*Frankie*), Lev Prigunov, Charlotte Cornwall, Emily Mortimer, Lucija Serbedzija, Tusse Silberg, Stefan Gryff, Malcolm Tierney, Christopher Rozycki, David Schneider, Benjamin Whitrow, Barbara Jefford, William Hope, Michael Cochrane, Roger Moore (*voice only – on car radio*).

Dir: Phillip Noyce. Pro: David Brown, Robert Evans, William J. MacDonald and Mace Neufeld. Ex Pro: Paul Hitchcock and Robert S. Baker. Screenplay: Jonathan Hensleigh and Wesley Strick, inspired by the character created by Leslie Charteris. Ph: Phil Meheux. Pro Des: Joseph Nemec III. Ed: Terry Rawlings. M: Graeme Revell; numbers performed by David Bowie, Dreadzone, Daft Punk, Superior, Luscious Jackson, The Smashing Pumpkins, Fluke, The Chemical Brothers, Underworld, Everything But The Girl, Orbital, Duran Duran, etc. Costumes: Marlene Stewart. (Paramount/Rysher Entertainment–UIP.) Rel: 18 April 1997. 116 mins. Cert 12. USA. 1997.

Scream

Days before the first anniversary of the grisly murder of Sidney Prescott's mother, a series of new killings terrorises the small community of Woodsboro, California. But Mrs Prescott's killer is on Death Row, so who is this new psycho stalking the students of Woodsboro High? Hoot might have been a more appropriate title for this unashamed knife-in-cheek homage to *Halloween*, *Prom Night* and their ilk. Stuffed to the gills with in-jokes and horror movie references, *Scream* attempts to have its cake and eat it by poking fun at the horror genre while giving us the heebie-jeebies. However, the gimmick of blatant imitation leaves little room for genuine unease (not helped by the

Stories from the cradle: Cillian Byrne in John Sayles' lyrical The Secret of Roan Inish *(from Metro Tartan)*

overtly 'spooky' music.) So, *Scream* is more fun and nasty than fun and scary, with a slew of terrific lines to keep genre fans awake at night trying to remember them.

David Arquette (*Deputy Dwight 'Dewey' Riley*), Neve Campbell (*Sidney Prescott*), Courteney Cox (*Gale Weathers*), Matthew Lillard (*Stuart*), Rose McGowan (*Tatum Reily*), Skeet Ulrich (*Billy Loomis*), Drew Barrymore (*Casey Becker*), W. Earl Brown (*Kenny*), Jamie Kennedy (*Randy*), Liev Schreiber (*Cotton Weary*), Henry Winkler (*Principal Himbry*), Lawrence Hecht, Lois Saunders, Joseph Whipp, C.W. Morgan, Frances Lee McCain, Linda Blair, Priscilla Pointer, Wes Craven.

Dir: Wes Craven. Pro: Cary Woods and Cathy Konrad. Ex Pro: Bob Weinstein, Harvey Weinstein and Marianne Maddalena. Co-Ex Pro: Stuart M. Besser. Co-Pro: Dixie J. Capp. Screenplay: Kevin Williamson. Ph: Mark Irwin. Pro Des: Bruce Alan Miller. Ed: Patrick Lussier. M: Marco Beltrami. Costumes: Cynthia Bergstrom. Special effects: KNB EFX Group, Inc. (Miramax/Dimension Films/ Woods Entertainment–Buena Vista.) Rel: 2 May 1997. 111 mins. Cert 18. USA. 1996.

The Secret Agent Club

A wimpish toy manufacturer is really a secret agent. Captured by evil arms dealer Lesley-Anne Down, his son and his mates set out to rescue him. This *True Lies* rip-off appropriately stars the poor man's Arnie, ex-wrestler Hulk Hogan. Shoddily made, the film will torture adults while single digit-aged kids will relish the *Home Alone*-style antics. For devotees of Hogan's acting (outside of the wrestling ring), *The Secret Agent Club* is better than the

lamentable *Mr Nanny* but not up to *Suburban Commando* standard. [*Simon Rose*]

Hulk Hogan (*Ray Chase*), Lesley-Anne Down (*Eve*), Barry Bostwick (*Vincent Scarletti*), Richard Moll (*Wrecks*), Matthew McCurley (*Jeremy Chase*), James Hong (*Mr Yamata*), Maurice Woods (*Sly*), Edward Albert, Lyman Ward, Danny McCue, Ashley Power, Jimmy Pham, Jack Nance, Rory Johnston, M.C. Gainey, Wild Bill Mock.

Dir: John Murlowski. Pro: Brian Shuster and James Ian Lifton. Ex Pro: Harry Shuster and Jordan Belfort. Co-Pro: David Silberg. Line Pro: Paula Major. Screenplay: Rory Johnston. Ph: Stephen Douglas Smith. Pro Des: James Scanlon. Ed: Leslie Rosenthal. M: Jan Hammer. Costumes: Cathryn Wagner. (Secret Agent/Hit Entertainment–Marquee Pictures/ Starlight Films.) Rel: 16 August 1996. 90 mins. Cert PG. USA. 1996.

The Secret of Roan Inish

When ten-year-old Fiona Conneely is sent to live with her grandparents on the remote coast of western Ireland, she is immediately transfixed by the tale of her little brother, Jaime, who was whisked out to sea in his cradle – never to be seen again. Later, she hears of the myth of the 'Selkies', half-human, half-seal creatures who live on the island of Roan Inish. Mysteriously drawn to the island, Fiona begins to make some startling discoveries of her own... A lyrical yet starkly unsentimental tale adapted by John Sayles from the 1957 children's novella *Secret of the Ron Mor Skerry* by Rosalie K. Fry, *Roan Inish* displays the director's familiar (and commendable) dramatic restraint. However, the film's matter-of-fact telling borders on the flat when it should be conjuring up magic. That leaves Haskell Wexler's luminous photography, Mason Daring's exquisite music and Jeni Courtney's beguiling central performance to admire, but that may not be enough for some viewers. Irish whimsy – without the whimsy.

Jeni Courtney (*Fiona*), Eileen Colgan (*Tess, Fiona's grandmother*), Mick Lally (*Hugh, Fiona's grandfather*), Richard Sheridan (*Eamon*), John Lynch (*Tadhg*), Cillian Byrne (*Jamie*), Pat Howey, Dave Duffy, Declan Hannigan, Brendan Conroy, Frankie McCafferty, Susan Lynch.

Dir, Screenplay and Ed: John Sayles.

Sisterz N the Hood: Jada Pinkett, Kimberly Elise, Queen Latifah and Vivica A. Fox embrace the hood of their car in F. Gary Gray's spunky, hackneyed Set It Off *(from Entertainment)*

Pro: Sarah Green and Maggie Renzi. Ex Pro: John Sloss, Glenn R. Jones and Peter Newman. Ph: Haskell Wexler. Pro Des: Adrian Smith. M: Mason Daring. Costumes: Consolata Boyle. (Skerry Movies/Jones Entertainment–Metro Tartan.) Rel: 9 August 1996. 103 mins. Cert PG. Ireland. 1993.

A Self-Made Hero - Un Heros Tres Discret

Deceived by his mother into believing that his father was a hero of the First World War, Albert Dehousse grows up with a false concept of heroism. Later, during the next war, Albert is shocked by the discovery that his wife has been harbouring English pilots, and so – on the very day of the Liberation – he runs off to Paris. There, he is befriended by a genuine hero of the Resistance who counsels Albert to try reinventing himself. This he does, infiltrating Resistance reunions, absorbing every detail of the patriots' former lives, swatting up on their history and, eventually, becoming the hero that France seems so desperately to need... While guiding things along nicely at a brisk clip, director Jacques Audiard lends his narrative a historic perspective by periodically cutting from the main

action to (fabricated) contemporary interviews. However, the film never gains the emotional hold it should as Mathieu Kassovitz gives such an uncharismatic reading of the hero. Resembling a cross between a young John Turturro and Daniel Auteuil, Kassovitz (who directed last year's *La Haine*) gives us little to care for or admire. This is a shifty, conniving little twerp whose sole attribute seems to be his ability to extemporise.

Mathieu Kassovitz (*Albert Dehousse*), Anouk Grinberg (*Servane*), Sandrine Kiberlain (*Yvette*), Albert Dupontel

Artificial Hero: Mathieu Kassovitz and Anouk Grinberg in Jacques Audiard's sly A Self-Made Hero *(from Artificial Eye)*

(*Captain Dionnet*), Bernard Bloch (*Ernst*), Francois Berleand (*Monsieur Jo*), Nadia Barentin, Wilfred Benaiche, Jerome Floch, David Fernandes, Jean-Louis Trintignant.
   Dir: Jacques Audiard. Pro: Patrick Godeau. Ex Pro: Francoise Galfre. Screenplay: Alain Le Henry and Audiard, based on the novel by Jean-Francois Deniau. Ph: Jean-Marc Fabre. Pro Des: Michel Vandestien. Ed: Juliette Welfling. M: Alexandre Desplat. Costumes: Caroline De Vivaise. (Aliceleo/Lumiere/France 3 Cinema/M6 Films/Initial Groupe/Canal Plus–Artificial Eye.) Rel: 4 April 1997. 106 mins. Cert 15. France. 1995.

Set It Off

The projects of Los Angeles; today. Frankie has just lost her job, Stony has lost her brother and Tisean has just lost her son. Cleo is about to lose her mind, so she goads her sisterz

from the 'hood to embark on a series of bank robberies to ease their path through life. After all, reasons Frankie, 'We'll just be takin' it from the system that's fuckin' us all anyway.' The system sucks, but can the girlz conquer it with guns and grit? Although the elements of the story are frequently schematic and hackneyed, four spunky actresses pump in plenty of fresh interest. The rap artist Queen Latifah – who recalls a female Ice Cube – is particularly engaging, while the dialogue throws in a few comic insights. Label it *Waiting to Exhale* meets *Dead Presidents*.

Jada Pinkett (*Stony*), Queen Latifah (*Cleopatra Simms*), Vivica A. Fox (*Frankie*), Kimberly Elise (*Tisean*), John C. McGinley (*Detective Strode*), Blair Underwood (*Keith*), Ella Joyce (*Det. Waller*), Anna Maria Horsford, Charlie Robinson, Chaz Lamar Shepard, Vincent And Van Baum, Thom Byrd, Samantha MacLachlan, WC, Lawrence Calhoun Jr, Dr Dre, Big Daddy Wayne.
    Dir: F. Gary Gray. Pro: Dale Pollock and Oren Koules. Ex Pro: Gray and Mary Parent. Co-Pro: Takashi Bufford and Allen Alsobrook. Screenplay: Bufford and Kate Lanier. Ph: Marc Reshovsky. Pro Des: Robb Wilson King. Ed: John Carter. M: Christopher Young; numbers performed by Parliament, Foxy, Yo-Yo and Ice Cube, Queen Latifah, Ramsey Lewis, Miles Davis, Phillis Hyman, Des'Ree, Sin, Seal, En Vogue, Bone Thugs-n-Harmony, Lori Petty, and Brandy, Gladys Knight, Tamia

The Self-Righteous Brother: Mike McGlone confronts Jennifer Aniston in Edward Burns' smart, *witty* She's the One *(from Fox)*

and Chaka Kahn. Costumes: Sylvia Vega Vasquez. (Peak Prods/New Line–Entertainment.) Rel: 24 January 1997. 130 mins. Cert 18. USA. 1996.

Shadow Conspiracy

Once again some dubious types are undermining the very fabric of the White House, killing off who they like in their mission to wrestle the Oval Office from the President. Unfortunately for them, the president's right-hand man is none other than Charlie Sheen, a sort of George Stephanopoulos with a built-in bulletproof vest. Having witnessed the assassination of a conspiracy buff (who dies in his arms, no less), Sheen becomes the prime target of humourless hitman Stephen Lang (reprising his role from *The Hard Way*). So Sheen ducks, Lang shoots and Linda Hamilton runs into the firing line as a conscientious reporter for *The Washington Herald*... Lumbered with one-dimensional characters, an overly familiar plot and endlessly improbable situations, director Cosmatos (*Rambo: First Blood Part II, Tombstone*) attempts to inject some cinematic style into his scenario, utilising flashy deep focus and colourful Washington locations – but to little avail. Then, what shred of credibility remains is stamped out by Bruce Broughton's over-excited score. *The Manchurian Candidate* this ain't.

Charlie Sheen (*Bobby Bishop*), Donald Sutherland (*Jake Conrad*), Linda Hamilton (*Amanda Givens*), Stephen Lang (*The*

Agent), Ben Gazzara (*Vice President Saxon*), Nicholas Turturro (*Grasso*), Stanley Anderson (*Attorney General Toyanbee*), Theodore Bikel (*Professor Yuri Pochenko*), Sam Waterston (*The President*), Gore Vidal (*Congressman Page*), Charles Cioffi, Paul Gleason, Terry O'Quinn, Henry Strozier, Dey Young, Richard Bauer, Penny Fuller, Walt MacPherson, Ramon Estevez.
    Dir: George Pan Cosmatos. Pro: Terry Collis. Ex Pro: Andrew G. Vajna and Buzz Feitshans. Co-Pro: Adi Hasak. Screenplay: Hasak and Ric Gibbs. Ph: Buzz Feitshans IV. Pro Des: Joe Alves. Ed: Robert A. Ferretti. M: Bruce Broughton. Costumes: April Ferry. Stunts/second unit dir: Vic Armstrong. (Cinergi Pictures–Entertainment.) Rel: 13 June 1997. 103 mins. Cert 15. USA. 1996.

She's the One

While Mickey and Francis Fitzpatrick are brothers biologically, they could not be further removed intellectually – although they both put their own happiness first. Mickey is smug, easy-going and self-righteous and seems content to be the sole white English-speaking cab driver in New York. Francis is stuck-up, selfish and arrogant and prides himself on his high-paying job on Wall Street. Then Mickey is swept off his feet by the beautiful, impulsive Hope and marries her in a whirlwind 24-hour romance. Meanwhile, Francis is taunted by his sexually frustrated wife and seems to be losing his mistress, the latter being Mickey's ex... Mining the same autobiographical themes of his first film (the $25,000 independent hit *The Brothers McMullen*), Edward Burns' sophomore outing arrives with 120 times the budget and a good deal more wit and polish. Again, Burns deals with sibling rivalry, adultery, marital discord, spontaneous love and, to a lesser extent, Catholic guilt. Yet while following the formula of romantic comedy (and very amusingly, too), Burns invests his characters with a stark honesty that bypasses the traditional glibness of the genre. Tom Petty supplies the evocative songs.

Jennifer Aniston (*Rene*), Maxine Bahns (*Hope*), Edward Burns (*Mickey Fitzpatrick*), Cameron Diaz (*Heather Davis*), John Mahoney (*Mr Fitzpatrick*), Mike McGlone (*Francis Fitzpatrick*), Anita Gillette (*Carol*), Leslie Mann (*Connie*), Amanda Peet (*Molly*), Frank Vincent (*Ron*), Robert Weil (*Mr De Lucca*), Malachy McCourt (*Tom*).

The lustre of genius: John Gielgud and Noah Taylor try a little Rachmaninov in Scott Hicks' powerful and funny Shine *(from Buena Vista)*

Dir and Screenplay: Edward Burns. Pro: Burns, Ted Hope and James Schamus. Ex Pro: Robert Redford and Michael Nozik. Co-Ex Pro: John Sloss. Line Pro: Alysse Bezahler. Ph: Frank Prinzi. Pro Des: William Barclay. Ed: Susan Graef. M: Tom Petty; seven numbers performed by Tom Petty, one by The Isley Brothers. Costumes: Susan Lyall. (Fox Searchlight Pictures/Good Machine/Marlboro Road Gang/South Fork Pictures/The Sundance Institute–Fox.) Rel: 14 February 1997. 96 mins. Cert 15. USA. 1996.

Shine

Australia; the 1950s-1990s. For David Helfgott, the piano is both his undoing and his salvation. Drilled by his Polish immigrant father from an early age, David develops into a child prodigy, winning competitions right, left and centre. But when he is invited to study in America, his father refuses to let him go. The latter expects only the best of David, yet will not facilitate the means for his son's creative fulfilment. Forced to

master Rachmaninoff's impossible third concerto, David becomes consumed by the composition, which ultimately grows into a musical manifestation of his father: the thread that forms David's ambiguous character... The Australian cinema has a tradition of producing remarkable films about 'special' people and/or social outcasts. Witness: *Stork*, *Man of Flowers*, *Annie's Coming Out*, *Bliss*, *Malcolm*, *Sweetie*, *An Angel At My Table*, *Golden Braid* and *Bad Boy Bubby*. Here director Scott Hicks explores the thin line between genius and insanity with extraordinary skill and compassion, allowing us an intimate glimpse into David's singular universe. While it's a privilege to see a film with two such outstanding actors as Armin Mueller-Stahl and John Gielgud, the cast is uniformly excellent, particularly Geoffrey Rush as the stammering, hyperkinetic older Helfgott. Powerful, funny, thought-provoking and terribly moving.

Armin Mueller-Stahl (*Peter Helfgott*), Noah Taylor (*David Helfgott, as an adolescent*), Geoffrey Rush (*David Helfgott, as an adult*), Lynn Redgrave (*Gillian*), John Gielgud

(*Professor Cecil Parkes*), Alex Rafalowicz (*David Helfgott, as a child*), Googie Withers (*Katharine Susannah Prichard*), Sonia Todd (*Sylvia*), Nicholas Bell (*Ben Rosen*), Justin Braine (*Tony*), Marta Kaczmarek (*Rachel*), Randall Berger (*Isaac Stern*), Beverly Dunn (*Beryl Alcott*), Chris Haywood, Gordon Poole, Danielle Cox, Rebecca Gooden, John Cousins, Maria Dafnero, David King, Helen Dowell.

Dir: Scott Hicks. Pro: Jane Scott. Screenplay: Jan Sardi, from a story by Hicks. Ph: Geoffrey Simpson. Pro Des: Vicki Niehus. Ed: Pip Karmel. M: David Hirschfelder; Rachmaninov, Chopin, Schumann, Paganini, Liszt, Rimsky-Korsakov, Vivaldi, Beethoven. Costumes: Louise Wakefield. (Australian Film Finance Corporation/Momentum Films/Pandora Cinema/BBC–Buena Vista.) Rel: 3 January 1997. 106 mins. Cert 12. Australia/UK. 1996.

Silence of the Hams - Il Silenzio dei Prosciutti

This supposed spoof of *The Silence of the Lambs* stars Billy Zane as FBI's Jo Dee Fostar seeking help from a Dr Animal Cannibal Pizza to track down a serial killer. Imagine the outtakes from Mel Brooks and *The Naked Gun* team stitched together at random and you get some idea of this mind-

Prank outsiders: Joseph Perrino, Geoffrey Wigdor, Brad Renfro and Jonathan Tucker watch their future self-destruct in Barry Levinson's stylistic, familiar Sleepers *(from PolyGram)*

bogglingly unfunny travesty of a movie. Dating from 1993, it beggars belief that this film should ever have been taken off the shelf. [*Simon Rose*]

Ezio Greggio (*Antonio Motel*), Dom DeLuise (*Dr Animal Cannibal Pizza*), Billy Zane (*Jo Dee Fostar*), Joanna Pacula (*Lily*), Charlene Tilton (*Jane*), Martin Balsam (*Detective Balsam*), Stuart Pankin, John Astin, Larry Storch, Bubba Smith, Rip Taylor, Phyllis Diller, Shelley Winters, Henry Silva, Marshall Bell, John Roarke, Joe Dante, John Carpenter, Irwin Keyes, Eddie Deezen, Peter DeLuise, Rudy De Luca, John Landis, David DeLuise, Al Ruscio, Raymond Serra.
    Dir, Ex Pro and Screenplay: Ezio Greggio. Pro: Greggio and Julie Corman. Ph: Jacques Haitkin. Pro Des: Jim Newport. Ed: Robert Barrere and Andy Horvitch. M: Parmer Fuller. Costumes: Leesa Evans. Make-up effects: Dave Barton. (Thirtieth Century Wolf/Silvio Berlusconi Communications–PolyGram.) Rel: 16 August 1996. 81 mins. Cert 15. Italy/USA. 1993.

Sleepers

1966-1981; Hell's Kitchen, New York. In New York slang a sleeper is a prison inmate who serves more than nine months. For Shakes, Michael, John and Tommy, four kids on the cusp of their teens, one reckless prank backfires, landing them in a correctional facility for a period of 'between nine and 18 months'. There, the boys' lives are irrevocably changed as they are subjected to mental abuse, rape and torture. Only the prospect of revenge maintains their hope for a better life...
Regardless of how true the events that form the narrative of *Sleepers* may be, Barry Levinson's handsomely crafted drama ploughs tired old territory: i.e. growing up in the Bronx alongside the usual recipe of gangsters, priests, delis and blah, blah, blah. Unfortunately, the writer-director fails to invest his characters with much distinction, so much so that when the young boys suddenly spring into Jason Patric, Brad Pitt & Co., we fail to recognise their pubescent counterparts. Not only that, but Levinson's stylistic flourishes further detract from any sense of reality, resulting in some emotional distance. As for the authenticity of this 'true story', many of the primary facts remain unsubstantiated, while the coy photographic gymnastics lead more to confusion than horror.

Kevin Bacon (*Sean Nokes*), Robert De Niro (*Father Bobby*), Dustin Hoffman (*Danny Snyder*), Jason Patric (*Lorenzo, aka Shakes*), Brad Pitt (*Michael*), Bruno Kirby (*Shakes' father*), Brad Renfro (*young Michael*), Ron Eldard (*John*), Billy Crudup (*Tommy*), Vittorio Gassman (*King Benny*), Terry Kinney (*Ferguson*), Frank Medrano (*Fat Mancho*), Jonathan Tucker (*young Tommy*), Geoffrey Wigdor (*young John*), Joe Perrino (*young Shakes*), Minnie Driver (*Carol*), Joe Attanasio, Eugene Byrd, George Georgiadis, Ben Hammer, Paul Herman, Pat McNamara, Wendell Pierce, Sean Patrick Reilly, Tom Signorelli, Patrick Tull, Aida Turturro, Joseph Urla.
    Dir and Screenplay: Barry Levinson, based on the controversial, semi-autobiographical bestseller by Lorenzo Carcaterra. Pro: Levinson and Steve Golin. Ex Pro: Peter Giuliano. Co-Pro: Carcaterra. Ph: Michael Ballhaus. Pro Des: Kristi Zea. Ed: Stu Linder. M: John Williams; numbers performed by Frankie Valli and The Four Seasons, Spencer Davis Group, The Trashmen, Doris Day, Soft Cell, The Beach Boys, Dean Martin, Love, Donovan, The Gap Band, Dusty Springfield, etc. Costumes: Gloria Gresham. Sound: Richard Beggs. Warner/PolyGram/Propaganda Films/Baltimore Pictures–PolyGram.) Rel: 3 January 1997. 147 mins. Cert 15. USA. 1996.

Some Mother's Son

1979-1981; Northern Ireland. When widowed schoolteacher Kathleen Quigley lends her car to her son to buy shoes, little does she realise what chain of events she is setting into motion. Unbeknownst to her Gerard Quigley is an active member of the IRA and is quickly apprehended for his part in a rocket attack on the British army (for which he used his mother's motor.) Sentenced to twelve years in the infamous Maze prison, Gerard quickly falls in with the ideals of his cellmate Bobby Sands and embarks on a hunger strike that is to capture the imagination of the nation. Meanwhile, Kathleen stands by, trying to reconcile herself to her son's convictions while watching him die... Shedding a fresh light on 'The Troubles' by focusing on the role of the mother, *Some Mother's Son* agitates an old nerve without anaesthetic. And with Helen Mirren's powerful interior performance leading the way, one cannot help but cry out for the plight of these persecuted people. As to be expected from the writers and producers of *In the Name of the Father*, the British are portrayed as ruthless caricatures, which doesn't exactly clarify the problem. Only Tim Woodward (excellent) as a level-headed English bureaucrat seems to project some kind of humanity, but then falls victim to his own altruism. Previously known as *Sons & Warriors*.

Helen Mirren (*Kathleen Quigley*), Fionnula Flanagan (*Annie Higgins*), Aidan Gillen (*Gerard Quigley*), David O'Hara (*Frank Higgins*), John Lynch (*Bobby Sands*), Tom Hollander (*Farnsworth*), Tim Woodward (*Harrington*), Ciaran Hinds (*Danny Boyle*), Geraldine O'Rawe (*Alice Quigley*), Gerard McSorley (*Father Daly*), Grainne Delany (*Theresa Higgins*), John Kavanagh (*Cardinal*), Oliver Maguire (*Frank Maguire*), Doreen Keogh (*Mother Superior*), Anthony Brophy (*Tom McLaughlin*), Dan Gordon, Ciaran Fitzgerald, Robert Lang, Peter Howitt, Bosco Hogan, Jimmy Keogh, Anna Megan, Alan Barry.

Dir: Terry George. Pro: Jim Sheridan, Arthur Lappin and Edward Burke. Assoc Pro: Helen Mirren. Screenplay: George and Sheridan. Ph: Geoffrey Simpson. Pro Des: David Wilson. Ed: Craig McKay. M: Bill Whelan; Handel, J.S. Bach; numbers performed by The Wooldridge Brothers, Patsy Cline, etc. Costumes: Joan Bergin. (Castle Rock/Hell's Kitchen–Rank/Castle Rock/Turner.) Rel: 10 January 1997. 112 mins. Cert 15. Ireland/USA. 1996.

Space Jam

Seeking a new attraction for his Moron Mountain theme park, a

In the Name of the Mother: Helen Mirren attempts to understand her dying son (Aidan Gillen) in Terry George's impassioned Some Mother's Son *(from Rank/Castle Rock/ Turner)*

The Comic, The Bunny and The Athlete: Bill Murray, Bugs Bunny and Michael Jordan confer in Joe Pytka's audacious Space Jam *(from Warner)*

despotic impresario dispatches four of his minions to planet Earth to kidnap the animated *dramatis personae* of the *Loony Tunes*. To save their skins, the cartoon characters propose a decisive basketball tournament and abduct hoop legend Michael Jordan from the real world to help them beat the aliens... Building on the concept of *Who Framed Roger Rabbit*, the makers of *Space Jam* raid the vaults of Warner

Brothers to parade the principal stars of the *Loony Tunes* against a number of real-life sporting icons. As the main attraction, Michael Jordan plays Michael Jordan as an extraordinarily talented athlete and jolly decent human being, a stunt that transcends even the vanity of a Streisand project. However, the film's anything-goes chutzpah truly exploits the potential of its material, packing in countless irreverent plugs that should delight everyone from small children to sports devotees. P.S. Considering how Michael Jordan holds his own against the menagerie of cartoon characters, it's surprising that his agent allowed Bugs Bunny to get top billing.

Bugs Bunny (*himself*), Michael Jordan (*himself*), Wayne Knight (*Stan Podolak*), Theresa Randle (*Juanita Jordan*), Manner 'Mooky' Washington (*Jeffery Jordan*), Eric Gordon (*Marcus Jordan*), Penny Bae Bridges (*Jasmine Jordan*), Brandon Hammond (*Michael Jordan, at ten*), Larry Bird (*himself*), Bill Murray (*himself*), Thom Barry (*James Jordan*), Charles Barkley (*himself*), Patrick Ewing (*himself*), Muggsy Bogues, Larry Johnson, Shawn Bradley, Ahmad Rashad, Del Harris, Vlade Divac, Cedric Ceballos, Jim Rome, Bebe Drake, Charles Oakley.
Voices: Billy West (*Bugs Bunny, Elmer Fudd*), Dee Bradley Baker (*Daffy Duck, Tazmanian Devil, Bull Dee*), Danny DeVito (*Swackhammer*), Bob Bergen (*Bert, Herbie, Marvin the Martian, Porky Pig, Tweety*), Bill Farmer (*Sylvester, Yosemite Sam, Foghorn Leghorn*), Kath Soucie (*Lola Bunny*), Dorian

Changing the past: Alison Elliott in Lee David Zlotoff's incredibly moving The Spitfire Grill *(from Rank/Castle Rock/ Turner)*

Harewood, T.K. Carter, Frank W. Welker.

Dir: Joe Pytka. Pro: Ivan Reitman, Joe Medjuck and Daniel Goldberg. Ex Pro: David Falk and Ken Ross. Co-Pro: Gordon Webb, Sheldon Kahn and Curtis Polk. Screenplay: Leo Benvenuti, Steve Rudnick, Timothy Harris and Herschel Weingrod. Ph: Michael Chapman. Pro Des: Geoffrey Kirkland. Ed: Kahn. M: James Newton Howard; numbers performed by Seal, R. Kelly, B. Real, Busta Rhymes, Coolio, LL Cool J & Method Man, Barry White and Chris Rock, Robin S, Spin Doctors, Salt 'n' Pepa, Dick Dale & His Del-Tones, etc. Animation Dirs: Bruce Smith and Tony Cervone. Visual Effects: Ed Jones. (Warner–Warner.) Rel: 21 March 1997. 87 mins. Cert U. USA. 1996.

Space Truckers

Deep Space; 2196. John Canyon is your typical trucker: independent, hard-bitten and more than capable of looking after himself. The only difference is that his rig – a giant, rusting Pachyderm 2000 – is rocket-powered and can travel anywhere in the solar system. When he's double-crossed by a corrupt multi-planetary corporation – The Company – he jumps at the next offer, to convey a shipment of sex toys to planet Earth. Taking his fiancée and a graduate of Space Trucker School along for the ride, Canyon quickly discovers that his cargo is nothing to be toyed with... Not since the first *Alien* has space seemed so lived-in, so probable – normal, even. Here, tacky Western-style bars turn up in outer space, intergalactic pilots sport denims and baseball caps and the cosmos is littered with satellite-powered neon advertising. Transporting the world of *Convoy* and *Smokey and the Bandit* to the future, *Space Truckers* never loses sight of its sense of humour. Even when the going gets grisly – with grim echoes of *RoboCop* – the violence is never more than jokey-suspenseful. And Charles Dance, as a bio-mechanical Captain Hook, is a hoot.

Dennis Hopper (*John Canyon*), Stephen Dorff (*Mike Pucci*), Debi Mazar (*Cindy*), Charles Dance (*Macanudo/Nabel*), Shane Rimmer (*Chairman E.J. Saggs*), George Wendt, Vernon Wells, Barbara Crampton, Birdy Sweeney, Sandra Dickinson.

Dir: Stuart Gordon. Pro: Gordon, Peter Newman and Ted Mann. Ex Pro: Guy Collins and Greg Johnson. Co-Pro: Morgan O'Sullivan. Screenplay: Mann. Ph: Mac Ahlberg. Pro Des: Simon Murton. Ed: John Victor Smith. M: Colin Towns; numbers performed by Chris Knight, Billy Swan, Rednex, etc. Costumes: John Bloomfield. Visual effects: Brian Johnson and Paul Gentry. (Pachyderm Productions/Internal/Mary Breen-Farrelly Prods–Entertainment.) Rel: 23 May 1997. 96 mins. Cert 12. USA/Ireland. 1996.

The Spitfire Grill

Drawn to the backwater town of Gilead, Maine, by its alleged rare rock formations, ex-con Percy Talbott knows she must build her life from scratch. Yet the natives of Gilead do not take kindly to strange criminals in their midst, cramping the young woman's attempts at rehabilitation. As it happens, Percy is about the only person prepared to fight for a better future in a town that has given up hope... Writer-director Lee David Zlotoff (who previously created the TV series *MacGyver*) credits three sources as the inspiration for his first screenplay: an article in the *Los Angeles Times* on Appalachian poverty, a report in *Newsweek* about prison staff recruited to operate tourist centres and the story of an inn in Maine that was raffled in an essay competition. Taking these three thematic strands, Zlotoff has fashioned an incredibly moving drama that focuses a sharp spotlight on the cruel injustices of intolerance. Utilising the achingly beautiful scenery of Vermont's Northeast Kingdom (affectionately caught by Rob Draper's camera), *The Spitfire Grill* (named after Burstyn's eatery) reveals the kind of depth of character found in a good novel. But it is Zlotoff's exemplary writing and the superlative playing of Burstyn, Harden, Patton and especially Alison Elliott that ennobles this wonderful film.

Ellen Burstyn (*Hannah Ferguson*), Marcia Gay Harden (*Shelby Goddard*), Will Patton (*Nahum Goddard*), Alison Elliott (*Percy Talbott*), Kieran Mulroney (*Joe Sperling*), Gailard Sartain (*Sheriff Gary Walsh*), Louise De Cormier (*Effy Katshaw*), Lisa Louise Langford (*Jolene*), John M. Jackson, Ida Griesemer, Sam Lloyd Snr, Jim Hogue, Patti Tippo (*Clare's voice-over*).

Dir and Screenplay: Lee David Zlotoff. Pro: Forrest Murray. Ex Pro: Warren G. Stitt. Co-Pro: Edward E. Vaughn and Marci Liroff. Ph: Rob Draper. Pro Des:

Howard Cummings. Ed: Margie Goodspeed. M: James Horner. Costumes: Louise Mingenbach. Sound: L. Mo Webber. (Castle Rock/Gregory Prods/Mendocino Corp-Rank–Castle Rock/Turner.) Rel: 30 May 1997. 116 mins. Cert 12. USA. 1996.

The Square Circle - Daayraa

If you thought *Kama Sutra* was bad, wait till you see this musical melodrama about a male transvestite who falls for a woman posing as a boy. Ruthlessly shredded to a palatable running time for Western tastes, this over-stylised, rural Indian tale makes little sense but does stand a few misconceptions of Hindi culture on their head. [*Ewen Brownrigg*]

Nirmal Pandey (*the transvestite*), Sonali Kulkarni (*the girl*), Faiyyaz (*madam*), Rekha Sahay (*bar owner*), Nina Kulkarni, Kalyani Karandikar.
Dir: Anol Palekar. Pro: Pravesh Sippy. Co-Pro: Dharam Priya Dass. Screenplay: Timeri N. Murari. Ph: Debu Deodhar. Pro Des: Prem Pillai. Ed: Waman Bhosle. M: Anand Milind. Costumes: Meena Naik. Choreography: Saroj Khan. (Gateway Entertainment–Blue Dolphin.) Rel: 13 June 1997. 108 mins. Cert 15. India. 1996.

The Starmaker - L'Uomo Delle Stelle

Sicily; 1953. Posing as a talent scout from Universalia Films in Rome, Joe Morelli charges the natives of Sicily 1,500 lire each to audition for him. Expropriating stolen equipment and outdated film stock, Morelli exploits people's universal desire 'to be in the movies', but steals more than just their money. Asked to improvise for the camera, the would-be 'stars' reveal their most inner selves, never to be offered up again... An odd little film, *The Starmaker* is for the most part nothing more than a series of auditions and scenic vistas of Sicily. Yet, armed with the bewitching rhythms of Ennio Morricone's music and the luminous photography of Dante Spinotti, director Giuseppe Tornatore – who previously explored the allure of the cinema in his Sicilian-set *Cinema Paradiso* – offers up a hypnotic cocktail. US title: *The Star Man*.

Sergio Castellitto (*Joe Morelli*), Tiziana Lodato (*Beata*), Franco Scaldati (*Brigadiere

Dreams are made of this: Sergio Castellito (right) directs a phantom audition in Giuseppe Tornatore's bewitching The Starmaker *(from Fox)*

Mastropaolo), Leopoldo Trieste (*mute*), Jane Alexander, Leo Gullotta, Mariarosa Parrello, Rita Lia, Vincent Navarra, Salvatore Billa, Peppino Tornatore, Simona Merito.
Dir: Giuseppe Tornatore. Pro: Vittorio and Rita Cecchi Gori. Ex Pro: Marion Cotone. Screenplay: Tornatore and Fabio

Born Borg: Alice Krige reveals her facelift in Jonathan Frakes' hugely appealing Star Trek First Contact *(from UIP)*

Rinaudo. Ph: Dante Spinotti. Pro Des: Francesco Bronzi. Ed: Massimo Quaglia. M: Ennio Morricone. Costumes: Beatrice Bordone. (Cecchi Gori Group Tiger Cinematografica/Summit Entertainment–Fox.) Rel: 10 January 1996. 106 mins. Cert 18. Italy. 1994.

The Star Man

See *The Starmaker*.

Star Trek First Contact

Earth/outer space; the 24th century/ 2063. Following the Third World War and the annihilation of 600 million people, planet Earth has never been

The art of sex: Liv Tyler simmers in Bernardo Bertolucci's irresistible Stealing Beauty *(from Fox)*

more vulnerable. Perfect timing, then, for the Borg – a highly advanced force of half-machine, half-organic aliens – to take over and do what they do best: to assimilate the biological and technical attributes of their victims. Shielded by a temporal wake, the *Starship Enterprise E* finds itself immune to the assimilation power of the Borg and immediately engages in battle. However, after destroying its adversary's mother ship, the *Enterprise* finds the enemy within its own walls... The eighth instalment in the celluloid *Star Trek* franchise, *First Contact* elevates the series to a new standard of sci-fi. Utilising some jaw-dropping effects (courtesy of Industrial Light & Magic), the film not only manages to sustain a high level of suspense (while injecting a good deal of humour), but simultaneously balances two narrative trajectories without losing its thread. In addition, Patrick Stewart, as the formidable Jean-Luc Picard, rallies a raw credibility to what so easily could have become a cardboard cut-out. The best *Star Trek* outing since *Star Trek IV: The Voyage Home*.

Patrick Stewart (*Captain Jean-Luc Picard*), Jonathan Frakes (*Director and Commander William Riker*), Brent Spiner (*android Lt Commander Data*), LeVar Burton (*Lt Commander Geordi La Forge*), Michael Dorn (*Lt Commander Worf*), Gates McFadden (*Dr Beverly C. Crusher*), Marina Sirtis (*Lt Commander Deanna Troi*), Alfre Woodard (*Lily Sloane*), James Cromwell (*Zefram Cochrane*), Alice Krige (*Borg Queen*), Neal McDonough, Marnie McPhail, Robert Picardo, Dwight Schultz (*Lt Reginald Endicott Barclay III*), Jack Shearer, Hillary Hayes, Julie Morgan, Don Stark.
Dir: Jonathan Frakes. Pro: Rick Berman. Ex Pro: Martin Hornstein. Screenplay: Brannon Braga and Ronald D. Moore, from a story by Berman, Braga and Moore, based upon the series created by Gene Roddenberry. Ph: Matthew F. Leonetti. Pro Des: Herman Zimmerman. Ed: John W. Wheeler. M: Jerry Goldsmith; numbers performed by Roy Orbison, Julie Morgan, and Steppenwolf. Costumes: Deborah Everton. Visual effects: John Knoll; Industrial Light & Magic. (Paramount–UIP.) Rel: 13 December 1996. 111 mins. Cert 12. USA. 1996.

Steal Big, Steal Little

Santa Barbara; today. Having discovered that her stepson Robby (Andy Garcia) has been skimming the profits from her 40,000-acre ancestral home, bohemian artist Mona Rowland-Downey changes her will so that Robby's identical twin brother, Ruben (Andy Garcia), gets her entire inheritance. On her death, Ruben starts to distribute her money to the homeless and offers half of it to Robby. But Robby wants the whole enchilada and thanks to his connections with a crooked bunch of local officials (judge, cops, business-men, lawyers) he gets Ruben thrown out on the street... For a film that harks back to the simple values of the past, *Steal Big, Steal Little* is anything but simple. Before the opening credits have ended the plot has become so confused that the film never entirely recovers. With his identical hairstyles, Garcia doesn't make it easy for us to know which brother he is playing – besides a fixed benevolent smile for Ruben and a stony stare for Robby. With the heavy-handed use of flashbacks within flashbacks (still during the opening credits), it's hard to differentiate between the two. Some fine special effects (particularly a scene in which both Garcias stand in a room full of mirrors) – and a priceless turn from Alan Arkin – struggle to prevail over the chaotic editing and meddlesome score.

Andy Garcia (*Ruben Partida Martinez/ Roberto Martin*), Alan Arkin (*Lou Perilli*), Rachel Ticotin (*Laura Martinez*), Joe Pantoliano (*Eddie Agopian*), Holland Taylor (*Mona Rowland-Downey*), Ally Walker (*Bonnie Martin*), David Ogden Stiers (*Judge Winton Myers*), Charles Rocket (*Sheriff Otis*), Richard Bradford (*Nick Zingaro*), Kevin McCarthy, Nathan Davis, Dominik Garcia-Lorido, Mike Nussbaum, Rita Taggart, Takaaki Ishibashi, Natalija Nogulich, Victor Rivers, Andy Romano, Fred Asparagus, Drucilla A. Carlson, Nina Beesley, Candice Daly, Cynthia Mace, Robert Harris, Buddy the dog.
Dir: Andrew Davis. Pro: Davis and Fred Caruso. Ex Pro: Mel Pearl. Co-Ex Pro: Larry Jackson. Screenplay: Davis, Lee Blessing, Jeanne Blake and Terry Kahn, from a story by Davis, Teresa Tucker-Davies and Frank Ray Perilli. Ph: Frank Tidy. Pro Des: Michael Haller. Ed: Don Brochu and Tina Hirsch. M: William Olvis. Costumes: Jodie Tillen. (Chicago Pacific Entertainment–Fox.) Rel: 13 December 1996. 115 mins. Cert 12. USA. 1995.

Stealing Beauty - Lo Ballo da Sola

Lucy Harmon, a 19-year-old girl from New York, returns to the scene of her conception in Tuscany, Italy, where she is to pose for a sculpture by a family friend from Dublin. However, the coterie of bohemian ex-pats and their obsession with Lucy's virginity alienates the girl from her hosts – until the beauty of the place takes its grip. But is beauty not a transient asset – as is Lucy's innocence? A man who truly understands the voice of cinema, Bertolucci juggles ideas, music and breathtaking vistas of Tuscany in a sensual cocktail. And so art, love, sex, poetry, conversation, chianti, marijuana, olive groves, Mozart, John Lee Hooker and above all beauty, cast their seductive spell. Bertolucci is the first to admit that he is a melodramatist, and his use of metaphor and operatic romantics may prove too much for some cinemagoers. Notwithstanding, *Stealing Beauty* is a heady celebration of cinema, art and hedonism that many will find irresistible.

Jeremy Irons (*Alex Parrish*), Liv Tyler (*Lucy Harmon*), Sinead Cusack (*Diana Grayson*), Jean Marais (*M Guillaume*), Donal McCann (*Ian Grayson*), D.W. Moffett (*Richard Reed*), Stefania Sandrelli (*Noemi*), Rachel Weisz (*Miranda Fox*), Carlo Cecchi (*Carlo Lisca*), Jason Flemyng (*Gregory*), Roberto Zibetti (*Nicolo Donati*), Joseph Fiennes, Anna Maria Gherardi, Ignazio Oliva, Leonardo Treviglio, Rebecca Valpy, Alessandra Vanzi.

Dir: Bernardo Bertolucci. Pro: Jeremy Thomas. Ex Pro: Yves Attal. Assoc Pro: Chris Auty. Screenplay: Susan Minot, from a story by Bertolucci. Ph: Darius Khondji. Pro Des: Gianni Silvestri. Ed: Pietro Scalia. M: Richard Hartley; Mozart; numbers performed by Liz Phair, Hoover, Isacc Hayes, Billie Holiday, Cocteau Twins, Lori Carson, Hole, Chet Baker, John Lee Hooker, Axiom Funk, Portishead, Nina Simone, Stevie Wonder, Sam Phillips, Mazzy Star, Roland Gift, etc. Costumes: Louise Stjernsward and Giorgio Armani. (Fiction Cinematografica/Recorded Picture Company/UGC Images–Fox.) Rel: 30 August 1996. 118 mins. Cert 15. Italy/UK/France. 1995.

Striptease

Due to the irresponsible behaviour of her husband, Erin Grant loses her secretarial post at the FBI. Then, because she is out of work, she loses custody of her seven-year-old daughter in the ensuing divorce. How unlucky can a momma get? A lot unluckier, as it happens. Forced to raise money to fight her custody battle, Erin takes a job as an exotic dancer at the Eager Beaver. There, matters get further complicated when a libidinous congressman (Burt Reynolds; appalling) falls in love with her and a fan is murdered when he offers to blackmail the former in order to help swing Erin's case... Demi Moore was paid a record $12.5m for her role as the muscular stripper and gives her worst performance since *Parasite* in 1982.

Moore in less: Demi Moore ripples her sinews in Andrew Bergman's risible Striptease *(from Rank)*

Tripping unevenly between farce and thriller, *Striptease* is neither funny nor gripping as the cast attempts to out-act each other. Besides his nervous tics, Armand Assante comes off best as a sympathetic cop, while the heavenly gruff Ving Rhames (*Pulp Fiction, Mission: Impossible*) grabs all the laughs by the scruff of their neck. As for the nudity, it's not a patch on the disrobing in *Showgirls*.

Demi Moore (*Erin Grant*), Armand Assante (*Al Garcia*), Ving Rhames (*Shad*), Robert Patrick (*Darrell Grant*), Burt Reynolds (*David L. Dilbeck*), Paul Guilfoyle (*Malcolm Moldovsky*), Rumer Willis (*Angela Grant*), Stuart Pankin (*Alan Mordecai*), Dina Spybey (*Monique Jr*), Pandora Peaks (*Urbana Sprawl*), Jerry Grayson, Robert Stanton, William Hill, Pasean Wilson, Barbara Alyn Woods, Kimberly Flynn, Siobhan Fallon, Gary Basaraba, Matthew Baron, Gianni Russo, Jose Zuniga, Anthony Jones, Eduardo Yanez, Frances Fisher, Teddy Bergman, Louis Seeger Crume, Keone Young, Anna Lobell.

Dir and Screenplay: Andrew Bergman, based on the book by Carl Hiaasen. Pro: Mike Lobell. Ex Pro: Joseph Hartwick. Ph: Stephen Goldblatt. Pro Des: Mel Bourne. Ed: Anne V. Coates. M: Howard Shore; numbers performed by The Spencer Davis Group, Light Crust Doughboys, Chynna Phillips, Soul Survivors, Blondie, Billy Idol, Billy Ocean, Annie Lennox, The Munchkins, Booker T and The MG's, Smokey Robinson and The Miracles, Herb Alpert & The Tijuana Brass, Pat Boone,

Lena on the beach: Melvil Poupaud and Aurelia Nolin in Eric Rohmer's engaging A Summer's Tale (from Artificial Eye)

Dean Martin, Joan Jett and The Blackhearts, Color Me Badd, Prince, Eurythmics, etc. Costumes: Albert Wolsky. Ms Moore's costumes: Nancy Natalie Cone. Ms Moore's make-up: Joanne Gair. Ms Moore's hair stylist: Enzo Angileri. Ms Moore's assistant: Mark Reinking. Ms Moore's personal trainer: Greg Joujon-Roche. Ms Moore's motion trainer: Tesh Ken Scott. Ms Moore's security: John Musser and Avi Korein. (Castle Rock–Rank–Castle Rock/Turner.) Rel: 20 September 1996. 117 mins. Cert 15. USA. 1996.

The Stupids

America's dumbest family – appropriately named the Stupids – are so retarded that they think their garbage is being stolen every week. Setting out to find the perpetrator of this heinous crime, Stanley Stupid stumbles across an arms deal aimed at world domination – but is too dumb to realise it. Ho, ho. Hard to believe that John Landis, director of *An American Werewolf in London* and *Trading Places*, served up this embarrassment, but it's true. Besides the traditional quota of guest stars, the film bears little resemblance to anything bordering on the film-maker's former expertise – just a desire to cash in on the new wave of moronic humour. Based on the highly popular children's books by

Harry Allard and James Marshall. [*Charles Bacon*]

Tom Arnold (*Stanley Stupid*), Jessica Lundy (*Joan Stupid*), Bug Hall (*Buster Stupid*), Alex McKenna (*Petunia Stupid*), Mark Metcalf (*Colonel*), Matt Keeslar (*Lieutenant*), Christopher Lee (*Evil Sender*), Max Landis, Gurinder Chadha, Mick Garris, Harvey Atkin, David Cronenberg, Constantin Costa-Gavras, Robert Wise, Frankie Faison, Mo Kelso, Atom Egoyan, Norman Jewison, Gillo Pontecorvo, Kevin Conway, Rick Avery.
    Dir: John Landis. Pro: Leslie Belzberg. Screenplay: Brent Forrester. Ph: Manfred Guthe. Pro Des: Phil Dagort. Ed: Dale Beldin. M: Christopher Stone. Costumes: Deborah Nadoolman. (Savoy Pictures/Imagine Entertainment–Rank.) Rel: 9 August 1996. 94 mins. Cert PG. USA. 1996.

The Substitute

Columbus High School; South Florida; today. Infiltrating a high school in South Florida – disguised as substitute teacher 'Mr Smith' – tough mercenary Tom Berenger embarks on a programme to stop some educational rot. His teacher girlfriend has been 'knee-capped' jogging, and Berenger wants to find out who's behind it. As it happens, the school is a front for a drug cartel and is run by the principal, an ex-cop. So, armed with chalk, a bullet-proof vest and a small army of mercenaries, Berenger sets out to teach his pupils a lesson they won't forget... Bringing a cheap action sensibility to the school of cinema of *Blackboard Jungle* and *Dangerous*

Minds, this formula video fodder should be ashamed of itself. It's extraordinary to think that the director previously brought us *F/X* and *School Ties*. [*Ewen Brownrigg*]

Tom Berenger (*Shale/Mr Smith*), Ernie Hudson (*Rolle*), Diane Venora (*Jane Hetzko*), Glenn Plummer (*Sherman*), Marc Anthony (*Juan Lacas*), Cliff De Young (*Wolfson*), William Forsythe (*Hollan*), Sharron Corley, Richard Brooks, Raymond Cruz, Rodney A. Grant, Luis Guzman, Willis Sparks, Jody Wilson.
    Dir: Robert Mandel. Pro: Morrie Eisenman and Jim Steele. Ex Pro: Devora Cutler and Steven Bakalar. Screenplay: Roy Frumkes, Rocco Simonelli and Alan Ormsby. Ph: Bruce Surtees. Pro Des: Ron Foreman. Ed: Alex Mackie. M: Gary Chang; Wagner; numbers performed by Mungo Jerry and Clement Campbell, Kid Frost, John Lee Hooker and Carlos Santana, Deliquent Habits, Paris, etc. Costumes: Patricia Field. (LIVE Film and Mediaworks/Dinamo/H20–Entertainment.) Rel: 9 August 1996. 114 mins. Cert 18. USA. 1996.

A Summer's Tale - Conte d'Ete

Gaspard, one of the most sullen and gauche teenagers to grace the screen in recent memory, is borrowing a friend's room in the seaside resort of Dinard, Brittany. There he awaits the arrival of Lena, a girl that he may or may not be in love with. As he kills time taking lengthy walks along the promenade, he meets up with a local student, Margot, and strikes up a tenuous friendship. She encourages him to seek out another girl, Solene, to help pass the time. But Gaspard is not so sure. In fact, he's not sure of anything... Gaspard is an unlikely cinematic protagonist. Like the character Isabelle Huppert played in Claude Goretta's *The Lacemaker*, he is one of life's 'non-people'. Yet beneath his awkward, uneasy manner, other agendas are at work. It is the ambiguity of Gaspard's character that holds this leisurely, slight work together, as a series of romantic accidents conspire to shake the boy up. In anybody else's hands, this slim story would have been whipped into melodramatic farce, but the 76-year-old Eric Rohmer keeps a tight control on credibility. Rohmer's art is to establish the reality of his scenario and then slip in a story. The concept works, but only for those who have the patience to see it through.

Melvil Poupaud (*Gaspard*), Amanda Langlet (*Margot*), Aurelia Nolin (*Lena*), Gwenaelle Simon (*Solene*), Aime Lefevre (*The Newfoundlander*), Alain Guellaff (*Uncle Alain*), Evelyne Lahana (*Aunt Maiwen*).

Dir and Screenplay: Eric Rohmer. Pro: Francoise Etchegaray. Ph: Diane Baratier. Ed: Mary Stephen. M: Philippe Eidel and Sebastien Erms. (Les Films du Losange/La Sept Cinema/Canal Plus/Sofilmka–Artificial Eye.) Rel: 27 September 1996. 113 mins. Cert U. France. 1996.

The Sunchaser

Michael Cimino's road movie brings together two men: the teenager Blue, a Navajo Indian with a fatal tumour who escapes after being imprisoned for killing his stepfather, and the doctor whom the convict seizes to drive him across country to a healing lake of legend. These roles are admirably played by Jon Seda and Woody Harrelson, and this is a 'Scope movie with a real feel for the epic. Where Jarmusch's tiresome *Dead Man* was terribly earnest in suggesting spiritual myth and transcendency as an answer to materialism, *The Sunchaser* just offers an entertaining evening out. But it's so capably handled that this engaging hokum ends up making its points rather well. Having been trashed by most critics, it could yet become a cult movie. [*Mansel Stimpson*]

Woody Harrelson (*Dr Michael Reynolds*), Jon Seda (*Brandon 'Blue' Monroe*), Anne Bancroft (*Dr Renata Baumbauer*), Alexandra Tydings (*Victoria Reynolds*), Talisa Soto (*Navajo woman*), Matt Mulhern, Richard Bauer, Victor Aaron, Lawrence Pressman, Michael O'Neill, Harry Carey Jr, Emil Alexander, Pam Morton, Mickey Jones, Brett Harrelson, Robert Downey (*telephone voices*).

Dir: Michael Cimino. Pro: Cimino, Arnon Milchan, Larry Spiegel, Judy Goldstein and Joseph S. Vecchio. Ex Pro: Michael Nathanson and Joseph M. Caracciolo. Screenplay: Charles Leavitt. Ph: Doug Milsome. Pro Des: Victoria Paul. Ed: Joe D'Augustine. M: Maurice Jarre; numbers performed by Esther Phillips, Los Lobos, Mary J. Blige, David Bowie, Roy Orbison, etc. Sound: Anthony R. Milch, Roland Thai, Brian Best and Frank Kniest. (Monarchy Enterprises/Regency Enterprises/Vecchio/Appledown–Warner.) Rel: 22 November 1996. 122 mins. Cert 15. USA. 1996.

Surviving Picasso

1943-1953; France. When the 23-year-old art student Francoise Gilot is invited up to Picasso's garret 'to see his etchings', she succumbs to the man's forthrightness and charm and soon moves in with him – much against the wishes of her autocratic father. Gradually, however, Francoise is to realise that she is not the only woman in Picasso's life as ex-wives and mistresses constantly emerge from the woodwork. But Francoise is unlike any other woman Picasso has known... While Ruth Prawer Jhabvala has fashioned a literate screenplay from Arianna Stassinopoulos Huffington's book, *Picasso: Creator and Destroyer*, distilling lots of fascinating detail, she has fallen prey to the age-old problem of screen biographies by failing to find a driving narrative to hang it all on. Picasso was, indeed, an extraordinary man: inspired, intelligent and driven, yet also arrogant, vain, selfish, tyrannical,

Selfish portrait: Anthony Hopkins returns to mimicry in James Ivory's laborious Surviving Picasso *(from Warner)*

cruel and mean, the latter short-comings all lovingly chronicled here. However, Hopkins, who contributed such fine work to Merchant Ivory's *Howards End* and *The Remains of the Day*, is unable to bring Jhabvala's lines alive and misses the mischievous magnetism of a man who was able to ensnare so many women (Ben Kingsley would've been a much more suitable choice.)

Anthony Hopkins (*Pablo Picasso*), Diane Venora (*Jacqueline Roque*), Joan Plowright (*Francoise's grandmother*), Natascha McElhone (*Francoise Gilot*), Julianne Moore (*Dora Maar*), Joss Ackland (*Henri Matisse*), Peter Eyre (*Jaime Sabartes*), Jane Lapotaire (*Olga Picasso*), Joseph Maher (*Daniel-Henry Kahnweiler*), Bob Peck (*M. Gilot, Francoise's father*), Dominic West (*Paulo Picasso*), Andreas Wisniewski, Allegra Di Capegna, Nigel Whitmey, Leon Lissek, Agapi Stassinopoulos, Susannah Harker, Dennis Boutsikaris, Vernon Dobtcheff, Sandor Eles, Brigitte Kahn, Stefan Gryff.

Dir: James Ivory. Pro: Ismail Merchant and David L. Wolper. Ex Pro: Donald Rosenfeld and Paul Bradley. Screenplay: Ruth Prawer Jhabvala. Ph: Tony Pierce-Roberts. Pro Des: Luciana Arrighi. Ed: Andrew Marcus. M: Richard Robbins. Costumes: Carol Ramsey. (Merchant Ivory/Wolper–Warner.) Rel: 26 December 1996. 122 mins. Cert 15. UK/USA. 1996.

Unearthing the truth: Brenda Fricker and Miranda Richardson probe into the life and death of Mary Swann *(from Guild)*

Swann

Nadeau, Ontario/Chicago/Toronto; today. Seldom is anything truly what it seems and the strange case of the little-known poet Mary Swann was anything but. When she is hacked to death by her husband on their farm in a remote corner of Ontario, her

Doing their thing: Johnathon Schaech and Liv Tyler in Tom Hanks' inviting That Thing You Do! *(from Fox)*

poetic scribblings are discovered by a local librarian, Rose Hindmarch, and are subsequently published to enormous acclaim. Soon the verse is attracting the attention of two rival biographers, including the successful journalist and columnist Sarah Maloney who embarks on a tenuous friendship with the intensely private Rose Hindmarch... Once one has gotten over the improbable pairing of the Lancashire-born Miranda Richardson and Dublin-born Brenda Fricker as a couple of North Americans, *Swann* settles into an intriguing little drama with an ambivalent agenda. Who is preventing Sarah from reaching her

publisher's deadline and why is Rose so protective of her friendship with the late Mary Swann?

Miranda Richardson (*Sarah Maloney*), Brenda Fricker (*Rose Hindmarch*), Michael Ontkean (*Stephen*), David Cubitt (*Ladner Brown*), Sean Hewitt (*Professor Morton Jimroy*), Sean McCann (*Homer*), John Neville (*Frederick Cruzzi*), Kyra Harper (*Jean*), Meg Hogarth (*Mrs Cruzzi*), Geny Walter (*Mary Swann*), John E. Nelles, Suzanne Coy.
   Dir: Anna Benson Gyles. Pro: Ann Scott and Christina Jennings. Screenplay: David Young, based on the novel by Carol Shields. Ph: Gerard Packer. Pro Des: John Dondertman. Ed: Robin Sales. M: Richard Rodney Bennett. Costumes: Elisabeth Beraldo. (Shaftesbury Films/Greenpoint/Majestic Films/Telefilm Canada/BBC Films, etc.–Guild.) Rel: 7 March 1997. 96 mins. Cert 15. Canada/UK. 1996.

That Thing You Do!

John F. Kennedy has been dead for four months, The Beatles have just made their historical appearance on *The Ed Sullivan Show* and a group of young guys from Erie, Pennsylvania, are themselves muscling in on the music scene. At least, they enjoy a good jam session in the garage. Then one fateful day Chad falls over and breaks his arm, so appliance salesman Guy Patterson is asked to take his place on drums in a high school talent show. The quartet – initially calling themselves The One-Ders (pronounced Wonders) – win the contest and their song, 'That Thing You Do!', begins its journey into the public consciousness... Part pastiche, part valentine, *That Thing You Do!* is a sweet, funny and snappy look at the mercurial world of instant stardom in the halcyon days of pop'n'roll. A likeable cast leap through their paces with aplomb, while the title song – selected for the film out of 300 submissions – holds up handsomely after repeated playings. Tom Hanks, who plays a supporting role as the group's manager, not only directs from his own original screenplay but also contributes nine of the numbers (including four solo compositions.) The perfect Tom Hanks film: boyish, easy-going and charming. And about as threatening as a strawberry soufflé.

Tom Everett Scott (*Guy Patterson*), Liv Tyler (*Faye Dolan*), Johnathon Schaech

The law versus justice: Charles S. Dutton and Matthew McConaughey in Joel Schumacher's riveting A Time to Kill *(from Warner)*

(*Jimmy*), Steve Zahn (*Lenny*), Ethan Embry (*The Bass Player*), Tom Hanks (*Mr White*), Charlize Theron (*Tina Powers*), Obba Babatunde (*Lamarr*), Giovanni Ribisi (*Chad*), Bill Cobbs (*Del Paxton*), Kevin Pollak (*Boss Vic Koss*), Holmes Osborne Jr (*Mr Patterson*), Chris Ellis, Alex Rocco, Peter Scolari, Rita Wilson, Chris Isaak, Robert Torti, Chaille Percival, Claudia Stedelin, Dawn Maxey, Lee Everett, Clint Howard, Kathleen Kinmont, Warren Berlinger, Jonathan Demme, Tracy Reiner, Gedde Watanabe, Marc McClure, Colin Hanks, Elizabeth Hanks.

Dir and Screenplay: Tom Hanks. Pro: Gary Goetzman, Jonathan Demme and Edward Saxon. Ph: Tak Fujimoto. Pro Des: Victor Kempster. Ed: Richard Chew. M: Howard Shore; numbers written by Hanks, Adam Schlesinger, Mike Piccirillo, etc. Costumes: Colleen Atwood. (Fox/ Clinica Estetico/Clavius Base–Fox.) Rel: 24 January 1996. 107 mins. Cert PG. USA. 1996.

Through the Olive Trees - Zire Darakhtan Zeyton

Koker, Northern Iran; June 1993. Concluding his trilogy that began with *Where Is My Friend's House?* and *And Life Goes On...*, writer-director Abbas Kiarostami zeros in on the lives of the actors who played the young bride and groom in his last film. Coaxing the original performers to play themselves, Kiarostami examines the whole process of filmmaking and the real drama that bubbled under the surface of *And Life Goes On....* The result, while leisurely, is fascinating in its detail, capturing the monotony and frustrations of a twentieth-century process at odds with the rural deprivation of Northern Iran. Furthermore, Kiarostami had to contend with the devastating aftermath of an earthquake which he utilises to fuel his narrative. Indeed, life must go on. Some critics found Kiarostami's meditations tedious, but I relished his attempts to recreate a reality born from fiction – and then dramatised – never less than utterly captivating. FYI: Kiarostami went on to write the screenplay for Jafar Panahi's sublime *The White Balloon*.

Mohamed Ali Keshavarz (*the director*), Farhad Kheradmand, Zarifeh Shiva, Hossen Rezai, Tahereh Ladania, Mahbanou Darabin, Hocine Redai, Zahra Nourouzi (*Kouly's wife*).

Dir, Pro, Screenplay and Ed: Abbas Kiarostami. Ph: Hossein Djafarian and Farhad Saba. (Farabi Cinema Foundation– Artificial Eye.) Rel: 27 December 1996. 103 mins. Cert U. Iran. 1994.

A Time to Kill

Mississippi; today. When his ten-year-old daughter is beaten and raped within an inch of her life, Carl Lee Hailey, a black factory worker, takes out his anger by gunning down the white perpetrators in cold blood – in front of a crowd of witnesses. With his motive inadmissible in court, an all-white jury assigned to his case and little money to defend himself, Carl Lee faces the gas chamber if he is found guilty of murder. In addition, he becomes the catalyst in a Ku Klux Klan revival. Enter young, pig-headed attorney Jake Brigance, who takes on Carl Lee's defence in spite of dwindling funds and death threats... Once again displaying his forté for blending a commercial blockbuster with a potent adult theme, Joel Schumacher punches some highly sensitive buttons with

Turf 'n' mirth: Rene Russo and Kevin Costner tee off in Ron Shelton's witty and poetic Tin Cup *(from Warner)*

consummate skill. While you can never forget that this is a Hollywood movie, the subject is incendiary enough, the facts credible enough and the material so well written that *A Time to Kill* leaves a powerful imprint. A masterful cast – particularly McConaughey, Bullock, Jackson and Spacey – deliver outstanding performances, and are well served by slick, invisible craftsmanship. This was John Grisham's first and favourite novel, and Schumacher's passionate, authoritative translation does it proud, lifting it well above the page-turning theatrics of *The Firm*, *The Pelican Brief* and *The Client*. FYI: When Grisham vetoed Brad Pitt, Woody Harrelson and Val Kilmer for the central role of Jake Brigance, Warner Brothers reluctantly accepted his choice of virtual unknown Matthew McConaughey (thank God.)

Sandra Bullock (*Ellen Roark*), Samuel L. Jackson (*Carl Lee Hailey*), Matthew McConaughey (*Jake Brigance*), Kevin

Spacey (*Rufus Buckley*), Brenda Fricker (*Ethel Twitty*), Oliver Platt (*Harry Rex Vonner*), Charles S. Dutton (*Sheriff Ozzie Walls*), Ashley Judd (*Carla Brigance*), Patrick McGoohan (*Judge Omar Noose*), Donald Sutherland (*Lucien Wilbanks*), Kiefer Sutherland (*Freddie Cobb*), Tonea Stewart (*Gwen Hailey*), Chris Cooper (*Deputy Looney*), Joe Seneca (*Reverend Isaiah Street*), Thomas Merdis (*Reverend Ollie Agee*), M. Emmet Walsh (*Willard Tyrell Bass*), Raeven Larrymore Kelly, John Diehl, Nicky Katt, Doug Hutchison, Kurtwood Smith, Tim Parati, Mark Whitman Johnson, Beth Grant, Anthony Heald, Alexandra Kyle, Terry Loughlin, Andy Stahl, Joe Bullen, Jonathan Hadary, Byron Jennings, Leonard Thomas, Bettina Rose.

Dir: Joel Schumacher. Pro: Arnon Milchan, Michael Nathanson, Hunt Lowry and John Grisham. Screenplay: Akiva Goldsman. Ph: Peter Menzies. Pro Des: Larry Fulton. Ed: William Steinkamp. M: Elliot Goldenthal. Costumes: Ingrid Ferrin. Sound design: Roland Thai. (Regency Enterprises–Warner.) Rel: 13 September 1996. 149 mins. Cert 15. USA. 1996.

Tin Cup

Although he has ended up teaching golf lessons at a run-down armadillo-plagued range in Salome, West Texas, Roy 'Tin Cup' McAvoy has

always lived his life for the moment. However, his long-time rival, David Simms, has gone on to become a wealthy and celebrated star of the PGA. When Simms turns up to offer him a job as his caddie – with a beautiful, leggy psychologist on his arm – Roy decides to seize the moment again... With the critical and commercial success of *Bull Durham* eight years ago, writer-director Ron Shelton proved that baseball and cinema could co-exist. Now he transforms the sedate, gentlemanly sport of golf into a game of extra-ordinary excitement, cunning and poetry. And, just as Kevin Costner brought a loose-limbed lyricism to his washed-up baseball veteran in the former, so he brings a poetic complexity to his talented but routed golfer – comparing a golf swing to 'a living sculpture' and explaining that the game itself is best realised by 'gaining control of your life and letting go at the same time'. A number of stock clichés of the sporting genre are observed, but then smartly revised, although Don Johnson's smarmy champion is a tad one-dimensional. Shelton's script is, as always, both witty and real, with no detail too small for inclusion (like the heated row over the location of a Waffle House.)

Kevin Costner (*Roy 'Tin Cup' McAvoy*), Rene Russo (*Dr Molly Griswold*), Cheech Marin (*Romeo Posar*), Don Johnson (*David Simms*), Linda Hart (*Doreen*), Dennis Burkley (*Earl*), Rex Linn (*Dewey*), Lou Myers, Richard Lineback, George Perez, Mickey Jones, Michael Milhoan, Gary McCord (*as himself*), Craig Stadler (*as himself*), Peter Jacobsen (*as himself*), Kevin Wilson, Sharon Costner, Bill Costner, Joe Costner.

Dir: Ron Shelton. Pro: Gary Foster and David Lester. Ex Pro: Arnon Milchan. Assoc Pro: Karin Freud and Kellie Davis. Screenplay: Shelton and John Norville. Ph: Russell Boyd. Pro Des: James Bissell. Ed: Paul Seydor and Kimberly Ray. M: William Ross; Vivaldi; numbers performed by Texas Tornados, Patty Loveless, Keb' Mo', Jimmie Vaughan, Los Lobos, George Jones, Bruce Hornsby, Buddy Guy, James House, Joe Ely, Mickey Jones, Tito and Tarantula, Mary Chapin Carpenter, Chris Isaak, Cheech Marin, Amanda Marshall, and Shawn Colvin. Costumes: Carol Oditz. (Regency Enterprises–Warner.) Rel: 18 October 1996. Cert 15. 135 mins. USA. 1996.

The Tit and the Moon - La Teta y la Luna

Tete is nine years old and is not enjoying his life. His father is training him to be an '*anxaneta*', a boy whose specialty is to climb to the summit of a human tower, or '*castell*', a sport unique to Catalonia. Worse still, Tete's mother has just given birth to a piglet and the boy has become unreasonably jealous of his mother's milk-yielding breast. And so he sets out to find his own breast to worship. Soon enough he finds his bosom of choice; a beautiful mammary gland that belongs to a French ballerina. But then Tete has to compete for her affections with a local flamenco singer and an ageing biker who farts on stage for a living... While proving to be every bit as unusual and earthy as his previous films *Jamon Jamon* and *Golden Balls*, the latest outing from the Catalan director Bigas Luna displays the additional ingredients of charm and magic. A constant surprise, the film is also funny and touching, helped not a little by a melodious score from Nicola Piovani and the haunting voice of Edith Piaf. A gem.

Mathilda May (*Estrellita - 'La Gabacha'*), Gerard Darmon (*Maurice - 'El Gabacho'*), Miguel Poveda (*Miguel - 'El Charmego'*), Biel Duran (*Tete*), Albert Folch (*father*), Laura Mana (*mother*), Genis Sanchez (*Stallone*), Xavier Masse, Xus Estruch, Victoria Lepori, Jane Harvey.

Dir: Bigas Luna. Pro: Andres Vicente Gomez. Co-Pro: Xavier Gelin and Stephane Marsil. Assoc Pro: Manuel Lombardero and Eduardo Campoy. Screenplay: Luna and Cuca Canals. Ph: Jose Luis Alcaine. Art: Aime Deude. Ed: Carmen Frias. M: Nicola Piovani. Costumes: Patricia Monne. (Lolafilms SA / Cartel SA/Hugo Films–Metro Tartan.) Rel: 12 July 1996. 85 mins. Cert 18. Spain/ France. 1994.

Tokyo Fist

Tsuda Yoshiharu is a meek, overworked insurance salesman who bumps into an old classmate from high school. The latter, now a professional boxer, moves in on Tsuda's girlfriend, prompting her to ram a hot nail through her ear lobe and then pierce her nipples. In distress, Tsuda takes up boxing and swears vengeance on his old chum... Having pushed the barriers of acceptable taste in *Tetsuo: The Iron Man* and *Tetsuo II: Body Hammer*, writer-producer-director-production designer-star-masochist Tsukamoto

The milk of human kindness: Biel Duran gets a mouthful of lactose in Bigas Luna's magical The Tit and the Moon *(from Metro Tartan)*

Shin'ya turns to the boxing arena to explore his demons. Nicely contrasting the clinical, blue-rinsed modernism of Tokyo's architecture with the age-old lust for bright red blood, Tsukamoto takes off on a personal, narcissistic odyssey of gratuitous violence in which he not only casts himself in the lead, but his brother, Kohji, as his nemesis. Besides the novelty of watching more spurting blood than in any previous boxing movie, this pretentious, incomprehensible exercise has little to offer.

Fujii Kahori (*Hizuru*), Tsukamoto Shin'ya (*Tsuda*), Tsukamoto Kohji (*Takuji*), Takenaka Naoto.

Dir, Pro, Screenplay, Ph, Pro Des and Ed: Tsukamoto Shin'ya, from a story by Tsukamoto and Hisashi Saito. Assoc Pro: Kiyo Joo. M: Chu Ishikawa. (Kaijyu Theater Co–Blue Dolphin.) Rel: 4 April 1997. 88 mins. Cert 18. Japan. 1995.

Total Eclipse

France/London/Abyssinia; 1871-1891. The French poet Paul Verlaine was a master of his craft and was just 14 when he sent his first poem to Victor Hugo. Eleven years later, a 16-year-old writer called Arthur Rimbaud (pronounced Rambo) sent his own verse to Verlaine, who was now living in Paris with his 18-year-old pregnant wife. Knocked out by the freshness and audacity of the latter's work, Verlaine invited Rimbaud to stay with him. Feeding each other's passion for their art, the

Zen and the art of psyche maintenance: Steve Buscemi in his pungent directorial debut, Trees Lounge *(from Electric)*

poets proceeded to embark on a tumultuous, all-consuming affair... Spiked with emotional sadism (both Rimbaud's taunting of Verlaine and Verlaine's psychological cruelty towards his wife) and punctuated by ungainly couplings, *Total Eclipse* is only rescued from total tedium by the unpleasantness of its material. Yet had such an ugly scenario been invested with an iota of credibility or style, it might have been worth the watch. As it is, the casting of the Californian Leonardo DiCaprio as Rimbaud and the Blackpool-born David Thewlis as Verlaine is as culturally intuitive as allowing John Rambo to rescue Afghanistan single-handed.

Leonardo DiCaprio (*Arthur Rimbaud*), David Thewlis (*Paul Verlaine*), Romane Bohringer (*Mathilde Verlaine*), Dominique Blanc (*Isabelle Rimbaud*), Nita Klein (*Rimbaud's mother*), Christopher Hampton (*The Judge*), Felicie Pasotti Cabarbaye, James Thieree, Emmanuelle Oppo, Christopher Chaplin, Kettly Noel.
  Dir: Agnieszka Holland. Pro: Jean-Pierre Ramsay Levi. Ex Pro: Jean-Yves Asselin, Staffan Ahrenberg and Pascale Faubert. Screenplay: Christopher Hampton. Ph: Yorgos Arvanitis. Pro Des: Dan Weil. Ed: Isabel Lorente. M: Jan. A.P. Kaczmarek. Costumes: Pierre-Yves Gayraud. (FIT Prods/Portman Prods/K2/ Capitol Films/Canal Plus–Feature Film Co..) Rel: 11 April 1997. 111 mins. Cert 18. France/UK/Belgium. 1995.

Trees Lounge

Valley Stream, Long Island, New York; the present. Writer-director Steve Buscemi, whose script was partly inspired by a John Cassavetes retrospective, notes, 'I tried to imagine what my life would be like if I had never moved to Manhattan and pursued acting; if I had just stayed in Valley Stream.' It's a naked contemplation, as Buscemi's alter ego, Tommy Basilio, does little but haunt the local bar of the title, hang out with some miserable low-lives and enter into a relationship with the 17-year-old daughter of an old friend. Having acted in four films by the Coen brothers, two by Tarantino and others by Scorsese, Altman and Jarmusch, Buscemi must have absorbed some directorial talent, if only by osmosis. In this, his directorial debut, there are no great lines, no unforgettable performances and no surprise plot twists. However, what Buscemi has learned from his directors is a confidence in his material which he shapes here with the hand of an experienced auteur. This is an atmospheric piece, tinged with the poignancy of unrealised dreams and distinguished by some proficient talent both in front of and behind the camera: Lisa Rinzler's evocative photography, Evan Lurie's perfectly integrated score and Chloe Sevigny's touching turn as the vulnerable, misplaced Debbie. But this is primarily Buscemi's triumph and the Coens, Tarantino and Altman must be proud.

Steve Buscemi (*Tommy Basilio*), Chloe Sevigny (*Debbie*), Anthony LaPaglia (*Rob*), Elizabeth Bracco (*Theresa*), Mark Boone Junior (*Mike*), Seymour Cassel (*Uncle Al*), Michael Buscemi (*Raymond Basilio*), Daniel Baldwin (*Jerry*), Carol Kane (*Connie*), Bronson Dudley (*Bill*), Eszter Balint (*Marie*), Kevin Corrigan (*Matthew*), Debi Mazar (*Crystal*), Suzanne Shepherd (*Jackie*), Rockets Redglare (*Stan*), Mimi Rogers (*Patty*), Annette Arnold, Steve Randazzo, Michael Imperioli, Samuel L. Jackson, Larry Gilliard, Charles Newmark, Victor Arnold, Irma St Paule, Brooke Smith.
  Dir and Screenplay: Steve Buscemi. Pro: Brad Wyman and Chris Hanley. Ex Pro: Nick Wechsler and Julie Silverman. Co-Pro: Kelley Forsyth and Sarah Vogel. Ph: Lisa Rinzler. Pro Des: Steve Rosenzweig. Ed: Kate Williams. M: Evan Lurie; numbers performed by The Ink Spots, Free, Argent, The Trees Lounge Kids, Brenda Lee, Mark Boone Junior, The Mills Brothers, Randy Bachman, Earl Hooker, Shane MacGowan & The Popes, The Platters, etc. Costumes: Mari-An Ceo. (Live Film and Mediaworks Inc./Live Entertainment/Seneca Falls–Electric.) Rel: 14 February 1997. 95 mins. Cert 15. USA. 1996.

Trigger Happy

In the nether world of Vic's swinging Rough-House nightclub, the word is out that Vic is about to be released from the loony bin. This is bad news for Vic's executive officers, who have been abusing their privileges in his absence. The volatile Ben 'Brass Balls' London has been riding roughshod over Vic's business interests (i.e. killing who he likes), while Mickey Holliday has been sleeping with the boss's girlfriend. But now Vic is out and his calm, benevolent air is not to be misinterpreted... A film based on the question of which star will die next is a pathetic excuse for a film. For with no basis in reality it doesn't matter who will live or die, although the billing is a good indication of who will hit the dust next. Further-more, the play on the characters' names – Mick, Vic and Nick – is a poor substitute for wit. Even the normally composed Jeff Goldblum looks seriously bemused here and for some inexplicable reason is constantly fiddling with his fly. US title: *Mad Dog Time.*

Ellen Barkin (*Rita Everly*), Gabriel Byrne (*Ben 'Brass Balls' London*), Richard Dreyfuss (*Vic*), Jeff Goldblum (*Mickey Holliday*), Diane Lane (*Grace Everly*), Larry Bishop (*Nick Falco*), Gregory Hines (*Jules Flamingo*), Kyle MacLachlan (*Jake Parker*), Burt Reynolds ('*Wacky' Jacky Jackson*), Henry Silva (*Sleepy Joe Carlisle*), Michael J. Pollard, Angie Everhart, Billy Idol, Juan Fernandez, Billy Drago, Christopher Jones ('*Nicholas Falco*'), Paul Anka, Rob Reiner, Richard Pryor, Joey Bishop.

Dir, Co-Pro and Screenplay: Larry Bishop. Pro: Judith Rutherford James. Ex Pro: Stephan Manpearl and Len Shapiro. Ph: Frank Byers. Pro Des: Dina Lipton. Ed: Norman Hollyn. M: Earl Rose; numbers performed by Frank Sinatra, Dean Martin, Paul Anka and Gabriel Byrne, and Sammy Davis Jr. Costumes: Ileane Meltzer. (Ring-A-Ding/ Dreyfuss/James/Skylight Films/ United Artists–First Independent.) Rel: 13 June 1997. 93 mins. Cert 15. USA. 1996.

Trojan Eddie

Trojan Eddie is a market hawker with a gift for the gab. On a good day he could sell you £50 worth of stuff you didn't even want. But Eddie works for John Power, a ruthless businessman with an iron grip on the local community of 'travellers'. Eddie wants out, to start his own business. But Power is a hard man to elude, and when Eddie inadvertently becomes involved in the tyrant's public disgrace his future looks decidedly unhealthy... I'm sorry, did somebody mention a story? Or characters to care about? Or, at the very least, some kind of point to the whole thing? I didn't think so. With Richard Harris in impassive, mono-lithic mode (his best impersonation of an Easter Island statue yet) and Stephen Rea supplying his entire range of hang-dog expressions, the film gets little help from its actors. A sombre, charmless and aimless experience.

Richard Harris (*John Power*), Stephen Rea (*Trojan Eddie*), Brendan Gleeson (*Ginger Power*), Sean McGinley (*Raymie*), Angeline Ball (*Shirley*), Brid Brennan (*Betty*), Aislin McGluckin (*Kathleen*), Stuart Townsend (*Dermot*), Angela O'Driscoll (*Carol*), Jason Gilroy, Maria McDermottroe, Sean Lawlor, Britta Smith, Jimmy Keogh, Billy Roche, Michael Collins.

Dir: Gillies MacKinnon. Pro: Emma Burge. Ex Pro: Alan J. Wands, Kevin Menton and Rod Stoneman. Co-Pro:

Seamus Byrne. Screenplay: Billy Roche. Ph: John de Borman. Pro Des: Frank Conway. Ed: Scott Thomas. M: John Keane. Costumes: Consolata Boyle. (Channel Four/Initial Films/Stratford/ Irish Film Board/Irish Screen, etc.–Film Four.) Rel: 21 March 1997. 105 mins. Cert 15. UK/Ireland. 1996.

Tromeo and Juliet

New York; today. The white son of a flatulent black man falls for the sexually abused daughter of a schlock film tycoon, causing swells of protest among their respective camps... Were it not for the concurrent release of so many legitimate Shakespearean films, this shocking spoof would barely have warranted a transfer on to Scotch video. As it is, all the hallmarks of *Troma* are here: shoddy production values, sub-amateur acting, gruesome rubber-and-soup effects and a spark of wit every 15 minutes or so. Juliet: 'Parting is such sweet sorrow.' Tromeo: 'No, it sucks.'

Jane Jensen (*Juliet Capulet*), Will Keenan (*Tromeo Que*), Valentine Miele (*Murray Martini*), Maximilian Shaun (*Cappy Capulet*), Steve Gibbons, Sean Gunn, Debbie Rochon, Wendy Adams, Lloyd

Rough trade: Stephen Rea attempts to barter his way out of trouble in Gillies MacKinnon's charmless Trojan Eddie *(from Film Four)*

Kaufman (*as the guy who finds his penis*), Lemmy (*the narrator*).

Dir: Lloyd Kaufman. Pro: Kaufman and Michael Herz. Ex Pro: Daniel Laikind, Grant Quasha and Robert Schiller. Co-Pro: Jonathan Foster and Robert Hersov. Assoc Pro: Andrew Weiner. Line Pro: Franny Baldwin. Screenplay: Kaufman and James Gunn. Ph: Brendan Flynt. Pro Des: Roshelle Berliner. Ed: Frank Reynolds. M: Willie Wisely; numbers performed by Thorn, Motorhead, Superchunk, The Willie Wisely Trio, Supernova, Ass Ponys, Jane Jensen, The Wesley Willis Fiasco, The Icons, Unsane, The Meatmen, etc. Costumes: Kyra Svetlovsky. Make-up effects: Louis Zakarian. Stunt nipple: Sandee Brockwell. (Troma Team–Troma Team.) Rel: 25 October 1996. 95 mins. Cert 18. USA. 1996.

True Blue

Following their rare defeat at the sculls of Cambridge in 1986, the Oxford University Boat Club face a gruelling year of pulling their socks up. Team mates must be chosen, differences patched up and a whole lot of training put into practice. However, tempers and nostrils flare, people quit and are fired and the dreaming spires of Oxford open one sleepy eye as the team prepares for mutiny. How can they get their act together before the next big race in March? A labour of love brimming with sincerity, *True Blue* cannot

disguise the fact that it is just 90 minutes of bickering followed by a quick boat race in the rain (with an inevitable outcome.) Who cares? Worse, the acting is decidedly uneven, the photography underlit and the subject matter unequivocally esoteric. *Chariots of Fire* it ain't.

Johan Leysen (*Daniel Topolski*), Dominic West (*Donald Macdonald*), Dylan Baker (*Michael Suarez, SJ*), Geraldine Somerville (*Ruth Macdonald*), Josh Lucas (*Dan Warren*), Brian McGovern (*Rick Ross*), Ryan Bollman (*Morrison Black*), Andrew Tees (*John Smythson*), Nicholas Rowe (*David Ball*), Clive Merrison (*Jack Garnet*), Robert Bogue, Noah Huntley, Edward Atterton, Jonathan Cake, Alexis Denisof, Patrick Malone, Andrew Clover, Tom Hollander, Danny Webb, Bill Nighy, Timothy Bateson, Helena Michell, Darcey Bussell, Daniel Topolski.
    Dir: Ferdinand Fairfax. Pro: Clive Parsons and Davina Belling. Ex Pro: Allan Scott. Line Pro: Al Burgess. Screenplay: Rupert Walters, based on the book by Daniel Topolski and Patrick Robinson. Ph: Brian Tufano. Pro Des: Alison Riva. Ed: Les Healey. M: Stanislas Syrewicz; 'Two Tribes' performed by Frankie Goes To Hollywood. Costumes: Delphine Roche-Gordon. (Channel Four/Booker Entertainment/The Arts Council of England/Film & General/Rafford–Film Four.) Rel: 15 November 1996. 118 mins. Cert 15. UK. 1996.

Mind over matter: Janeane Garofalo and Uma Thurman make the perfect woman (for Ben Chaplin) in Michael Lehmann's winning The Truth About Cats & Dogs *(from Fox)*

The Truth About Cats and Dogs

Veterinarian Abby Barnes hosts a radio talk show called 'The Truth About Cats and Dogs'. Bright, talented and funny, Abby hides behind the power of her voice and inadvertently seduces one caller – an English photographer called Brian – into a blind date. Developing cold feet, she convinces the tall, blonde and beautiful (if scatty) Noelle Slusarsky to stand in for her at the last minute. The evening is a success but is nothing compared to the subsequent seven-hour phone call in which Brian and the real Abby exchange their most intimate feelings. Brian is now well and truly hooked, but then he does think Abby looks like a tall, blonde supermodel... Updating and sexually reversing the concept of *Cyrano de Bergerac*, *The Truth About Cats and Dogs* takes a fresh spin on an old theme and pumps it with charm and humour. At heart an endearingly old-fashioned romantic comedy, the film never resorts to sentimentality thanks to a scalpel-honed turn from the sublime Janeane Garofalo (*Reality Bites, Bye Bye Love*) in her first starring role. Sweet, smart and very funny.

Uma Thurman (*Noelle Slusarsky*), Janeane Garofalo (*Abby Barnes*), Ben Chaplin (*Brian*), Jamie Foxx (*Ed*), James McCaffrey (*Roy*), Hank (*Hank*), Richard Coca, Stanley DeSantis, Antoinette Valente, Mitch Rouse, La Tanya M. Fisher.

Dir: Michael Lehmann. Pro: Cari-Esta Albert. Ex Pro: Richard Hashimoto and Audrey Wells. Screenplay: Wells. Ph: Robert Brinkman. Pro Des: Sharon Seymour. Ed: Stephen Semel. M: Howard Shore; numbers performed by Sting and Ranking Roger, Paul Weller, The Robert Cray Band, The Brand New Heavies, Blues Traveler, Aaron Neville, Ben Folds Five, Al Green, Suzanne Vega, Cowboy Junkies, Dionne Farris, Squeeze, and Jill Sobule. Costumes: Bridget Kelly. (Fox/Noon Attack–Fox.) Rel: 19 July 1996. 97 mins. Cert 15. USA. 1996.

Turbulence

Flight 47, Boeing 747-200; Christmas Eve. Trapped by planted evidence, Ryan Weaver, a man suspected of raping and strangling five blonde women, is rounded up by police in New York. Escorted on to a Los Angeles-bound 747 by four federal agents, Weaver finds himself in the company of a brutal bank robber and just 11 other passengers. A storm is brewing, but the outside conditions are nothing compared to what is about to take place on the plane... Following an intriguing build-up in which the viewer is led up a few short garden paths, *Turbulence* buckles down to its white knuckle objective. Flying into the direct path of such movies as *Airport 1975*, *Passenger 57* and *Executive Decision*, the film is not entirely original, is far-fetched and buffets logic once too often. Furthermore, by casting Hollywood's favourite psycho – Ray Liotta (*Something Wild, Unlawful Entry*) – as the psycho is not exactly subtle casting. None the less, there are some terrific moments, although most arrive too late in the flight.

Ray Liotta (*Ryan Weaver*), Lauren Holly (*Teri Halloran*), Brendan Gleeson (*Stubbs*), Ben Cross (*Captain Sam Bowen*), Hector Elizondo (*Lt Aldo Hines*), Rachel Ticotin (*Rachel Taper*), Jeffrey DeMunn (*Brooks*), John Finn (*Sinclair*), Catherine Hicks (*Maggie*), Heidi Kling (*Betty*), J. Kenneth Campbell, Gordy Owens, James MacDonald, Grand L. Bush, Bill Cross, Cooper Huckabee.
    Dir: Robert Butler. Pro: Martin Ransohoff and David Valdes. Ex Pro: Keith Samples. Assoc Pro: D. Scott Easton. Screenplay: Jonathan Brett, and (uncredited) Steven E. De Souza and John Herzfeld. Ph: Lloyd Ahern. Pro Des: Mayling Cheng. Ed: John Duffy. M: Shirley Walker. Costumes: Robert Turturice. Visual effects: Mark Vargo.

(Rysher Entertainment–Entertainment.) Rel: 30 May 1997. 100 mins. Cert 18. USA. 1997.

Twelfth Night

Identical twins, Viola and Sebastian, are shipwrecked off the coast of Illyria, believing each other drowned. As Orsino, the Duke of Illyria, discourages the presence of women in his court, Viola disguises herself as a page boy and quickly gains the confidence of the duke. Dispatched to woo the mourning Olivia on his behalf, Viola finds herself at the centre of a whirligig of mistaken identity – not helped by her own desire for Orsino and Olivia's misplaced passion for herself... Once one has got over the wintry climate (frosty breath, fallen leaves everywhere) of this budget-strapped recreation of Shakespeare's fanciful kingdom, this wonderful play casts its spell. Of course, Ben Kingsley's Feste does remind us that 'the rain it raineth every day'. Talking of Kingsley, a marvellous cast – vivaciously led by Imogen Stubbs (the director's wife) – looks to the manner born. Indeed, were not Richard E. Grant and Mel Smith born to play Augecheek and Sir Toby Belch? Filmed on location in Cornwall.

Helena Bonham Carter (*Olivia*), Richard E. Grant (*Sir Andrew Aguecheek*), Nigel Hawthorne (*Malvolio*), Ben Kingsley (*Feste*), Mel Smith (*Sir Toby Belch*), Imelda Staunton (*Maria*), Toby Stephens (*Orsino*), Imogen Stubbs (*Viola*), Steven Mackintosh (*Sebastian*), Nicholas Farrell (*Antonio*), Peter Gunn (*Fabian*), Sid Livingstone, Timothy Bentinck, James Walker.

Dir and Screenplay: Trevor Nunn. Pro: Stephen Evans and David Parfitt. Ex Pro: Greg Smith. Line Pro: Mark Cooper. Ph: Clive Tickner. Pro Des: Sophie Becher. Ed: Peter Boyle. M: Shaun Davey. Costumes: John Bright. (Fine Line/Renaissance–Entertainment.) Rel: 25 October 1996. 133 mins. Cert U. UK/USA. 1996.

Twin Town

Dylan Thomas described Swansea as an 'ugly lovely town'. Corrupt Scottish cop Terry Walsh thinks 'pretty shitty city' is closer to the truth. A nondescript district in south west Wales that boasts such tourist attractions as a disco, massage parlour and Wimpy, Swansea is

The fools of love: Helena Bonham Carter, Imogen Stubbs and Toby Stephens get hopelessly mixed-up in Trevor Nunn's bewitching Twelfth Night *(from Entertainment)*

under siege from two substance-abusing, trivia-obsessed brothers who get off on stealing cars, urinating on karaoke contestants and cutting the head off a treasured poodle. Grimly determined to bring the 'twins' to justice, Terry Walsh is not above a bit of underhand chicanery to nail the bastards... Exhibiting some technical skill as a director and a sense for black comedy as a writer (in collaboration with Paul Durden), former actor Kevin Allen kickstarts a terrific scenario and then doesn't know where to go with it. Without a single redeemable character in sight, this vivid, Welsh answer to *Trainspotting* descends into arch unpleasantness. Personally, I can't see a single reason to recommend the film to anyone – and feel exceedingly guilty for enjoying it as much as I did.

Dougray Scott (*Terry Walsh*), Dorien Thomas (*Greyo*), William Thomas (*Bryn Cartwright*), Sue Roderick (*Lucy Cartwright*), Rhys Ifans (*Jeremy Lewis*), Llyr Evans (*Julian Lewis*), Di Botcher (*Jean Lewis*), Huw Ceredig (*Fatty Lewis*), Rachel Scorgie (*Adie Lewis*), Jenny Evans (*Bonny Cartwright*), Brian Hibbard (*Dai Rees*),

Morgan Hopkins (*Chip*), Paul Durden (*taxi driver*), Kevin Allen (*TV presenter*), Biddug Williams, Ronnie Williams, David Hayman, Sion Tudor Owen, Danny Durden, Brian Hancock, Bhasker Patel, Keith Allen, Charlie (*Cantona*), Snowy (*Fergie*).

Dir: Kevin Allen. Pro: Peter McAleese. Ex Pro: Andrew Macdonald and Danny Boyle. Screenplay: Allen and Paul Durden. Ph: John Mathieson. Pro Des: Pat Campbell. Ed: Oral Norrie Ottey. M: Mark Thomas; numbers performed by Petula Clark, Mungo Jerry, Dana, Martin Ace, Dodgy, Moloko, Super Furry Animals, etc. Costumes: Rachael Fleming. (PolyGram/Figment Films/Agenda/Aimimage–PolyGram.) Rel: 11 April 1997. 99 mins. Cert 18. UK. 1997.

Twister

Dropping by Tornado Alley, Oklahoma, to get his divorce papers signed by his estranged wife, weatherman Bill Harding and his new fiancée Melissa encounter a motley crew of hurricane chasers. The soon-to-be ex-Mrs Harding, Jo, has patented an 'instrument tank' to study the behaviour of twisters, but for it to work she has to place it directly in the path of an oncoming 'finger of God'. Just then, Bill and Melissa get caught up in what promises to be the most terrifying and devastating force of nature in 50 years... Generating the same fascination with and horror of

The Thief, The Cook: Danny Aiello cooks up a storm in John Herzfeld's deliciously perverse 2 days in the Valley *(from Entertainment)*

tornadoes as *Jaws* and *Jurassic Park* achieved with sharks and dinosaurs, *Twister* came screaming into cinemas with the fury of the genuine article. Fuelled by real-life reports in the US press of destructive cyclones, this rollercoaster ride of special effects tore into the box-office with super-natural intensity. Co-executive-produced by Steven Spielberg and co-scripted by Michael Crichton and his wife, *Twister* delivers the goods and more. You'll believe a cow can fly. And a harvester. And a house.

Helen Hunt (*Jo Harding*), Bill Paxton (*Bill Harding*), Jami Gertz (*Melissa*), Cary Elwes (*Dr Jonas Miller*), Lois Smith (*Aunt Meg*), Philip Seymour Hoffman (*Dusty*), Alan Ruck, Sean Whalen, Scott Thomson, Todd Field, Joey Slotnick, Wendle Josepher, Jeremy Davies, Zach Grenier, Nicholas Sadler, Anthony Rapp, Jake Busey, Richard Lineback, Rusty Schwimmer, Taylor Gilbert, Bruce Wright, Anneke De Bont.

Dir: Jan De Bont. Pro: Kathleen Kennedy, Ian Bryce and Michael Crichton. Ex Pro: Steven Spielberg, Walter Parkes, Laurie MacDonald and Gerald R. Molen. Screenplay: Crichton & Annie-Marie Martin and (uncredited) Steven Zaillian and Joss Whedon. Ph: Jack N. Green. Pro Des: Joseph Nemec III. Ed: Michael Kahn. M: Mark Mancina; numbers performed by Tori Amos, Eric Clapton, Mark Knopfler, Stevie Nicks and Lindsey Buckingham, Red Hot Chili Peppers, Deep Purple, Goo Goo Dolls, Soul Asylum, Belly, Van Halen, Lisa Loeb and Nine Stories, Alison Krauss & Union Station, k.d. lang, etc. Costumes: Ellen Mirojnick. Visual effects: Stefen Fangmeier; Industrial Light & Magic. Weather consultant: Vince Miller. (Universal/Warner/Amblin–UIP.) Rel: 26 July 1996. 113 mins. Cert PG. USA. 1996.

2 days in the Valley

San Fernando Valley, Los Angeles; the present. A down-on-his-luck hitman has been double-crossed, an Olympic skier wakes up to find the corpse of her ex-husband beside her, a failed movie director's attempts at suicide are repeatedly foiled and a vice cop cannot seem to make the jump to homicide. Meanwhile, a cold-blooded manipulator, Lee Woods, is about to make a killing... A smart, forceful comedy that blends Woody Allen with Quentin Tarantino, *2 days in the Valley* is a gift to its cast, a fine ensemble of actors who return the favour in kind. Director-scenarist John Herzfeld, who began writing his screenplay in LA's Veteran's Cemetery (because, he says, he was inspired by the name on a headstone), deftly pays out a handful of story strands that gradually snake together, tightening round the throat of the film like a rope. Danny Aiello is particularly winning as the hitman who tries to retain his toughness in the face of escalating odds (bees, dogs and a mercurial hairpiece), while James Spader makes a deliciously icy villain.

Danny Aiello (*Dosmo Pizzo*), Greg Cruttwell (*Allan Hopper*), Jeff Daniels (*Alvin Strayer*), Teri Hatcher (*Becky Foxx*), Glenne Headley (*Susan Parish*), Peter Horton (*Roy Foxx*), Marsha Mason (*Audrey Hopper*), Paul Mazursky (*Teddy Peppers*), James Spader (*Lee Woods*), Eric Stoltz (*Wes Taylor*), Charlize Theron (*Helga Svelgen*), Keith Carradine (*Det. Creighton*), Louise Fletcher (*Evelyn*), Kathleen Luong (*Midori*), Austin Pendelton, Michael Jai White, Cress Williams, Lawrence Tierney, Micole Mercurio, Coby (*Bogey, a dog*), Mark Goldstein (*Marc, the pitbull*).

Dir and Screenplay: John Herzfeld. Pro: Jeff Wald and Herb Nanas. Ex Pro: Keith Samples and Tony Amatullo. Co-Pro: Jim Burke. Ph: Oliver Wood. Pro Des: Catherine Hardwicke. Ed: Jim Miller and Wayne Wahrman. M: Anthony Marinelli; Donizetti; numbers performed by Wilson Pickett, Junior Wells, The Crying Knobs, Morphine, Scott Reeder, Lyle Lovett, Georgia Hubley and Lois Maffeo, Martin Sexton, Otis Redding, The Time, and Taj Mahal. Costumes: Betsy Heimann. (Rysher Entertainment/Redemption–Entertainment.) Rel: 18 October 1996. 104 mins. Cert 18. USA. 1996.

Two Much - Loco de Amor

Miami; today. Astonishingly unfunny farce in which Art Dodger, a Latino con artist, finds himself romantically involved with two Mafia molls, the sisters Betty and Liz

Kerner. So Art invents a twin brother, Bart, so that he can have his cake and choke on it. It's tragic to think that the director's last venture, *Belle Epoque*, actually won an Oscar for Best Foreign Film, although it's comforting to know that his stars, Antonio Banderas and Melanie Griffith, moved on to marital bliss. [*Charles Bacon*]

Melanie Griffith (*Betty Kerner*), Antonio Banderas (*Art/Bart Dodger*), Darryl Hannah (*Liz Kerner*), Danny Aiello (*Gene Palletto*), Joan Cusack (*Gloria Fletcher*), Eli Wallach (*Sheldon Dodge*), Gabino Diego (*Manny*), Austin Pendleton, Allan Rich, Vincent Schiavelli, Phil Leeds.
   Dir: Fernando Trueba. Pro: Cristina Huete. Ex Pro: Ted Field, Adam Leipzig and Robert W. Cort. Line Pro: Angelica Huete. Screenplay: Fernando and David Trueba, from the novel by Donald E. Westlake. Ph: Jose Luis Alcaine. Pro Des: Juan Botella. Ed: Nena Bernard. M: Michel Camilo. Costumes: Lala Huete. (Sogetel/Lola Films/Interscope Communications/PolyGram/Andres Vicente Gomez–Poly-Gram.) Rel: 13 December 1996. 118 mins. Cert PG. Spain/USA. 1995.

The Van

Barrytown, Dublin; 1989. When bakery worker Bimbo is 'let go' from his job he refuses to succumb to the indignity of unemployment. So he sets his sights on renovating the world's dirtiest van for use as a 'chipper', a mobile take-away facility dispensing fish 'n' chips, hamburgers and soft drinks. Inviting his best friend Larry to share his venture, Bimbo discovers that the reversal of roles – his sudden seniority over Larry – may have a devastating effect on their friendship... Although cited as a sequel to *The Commitments* and *The Snapper*, Stephen Frears' adaptation of Roddy Doyle's third novel only shares the location of the fictitious Dublin suburb of Barrytown. True, the omnipresent pub, TV and kitchen sink are still familiar ingredients, but the characters are different – in spite of Colm Meaney's third appearance as a volatile working-class family man on his uppers. Produced on a much bigger budget than *The Snapper* (which was made for TV), *The Van* looks terrific, but lacks the narrative momentum and sharp dialogue of the former. Still, there's much to enjoy and Doyle's knack for distilling the poetic in the everyday is still very much in evidence.

Colm Meaney (*Larry*), Donal O'Kelly (*Bimbo*), Ger Ryan (*Maggie*), Caroline Rothwell (*Mary Ellen*), Neili Conroy (*Diane*), Ruaidhri Conroy (*Kevin*), Brendan O'Carroll (*Weslie*), Marie Mullen (*Vera*), Jon Kenny (*Gerry McCarthy*), Stuart Dunne, Jack Lynch, Laurie Morton, Jill

Engaged to be harried: Anne Heche shows off her new ring to Catherine Keener in Nicole Holofcener's observant and heartfelt Walking and Talking *(from Electric)*

Doyle, Ronan Wilmot, Stanley Townsend, David Byrne.
   Dir: Stephen Frears. Pro: Lynda Myles. Co-Pro and Screenplay: Roddy Doyle. Ph: Oliver Stapleton. Pro Des: Mark Geraghty. Ed: Mick Audsley. M: Eric Clapton and Richard Hartley; numbers performed by Swinging Blue Jeans, The Ventures, etc. Costumes: Consolata Boyle. (Fox Searchlight/BBC Films/Beacon Pictures/Deadly Films–Fox.) Rel: 29 November 1996. 100 mins. Cert 15. Ireland/UK. 1996.

Walking and Talking

New York City/Queens; New York; today. On the verge of turning 30, Amelia and Laura are best friends since childhood whose paths are suddenly taking separate forks. Laura has accepted a proposal of marriage from her boyfriend, Frank, and Amelia finds herself left behind, both as a soulmate and romantic being. In a desperate attempt to fill the encroaching void, she takes up with a clerk from the local video store who quickly sees through her capricious agenda. Meanwhile, Laura is finding the prospect of permanent commitment a terrifying and lonely

Dogface in a dollhouse: Heather Matarazzo displaying her eye-assaulting dress sense in Todd Solondz's misanthropic Welcome to the Dollhouse *(from Artificial Eye)*

option... Presenting complex characters with fascinatingly ordinary lives, first-time writer-director Nicole Holofcener exhibits a remarkable talent for extracting the truth from her scenario. Observant, compassionate and heartfelt, *Walking and Talking* artfully needles its way into our affections, overturning stereotypes and pinpointing the inexorable misunderstandings of well-meaning people trapped in their own lives. A minor triumph that is as funny as it is poignant. FYI: The story was inspired by the director's own diaries, when she was living as a single woman in New York.

Catherine Keener (*Amelia*), Anne Heche (*Laura*), Liev Schreiber (*Andrew*), Todd Field (*Frank*), Kevin Corrigan (*Bill*), Randall Batinkoff (*Peter*), Lawrence Holofcener (*Andrew's father*), Spatz (*Blue Jeans, the cat*), Brenda Thomas Denmark, Vincent Pastore, Joseph Siravo, Rafael Alvarez, Lynn Cohen, Nitza Wilon, Allison Janney, Alice Drummond.
Dir and Screenplay: Nicole Holofcener. Pro: Ted Hope and James Schamus. Ex Pro: Dorothy Berwin and Scott Meek. Ph: Michael Spiller. Pro Des: Anne Stuhler. Ed: Alisa Lepselter. M: Billy Bragg; numbers performed by Billy Bragg, Soul Defenders, Yo La Tengo, Liz Phair, Joan Osborne, REM, etc. Costumes: Edi Giguere. (Zenith/Good Machine/Channel Four/TEAM/Pandora/Mikado/Electric–

Electric.) Rel: 17 January 1997. 86 mins. Cert 15. USA. 1996.

Welcome to the Dollhouse

New Jersey; today. Nicknamed everything from 'Dog Face' to 'Lesbo', 11-year-old Dawn Wiener longs to be popular. But with the dress sense of the visually impaired and a spiteful mother who plays favourites with her children, Dawn is a lost cause. Ostracised by her peers, she adopts odd notions of love, friendship and sex and settles for romance in the form of a promised rape from the class drug dealer... A huge success at Sundance (where it won the Grand Jury prize), this bleak, cruel black comedy blends the garish production values of John Waters with the rebellious edge of *Heathers*. But here there is no hip talk, no gross-out humour; just an unblinking stare at the emotional implosion of a child denied love, guidance and sartorial advice. Heather Matarazzo is commendably po-faced as Dawn, retaining the integrity of a film that only reveals its comedic agenda through its mischievous use of classical music.

Heather Matarazzo (*Dawn Wiener*), Brendan Sexton Jr (*Brandon McCarthy*), Matthew Faber (*Mark Wiener*), Eric Mabius (*Steve Rodgers*), Daria Kalinina (*Missy Wiener*), Dimitri Iervolino (*Ralphy*), Angela Pietropinto (*Mrs Wiener*), Bill Buell (*Mr Wiener*), Victoria Davis, Rica Martens, Zsanne Pitta.

Catwalk: Zinedine Soualem and Garance Clavel in Cedric Klapisch's delightful When the Cat's Away *(from Artificial Eye/Mayfair)*

Dir, Pro and Screenplay: Todd Solondz. Ex Pro: Donna Bascom. Co-Pro: Dan Partland and Ted Skillman. Assoc Pro: Jason Kliot and Joana Vicente. Ph: Randy Drummond. Pro Des: Susan Block. Ed: Alan Oxman. M: Jill Wisoff; Tchaikovsky, Chopin, Grieg; numbers performed by Daniel Rey. Costumes: Melissa Toth. (Suburban Pictures–Artificial Eye.) Rel: 24 January 1997. 88 mins. Cert 15. USA. 1995.

When the Cat's Away - Chacun Cherche Son Chat

The 'Bastille' district, Paris; today. Sometimes we reveal ourselves most acutely when we are searching for something we have lost. Chloe has lost her cat and is plunged into a circuitous exploration of Parisian highways and byways, both physical and psychological. A timid make-up artist, Chloe shares an apartment with a homosexual, a set-up that exposes her to libertine ways, yet shields her from her own sexuality... A series of neatly realised sketches, *When the Cat's Away* explores the changing personality of Chloe as she unwittingly becomes a bridge between the old guard of Paris (the cat women) and the new (the fashion world and gay culture.) Ultimately, however, the film works best as a sketch of Paris itself – and a delightful and constantly surprising sketch it is. FYI: The film was inspired by a real story, with Renee 'Le Calm' – as the cat-loving Mme Renee – virtually playing herself.

Garance Clavel (*Chloe*), Zinedine Soualem (*Djamel*), Renee La Calm (*Mme Renee*), Olivier Py (*Michel*), Arapimou (*Grigri, Chloe's cat*), Rambo (*Rambo, Mme Renee's cat*), Joel Brisse (*Benoit 'Bel Canto,' the*

painter), Franck Manzoni (*Claude*), Andree Damant, Simon Abkarian, Frederic Augray, Denis Falgoux, Danielle Hoisnard.

Dir and Screenplay: Cedric Klapisch. Pro: Farid Lahouassa, Aissa Djabri and Manuel Munz. Ph: Benoit Delhomme. Pro Des: Francois Emmanuelli. Ed: Francine Sandberg. M: various; 'Glory Box' performed by Portishead. Costumes: Pierre Yves Gayraud. (Vertigo Films/France 2/Canal Plus–Artificial Eye/Mayfair.) Rel: 25 October 1996. 95 mins. Cert 15. France. 1995.

When We Were Kings

Muhammad Ali declares, 'I'm so mean I make medicine sick.' Spike Lee talks of the changing attitudes towards the African-American. James Brown sings 'Gonna Have a Funky Good Time'. And, shortly before the arrival of the international media to Zaire, President Mobutu Sese Seko executes one hundred prisoners. Chronicling the weeks leading up to the historical '94 WHB title bout between Ali and George Foreman, director Leon Gast has transformed over 300,000 feet of film into a vivid document of an extraordinary time. Originally conceived as an 'Afro-American Woodstock', the film has emerged as a portrait of a charismatic icon at the most crucial point in his professional, psycho-logical and religious life. Winner of the 1996 Oscar for Best Documentary.

Muhammad Ali, George Foreman, James Brown, B.B. King, Spike Lee, Norman Mailer, George Plimpton, Don King, President Mobutu Sese Seko, Thomas Hauser, Malik Bowens, Llòyd Price, Miriam Makeba, The Spinners, Jazz Crusaders, etc.

Dir: Leon Gast. Pro: Gast, David Sonenberg and Taylor Hackford. Co-Pro: Keith Robinson and Vikram Jayanti. Ex Pro: Sonenberg. Ph: Maryse Alberti, Paul Goldsmith, Kevin Keating, Albert Maysles and Roderick Young. Ed: Gast, Hackford, Robinson and Jeffrey Levy-Hinte. M: numbers performed by Jazz Crusaders, The Spinners, B.B. King, James Brown, OK Jazz, Brian McKnight and Diana King, The Fugees & Friends, and Abba. (PolyGram/Das Films–PolyGram.) Rel: 16 May 1997. 87 mins. Cert PG. USA. 1996.

White Man's Burden

We know it is an unequal world: the cultural underclass is invariably trapped in demeaning jobs, are

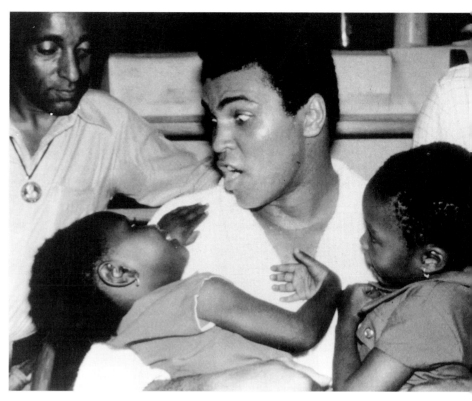

Cry, the Beloved Fighting: Muhammad Ali scares some local children from Zaire in Leon Gast's riveting documentary When We Were Kings *(from PolyGram)*

poorly represented by TV role models and are forever victimised by the police. All this is true for Louis Pinnock, a loyal factory worker struggling to build a life of dignity for himself and his family. Then, in an unguarded moment, he makes one small mistake, and watches as his life unravels... Louis Pinnock is just like any number of society's underdogs, except in this instance he is white as writer-director Desmond Nakano views America in the negative, with John Travolta cast as the victim and Harry Belafonte as the affluent agent of his undoing. A neat, creditable idea is pushed a little too far, maybe, but Travolta and Belafonte distinguish it with resonant performances, although the film's finale collapses into mediocrity. [*Ewen Brownrigg*]

John Travolta (*Louis Pinnock*), Harry Belafonte (*Thaddeus Thomas*), Kelly Lynch (*Marsha Pinnock*), Margaret Avery (*Megan Thomas*), Tom Bower (*Stanley*), Andrew Lawrence (*Donnie*), Bumper Robinson, Tom Wright, Sheryl Lee Ralph, Judith Drake, Tom Nolan, Michael Beach, Thom

Barry, Carrie Snodgress, Bert Remsen, Seth Green, Alexis Arquette, Kerry Remsen, Googy Gress, Lawrence Bender.

Dir and Screenplay: Desmond Nakano. Pro: Lawrence Bender. Ex Pro: Yves Marmon. Assoc Pro: Joann Fregalette Jansen. Ph: Willy Kurant. Pro Des: Naomi Shohan. Ed: Nancy Richardson. M: Howard Shore; numbers performed by Blues Traveller, Hootie & The Blowfish, Cracker, Bush, Meat Puppets, etc. Costumes: Isis Mussenden. (UGC/Band Apart–Fox.) Rel: 7 February 1997. 89 mins. Cert 15. USA/France. 1995.

William Shakespeare's Romeo + Juliet

Two households, both alike in dignity, from ancient grudge break to new mutiny, where civil blood makes civil hands unclean. Not to mention the complications arising from a pair of star-cross'd lovers... While eponymously attributed to the Bard, this pop promo for the iambic pentameter is anything but. No, this is truly Baz Luhrmann's *Romeo + Juliet*, and every zoom, jump cut and note bears his stamp. Updating and relocating Shakespeare's play to contemporary Mexico City, the film replaces *The Chorus* with a TV newscaster and switches guns for rapiers, but it does retain the original dialogue, albeit shaved to the bone.

Strictly Luhrmann: Leonardo DiCaprio and Claire Danes in William Shakespeare's Romeo + Juliet, *arguably the most daring and electrifying translation of Shakespeare to the modern screen – ever (from Fox)*

Luhrmann, who made his screen debut with *Strictly Ballroom* four years previously, exhibits an extraordinary command of his imagery, his visuals matching in ingenuity the powerful poetry of the prose. As Romeo, Leonardo DiCaprio certainly looks the part, and injects plenty of passion, but it is Claire Danes as Juliet who truly brings the text alive. Ultimately, however, the film impresses more than it moves.

Leonardo DiCaprio (*Romeo Montague*), Claire Danes (*Juliet Capulet*), Brian Dennehy (*Ted Montague*), John Leguizamo (*Tybalt*), Pete Postlethwaite (*Father Laurence*), Paul Sorvino (*Fulgencio Capulet*), Diane Venora (*Gloria Capulet*), Dash Mihok (*Benvolio*), Christina Pickles (*Caroline Montague*), Vondie Curtis-Hall (*Captain Prince*), Paul Rudd (*Dave Paris*), Jesse Bradford (*Balthasar*), Miriam Margolyes (*Nurse*), Harold Perrineau (*Mercutio*), Edwina Moore (*anchorwoman*), Zak Orth, Jamie Kennedy, M. Emmet Walsh, Des'ree.
   Dir: Baz Luhrmann. Pro: Luhrmann and Gabriella Martinelli. Co-Pro: Martin Brown. Screenplay: Luhrmann and Craig Pearce, from an idea by William Shakespeare. Ph: Donald McAlpine. Pro

Des: Catherine Martin. Ed: Jill Bilcock. M: Nellee Hooper, Craig Armstrong and Marius De vries; Mozart; numbers performed by Garbage, Everclear, Gavin Friday, One Inch Punch, Des'ree, Butthole Surfers, The Cardigans, Kym Mazelle, Quindon Tarver, Mundy, Radiohead, Stina Nordenstam, and The Wannadies. Costumes: Kym Barrett. (Fox/Bazmark–Fox.) Rel: 28 March 1997. 120 mins. Cert 12. USA. 1996.

The Wind in the Willows

Admitting that he found Kenneth Grahame's classic children's book of 1908 'placid and episodic', writer-director Terry Jones has taken considerable liberties with the work in its first feature-length adaptation. Casting human actors in the roles of the animals, Jones has followed the undisguised anthropomorphism of the book although he quickly dispenses with the original's lyricism in favour of a nightmarish scenario in which the wily, sadistic weasels attempt to commandeer and then blow up Toad Hall. The starry cast makes the most of its opportunities, with Eric Idle and Nicol Williamson particularly effective as Rat and Badger and John Cleese contributing a classic cameo as Toad's aggressive lawyer. However, Jones' own irritating interpretation of Toad (echoing his Monty Python creations) all but ruins the film in spite of some

delightful moments of incidental humour.

Steve Coogan (*Mole*), Eric Idle (*Rat*), Terry Jones (*Mr Toad*), Antony Sher (*Chief Weasel*), Nicol Williamson (*Badger*), John Cleese (*Mr Toad's lawyer*), Stephen Fry (*the judge*), Bernard Hill (*the engine driver*), Michael Palin (*the sun*), Nigel Planer (*car salesman*), Julia Sawalha (*the jailer's daughter*), Victoria Wood (*tea lady*), Robert Bathurst (*St John Weasel*), Richard James (*Geoffrey Weasel/Mole's clock*), Don Henderson, Keith-Lee Castle, Roger Ashton-Griffiths, Sarah Crowden, Peter Whitfield.
   Dir and Screenplay: Terry Jones. Pro: John Goldstone and Jake Eberts. Ph: David Tattersall. Pro Des and Costumes: James Acheson. Ed: Julian Doyle. M: John Du Prez; songs: Du Prez, Andre Jacquemin, Terry Jones and Dave Howman. Choreography: Arlene Phillips. Sound Design: Jacquemin. Tails and Ears: Vin Burnham. (Allied Filmmakers–Guild.) Rel: 18 October 1996. 87 mins. Cert U. UK. 1996.

Your Beating Heart - Un Coeur Qui Bat

Paris; 1991. Mado, a sometime radio actress, lives on a houseboat on the Seine with her husband, the father of her 17-year-old son. Meeting the stare of a handsome stranger on the Metro, she agrees to go to a hotel with him and they make love. He gives her his number and, to her surprise, she calls him back. He is an unknown quantity; an unpredictable man with no apparent background. They fall in love – sort of. A tedious extramarital Parisian love story from Francois Dupeyron, who directed and co-scripted (with his wife Dominique Faysse) the equally tiresome *A Strange Place To Meet*, with Catherine Deneuve and Gerard Depardieu. This time Mme Faysee takes the starring role, enthusiastically engaging in some very frank sex scenes as the adulterous wife.

Dominique Faysse (*Mado*), Thierry Fortineau (*Yves*), Jean-Marie Winling (*Jean*), Christophe Pichon (*Stephane*), Steve Kalfa (*Luc*), Coralie Seyrig, Regis Le Rohellec, Daniel Laloux.
   Dir and Screenplay: Francois Dupeyron. Pro: Rene Cleitman. Ex Pro: Bernard Bouix. Ph: Yves Angelo. Pro Des: Carlos Conti. Ed: Francoise Collin. M: Jean-Pierre Drouet. (Hachette Premiere/UGC/Avril SA/FR3 Films/Canal Plus–Artificial Eye.) Rel: 24 January 1997. 100 mins. Cert 15. France. 1991.

Video Releases

Compiled by Charles Bacon

(from July 1996 through to June 1997)

❏: denotes films released theatrically in
the US
✳: denotes films of special merit

Additional reviews
by James Cameron-Wilson

Aladdin and the King of Thieves ❏

Now that Robin Williams has patched up his differences with Disney, his return as the genie for the second sequel to *Aladdin* makes this one of the unexpected delights of the year. Having taken a noticeable back seat in *The Return of Jafar*, the genie is much in evidence here, packing in a number of unlikely impressions, including blink-or-miss sketches of Sylvester Stallone, Marlon Brando, Forrest Gump, Pumbaa, RoboGenie and an uncanny impersonation of Mrs Doubtfire. The story itself – in which Aladdin discovers that his father is the leader of the Forty Thieves – serves as a solid prop for an entertaining cocktail of action, songs and comic diarrhoea. [JC-W]

Other voices: Gilbert Gottfried (*Iago*), Jim Cummings, Jerry Orbach, John Rhys-Davies, Scott Weinger (*Aladdin*), Linda Larkin (*Jasmine*), Clyde Kusatsu, CCH Pounder. Dir: Tad Stones. U. March 1997 (Disney).

The Arrival ❏

Silly UFO drama in which a radio astronomer (Charlie Sheen) smells a conspiracy and hightails it to Mexico to find some locals acting very strangely. Amazingly, Sheen keeps a straight face.

Aladdin and the King of Thieves *(from Disney)*

Also with Ron Silver, Lindsay Crouse, Teri Polo, Richard Schiff. Dir and Screenplay: David Twohy. 12. February 1997 (Entertainment).

Back of Beyond ❑

In spite of some captivating scenery (the 'Red Centre' of Australia) and a beguiling villain from the estimable Colin Friels, this poorly conceived romantic-mystical thriller is incredibly uninteresting.

With Paul Mercurio, Dee Smart. Dir: Michael Robertson. 15. August 1996 (Imagine Home Entertainment).

Big Bully ❑

While this looks like it might be every bit as awful as a lot of broad American comedies dumped on to video abroad, it's not. However, as a vehicle for the director of *Forever Young* and the writer of *Grumpy Old Men*, it should've been a lot better. The story of childhood hatchets dug up in middle age, the film has some good lines and a handful of slick character sketches but wafts aimlessly around the dark core it so desperately needs to mine.

With Rick Moranis, Tom Arnold, Julianne Phillips, Carol Kane, Jeffrey Tambor, Curtis Armstrong, Don Knotts, Stuart Pankin. Dir: Steve Miner. Screenplay: Mark Steven Johnson. M: David Newman. PG. October 1996 (Warner).

The Big Green ❑

Hackneyed, lightweight comedy about a class of losers who locate the meaning of life on the football pitch. Any kid who's seen *The Mighty Ducks* (or a variety of similar confections) will guess the outcome, although the young cast does its best to pretend this is happening for the first time.

With Steve Guttenberg, Olivia d'Abo, Jay O. Sanders, John Terry, Chauncey Leopardi, Bug Hall. Dir and Screenplay: Holly Goldberg Sloan. M: Randy Edelman. U. August 1996 (Buena Vista).

Billy Madison ❑

Yet another moron-from-hell farce from America, this one also features yet another starring debut from a *Saturday Night Live* alumnus. A cross-fertilisation of *Tommy Boy* and *Richie Rich*, *Billy Madison* stars the zany Adam Sandler as a privileged 27-year-old dimwit due to inherit his father's billion-dollar Madison Hotels empire. But for silly Billy to show that he's up for the job he has to plough through school again – and this time graduate without bribes. First and second grade are a cinch, but from third grade up Billy finds the going getting rougher... Eerily, the film does get funnier in its second half when a handful of spontaneous moments grab the funny bone. Ultimately, though, the comedy's success rests on whether or not one finds Adam Sandler's juvenile lunacy amusing. [JC-W]

Also with Bradley Whitford, Josh Mostel, Bridgette Wilson, Darren McGavin, Steve Buscemi (*as Danny McGrath*). Dir: Tamra Davis. Screenplay: Tim Herlihy and Adam Sandler. Penguin Design: Arlene Smith. PG. June 1997 (CIC).

Bio-Dome ❑

Two stupid dudes find themselves trapped in a scientifically sealed dormitory of the future and, natur-ally, create havoc. Irredeemable.

With Pauly Shore, Stephen Baldwin, William Atherton, Joey Adams, Henry Gibson, Kylie Minogue, Patricia Hearst, Roger Clinton. Dir: Jason Bloom. 12. January 1997 (MGM/UA).

Black Sheep ❑

Chris Farley, in a valiant attempt to make Jim Carrey and Adam Sandler look like Jung and Freud, plays the moronic, accident-prone brother of the bright, dashing and handsome Al Donnelly (Tim Matheson), candi-date for the office of governor of Washington state. But, like a jumble of Billy Carter, Ron Reagan Jr and Roger Clinton, Farley incessantly besmirches his brother's name... Besides the total lack of wit, *Black Sheep* refuses to convey any semblance of logic or credibility. For laughs we have Farley trapping his thumbs in a car boot, stapling his hand to a campaign poster and – the height of comic ingenuity – walking into a tree. A crime against cinema. From the director of *The Beverly Hillbillies* and *The Little Rascals*. [JC-W]

Also with David Spade, Christine Ebersole, Gary Busey, Grant Heslov, Timothy Carhart, Bruce McGill. Dir: Penelope Spheeris. 12. March 1997 (CIC).

Body Language

Muscular albeit familiar 'erotic' thriller in which Tom Berenger plays an attorney whose affair with the wife of a trailer park thug lands him into decidedly hot water.

Also with Nancy Travis, Heidi Schanz, Robert Patrick. Dir: George Case. 18. July 1996 (Hi-Fliers).

Bordello of Blood ❑

Adolescent, exploitative spin-off from the *Tales of the Crypt* series in which a wise-cracking cop tracks down a missing punk and unearths a brothel of vampires. Old tricks are generously splattered with fresh gore and female flesh, but *From Dusk Till Dawn* did it with much more style.

With Dennis Miller, Erika Eleniak, Angie Everhart, Chris Sarandon, Corey Feldman, Aubrey Morris, William Sadler, Whoopi Goldberg. Dir: Gilbert Adler. Ex Pro: Richard Donner, David Giler, Walter Hill, Joel Silver, Robert Zemeckis. 18. May 1997 (CIC).

Bottle Rocket ❑ ✳

Three young men search for love, friendship and criminal kudos in suburban Dallas. A refreshingly grounded, low-key comedy from first-time director Wes Anderson and writer-star Owen C. Wilson, *Bottle Rocket* exudes a natural charm and some winning performances from its unknown cast and James Caan. A joy.

Also with Luke Wilson (*brother of Owen C.*), Robert Musgrave. 15. October 1996 (Columbia TriStar).

A Boy Called Hate ❑

An affectingly acted, credible lovers-on-the-run drama starring Scott Caan (son of James) who finds himself pursued by police when he shoots a man for molesting a teenager (Missy Crider). As it happens, the man is an assistant DA and uncle to the girl and survives his wounds to make Scott's life hell.

Also with James Caan, Elliott Gould, Adam Beach. Dir and Screenplay: Mitch Marcus. M: Pray For Rain. 15. January 1997 (Imagine).

Bullet to Beijing

A British-Canadian-Russian co-production, *Bullet to Beijing* resurrects Harry Palmer, the jaded spy that made Michael Caine's name all of 30 years ago. Here he's led on a wild goose chase to Russia where he gets caught in a ridiculous plot made all the more impenetrable by George Mihalka's laborious direction. Followed by *Midnight in St Petersburg*. Aka *Len Deighton's Bullet to Beijing*.

With Michael Caine, Jason Connery, Mia Sara, Michael Sarrazin, Michael Gambon, Burt Kwouk, Sue Lloyd, Patrick Allen. Ex Pro and Screenplay: Harry Alan Towers. M: Rick Wakeman. 15. April 1997 (Buena Vista).

Celtic Pride ❑

Embarrassing comedy in which two basketball fans kidnap an NBA player (Damon Wayans) in order to heighten the chances of their team winning. Obnoxious characters and a lethargic pace don't help matters.

Also with Daniel Stern, Dan Aykroyd, Gail O'Grady, Paul Guilfoyle, Christopher McDonald. Dir: Tom De Cerchio. 15. February 1997 (Buena Vista).

Citizen X ✳

Mesmerising, atmospheric TV movie chronicling the sickening exploits of

Russia's most notorious serial killer, whose 52 murders (committed in 1989-1990) were swept under the carpet by Soviet officials. Acting, direction and photography are all of the first order.

With Stephen Rea, Donald Sutherland, Jeffrey DeMunn, Max Von Sydow, Joss Ackland, John Wood, Ion Caramitru, Imelda Staunton. Dir and Screenplay: Chris Gerolmo. Ph: Robert Fraisse. M: Randy Edelman. 18. August 1996 (20.20 Vision).

Clive Barker's Lord of Illusions

See *Lord of Illusions*.

Coach ❑

Yet another formulaic comedy in which an unlikely instructor ends up triumphing over impossible odds. Here, Rhea Perlman is the scrappy trainer who gets her team of black basketball players to do what she says. Still, the acting is better than usual for this type of thing. US title: *Sunset Park*.

Also with Fredro Starr, Carol Kane, Terrence DaShon Howard. Dir: Steve Gomer. Pro: Danny DeVito. 15. March 1997 (20.20 Vision).

Crime of the Century ✳

Highly effective revision of the Lindburgh kidnapping case casts Stephen Rea as the 'wrongfully'

accused German carpenter Bruno Richard Hauptman, who is condemned for his part in the botched abduction of the celebrated aviator's 18-month-old son. Strong performances, credible dialogue and crisp production design make this one of the most engrossing TV movies of the year.

Also with Isabella Rossellini (excellent), J.T. Walsh, Allen Garfield, Michael Moriarty, David Paymer, Don Harvey, Gerald S. O'Loughlin, Bert Remsen, John Harkins, Barry Primus, Brad Greenquist. Dir: Mark Rydell. Screenplay: William Nicholson, based on the book *The Airman and the Carpenter* by Ludovic Kennedy. 15. May 1997 (Columbia TriStar).

DROP Squad ❑

Misconceived satire-cum-thriller in which a black gang resort to discussion and torture to re-programme those brothers who have sold out to 'Whitey', a scheme dubbed the Detention and Restoration Of Pride. Unpleasant, confused and melodramatic.

With Eriq LaSalle, Vondie Curtis-Hall, Ving Rhames, Kasi Lemmons, Leonard Thomas, Billy Williams, Vanessa Williams, Spike Lee. Dir: D. Clark Johnson. Ex Pro: Spike Lee. 15. July 1996 (CIC).

D3: The Mighty Ducks ❑

Third outing in the ice hockey franchise featuring a swarm of irritating kids and their will to win over impossible odds. The gimmick here is that the team's hormones are acting up and they've been transplanted to a posh private school. Based on the measure that a film succeeds if it achieves what it sets out to accomplish, this predictable sequel fires on all mushy cylinders.

With Emilio Estevez, Jeffrey Nordling (*the new coach*), Joshua Jackson, David Selby, Heidi King, Joss Ackland, Elden Ryan Ratliff. Dir: Robert Lieberman. Screenplay: Steven Brill and Jim Burnstein. M: J.A.C. Redford. PG. June 1997 (Walt Disney).

Ed ❑

The big screen break for Matt LeBlanc, who plays Joey in TV's *Friends*, is a genuine humiliation for all concerned. LeBlanc plays an insecure baseball player whose life is

The three stars of Bottle Rocket *contemplate love, friendship and crime in Wes Anderson's winning* Bottle Rocket *(Columbia TriStar Home Video)*

turned around when he's hired to look after the club's third baseman, who happens to be a chimpanzee. Nothing makes sense, least of all the direction of Bill Couturie, who previously made the highly acclaimed documentary *Dear America: Letters Home From Vietnam*.

Also with Jayne Brook, Bill Cobbs, Jack Warden, Charlie Schlatter. M: Stephen Endelman. PG. January 1997 (CIC).

A Family Thing ❑

In this instance the 'family thing' is a case of discovering that you're half black, as Southern tractor salesman Robert Duvall realises when he finds out that his late mother was Afro-American. James Earl Jones co-stars as Duvall's half-brother, a Chicago cop who's no happier at having a white sibling. Thanks to the towering performances of Jones and Duvall, the film's clunky narrative devices and patronising air is largely overcome.

Scripted by Billy Bob Thornton and Tom Eppersdon, who previously collaborated on the far superior *One False Move*. Also with Michael Beach, Irma P. Hall, Grace Zabriskie, Regina Taylor. Dir: Richard Pearce. Pro: Robert Duvall, Todd Black and Randa Haines. 15. February 1997 (MGM/UA/Warner).

First Do No Harm

So it's come to this: America's First Lady of the Screen reduced to a video première. Not only that, but Meryl Streep is outclassed by young Deth Adkins, who plays an epileptic boy in this true story of a mother's fight to help her son.

Also with Fred Ward. Dir and Pro: Jim Abrahams. 15. April 1997 (Odyssey Platinum).

Frankie the Fly ❑

Overly familiar story of a dogsbody for the Mob who finds himself smitten with a porn star and is asked to place bets for her troubled director. If it weren't for Dennis Hopper's dedicated performance as the loser who wants to 'be somebody', this sloppy, mean-spirited black comedy would be a total bust. US title: *The Last Days of Frankie the Fly*.

Also with Daryl Hannah, Michael Madsen, Kiefer Sutherland, Dayton Callie. Dir:

Peter Markle. Screenplay: Dayton Callie. 18. June 1997 (FoxGuild).

Freeway ❑

Genuinely nasty road movie in which a troubled teenage runaway becomes embroiled with a serial killer posing as a child psychiatrist. Taking his cue from *Little Red Riding Hood*, first-time writer-director Matthew Bright winks broadly at his audience while shovelling on the cruelty. Offensive, exaggerated melodrama.

With Kiefer Sutherland, Reese Wither-spoon, Brooke Shields, Wolfgang Bodison, Dan Hedaya, Amanda Plummer, Bokeem Woodbine, Sidney Lassick. M: Danny Elfman. 18. April 1997 (Hi-Fliers).

Gold Diggers: The Secret of Bear Mountain ❑

A hurriedly assembled adventure yarn that resembles a thousand better outings, this is the story of two girls – city slicker Christina Ricci and tomboy rebel Anna Chlumsky – whose mutual love for Winnie the Pooh empowers them for a world of insincere adults stuck with unutterable dialogue. Filmed in British Columbia, which doubles for the Pacific Northwest.

Also with Polly Draper, Brian Kerwin, Diana Scarwid (*as Chlumsky's alcoholic mother*), David Keith. Dir: Kevin James Dobson. PG. October 1996 (CIC).

Gotti

Disappointing biography of 'the Teflon Don', which refuses to take sides in this brutal tale of the gangster who killed his way to the top of the Mob. While Armand Assante (as John Gotti), Anthony Quinn (his mentor) and William Forsythe (his snitch) give good value for money, the film is otherwise shortchanged by flavour and suspense.

Also with Richard S. Sarafian, Vincent Pastore, Frank Vincent, Marc Lawrence, Al Waxman, Alberta Watson. Dir: Robert Harmon. Screenplay: Steve Shagan. M: Mark Isham. 18. June 1997 (Hi-Fliers).

The Grave ❑

Laborious, familiar tale in which two convicts break out of a prison farm in North Carolina to find treasure

buried in a grave. Only some neat dialogue (written by the director in collaboration with his brother) and a bit of unexpected nastiness spice up the creaky action.

With Craig Sheffer, Gabrielle Anwar, Josh Charles, John Diehl, Anthony Michael Hall, Max Perlich, Donal Logue, Keith David, Eric Roberts. Dir: Jonas Pate. Screenplay: Jonas Pate and Josh Pate. 18. February 1997 (BMG).

Grumpier Old Men ❑ ✳

Unexpectedly delightful, funny and charming sequel to the 1993 hit (*Grumpy Old Men*) which reunites the original cast to fruitful effect. This time Sophia Loren guest stars as an Italian outsider who attempts to transform a bait shop into a restaurant, throwing a fresh spanner into the competitive and volatile relationship enjoyed by Jack Lemmon and Walter Matthau. It's a joy to see such a well matured cast employed to such fine – and unpatronising – effect.

Also with Ann-Margret (*as Lemmon's new wife*), Burgess Meredith, Kevin Pollak, Daryl Hannah, Ann Guilbert. Dir: Howard Deutch. Screenplay: Mark Steven Johnson. M: Alan Silvestri. 12. October 1996 (Warner).

Heavyweights ❑

Offensive, feeble-minded comedy set in a summer camp for fat children. Need one say more?

With Tom McGowan, Aaron Schwartz, Ben Stiller, Jeffrey Tambor. Dir and Screenplay: Steven Brill. PG. July 1996 (Buena Vista).

Hotel Sorrento ❑

Absorbing, well-acted Australian drama in which three sisters are reunited at their childhood home following their father's death. Based on the play by Hannie Rayson.

With Caroline Goodall, Caroline Gillmer, Tara Morice, Joan Plowright, John Hargreaves, Ben Thomas, Ray Barrett. Dir: Richard Franklin. 15. January 1997 (PolyGram).

The Hunted ❑

A step back for the martial arts genre, this silly, gruesome actioner stars Christopher Lambert as a New York businessman who unwittingly

The Rod Couple: Jack Lemmon and Walter Matthau team up for the nth time in Howard Deutch's enjoyable Grumpier Old Men *(from Warner Video)*

becomes a pawn in a centuries-old spat between a ninja crime lord and a samurai warrior. Duff dialogue, poor jokes and some theatrical acting don't exactly help.

Also with John Lone, Joan Chen, Yoshio Harada. Dir and Screenplay: J.F. Lawton. 18. August 1996 (CIC).

If Lucy Fell ❑

Predictable, silly romantic comedy in which two Manhattan room-mates plot to jump off the Brooklyn Bridge if their respective romantic lives fail to pick up. Writer-director-star Eric Schaeffer previously wrote, directed and starred in the equally inept *My Life's in Turnaround.*

Also with Sarah Jessica Parker, Ben Stiller, Elle Macpherson, James Rebhorn, Robert John Burke, Bill Sage. 15. December 1996 (Columbia TriStar).

If These Walls Could Talk

Breast-beating anthology in which three different women – in three separate time zones – struggle to deal with their unexpected pregnancies.

Produced by Demi Moore, the trilogy dictates its emotional agenda with well-acted conviction by a powerhouse cast. Demi plays a widowed nurse in 1952, Sissy Spacek a mother of four in 1972 and Anne Heche a contemporary student of architecture.

Also with: Catherine Keener, Jason London, Shirley Knight, CCH Pounder, Robin Gammell, Xander Berkeley, Joanna Gleason, Harris Yulin, Jada Pinkett, Cher, Diana Scarwid, Lindsay Crouse, Rita Wilson, Eileen Brennan, Craig T. Nelson. Dirs: Nancy Savoca (episodes 1 & 2), Cher (3). M: Cliff Eidelman. 15. March 1997 (Medusa).

In the Army Now ❑

Predictably dire entry in the singular genus of boot camp comedy that has, more successfully, included *Private Benjamin* and *Stripes.* Here, Pauly Shore plays the world's least likely soldier who ends up in Chad as an expert in water purification.

Also with Andy Dick, Lori Petty, David Alan Grier, Esai Morales, Lynn Whitfield, Art LaFleur, Brendan Fraser. Dir: Daniel Petrie Jr. M: Robert Folk. PG. August 1996 (Buena Vista).

It's My Party ❑

Discovering that he is dying of Aids, successful architect Nick Stark invites his family and friends to a 'going out' party before he tops himself. There are still a few loose ends to tie up – a reconciliation with his father and ex-boyfriend, etc. – and Nick is determined to go out in style. Mercilessly manipulative, Randal Kleiser's meandering film constantly sounds two notes: maudlin and flip. Borrowing wads of dialogue from other movies and inventing a few clumsy notes of exposition itself (Nick: 'I got it.' Boyfriend: 'You tested positive?'), *It's My Party* is mushy, recycled and contrived, like a *Love Story* for the Aids generation. Here's a clue: Olivia Newton-John sings the closing number. [JC-W]

With Eric Roberts (*Nick Stark*), Gregory Harrison, Marlee Matlin, Margaret Cho, Lee Grant, Bronson Pinchot, Olivia Newton-John, Bruce Davison, Paul Regina, George Segal, Devon Gummersall, Dimitra Arlys, Roddy McDowall. 15. November 1996 (MGM/UA).

Joe's Apartment ❑

From the suits that brought us Beavis and Butt-Head comes the very first live-action musical comedy featuring all-singing, all-dancing cockroaches. While obviously one leg short of a centipede, this revolting curiosity item does have its moments, although it outstays its modest running time by a good half-hour.

With Jerry O'Connell, Megan Ward, Jim Sterling, Robert Vaughn, David Huddleston. Dir and Screenplay: John Payson. M: Carter Burwell. 12. March 1997 (MTV/Warner).

John Woo's Once a Thief
See *Violent Tradition*.

Jury Duty ❑
Pauly Shore trumps his own nadir with this tasteless, brainless farce about an idiot who causes chaos in court. Any characters or names that bear any similarity to any actual event or actual person involved in the O.J. Simpson trial is entirely coincidental and unintentional.

Also with Tia Carrere, Stanley Tucci, Brian Doyle-Murray, Abe Vigoda, Charles Napier, Richard Edson, Richard Riehle, Alex Datcher, Shelley Winters, Andrew Dice Clay. Dir: John Fortenberry. 12. September 1996 (Columbia TriStar).

Kabloonak ✳
A powerful and touching film that chronicles the treacherous lengths that the documentary filmmaker Robert Flaherty went to to make his classic 1922 documentary *Nanook of the North*. As the wilful Flaherty, Charles Dance gives one of his best performances in years and is well matched by Adamie Quasiak Inukpuk as the Inuit hunter Nanook, although it is the stunning Arctic scenery that clings to the memory. Aka *Nanook*.

Dir: Claude Massot. 15. September 1996 (PolyGram).

Kazaam ❑
Extraordinary cross between a gritty inner-city fable and a modern-day fantasy in which a troubled teenager is befriended by a 3,000-year-old genie who's been trapped in a ghetto-blaster. Huh? Basketball star Shaquille O'Neal works hard to milk magic from his role as the rapping genie and easily overshadows his more experienced co-stars who are stuck with stock characters.

Also with Francis Capra, Ally Walker. Dir: Paul Michael Glaser. M: Christopher Tyng. 12. February 1997 (PolyGram).

Kicking and Screaming ❑
What on earth do you do when you graduate from college in America? Well, there are a number of films that show you the ropes (both slippery and supportive), but this debut outing from 25-year-old director Noah Baumbach adds little freshness to the genre. Here, a group of college friends deliberate on how best to motivate their lives as they ape various situations smugly stolen from other movies. To be fair, it is occasionally amusing, but is more often calculated to a fault.

With Josh Hamilton, Olivia d'Abo, Carlos Jacott, Chris Eigeman, Eric Stoltz, Jason Wiles, Parker Posey, Cara Buono, Elliott Gould, Catherine Kellner, Noah Baumbach. 15. November 1996. (Entertainment).

The Last Days of Frankie the Fly
See *Frankie the Fly*.

Len Deighton's Bullet to Beijing
See *Bullet to Beijing*.

The Limbic Region
Taut, unsettling thriller in which a dying ex-cop (Edward James Olmos) takes the chief suspect in a murder case on the drive of a lifetime. Olmos is spectacular.

Also with George Dzunda, Roger R. Cross, Gwyneth Walsh. Dir: Michael Pattinson. M: Gary Chang. 18. April 1997 (MGM/UA).

Liz: The Elizabeth Taylor Story
Shamefully entertaining biography of the serial wife and food-loving superstar which steadfastly ignores the psychological depths of its subject. From the director of *Diana: Her True Story*.

With Sherilyn Fenn (*as Liz*), Angus Macfadyen (*Richard Burton*), Nigel Havers (*Michael Wilding*), Ray Wise (*Mike Todd*), Michael McGrady (*Larry Fortensky*), William McNamara (*Montgomery Clift*). Dir: Kevin Connor. 12. July 1996 (Odyssey).

Lord of Illusions ❑
From the man who brought us *Hellraiser* and *Nightbreed*, this horror opus lacks the outrageous shock value of Clive Barker's earlier films, but replaces it with more sophisticated production values (not to mention some splendid make-up effects). The upshot is that genre fans will be less interested, while the unsuspecting may well still throw up. Scott Bakula stars as a tough private dick whose investigations lead him to an illusionist whose sleight of hand conceals genuine sorcery. Based on Barker's 1985 short story *The Last Illusion*.

Also with Kevin J. O'Connor, Famke Janssen, Vincent Schiavelli, Sheila Tousey, Daniel Von Bargen. Dir and Screenplay: Clive Barker. 18. August 1996 (MGM/UA).

Edward James Olmos in Michael Pattinson's unsettling The Limbic Region *(from (MGM/UA)*

The Machine ❏

Powerfully atmospheric, efficiently rendered thriller in which a scientist obsessed by the workings of the brain traps himself in the body of a killer with the help of a remarkable machine. As the French rarely venture into such territory, it's a shame that the film is so badly dubbed.

With Gerard Depardieu, Nathalie Baye, Didier Bourdon, Claude Berri. Dir and Screenplay: Francois Dupeyron, from the novel by Rene Belletto. 18. October 1996 (PolyGram).

Major Payne ❏

Appalling, insulting remake of the 1955 Charlton Heston vehicle *The Private War of Major Benson*, in which Damon Wayans (who also co-scripted and serves as executive producer) plays a foul-mouthed autocrat who whips a team of underage cadets into shape.

Also with Karyn Parsons, William Hickey, Michael Ironside, Albert Hall. Dir: Nick Castle. 12. October 1996 (CIC).

Mallrats ❏ ✳

Breezy, compassionate and delight-fully shocking satire from the creator of *Clerks*, which chronicles the romantic breakdown of two slackers who lose their girlfriends on the same day. Performances, dialogue and above all the filmmaker's wayward attitude are all on the nose.

With Shannen Doherty, Jeremy London, Jason Lee, Claire Forlani, Michael Rooker, Priscilla Barnes, Renee Humphrey, Kevin Smith, Ben Affleck, Joey Lauren Adams. Dir and Screenplay: Kevin Smith. M: Ira Newborn. 18. August 1996 (CIC).

Man With a Gun ❏

Mean and moody Michael Madsen is the man with the gun, a hitman who accepts an assignment to knock off gangster's moll Jennifer Tilly, a former flame. Tilly, however, has a few tricks up her own sleeve... Methodical, familiar *film noir* fare based on High C. Rae's novel *The Shroud Society*.

Also with Gary Busey, Robert Loggia, Bill Cobbs. Dir: David Wyles. 18. July 1996 (Fox Guild).

Mrs Winterbourne ❏

Earnest, somewhat contrived comedy based on the story by Cornell Woolrich, in which, following a train crash, a heavily pregnant piece of white trash is mistaken for an upmarket Bostonian. Likeable performances save the day in this tale that was previously filmed as *No Man of Her Own* (with Barbara Stanwyck) and *I Married a Shadow* (with Nathalie Baye).

With Shirley MacLaine, Ricki Lake, Brendan Fraser, Miguel Sandoval, Loren Dean, Paula Prentiss. Dir: Richard Benjamin. 15. May 1997 (Columbia TriStar).

Mr Wrong ❏

An unlikely big-screen introduction to the winning talents of TV's Ellen DeGeneres, who plays a career gal looking for her ideal man, a figment who turns out to be a psychotic Bill Pullman. The latter manfully trips over the numerous bumps of an uneven script, while Ms DeGeneres manfully falls back on her larger-than-life personality.

Also with Joan Cusack, Dean Stockwell, Joan Plowright, Robert Goulet, Polly Holliday. Dir: Nick Castle. 12. June 1997 (Buena Vista).

Nanook

See *Kabloonak*.

Nina Takes a Lover ❏

Nina takes a lover (while her husband's away) in this hackneyed look at sex, love and infidelity. Yawn.

With Laura San Giacomo, Paul Rhys, Michael O'Keefe, Cristi Conaway, Fisher Stevens. Dir: Alan Jacobs. 18. March 1997 (Columbia–TriStar).

Of Love and Shadows

Based on the novel that Isabel Allende wrote after her bestseller *The House of the Spirits* (and its subsequent, disastrous transition to celluloid), *Of Love and Shadows* juggles passion and intrigue with some conviction in this romance set in the aftermath of the 1973 Chilean coup. Forcibly acted by a largely Spanish-speaking cast, the film marks an auspicious directorial debut for co-producer Betty Kaplan

although, at times, the plot disappears up its own alimentary canal.

With Jennifer Connolly, Antonio Banderas, Stefania Sandrelli, Camilo Gallardo. 15. January 1997 (Entertainment).

Once a Thief

See *Violent Tradition*.

Operation Dumbo Drop ❏

Dumbo meets *Platoon* in this unlikely family film set in Vietnam, in which, as a strategic good-will measure, some American soldiers attempt to transport an elephant to a Vietnamese village. Cynics may carp, but children should enjoy this polished, sentimental revision of a brutal slice of American history.

With Danny Glover, Ray Liotta, Denis Leary, Doug E. Doug, Corin Nemec, Tcheky Karyo, Marshall Bell. Dir: Simon Wincer. M: David Newman. PG. August 1996 (Buena Vista).

The Plague

Straightforward but incoherent adaptation of Albert Camus' novel in which a committed doctor, TV cameraman and female reporter face a bubonic plague in a South American city. The best thing that came out of this was the short-lived relationship between co-stars William Hurt and Sandrine Bonnaire.

Also with Jean-Marc Barr, Robert Duvall, Raul Julia, Victoria Tennant. Dir: Luis Puenzo. 15. July 1996 (First Independent).

Proteus

Risible monster flick in which a humanoid shark hunts down a gang of drug smugglers on an oil rig. Directed by special effects maestro Bob Keen, the thriller makes the most of its limited budget but is under-mined by a flabby script and uninteresting human characters. Filmed on London's River Thames.

With Craig Fairbrass, Toni Barry, Jenifer Calvert, Doug Bradley. Pro: Paul Brooks. 18. December 1996 (PolyGram).

The Rich Man's Wife ❏

Highly derivative if occasionally entertaining thriller in which a faithless wife finds herself implicated in the murder of her unfaithful husband. Peter Greene supplies some fun as a psychotic killer but the rest of the cast can do little with such routine material. Beautifully photographed, though.

Also with Halle Berry, Christopher McDonald, Clive Owen, Charles Hallahan, Frankie Faison, Clea Lewis. Dir and Screenplay: Amy Holden Jones. Ph: Haskell Wexler. 18. May 1997 (Hollywood).

Roommates ❏

Loosely based on fact, this routine tearjerker stars Peter Falk as a grizzled Polish immigrant who adopts his own grandson and won't leave him alone. Falk's performance, aided by admirable make-up, saves the day.

Also with D.B. Sweeney, Julianne Moore, Ellen Burstyn, Jan Rubes, Frankie Faison, Noah Fleiss, Ernie Sabella. Dir: Peter Yates. PG. February 1997 (Buena Vista).

Savage Hearts

Jokey, frequently gripping (and violent) action yarn in which a drifter gets caught up with two femme fatales in a breezy flight from the police and drug barons. Nice, too, to see a chase thriller set in the picturesque heart of England.

With Jamie Harris, Maryam d'Abo, Myriam Cyr, Richard Harris, Stephen Marcus, Angus Deayton, Julian Fellowes, Jerry Hall. Dir and Screenplay: Mark Ezra. 18. January 1997 (BMG).

Search and Destroy ❏

In spite of a wonderful cast, this misconceived directorial debut from 'visual artist' David Salle backfires on all levels. Adapted from Howard Korder's play, the film courts eccentricity with dwindling success as a Florida businessman (Griffin Dunne) struggles to maintain his status quo in the face of horrific odds. Vaguely resembling Scorsese's *After Hours*, the film lacks none of the former's dark style and lunges hope-lessly from slapstick to satire to brutal violence.

Also with Illeana Douglas, Dennis Hopper, Christopher Walken, John Turturro, Rosanna Arquette, Ethan Hawke, Martin Scorsese. Dir: David Salle. M: Elmer Bernstein. 15. July 1996 (Fox Guild).

The Siege at Ruby Ridge

Morally dubious take on the real-life 1992 siege initiated by the FBI to smoke out a family of white separatists. Good performances – particularly from Laura Dern and Randy Quaid as neo-Nazi zealots – enliven the laborious running time.

Also with Diane Ladd, Joe Don Baker, Kirsten Dunst. 15. February 1997 (BMG).

The Stars Fell On Henrietta ❏

A drifter specialising in the location of black gold in Depression-era Texas leads a family astray when he tells them that they're sitting on top of an oil field. Produced by Clint Eastwood, this earnest, uneven drama strains to connect emotionally but falls rather flat, in spite of Bruce Surtees' handsome photography and yet another superbly detailed performance from Robert Duvall as the dignified hobo.

Also with Aidan Quinn, Frances Fisher, Brian Dennehy, Lexi Randall, Francesca Ruth Eastwood. Dir: James Keach. PG. September 1996 (Warner).

Strictly Business ❏

Released in the US in early November of '91, this silly romantic comedy has, presumably, been rescued from obscurity here by the presence of Halle Berry and Samuel L. Jackson in subservient roles. The former makes a grand entrance in the Bo Derek tradition from *10*, as a restaurant hostess who catches the eye of a nerdy workaholic who has to loosen up his act in order to ensnare the babe. Joseph C. Phillips makes an engaging and handsome lead as the love-struck geek, with a fine sense of comedy timing, while director Kevin Hooks keeps the action light on its feet.

Also with Tommy Davidson, Anne Marie Johnson, David Marshall Grant, Jon Cypher, Kevin Hooks. M: Michel Colombier. 15. January 1997 (First Independent).

Sugartime

Fact-based HBO movie that fails to fully illuminate the romance of singer Phyllis McGuire (of The McGuire Sisters) and Chicago gangster Sam Giancana. Still, there's

fun to be had in spotting the famous names – the Kennedys, Fidel Castro, Frank Sinatra, Rowan and Martin, J. Edgar Hoover – in this most unlikely of alliances. From the director of *Dangerous Minds*.

With John Turturro (*Giancana*), Mary-Louise Parker (*McGuire*), Maury Chaykin, Elias Koteas, Louis Del Grande. Dir: John N. Smith. M: Sidney James. 18. December 1996 (20.20 Vision).

Sunset Park

See *Coach*.

The Sunshine Boys

Mediocre TV remake of Neil Simon's Broadway comedy with Woody Allen and Peter Falk miscast in the roles immortalised by Walter Matthau and George Burns in the 1975 film.

With Sarah Jessica Parker. Dir: John Erman. U. January 1997 (Fox Guild).

Tall Tale: The Unbelievable Adventure ❏

A young farm boy (Nick Stahl) inveigles the assistance of Western legends Pecos Bill, Paul Bunyan, John Henry and Calamity Jane to help save his father's property from an evil land developer (Scott Glenn). A dud at the US box office, this Disney fantasy is actually quite enjoyable, stylish and rather fun. From the director of *Benny & Joon* and *Diabolique*.

Also with Patrick Swayze, Oliver Platt, Roger Aaron Brown, Stephen Lang, Jared Harris, Catherine O'Hara, Moira Harris, Joe Grifasi, John P. Ryan, Scott Wilson, Burgess Meredith. Dir: Jeremiah Chechick. PG. July 1996 (Buena Vista).

Theodore Rex

Unbelievable mess in which Whoopi Goldberg plays a futuristic cop who teams up with a talking, cookie-devouring dinosaur to solve a case of the old 'dinocide'. While obviously aimed at a very, very young audience, this limp comedy even trips up here as some of the scenes are unnecessarily strong.

Also with Armin Mueller-Stahl, Juliet Landau, Bud Cort, Stephen McHattie, Richard Roundtree. Dir: Jonathan Betuel. PG. December 1996 (Entertainment).

Tom and Huck ❑

Just two years after the pedestrian *Adventures of Huck Finn* comes this *ninth* version of the Mark Twain story, which might just stagger two year olds with its fresh approach to the subject. Still, Brad Renfro makes an engaging Huckleberry Finn, which should teach Elijah Wood a lesson.

Also with Jonathan Taylor Thomas (*Tom Sawyer*), Eric Schweig, Charles Rocket, Amy Wright, Micheal McShane. Dir: Peter Hewitt. PG. February 1997 (Walt Disney).

To Sir With Love 2

Thirty years after Sidney Poitier befriended Lulu and Judy Geeson in an East London classroom, the saintly teacher slips over to Chicago to distribute more of his unwavering sincerity. Once again Poitier manages to take a contrived scenario by the horns and bring it alive, no thanks to an implausible script.

Also with Christian Payton, Dana Eskelson, Daniel J. Travanti, and (in cameos) Lulu and Judy Geeson. Dir: Peter Bogdanovich. 15. February 1997 (Odyssey).

Truman ✳

Rousing, thoroughly engaging portrait of America's 33rd president, Harry S. Truman, played to the hilt by Gary Sinise.

Also with Diana Scarwid, Richard Dysart, Colm Feore, James Gammon, Tony Goldwyn, Pat Hingle, Harris Yulin, Zeljko Ivanek, David Lansbury, Lois Smith. Dir: Frank Pierson. 15. May 1997 (Third Millennium).

The Turn of the Screw

Painfully inept Franco-British update of Henry James' 1898 masterpiece in which a love-struck governess discovers that her young charges are possessed by ghosts.

With Patsy Kensit, Stephane Audran, Julian Sands, Marianne Faithful. Dir and Screenplay: Rusty Lemorande. Ph: Witold Stok. Costumes: Amy Roberts. 18. September 1996 (20.20 Vision).

Under the Piano

Earnest but somewhat plodding dramatisation of a true story in which a young woman attempts to help her musically gifted but autistic sister survive the real world.

With Amanda Plummer, Megan Follows, Teresa Stratas. Dir: Stefan Scaini. 15. September 1996 (Odyssey).

Violent Tradition ✳

Entertaining, funny and gripping action-comedy-cum-love story from Hong Kong's finest, in which a trio of crime busters – two guys and one gal – find that romance gets in the way of duty. A loose remake of Woo's 1991 movie *Once a Thief*. UK title: *John Woo's Once a Thief*.

With Sandrine Holt, Ivan Sergei, Nicholas Lea, Jennifer Dale. Dir: John Woo. 18. January 1997 (BMG).

Virtuosity ❑

By the year 1999 virtual reality has become so real that should the crucial safeguard malfunction a participant could die from shock. And so, barely minutes into this techno-shocker, does the unimaginable happen. But worse is yet to come. At the government's Law Enforcement Technology Advancement Center, the computer-generated Sid 6.7 escapes the virtual reality simulator built to house him. Programmed to kill and outwit the most advanced of law enforcement procedures, Sid 6.7 plugs into the personality components of Hitler, Charles Manson, John Wayne Gacy and other miscreants for his human profile. So it's up to Denzel Washington, who outwitted the bastard in VR, to tackle him in the real world... A terrific concept is brought vividly to life with high-tec computer graphics, courtesy of the director of *The Lawnmower Man*. Yet watching real people die like blips on a computer screen does leave a nasty taste on the mouse. [JC-W]

With Denzel Washington (*Parker Barnes*), Kelly Lynch, Russell Crowe (*Sid 6.7*), Stephen Spinella, William Forsythe, Louise Fletcher. Dir: Brett Leonard. M: Christopher Young. FX: Chris Walas. 15. September 1996 (CIC).

Wild Bill

Jeff Bridges gives another outstanding performance as the legendary gunman Wild Bill Hickok and Ellen Barkin supplies lively support as Calamity Jane. However, in spite of a number of memorable scenes, the film fails to gather dramatic momentum or to find an emotional grip, stumbling into arty pretension. Based on the play *Fathers and Sons* by Thomas Babe and the novel *Deadwood* by Peter Dexter.

With John Hurt, Diane Lane, David Arquette, Christina Applegate, Bruce Dern, James Gammon, Marjoe Gortner, James Remar, Keith Carradine (*as Buffalo Bill*). Dir and Screenplay: Walter Hill. 15. July 1996 (MGM/UA).

Other Video Releases:

Abduction of Innocence. Dirk Benedict, Katie Wright, Lucie Arnaz. 15. April 1997 (Odyssey).

After the Silence. JoBeth Williams, Kellie Martin. Dir: Fred Gerber. 15. January 1997 (Odyssey).

Alien Within. Roddy McDowall, Alex Hyde-White, Melanie Shatner, Don Stroud. Dir: Scott Levy. 18. November 1996 (CIC).

Alligator Eyes. Annabelle Larsen. 15. January 1997 (Imagine).

All She Ever Wanted. Marcia Cross, James Marshall, Leila Kenzle, Bruce Kirby, Carrie Snodgress, CCH Pounder. Dir: Michael Scott. 12. September 1996 (Odyssey).

American Yakuza 2: Back to Back. Ryo Ishibashi, Michael Rooker, John Laughlin, Danielle Harris. Dir: Roger Nygard. 18. October 1996 (Medusa).

Amityville Dollhouse. Robin Thomas. Dir: Steve White. 18. October 1996 (Hi-Fliers).

Animal Instincts: The Seductress. Wendy Schumacher. 18. February 1997 (Hi-Fliers).

Badge of Betrayal. Harry Hamlin, Gordon Clapp. 12. April 1997 (Odyssey).

Baja. Molly Ringwald, Lance Henriksen, Donal Logue, Corbin Bernsen. Dir: Kurt Voss. 18. December 1996 (Hi-Fliers).

Beastmaster III: The Eye of Braxus. Marc Singer, David Warner, Tony Todd, Lesley-Anne Down. Dir: Gabrielle Beaumont. PG. July 1996 (CIC).

Bloodhounds. Corbin Bernsen, Christine Harnos. 15. March 1997 (CIC).

Blood Money. James Brolin, Billy Drago, Traci Lords. 18. September 1996 (First Independent).

Bloodsport II. Daniel Bernhardt, Pat Morita, James Hong. 18. November 1996 (20.20).

Blue Rodeo. Kris Kristofferson, Ann-Margret. Dir: Peter Werner. PG. March 1997 (Warner).

Body of Influence 2. Jodie Fisher. 18. January 1997 (Hi-Fliers).

Born Free: A New Adventure. Jonathan Brandis, Linda Purl, Ariana Richards, Chris Noth. Dir: Tommy Lee Wallace. U. February 1997 (Odyssey).

Bounty Hunters. Michael Dudikoff. Dir: George Erschbamer. 15. March 1997 (Entertainment).

Bugs. Maud Adams, Clint Howard. Dir: Bryan Yuzna. 18. August 1996 (Guild).

Caged Hearts. Carrie Genzel, Tane McClure. 18. March 1997 (Marquee).

Campfire Tales. Christine Taylor (from *The Brady Bunch Movie*). 18. May 1997 (Medusa).

A Case For Life. Valerie Bertinelli, Mel Harris, Karl Malden. Dir: Eric Laneuville. 12. September 1996 (Odyssey).

Castle Freak. Jeffrey Combs, Barbara Crampton. Dir: Stuart Gordon. 18. July 1996 (EV).

Cemetary Man. Rupert Everett. Dir: Michael Soavi. 18. August 1996 (Entertainment).

The Chain. Gary Busey, Victor Rivers. 18. October 1996 (Columbia TriStar).

Chase Moran. Bruce Campbell, Joseph Culp. 18. October 1996 (First Independent).

Chasing the Dragon. Markie Post, Dennis Boutsikaris, Noah Fleiss, Peter Frechette, Deirdre O'Connell. Dir: Ian Sander. 15. February 1997 (Odyssey).

A Child is Missing. Henry Winkler, Roma Downey. 12. August 1996 (Hi-Fliers).

A Child's Wish. John Ritter, Tess Harper, Anna Chlumsky, Bill Clinton. Dir: Waris Hussein. PG. June 1997 (Odyssey).

Cold Blooded. Jason Priestley, Peter Riegert, Kimberly Williams. 18. September 1996 (PolyGram).

The Cold Light of Day. Richard E.

Grant, Simon Cadell, Lynsey Baxter. Dir: Rudolf Van Den Berg. 18. October 1996 (PolyGram).

Conspiracy of Fear. Andrew Lowery, Leslie Hope, Christopher Plummer. Dir: John Eyres. 18. February 1997 (Columbia TriStar).

Cover Me. Paul Sorvino, Rick Rossovich. 18. January 1997 (Fox Guild).

Coyote Run. Michael Pare, Peter Greene. 18. April 1997 (Entertainment).

Crash Dive. Michael Dudikoff, Frederic Forrest. 15. April 1997 (Columbia TriStar).

Crimes of Silence. Michele Greene, William R. Moses, Lynda Carter. Dir: James A. Contner. 15. December 1996 (Odyssey).

Criminal. Ralph Feliciello. 15. September 1996 (Screen Edge).

Criminal Passion. Joanna Cassidy, Jere Burns. Dir: Reza Badiyi. 15. October 1996 (Odyssey).

Crossworlds. Rutger Hauer, Josh Charles, Stuart Wilson. Dir: Krishna Rao. 15. January 1997 (Hi-Fliers).

The Crying Child. Mariel Hemingway, Finola Hughes. 12. February 1997 (CIC).

Cupid. Zach Galligan, Ashley Laurence, Mary Crosby. 15. April 1997 (First Independent).

Daddy's Girl. William Katt, Michele Greene, Roxana Zal, Mimi Craven. 18. October 1996 (First Independent).

Danielle Steel's Mixed Blessings. Scott Baio, Alexandra Paul. 12. July 1996 (20.20).

Danielle Steel's No Greater Love. Kelly Rutherford, Simon MacCorkindale, Chris Sarandon. PG. July 1996 (20.20).

Dark Angel: The Ascent. Daniel Markel, Charlotte Stewart. 18. December 1996 (CIC).

Dark Breed. Jack Scalia, Jonathan Banks. Dir: Richard Pepin. 18. November 1996 (FoxGuild).

Darkman III: Die Darkman Die. Jeff Fahey, Arnold Vosloo, Darlanne Fluegel. Dir: Bradford May. 15. November 1996 (CIC).

Dead Ahead. Stephanie Zimbalist, Sarah Chalke. 15. April 1997 (CIC).

Dead By Sunset. Ken Olin, Lindsay Frost, Annette O'Toole, John Terry. Dir: Karen Arthur. 18. July 1996 (Odyssey).

Dead Innocent. Genevieve Bujold, Graham Greene. Dir: Sara Botsford. 18. February 1997 (Third Millennium).

Death and Vengeance. Brian Dennehy, Susan Ruttan, Charles S. Dutton, Joe Morton, Anthony Zerbe. Dir: Dennehy. 15. June 1997 (Odyssey).

Death Benefit. Peter Horton, Wendy Makkena, Carrie Snodgress, Elizabeth Ruscio. 12. November 1996 (CIC).

Deceptions. Harry Hamlin, Nicollette Sheridan, Robert Davi. Dir: Ruben Preuss. 18. September 1996 (Encore).

The Deidre Hall Story. Deidre Hall, Daniel Hugh Kelly. Dir: John Patterson. 12. August 1996 (Odyssey).

The Demolitionist. Nicole Eggert, Richard Grieco, Bruce Campbell, Heather Langenkamp, Jack Nance, Tom Savini. 15. November 1996 (Hi-Fliers).

Demon House. Amelia Kinkade. 18. May 1997 (Hi-Fliers).

The Dentist. Corbin Bernsen. Dir: Brian Yuzna. 18. November 1996 (Hi-Fliers).

Donor Unknown. Peter Onorati, Alice Krige, Clancy Brown. 15. October 1996 (CIC).

Don't Look Back. Eric Stoltz, Josh Hamilton, John Corbett, Billy Bob Thornton, Amanda Plummer. 18. June 1997 (Entertainment).

Double Dragon. Robert Patrick, Mark Dacascos, Scott Wolf, Alyssa Milano, Julia Nickson. Dir: James Yukich. 12. March 1997 (Columbia TriStar).

Downhill Willie. Fred Stoller, Keith Coogan. 12. October 1996 (Medusa).

Down, Out and Dangerous. Richard Thomas, Bruce Davison. 15. September 1996 (CIC).

Ebbie. Susan Lucci. Dir: George Kaczender. PG. December 1996 (Odyssey).

An Element of Truth. Donna Mills, Peter Riegert, Robin Thomas. Dir: Larry Peerce. 15. November 1996 (Odyssey).

Embrace of the Vampire. Martin Kemp, Alyssa Milano, Charlotte Lewis, Jennifer Tilly. Dir: Anne Goursaud. 18. March 1997 (Medusa).

Escape Clause. Andrew McCarthy, Paul Sorvino. Dir: Brian Trenchard-Smith. 18. February 1997 (MGM/UA).

Another true story: Brian Dennehy as real-life Chicago cop Jack Reed in the fifth film based on the exploits of the tough sergeant, Death and Vengeance *(from Odyssey), directed by Dennehy himself*

Every Woman's Dream. Jeff Fahey, Kim Cattrall. Dir: Steven Schachter. Screenplay: Schachter, Martin Davidson, William H. Macy. 15. April 1997 (Medusa).

Evil Has a Face. Sean Young, William R. Moses, Chelcie Ross. Dir: Rob Fresco. 15. February 1997 (CIC).

The Ex. Yancy Butler, Suzy Amis, Nick Mancuso. Dir: Mark L. Lester. 15. March 1997 (Hi-Fliers).

Exit in Red. Mickey Rourke, Carre Otis, Annabel Schofield, Anthony Michael Hall. Dir: Yurek Bogayevicz. 18. December 1996 (20.20).

Family of Cops. Charles Bronson, Daniel Baldwin, Lesley-Anne Down. 15. July 1996 (Hi-Fliers).

Family Rescue. George C. Scott, Ally Sheedy, Rachael Leigh Cook. Dir: Graeme Campbell. 15. October 1996 (Odyssey).

Fast Money. Yancy Butler, Matt McCoy. 18. September 1996 (Fox Guild).

Father and Scout. Bob Saget, Brian Bonsall, David Graf, Troy Evans. Dir: Richard Michaels. U. July 1996 (EV).

The Final Cut. Sam Elliott, Anne Ramsey, Amanda Plummer, John Hannah. Dir: Roger Christian. 18. July 1996 (Medusa).

Final Vendetta. Bridgitte Wilson, Peter Boyle. 18. April 1997 (BMG).

Firestorm. John Savage, Robert Carradine, Bentley Mitchum, Paul Williams. Dir: John Shepphird. 18. December 1996 (First Independent).

Fist of the North Star. Gary Daniels, Chris Penn, Malcolm McDowell, Melvin Van Peebles. Dir: Tony Randel. 18. September 1996 (20.20).

Flynn. Guy Pearce, Steven Berkoff, John Savage in biog of Errol Flynn. Dir: Frank Howson. 18. January 1997 (Medusa).

Forgotten Sins. William Devane, John Shea, Bess Armstrong, Tim Quill, Gary Grubbs. Dir: Dick Lowry. 15. June 1997 (Odyssey).

Formula For Death See *Robin Cook's Formula For Death.*

French Exit. Jonathan Silverman, Madchen Amick. 15. June 1997 (Fox Guild).

Fugitive From Justice. Chris Noth, Loryn Locklin, Megan Gallagher, Daniel Roebuck, Stepfanie Kramer, Natalie Cole, Peter MacNicol. Dir: Chuck Bowman. 15. October 1996 (Odyssey).

The Glass Cage. Charlotte Lewis, Richard Tyson, Eric Roberts. 18. December 1996 (Fox Guild).

Gone In the Night. Shannen Doherty, Kevin Dillon, Dixie Carter, Timothy Carhart, Michael Brandon, Edward Asner. Dir: Bill L. Norton. 15. November 1996 (Odyssey).

Gridlock. David Hasselhoff, Miguel Fernandez, Kathy Ireland. 15. August 1996 (Hi-Fliers).

Harmful Intent See *Robin Cook's Harmful Intent.*

The Haunted Heart. Diane Ladd. 15. May 1997 (FoxGuild).

Hawk's Vengeance. Gary Daniels. 18. January 1997 (Entertainment).

Head of the Family. Blake Bailey. 18. April 1997 (Entertainment).

Hellraiser IV: Bloodline. Bruce Ramsey, Doug Bradley, Valentina Vargas. Dir: Alan Smithee. 18. May 1997 (Buena Vista).

Here Comes the Son. Scott Bakula, Chelsea Botfield. Dir: Paul Schneider. 12. January 1997 (Odyssey).

Her Last Chance. Kellie Martin, Patti LuPone, Jonathan Brandis. Dir: Richard A. Colla. 15. December 1996 (Odyssey).

Holiday Affair. David James Elliott, Cynthia Gibb. Dir: Alan Myerson. PG. November 1996 (Odyssey).

Hostile Advances: The Kerry Ellison Story. Rena Sofer, Victor Garber, Sean McCann, Karen Allen. Dir: Allan Kroeker. 15. September 1996 (Odyssey).

Human Time Bomb. Bryan Gennesse, Joe Lara. 18. July 1996 (Fox Guild).

If Looks Could Kill. Antonio Sabata Jr, Brad Dourif. 18. June 1997 Fox Guild).

Illegal in Blue. Dan Gauthier, Stacey Dash. 18. June 1997 (Marquee).

Indecent Seduction: A True Story. Gary Cole, Mary Kay Place, Nicholle Tom, Mac Davis. Dir: Alan Metzger. 15. February 1997 (Odyssey).

Innocent Victims. Rick Schroder, John Corbett, Tom Irwin, Howard Hessemann, Rue McClanahan, Hal Holbrook. Dir: Gilbert Cates. 12. August 1996 (Odyssey).

In the Blink of an Eye. Veronica Hamel, Mimi Rogers, Polly Bergen. Dir and Pro: Micki Dickoff. 12. July 1996 (Odyssey).

The Killing Jar. Brett Cullen, Tamlyn Tomita. 18. April 1997 (Fox Guild).

Leapin' Leprechauns 2. John Bluthal, Madeleine Potter, Sylvester McCoy, James Ellis. U. February 1997 (CIC).

Lethal Tender. Jeff Fahey, Kim Coates, Gary Busey. 15. February 1997 (Hi-Fliers).

The Little Death. Brent Fraser, Pamela Gidley, J.T. Walsh, Dwight Yoakam, Richard Beymer. Dir: Jan Verheyen. 18. October 1996 (PolyGram).

Little Witches. Jennifer Rubin, Zelda Rubinstein, Jack Nance. Dir: Jane Simpson. 18. March 1997 (Hi-Fliers).

Lurking Fear. Jon Finch, Blake Bailey, Ashley Laurence, Jeffrey Combs, Vincent Schiavelli. 18. December 1996 (CIC).

The Maddening. Burt Reynolds, Angie Dickinson, William Hickey, Mia Sara. Dir: Danny Huston. 18. September 1996 (Entertainment).

Magic In the Mirror. Jaimee Renee Smith. Dir: Ted Nicolaou. U. April 1997 (CIC).

Marked Man. Roddy Piper. 18. August 1996 (First Independent).

Marshal Law. Jimmy Smits, James LeGros, Kristy Swanson. Dir: Stephen Cornwell. 18. April 1997 (MGM/UA).

Maternal Instincts. Delta Burke, Beth Broderick. 15. March 1997 (CIC).

Mercenary. Olivier Gruner, John Ritter, Robert Culp. Dir: Avi Nesher. 18. May 1997 (Buena Vista).

Midnight Hour. Paula Barbieri, Andrew Stevens. 18. August 1996 (Hi-Fliers).

Midnight in St Petersburg. Michael Caine, Jason Connery, Michael Gambon, Michael Sarrazin. Dir: Doug Jackson. 15. April 1997 (Buena Vista).

Miracle at Christmas: Ebbie's Story. Susan Lucci, Wendy Crewson. Dir: George Kaczender. PG. December 1996 (Odyssey).

Mondo Topless. Babette Bardot. Dir: Russ Meyer. 18. September 1996 (Troma).

Mortal Fear See *Robin Cook's Mortal Fear*.

Murder In a College Town. Kate Jackson, Drew Ebersole, Gary Basaraba, Sean McCann. Dir: Bradley Wigor. 15. June 1997 (Odyssey).

Mystery Science Theatre 3000: The Movie. Michael J. Nelson. Dir: Jim Mallon. PG. March 1997 (CIC).

Naked Souls. Sci-fi. Pamela Anderson, Brian Krause, David Warner, Dean Stockwell. Dir: Lyndon Chubbock. 18. September 1996 (PolyGram).

Natural Enemy. Donald Sutherland, William McNamara, Lesley Ann Warren, Joe Pantoliano, Tia Carrere. Dir: Douglas Jackson. 18. March 1997 (Fox Guild).

Nemesis 3: Timelapse. Norbert Weisser, Tim Thomerson. 18. August 1996 (Columbia TriStar).

Never Say Die. Frank Zagarino, Billy Drago. 18. July 1996 (Fox Guild).

Nick and Jane. James McCaffrey, Dana Wheeler-Nicholson, Lisa Gay Hamilton, David Johansen. Dir: Rich Mauro. 15. April 1997 (Columbia TriStar).

Nothing Lasts Forever. Gail O'Grady, Brooke Shields, Vanessa Williams. 15. September 1996 (FoxGuild).

No Way Back. Russell Crowe, Helen Slater, Michael Lerner. Dir: Frank Cappello. 18. January 1997 (Columbia TriStar).

The Nurse. Lisa Zane, Jay Underwood. 18. March 1997 (First Independent).

An Occasional Hell. Tom Berenger, Valeria Golino, Kari Wuhrer, Robert Davi, Stephen Lang, Geoffrey Lewis, Diana Scarwid. Dir: Salome Breziner. 18. March 1997 (BMG).

Once a Thief. Chow Yun Fat, Leslie Cheung. Dir: John Woo. 18. September 1996 (Made in Hong Kong).

One Woman's Courage. Patty Duke, James Farentino, Margot Kidder, Dennis Farina. Dir: Charles Robert Carner. 15. August 1996 (Odyssey).

Orbit. Joe Estevez, Bentley Mitchum, Carrie Mitchum, Chris Mitchum, Jan-Michael Vincent, Caspar Van Dien. Dir: Mario Van Cleef. 15. January 1997 (FoxGuild).

The People Next Door. Michael O'Keefe, Nicollette Sheridan, Ernie Lively, Faye Dunaway. Dir: Tim Hunter. M: David Mansfield. 15. March 1997 (Odyssey).

Phoenix II. Marc Singer, Matthias Hues. 18. April 1997 (Fox Guild).

Playback. Harry Dean Stanton, Tawny Kitaen, George Hamilton. 18. January 1997 (FoxGuild).

Power 98. Eric Roberts, Jason Gedrick, Jennie Garth. 18. September 1996 (Hi-Fliers).

Precious Find. Rutger Hauer, Brion James. Dir: Philippe Mora. 15. November 1996 (Medusa).

Prescription For Murder. Adam Baldwin, Barbara Carrera, Don Harvey, Nina Siemaszko, Nicholas Sadler. Pro: Roger Corman. 18. September 1996 (Medusa).

Prey of the Jaguar. Maxwell Caulfield, Trevor Goddard, Linda Blair, Stacy Keach, Paul Bartel. Dir: David DeCoteau. 18. November 1996 (First Independent).

The Price of Love. Peter Faginelli. 15. April 1997 (PolyGram).

Profile For Murder. Lance Henriksen, Joan Severance. 18. June 1997 (Medusa).

Public Enemy #1. Theresa Russell, Frank Stallone, Dan Cortese, Eric Roberts. Dir: Mark L. Lester. 15. June 1997 (BMG).

Race Against Time. Patty Duke, Richard Crenna. Dir: Fred Gerber. 12. January 1997 (Odyssey).

The Rage. Lorenzo Lamas, Gary Busey, Roy Scheider. Dir: Sidney J. Furie. 18. June 1997 (BMG).

Rattled. William Katt, Shanna Reed, Ed Lauter. Dir: Tony Randel. PG. February 1997 (CIC).

Raven. Burt Reynolds, Matt Battaglia. Dir: Russell Solberg. 18. June 1997 (Marquee).

Red Blooded. Kari Salin, Burt Young David Keith. 18. February 1997 (Medusa).

The Return of Swamp Thing. Dick Durock, Heather Locklear, Louis Jourdan, Sarah Douglas. 15. February 1997 (Imagine Independents).

The Road to Galveston. Cicely Tyson, Piper Laurie, Tess Harper. PG. October 1996 (CIC).

Robin Cook's Formula For Death. Nicollette Sheridan, William Devane, Stephen Caffrey, Barry Corbin, William Atherton. Dir: Armand Mastroianni. 15. February 1997 (Odyssey).

Robin Cook's Harmful Intent. Tim Matheson, Emma Samms, Robert Pastorelli, Alex Rocco. Dir: John Patterson. M: Lee Holdridge. 15. February 1997 (Odyssey).

Robin Cook's Mortal Fear. Joanna Kerns, Gregory Harrison, Max Gail, Tobin Bell, Robert Englund. Dir: Larry Shaw. 12. February 1997 (Odyssey).

Roseanne. Garish biog of the TV star, with Denny Dillon, David Graf. Dir: Paul Schneider. 15. May 1997 (PolyGram).

Rumplestiltskin. Kim Johnston Ulruch. 18. August 1996 (First Independent).

Sabotage. Mark Dacascos, Tony Todd, Graham Greene, John Neville. Dir: Tibor Takacs. 18. April 1997 (BMG).

Savage. Olivier Gruner, Jennifer Grant. Dir: Avi Nesher. 18. June 1997 (Buena Vista).

Sci-Fighters. Roddy Piper, Billy Drago. Dir: Peter Svatek. 18. February 1997 (Hi-Fliers).

Search for Justice. Peggy Lipton, Susan Ruttan. Dir: Noel Nosseck. 15. November 1996 (Odyssey).

Serpent's Lair. Jeff Fahey, Lisa B. 18. January 1997 (Hi-Fliers).

The Shell Seekers. Angela Lansbury, Sam Wanamaker, Anna Carteret, Michael Gough, Patricia Hodge, Denis Quilley, Sophie Ward, Irene Worth. Dir: Waris Hussein. U. August 1996 (Odyssey).

Sgt Kabukiman NYPD. Rick Gianasi. 18. July 1996 (Troma).

The Silencers. Jack Scalia, Dennis Christopher. Dir: Richard Pepin. 18. April 1997 (Marquee).

Silent Lies. Elizabeth Anne Allen. 18. June 1997 (First Independent).

Silent Trigger. Dolph Lundgren, Gina Bellman. Dir: Russell Mulcahy. 18. February 1997 (Buena Vista).

Silver Strand. Gil Bellows, Nicollette Sheridan. Dir: George Miller. Screenplay: Douglas Day Stewart. 15. July 1996 (MGM/UA).

Skyscraper. Anna Nicole Smith. Dir: Raymond Martino. 18. May 1997 (Medusa).

Smoke Jumpers. Adam Baldwin, Lindsay Frost, Timothy Carhart. Dir: Dick Lowry. PG. June 1997 (Odyssey).

The Soft Kill. Corbin Bernsen, Brion James, Matt McCoy. 18. October 1996 (Hi-Fliers).

Sometimes They Come Back...Again. Alexis Arquette, Michael Gross, Hilary Swank. Dir: Adam Grossman. 18. August 1996 (Hi-Fliers).

Son of the Morning Star. Gary Cole, Rosanna Arquette, Dean Stockwell, Rodney A. Grant, Terry O'Quinn, David Strathairn. Dir: Mike Robe. Screenplay: Melissa Mathison. PG. February 1997 (Odyssey).

Space Marines. Billy Wirth, Edward Albert. 15. June 1997 (Third Millennium).

Specimen. Mark Paul Gosselaar, Michelle Johnson. Dir: John Bradshaw. 18. November 1996 (Fox Guild).

Spill. Brian Bosworth, Leah Pinsent. Dir: Alan A. Goldstein. 12. February 1997 (Entertainment).

Stalker: Shadow of Obsession. Veronica Hamel, Jack Scalia. 18. September 1996 (Medusa).

The Stendhal Syndrome. Asia Argento. Dir: Dario Argento. 18. February 1997 (Fox Guild).

The Stepford Husbands. Donna Mills, Michael Ontkean, Cindy Williams, Sarah Douglas, Louise Fletcher. Dir: Fred Walton. 15. March 1997 (Odyssey).

Stolen Innocence. Tracey Gold, Thomas Calabro, Bess Armstrong, Nick Searcy, Terence Knox. Dir: Bill L. Norton. 15. March 1997 (Odyssey).

Stolen Women. Western with Janine Turner, Patrick Bergin. PG. June 1997 (Fox Guild).

Stolen Youth. Sharon Lawrence, Brian Austin Green, Harley Jane Kozak, John Getz. Dir: Christopher Leitch. 15. May 1997 (Odyssey).

Strange Affair. Judith Light, Jay Thomas, Linda Sorensen, William Russ. Dir: Ted Kotcheff. 15. February 1997 (Odyssey).

Strip Show. Kimberley Kelly. 18. November 1996 (Hi-Fliers).

Tales You Live, Heads You Die. Corbin Bernsen, Tim Matheson. 15. August 1996 (CIC).

Temptress. Kim Delaney, Chris Sarandon, Corbin Bernsen. 18. December 1996 (Fox Guild).

Terminal Justice. Lorenzo Lamas, Chris Sarandon, Peter Coyote. 18. September 1996 (Hi-Fliers).

Tiger Heart. T.J. Roberts. 15. January 1997 (Fox Guild).

The Time Master. Jesse Cameron-Glickenhaus, Noriyuki 'Pat' Morita, Joanna Pacula. Dir: James Glickenhaus. 12. January 1997 (First Independent).

The Tomorrow Man. Julian Sands, Giancarlo Esposito, Craig Wasson. 12. October 1996 (FoxGuild).

Too Fast, Too Young. Michael Ironside. 18. December 1996 (Hi-Fliers).

Tough and Deadly. Billy Blanks, Roddy Piper. 18. October 1996 (Guild).

Tracks of a Killer. Wolf Larsen, James Brolin, Kelly LeBrock. 18. September 1996 (Medusa).

Tremors 2: Aftershocks. Fred Ward, Helen Shaver, Michael Gross. Dir: S.S. Wilson. 12. August 1996 (CIC).

True Crime. Alicia Silverstone, Kevin Dillon. Dir: Pat Verducci. 18. October 1996 (Hi-Fliers).

Unabomber. Robert Hays, Dean Stockwell, Tobin Bell. Dir: Jon Purdy. 15. May 1997 (Odyssey).

Uncle Sam. Isaac Hayes, Timothy Bottoms. 18. March 1997 (BMG).

Unlikely Suspects. Shanna Reed, Sarah Chalke, Gwyneth Walsh. Dir: Joseph L. Scanlan. 15. May 1997 (Odyssey).

Upper Cut. John Savage. 18. May 1997 (Third Millennium).

The Vampire Journals. Jonathon Morris. 18. May 1997 (Entertainment).

Voice From the Grave. Kevin Dobson, Megan Ward, John Terlesky, Michael Riley. Dir: David S. Jackson. 15. May 1997 (Odyssey).

What Love Sees. Richard Thomas, Annabeth Gish. Dir: Michael Switzer. PG. March 1997 (Odyssey).

When Friendship Kills. Lynda Carter. Dir: James A. Contner. PG. December 1996 (Odyssey).

Where's the Money Noreen? Julianne Phillips, A. Martinez. 12. December 1996 (CIC).

While Justice Sleeps. Cybill Shepherd, Tim Matheson. Dir: Alan Smithee. 15. August 1996 (Odyssey).

Whiskey Down. Virginia Madsen, Sean Patrick Flanery, Ernie Hudson, Jon Polito, Carroll Baker. Dir: Gary Auerbach. 15. May 1997 (PolyGram).

Wild Justice. Manon Prysor. 18. January 1997 (First Independent).

Within the Rock. Xander Berkley. 18. December 1996 (Hi-Fliers).

A Woman Scorned 2. Tane McClure, Andrew Stevens. 18. February 1997 (Medusa).

Yesterday's Target. Malcolm McDowell, Daniel Baldwin, T.K. Carter. 15. March 1997 (Marquee).

Movie Quotations of the Year

'What can I say? I'm a bad man. But sometimes it's fun to be bad.'

> Dennis Hopper, 61, defending his liaison with a 17-year-old student, in *Acts of Love*

'I want to fuck you with all the lights on.'

> Crippled farmer and teacher Dennis Hopper to Amy Irving, in *Acts of Love*

Meg Ryan, to Matthew Broderick: 'What's your name?' Broderick: 'Mike.' Ryan (unbelieving): 'What's your name, Mike?' Broderick: 'Sam.'

> From *Addicted To Love*

'It's the longest orgasm I've ever heard.' Meg Ryan (who knows a thing or two about moaning), eavesdropping on Kelly Preston's ecstasy.

> From *Addicted To Love*

'Why would I have sex with a hamburger when I can make love to a steak?' Restaurateur Tcheky Karyo defending Kelly Preston's accusation of his infidelity.

> From *Addicted To Love*

'Sister, you ain't booked the seat yet, so don't pack the bags.'

> Jason Flemyng, ticking off his friend with Aids (Anthony Higgins), for talking about his impending death - in *Alive and Kicking*

'You don't not love me more than I don't not love you.'

> Antony Sher entering into a somewhat philosophical romantic debate with his lover Jason Flemyng – in *Alive and Kicking*

'Whatever it is they tell you, it is the size of your gun that counts.'

> From Arnold Schwarzenegger, in *Batman and Robin*

Robert Carlyle: 'I thought you were a fucking pacifist.' Scott Glenn, picking up a rifle: 'Yeh. I resigned.'

> From *Carla's Song*

Steve Buscemi, calmly observing the hijinks around him: 'Define irony. A bunch of guys on a plane dancing to a song made famous by a bunch of guys who died on a plane.'

> From *Con Air*

John Malkovich, holding a gun to the head of Nicolas Cage's soft toy: 'Make a move and the bunny gets it!'

> From *Con Air*

'It''s all very satisfying – but I don't see why.'

> James Spader, admiring the carnage following a reenactment of James Dean's fatal car crash, in *Crash*

'If you're not confused, you don't know what's going on.'

> Brad Pitt illuminating the 'Irish Question' in *The Devil's Own*

'Did you hear about the Irishman who tried to blow up a car? He burnt his lips on the tail pipe.'

> Greg Salata in *The Devil's Own*

'It's not an American story, it's an Irish one.'

> Brad Pitt's explanation for his deeds – to Harrison Ford – in *The Devil's Own*

'On Mars the best cooks are going to be men. And that's a fact.'

Al Pacino, offering some remarkable insight, in *Donnie Brasco*

'That woman has enough drugs to relax China.'

Sharon Stone in *Diabolique*

Isabella Adjani: 'Nicole, why did you kill him?' Sharon Stone: 'He underestimated me.'

From *Diabolique*

'It's not your fault. It's men. Testosterone. They should put it in bombs.'

Kathy Bates, attempting to assuage Mlle Adjani's guilt over her marriage, in *Diabolique*

'I may have chewed in self-defence – but I never swallow.'

The benign dragon voiced by Sean Connery in *DragonHeart*

'Come and get me.'

Arnold Schwarzenegger's priceless invitation to the bad guys, in *Eraser*

'You're luggage!'

Arnold Schwarzenegger, as he blows a crocodile to kingdom come, in *Eraser*

'Baseball's better than life. It's fair.'

Robert De Niro in *The Fan*

'Mr Sylvester Stallone did not get to where he is today by doing Jane Austen.'

John Cleese, as zoo director Rollo Lee, pointing out the commercial advantage of violent entertainment in *Fierce Creatures*

'Rollo, I don't like you. You're weird and unattractive.'

A plain dealing Kevin Kline to John Cleese, in *Fierce Creatures*

'This is the sort of conversation two people have when one of them is a woman.'

Kevin Kline, exasperated at the way his courtship is going, to Jamie Lee Curtis – in *Fierce Creatures*

'Freudian slit.'

A flustered John Cleese apologising to Jamie Lee Curtis for his inadvertent double entendre – in *Fierce Creatures*

Wise guy: Al Pacino dishing out the advice in Donnie Brasco

'It's important to have enemies. They keep you strong.'

Shirley MacLaine in *The Evening Star*

Aurora Greenway to Garrett Breedlove: 'Do you mind ageing?' Breedlove: 'No – because I do it so well.'

Shirley MacLaine and Jack Nicholson in *The Evening Star*

'I would say life would be quite pointless without the movies.'

Vincent Gallo in *The Funeral*

'Everybody's got a plan until they're hit.'

Michael Douglas reprising his favourite boxing motto, in *The Ghost and The Darkness*

Lt Col. John H. Patterson to big game hunter Remington: 'Have you *ever* failed?' Remington, profoundly: 'Only in life.'

Val Kilmer and Michael Douglas in *The Ghost and The Darkness*

'Wait till you see your father's organ. He can't keep his hands off it.'

Anne Bancroft telling Holly Hunter about the latest obsession of Charles Durning, in *Home For the Holidays*

'We don't have to like each other, Jo. We're family.'

Holly Hunter telling her sister – Cynthia Stevenson – like it is, in *Home For the Holidays*

'What do I want to be when I grow up? Alive.'

A fast-growing Robin Williams in *Jack*

'Just jump right into my nightmare. The water is warm.'

Tom Cruise, exasperated that fiancée Kelly Preston is only making matters worse, in *Jerry Maguire*

'This guy would go home with a gardening tool if it showed interest.'

Bonnie Hunt airing her opinion of Tom Cruise's libido, in *Jerry Maguire*

'I love him for the man he wants to be.'

Renee Zellweger (on Tom Cruise) in *Jerry Maguire*

'Men are the enemy. But I still love the enemy.'

Renee Zellweger, at a meeting for divorced women, in *Jerry Maguire*

'You complete me.'

Tom Cruise's winning words of courtship in *Jerry Maguire*

Renee Zellweger, interrupting Tom Cruise's verbal flow of apology and adulation: 'Aw, shut up. You had me at "hello".'

From *Jerry Maguire*

'Call me Snake.'

Kurt Russell's catchphrase in *John Carpenter's Escape From L.A.*

'Thanks for not killing me, man. I owe you one.'

Peter Fonda to Kurt Russell in *John Carpenter's Escape From L.A.*

'The more things change, the more they stay the same.'

A philosophical Kurt Russell in *John Carpenter's Escape From L.A.*

'I enjoy three things: eating meat, riding meat and putting meat into meat.'

A somewhat carnal King Raj (Naveen Andrews) in *Kama Sutra*

Irate driver: 'What's your problem, schmuck?' Jim Carrey (who cannot tell a lie): 'I'm an inconsiderate prick.'

In *Liar Liar*

Passer-by: 'How's it hanging?' Jim Carrey (who cannot tell a lie): 'Short, shrivelled and slightly to the left.'

In *Liar Liar*

The wisdom of the Irish: Liam Neeson as
Michael Collins

'A woman's face never looks quite so
beautiful as when it's distended in
pain.'

A sadistic David Morse preparing
himself for the pleasures of torture, in
The Long Kiss Goodnight

'The last time I got blown, candy bars
cost a nickel.'

Samuel L. Jackson in *The Long Kiss
Goodnight*

Passer-by to Geena Davis: 'Want some
company?' Davis, forging ahead: 'No,
I'm saving myself until I get raped.'

From *The Long Kiss Goodnight*

Geena Davis, summing up Samuel L.
Jackson's skill as a marksman: 'You
couldn't hit a lake if you were
standing on the bottom.'

From *The Long Kiss Goodnight*

Jeff Goldblum to his daughter: 'If you
want some good parental advice: don't
listen to me.'

From *The Lost World: Jurassic Park*

Julianne Moore (placating her
boyfriend, Jeff Goldblum): 'I'll be back
in five or six days.' Goldblum, not
placated: 'No. You'll be back in five or
six pieces.'

From *The Lost World: Jurassic Park*

Coroner Linda Fiorentino, pissed off
with the attitude of her co-workers: 'I
hate the living.'

From *Men in Black*

'He asked me to some Alzheimer's
benefit. I told him to forget it.'

Lauren Bacall, on turning down a date,
in *The Mirror Has Two Faces*

'I want peace and quiet so much I
could die for it.'

Liam Neeson as Irish revolutionary
Michael Collins

'I hate them [the English] for making
hate necessary.'

Liam Neeson as Irish revolutionary
Michael Collins

'Never buy what's for sale.'

Bernard Tapie's business philosophy, in
Men Women: A User's Manual

'My dear, we're not intimate. We just
have sex together.'

Debbie Reynolds, 64, re her gentleman
caller, in *Mother*

'For the first time I don't see you as a
mother. I see you as a failure. That's
wonderful.'

Albert Brooks to his *Mother*, Debbie
Reynolds

John Brown, Queen Victoria's servant,
to The Prince of Wales: 'Are you deaf
as well as stupid?' The Prince of
Wales, outraged: 'Do you know to
who you are talking?' John Brown,
correcting him: 'To whom.'

Billy Connolly and David Westhead in
Mrs Brown

'I wish I could find a fish that would
appreciate my chocolate layer.'

George Clooney tying himself up in
metaphors in front of his psychiatrist, in
One Fine Day

Cruella DeVil, to her assistant,
Frederick: 'What sort of sycophant are
you?' Frederick: 'What sort of
sycophant would you like me to be?'

Glenn Close and Hugh Fraser in *101
Dalmatians*

'More good women have been lost to
marriage than war, famine and
disease.'

Glenn Close in *101 Dalmatians*

'You may have won the battle. But I'm
about to win the wardrobe.'

Glenn Close to a barn full of animals in
101 Dalmatians

'Fortunately, he has consumption. I
say fortunately, because it gives him
something to do.'

Barbara Hershey, taking a philosophical
view of Martin Donovan's malady, in
The Portrait of a Lady

'You're not the only person in this
club who's slept with every woman in
this club.'

Libidinous striptease artist Courtney
Love to club owner Woody Harrelson, in
The People vs. Larry Flynt

'All I'm guilty of is bad taste.'

Larry Flynt (Woody Harrelson), the
prosecuted publisher of *Hustler*
magazine, in *The People vs. Larry Flynt*

'I like a joke as much as the next fat
person.'

A humourless Pam Ferris in *Roald Dahl's
Matilda*

'This dress is a celebration of the
genetic betrayal that is my legacy.'

Janeane Garofalo, not happy with her
new outfit, in *Romy and Michele's High
School Reunion*

'Domestic violence was a cottage
industry in the Bronx.'

Jason Patric on the soundtrack of *Sleepers*

'What kind of Mickey Mouse
organisation would name their team
The Ducks?'

Aspiring basketball player and Warner
Brothers' franchise Bugs Bunny, in *Space
Jam*

Paul Guilfoyle, assistant to libidinous
congressman David Dilbeck (Burt
Reynolds), explaining his position to
Demi Moore: 'I am David Dilbeck's
right hand.' Moore: 'You must be a
very busy man.'

From *Striptease*

*Dress sense: Glenn Close knocking out the
one-liners in* 101 Dalmatians

A distressed Drew Barrymore, to anonymous caller: 'What do you want?' Voice on the other end: 'To see what your insides look like.'

From *Scream*

'You can only hear that Richard Gere gerbil story so many times before you start believing it.'

Rose McGowan, in *Scream*

'What do I have to do to prove I'm not a killer?'

Skeet Ulrich – just before he's knifed from behind – in *Scream*

'Movies don't create psychos. Movies make psychos more creative!'

Matthew Lillard in *Scream*

'You really called the police? My mom and dad are going to be really mad at me.'

The teenage serial killer, in *Scream*

'Your twenties are for having sex with all the wrong people.'

Bette Midler - to twentysomething daughter Paula Marshall – in *That Old Feeling*

'Shrinks don't fight. They just listen you to death.'

Jennifer Aniston on living with a psychiatrist, in *'Til There Was You*

'My cat eats like a Jew.'

Non sequitur from Alice Drummond – in *'Til There Was You*

'How would you like me to use your guts to Jackson Pollock the streets?'

Maximilian Shaun (waving a crossbow) in *Tromeo & Juliet*

Juliet: 'Parting is such sweet sorrow.' Tromeo: 'No, it sucks.'

Jane Jensen and Will Keenan in *Tromeo & Juliet*

'Rugby. Tom Jones. Male voice choirs. Shirley Bassey. Llanfairpwllgwyngellgogerythgwyrobollantisilioaagogogoch. Snowdonia. Prince of Wales. Anthony Hopkins. Daffodils. Sheep. Sheep lovers. Coal. Slate quarries. The Blaenau Ffestiniog Dinkey-Dooey Miniature Railway. Now if that's your idea of thousands of years of Welsh culture, you can't blame us for trying to liven the place up a bit can you?'

From *Twin Town*

'The coast is toast.'

From *Volcano*

And, some of the year's most memorable tag lines:
(those blurbs dreamed up by marketing people to put on movie posters)

'He will erase your past to protect your future.'

From *Eraser*

'Life gets complicated when you love one woman and worship eleven men.'

From *Fever Pitch*

'Something has survived.'

From *The Lost World: Jurassic Park*

'He's an angel. Not a saint.'

From *Michael*

'Protecting the earth from the scum of the universe.'

From *Men in Black*

'Sex, bugs and rock 'n'roll.'

From *Microcosmos*

'Golf pro. Love amateur.'

From *Tin Cup*

Quotes, off-screen
(that is, famous lines not scripted)

'If I die before him, I want a little bit of my ashes put in his food so that I can finally live inside him.'

Drew Barrymore, talking of her one true love, her cat

'Casting directors are amazing dating services. They find two people who have excellent chemistry. So I always tell people that if you go on a set and you have that tingle, give it two weeks. By the end of the second week, you'll see them picking their nose or something.'

Sandra Bullock, whose boyfriends number co-stars Tate Donovan and Matthew McConaughey

'When you are called a character actress, it's because you're too ugly to be called a leading lady.'

Kathy Burke, winner of the best actress award at Cannes for Gary Oldman's *Nil By Mouth*

'My favourite review described me as the cinematic equivalent of junk mail. I don't know what that means, but it sounds like a dig.'

Steve Buscemi, ubiquitous

Jim Carrey, asked what it is about comedians that attracts beautiful women: 'A surface-to-air missile-type dick. Look at Milton Berle, Charlie Chaplin. I mean, I'm sure there's probably some real little-dick comics out there with tremendous senses of humour who make pithy, witty Oscar Wilde-type comments. Ah, but the rest of us...'

'Other actors have their alcohol, women, horses or their dope. Me, I have my restaurants. Every time I get depressed, I open a restaurant.'

Michael Caine

'Can you imagine me with a woman old enough to be my wife? Forget it. My girlfriend is 25 years old.'

Tony Curtis, 72

'Our *Romeo + Juliet* is hardcore. I wouldn't have done it if I'd had to jump around in tights.'

Leonardo DiCaprio on his vision of Shakespeare

'It's no big deal, kissing a fella, except they should shave more often.'

Ian Hart on his gay scenes with Martin Donovan in *Hollow Reed*

'I knew Michelle Pfeiffer and I would work together someday – I'm just so glad it was while we were both ambulatory. I figured we would both be in *On Golden Pond II* or something like that.'

Peter Gallagher, who shares the screen with Ms Pfeiffer in *To Gillian On Her 37th Birthday*

'The strangest thing is, I thought I was elderly, past my peak, in 1944.'

Sir John Gielgud, 92

'I used to be the "*Cape Fear* actress", then the "*To Die For* actress". Now I'm "indie staple". My favourite was someone called me "diva in development".'

Ileanna Douglas, star of *Grace of My Heart*

'The last time I went out without make-up he looked at me as if to say,"Have I really married this old bag?"'

Old bag Melanie Griffith on gorgeous new husband Antonio Banderas

'Journalists will ask you a question like, "What are your deepest secrets?" You know, it's funny. I'd like to discuss this in a national magazine?'

Tom Hanks

'I've been mistaken for Jane Fonda, Sigourney Weaver, Mia Farrow. Once someone asked me if I was Barbara Hershey's daughter! That was a new one.'

Barbara Hershey, 49

'I feel like such a phony, being in Los Angeles in my blue jeans. I should be back in Wales, worrying.'

Anthony Hopkins

'I have three lives... actress, model, producer. Sometimes I'm aware that there's a fourth life which is somewhat neglected, which is living a bit.'

Busy bee Elizabeth Hurley

Ileanna Douglas, diva in development

Director Tom Hanks, refusing to reveal his soul

'I have heard people say that it will not get a distributor to release it. If it does not find one, I will leave the country.'

Jeremy Irons, threatening to leave his homeland should *Lolita* fail to be released in the UK

'If I were doing a movie about a 13 year old getting chopped up and eaten by cannibals, there'd be no problem.'

Adrian Lyne on the censorship and releasing problems of his film *Lolita*

'There were ex-boxers, ex-football players and ex-convicts on the set. And without getting homoerotic about it – stopping short of Michelangelo – it amuses me to be around guys like that.'

John Malkovich, on his fellow cast members in *Con Air*

'I was very disappointed with the movie business, and I swore an oath that I wouldn't work again until a woman was paid $12 million to star in a film. Finally, the Demi Moore thing happened.'

Bill Murray, explaining his relative absence from the big screen

'It's always strange being a kid on the set. You're treated like an equal when you're working, but then when you break, the other actors get to go back to their trailers and drink beer and I have to, like, go to school.'

Natalie Portman, 14-year-old star of *Leon, Heat, Beautiful Girls* and *Mars Attacks!*

'I have a certain detachment sometimes which people take for bad acting. I really am the critics' whipping boy.'

Keanu Reeves, biker dude, musician and Hamlet

'I've never done anything for money and that is why I got money. When you do stuff for money, you never get money.'

Roseanne, who received $500,000 an episode for TV's *Roseanne*

'I'm 44, and I think it's more important to say, "I'm 44 and I look beautiful" than to say, "I'm 44, but I look 28," and never accept your age.'

Isabella Rossellini

'I only went to R-rated movies. I would refuse to go to PG movies. Who wants to see people talk and have a good time? I wanted to see violence and hanky-panky.'

Arnold Schwarzenegger on his childhood cinemagoing habits

'I don't date much. It's not that I don't want to, it's just that nobody asks me.'

Alicia Silverstone, superbabe

'I believe anyone who is married and raising children is successful. Everything else is just gravy.'

Damon Wayans

'Reviews are mostly for people who still read. I don't know any actors or people in showbusiness who have any serious interest in what is written about our world.'

Bruce Willis, dismissing the negative reviews for *The Fifth Element*

'I had to sleep with him to get the part, which wasn't bad at all. I went back and did it again.'

Rita Wilson – aka Mrs Tom Hanks – on landing her role in *That Thing You Do!*

'I had to be fitted with a prosthetic, which was wonderful. I had these three gorgeous men smearing Nivea all over my bottom, all over my tummy. All over...well, everywhere.'

Kate Winslet, on the preparation for her childbirth sequence in *Jude*

Faces of the Year

Jennifer Aniston

Unlike other overnight TV sensations, Jennifer Aniston edged her way stealthily on to the big screen. First she took a supporting role in the low-budget *Dream for an Insomniac* – as an aspiring actress; played Rene, the jilted wife who has an affair with her vibrator in Edward Burns' smart and sassy *She's the One*;

Jennifer Aniston

and was Jeanne Tripplehorn's snotty best friend in *'Til There Was You*. Then, having found that the water was warm, the actress plunged into the deep end with the starring role in Fox's romantic comedy *Picture Perfect* – for which she was paid a handsome $3 million. This she followed with another lead, in Nicholas Hytner's New York-set dramatic comedy *The Object of My Affection*, with Stephen Baldwin, Alan Alda and Nigel Hawthorne in support. Before earning household stardom as the terminally spoiled Rachel Green in TV's *Friends*, the erstwhile Jennifer Anistonapoulos appeared in two other sitcoms, *Molloy* and *Ferris Bueller*, and was cast in the execrable horror film *Leprechaun* (1993). Being that rare combination of a fine comic actress with the looks to match, Aniston seems set for a heady career in romantic comedy. While she may yet choose to work with the likes of Wim Wenders or Terence Davies, we should enjoy her exquisite comic timing and sunny countenance while we can.

Billy Crudup

Exhibiting the requisite cut-glass jaw-line and sulky demeanour of the fashionable hunk club, Billy Crudup resembles a young Patrick Swayze with a dash of Rob Lowe. A graduate of the University of North Carolina, Crudup won a fistful of prizes for his Broadway debut in Tom Stoppard's *Arcadia* and then made his film debut opposite Brad Pitt and Jason Patric in

Anne Heche with Johnny Depp in Donnie Brasco

Sleepers – as the ex-con who murders Kevin Bacon in cold blood. He then got to sing in Woody Allen's first musical, *Everyone Says I Love You*, made love to Liv Tyler, Jennifer Connelly and Joanna Going in *Inventing the Abbots*, and played the legendary runner Steve Prefontaine in Robert Towne's *Pre*. He was an ex-con again (who sleeps with his brother's wife) in the fresh, low-budget *Grind*, he teamed up with Denis Leary and Kelly Lynch in Ted Demme's *Noose* and then joined Woody Harrelson in Stephen Frears' Western *The HiLo Country*.

Anne Heche

Having displayed a remarkable talent in *The Juror* (as Demi Moore's ill-fated girlfriend), *Walking and Talking* and *Donnie Brasco*, Anne Heche hit the headlines just as her first biggie – *Volcano* – engulfed US cinemas. Previously linked to Steve Martin, Heche leaped out of the closet in April of '97 and into the

Billy Crudup

arms of TV star Ellen DeGeneres. The couple then exchanged rings in a declaration of their love and attended a public function in which they made no bones about their affection in front of President Clinton. Brought up in a resolutely Baptist family, Heche was 13 when her father – an evangelical preacher and homosexual – died of Aids. Then, just three months later, her brother was killed in a car crash. An Emmy-winning, four-year veteran of the daytime soap *Another World* – in which she played the good-and-evil twins Victoria and Marley – Heche clocked up film appearances in the TV movie *O Pioneers!*, *An Ambush of Ghosts* (with Stephen Dorff), *The Adventures of Huck Finn* (as Mary Jane Wilks), *Against the Wall* (for TV), *I'll Do Anything*, *Milk Money*, *Kingfish: A Story of Huey P. Long* (TV), *Wildside*, *Pie in the Sky* and *If These Walls Could Talk* (TV). She'll next be seen alongside Robert De Niro, Dustin Hoffman and Woody Harrelson in Barry Levinson's *Wag the Dog* and opposite Harrison Ford in the romantic comedy *6 Days, 7 Nights*.

She also wrote, produced and directed a short called *Stripping For Jesus*.

Jennifer Lopez

Not since the days of Dolores Del Rio and Carmen Miranda has a Latino actress made such an impact on Hollywood. In April of 1997, Jennifer Lopez was top-billed in two movies in the American top ten, a feat rarely equalled by any star, let alone a former 'fly girl' of Puerto Rican extraction. Born in the Bronx, New York, Lopez started acting classes in 1990 and was quickly signed up as a dancer (under the tutelage of Rosie Perez) on the TV revue *In Living Color* featuring Jim Carrey. Since then she's gone from strength to strength, being nominated for an Independent Spirit award for her role as a young Mexican mother in the multi-generational epic *My Family/Mi Familia*, executive-produced by Francis Ford Coppola. She followed this with the female lead in *Money Train* (whose affections are vied for by Wesley Snipes and Woody Harrelson), the role of Robin

Matthew McConaughey in A Time to Kill

Jennifer Lopez

Williams' teacher in *Jack* (directed by Coppola) and the part of the seductive nanny who pits Jack Nicholson against stepson Stephen Dorff in *Blood and Wine*. She was then paid $1 million to play the murdered Tejano singer *Selena* Quintanilla, a role that won her bouquets of praise, followed by top-billing in the jungle thriller *Anaconda* (with Ice Cube, Jon Voight and Eric Stoltz in support). It was the latter two titles that found her firmly ensconced in the top ten. 'I want to be the Latina in American cinema,' the actress declares. 'We need somebody to be a star for the times.' Keeping up steam, she'll next be seen wedged between Sean Penn and Nick Nolte in Oliver Stone's *Stray Dogs* and then joins George Clooney in *Out of Sight*.

Matthew McConaughey

The hottest new star of the year, Matthew McConaughey instigated a bidding war after John Grisham gave him the thumbs up for the lead in *A Time to Kill*. Universal wanted

McConaughey for *The Jackal*, Fox wanted him for *Speed 2* and Warners got him to star opposite Jodie Foster in their sci-fi spectacular *Contact*. Spielberg also jumped and signed the handsome newcomer up for his slave epic, *Amistad*, while Sandra Bullock coaxed the young Texan into more domestic duties (believe what you like: the couple were holding hands in public and do their grocery shopping together). A native of Longview, Texas, the actor segued from film school into Richard Linklater's *Dazed and Confused*, playing the perennial pothead Wooderson, who marvels: 'That's what I love about freshman girls, man – I get older, they stay the same age.' He then notched up roles in *My Boyfriend's Back*, *Angels in the Outfield*, *Boys on the Side*, *The Return of the Texas Chainsaw Massacre*, *Larger Than Life* and *Lone Star*. Returning full circle, McConaughey will next be seen in Linklater's *The Newton Boys* – set in Texas.

Edward Norton with Woody Harrelson in The People vs. Larry Flynt

Edward Norton

Edward Norton was a star from the word go. As the stuttering Southern altar boy accused of hacking an archbishop to death in *Primal Fear* – his very first performance on celluloid – he was not only nominated for an Oscar but actually won the coveted Golden Globe award. The same year he sang 'Just You, Just Me' and 'My Baby Just Cares For Me' in Woody Allen's first musical, *Everyone Says I Love You*, and then played the crusading lawyer Alan Isaacman in the critically celebrated *The People vs. Larry Flynt*. For this stunning hat trick the Yale graduate won citations from the Los Angeles Film Critics' Association and the National Board of Review for best supporting actor of 1996. He was now so hot that he turned down the lead in Clint Eastwood's *Midnight in the Garden of Good and Evil* in order to play a neo-Nazi skinhead in New Line's *American History X*. He was also due to star opposite Sean Connery in *The Runaway Jury*, from the bestselling novel by John Grisham.

Parker Posey

Sassy, bright and sharp as a sickle, this Mississippi native was the 'It' girl of the 1997 Sundance Film Festival, appearing in all of *The House of Yes*, *subUrbia* and *Clockwatchers*. For her fresh and varied contribution the jury duly voted her 'best performer'. However, while 1997 shaped up to be her annus miraculosus, Posey is no newcomer. She was in *Coneheads* and *Joey Breaker* and played the bitchy, tyrannical high school senior – Darla – in Richard Linklater's *Dazed and Confused*. And, in 1995, she warmed Sundance up with her roles in *Party Girl* and *The Doom Generation*. 'Some days I was so busy,' she marvelled, 'I couldn't even smoke a full pack of cigarettes!' Catch her, too, in *Sleep With Me*, *Mixed Nuts*, *Amateur*, *Flirt*, *Kicking and Screaming*, *The Daytrippers*, *Basquiat*, *Waiting For Guffman* and *Dinner at Fred's*. What a girl.

Howard Stern

A healthy combination of Woody Allen, Jeff Goldblum and Alice

Parker Posey (right) with Steve Zahn in Richard Linklater's subUrbia

Howard Stern

Cooper, shock jock Howard Stern made a triumphant screen debut in a film based on his own memoirs – in which he portrayed himself. This bizarre novelty aside, Stern exhibits enough ease in front of the camera to guarantee a wicked film career: perhaps, even, playing other people. As chronicled in his cine-autobiography, *Howard Stern's Private Parts*, the super-nerd started out as a small-town DJ, moving his way up through Detroit and Washington DC to the Big Apple, where he ended up hosting America's No. 1 talk show (and the biggest daily syndicated radio show in the world). With a fondness for offering up the most intimate moments of his own life as a progressive soap opera – not to mention inviting listeners to reach orgasm on air – Stern courted the ire of his employers and landed incredible ratings. He is certainly an anomaly, but a funny enough one to blast off his own celluloid trajectory.

Billy Bob Thornton as he appears in Sling Blade

demonstrate in print the exact brilliance of her riposte to Cruise's gushing 'please take me back' speech, but when she cuts him short with a terse, 'Aw, shut up – you had me at "hello",' the audience went ballistic. A native of small-town Katy, Texas, the actress made her film debut in Richard Linklater's *Dazed and Confused* and moved on to roles in *My Boyfriend's Back*, the TV movie *Murder In the Heartland*, *Reality Bites*, *8 Seconds*, *Shake Rattle and Rock!* (TV), *Love and a .45 and Empire Records*, before landing the lead opposite Matthew McConaughey (qv) in the efficient chiller *Return of the Texas Chainsaw Massacre* (1995). She then played the real-life love of the *Conan the Barbarian* creator Robert E. Howard (Vincent D'Onofrio) in the widely praised 1930's romance *The Whole Wide World*. In spite of glowing reviews for the latter, she still had to audition for *Jerry Maguire* – and won the part over Winona Ryder, Mira Sorvino and Marisa Tomei. Since then she's starred in the New York drama *A Price Below Rubies* (as an adulterous Hasidic Jew), with Christopher Eccleston, and turned down the female lead in Roland Emmerich's *Godzilla*.

Renee Zellweger

Billy Bob Thornton

Billy Bob Thornton has been around for longer than he'd care to admit. But like Stallone with *Rocky*, it took him writing his own vehicle before anybody would notice. Unlike Stallone, Thornton actually directed the thing as well. The story of a retarded man who bonds with a young boy from a dysfunctional family, *Sling Blade* knocked critics sideways, both for Thornton's empathic writing and for his committed performance as the gentle nut. The film earned him an Oscar nomination for best actor and won him the award for his screenplay. Before that, the jobbing actor from Arkansas was best known for co-writing and co-starring in *One False Move*, one of the most quietly acclaimed films of 1992. Within the business, he was also known for his string of failed marriages. Then, three weeks after nabbing the Academy Award, his fourth wife, Pietra, filed for divorce, claiming he had threatened to kill her (yet they looked cosy enough on Oscar night). Notwithstanding, he's now hellish in demand, has top billing in Alex Cox's *The Winner* (with Rebecca DeMornay and Michael Madsen), the lead in *Homegrown* (co-starring Jon Bon Jovi, Judge Reinhold, John Lithgow and Jamie Lee Curtis) and is playing a character inspired by James Carville in Mike Nichols' *Primary Colors*.

Renee Zellweger

It's hard to believe in light of all the ballyhoo and glittering prizes dumped on Tom Cruise as *Jerry Maguire* that his leading lady, Renee Zellweger, actually skewered better reviews. Delivering all the prerequisites for an outstanding performance, Ms Zellweger gave us passion, intelligence, vulnerability and perfect comic timing, all wrapped up in a highly attractive package. Sadly, it's difficult to

Film World Diary

July 1996 - June 1997

James Cameron-Wilson

July 1996

Independence Day grosses $104.3 million in its first week, shattering US box-office records ✳ The character actor **Harry Morgan** (*High Noon*, *The Apple Dumpling Gang*, TV's *M*A*S*H*), 81, is arrested on charges of beating his wife. After spending a night in Los Angeles county jail, he is released on $5,000 bail with the prospect of a year's imprisonment ✳ **Marlon Brando**, 72, announces plans to move to London, saying, 'I love London and I love Britain because it remains the last bastion of the English language' ✳ Following his third drug-related arrest in one month, **Robert Downey Jr** is jailed in Malibu ✳ **Gregory Peck**, 80, is hospitalised in the Czech town of Karlovy Vary, after receiving a lifetime achievement award. He is operated on for appendicitis ✳ **Dudley Moore**'s house in Los Angeles is ransacked by his wife, Nicole Rothschild ✳ ITV pledges to invest more than £100 million in British films over a five-year period, producing 'at least' ten features a year ✳ *The Rock* grosses $100 million in the US ✳ Three of the current top four films at the American box office are starring Afro-American actors: **Will Smith** in *Independence Day*, **Eddie Murphy** in *The Nutty Professor* and **Denzel Washington** in *Courage Under Fire*. In the other hit, *Phenomenon*, **Forest Whitaker** also has a decent featured role ✳ *Independence Day* grosses $200m in the US ✳ **Sean Penn** replaces **Jodie Foster** (!) in **David Fincher**'s *The Game*, also starring **Michael Douglas** ✳ *The Nutty Professor* grosses $100m in the US ✳ **Patsy Kensit** announces her engagement to **Liam Gallagher** of Oasis ✳ According to an American magazine, **Nicolas Cage** has threatened **Patricia Arquette** with divorce because of her close relationship with actor-director **Ben Stiller**.

August 1996

Robert Downey Jr enters drug rehab after being released from prison on $25,000 bail ✳ *Mission: Impossible* grosses more than $300 million worldwide ✳ **Tom Cruise** and **Nicole Kidman** entertain the five survivors of a burning yacht on their own 230ft craft, *Talitha G*. The celebrity couple were holidaying nearby – off the coast of Capri – when they came to the aid of the survivors stranded in their lifeboat ✳ **Emmanuelle Beart**, the incredibly lovely French actress (*Manon des*

Sources, Mission: Impossible), ties herself to railings of the Saint Bernard church in Paris to protest the deportation of illegal immigrants ✳ **Jeremy Irons** finds himself at the centre of a controversy when he is approached to play the Pakistani Muslim leader Mohammed Ali Jinnah in *Jinnah*. The film's writer-producer, Professor Akbar Ahmad, says that Irons is ideal for the part, pointing out that the actor to play Jinnah would have to be 'lean, with high cheek bones, tall, fairly aquiline and speak good English.' Ahmad also stresses that he needs a bankable star in order to secure the financing and has also approached **Vanessa Redgrave** to play Jinnah's sister, Fatimà. However, Asian actors and filmmakers and British Equity are outraged ✳ Talking of **Vanessa Redgrave**, the actress becomes the proud grandmother of Daniel Jack, the second son born to **Natasha Richardson** and her husband **Liam Neeson** ✳ **Dudley Moore** hires a bodyguard to protect him from the violent outbursts of his wife, Nicole Rothschild ✳ **Anthony Hopkins** collapses from hypothermia on the set of *Bookworm* ✳ *Independence Day* grosses £6,824,163 in its first weekend in the UK, smashing the previous box-office record (£4,875,000) set by *Jurassic Park* ✳ **Jan-Michael Vincent** (*Hooper, Big Wednesday, Xtro II*) suffers a broken neck in a car crash. Later he is charged with drunken driving ✳ Warner Brothers pays **John Grisham** a staggering $8 million for the film rights to his runaway bestseller *The Runaway Jury* ✳ **Dudley Moore**'s wife, Nicole Rothschild, enters a drug rehabilitation clinic ✳ **Liam Neeson** undergoes emergency surgery in Padua, Italy, after collapsing from a suspected case of diverticulitis, a complaint of the colon. He was attending the Venice Film Festival to launch *Michael Collins*.

Jeremy Irons: driving me crazy (August, September)

September 1996

Returning from their holiday in Cork, **Jeremy Irons** and his wife **Sinead Cusack** cause three cars to crash on the M4 when their horsebox overturns. Thankfully, nobody is seriously hurt – although the horse temporarily escapes ✳ With much ballyhoo, Planet Hollywood opens in Moscow, the glitzy $1 million opening attended by **Arnold Schwarzenegger**, **Gerard Depardieu**, **Luke Perry**, various Russian actors, PR personnel and shadowy underworld figures. But although the vodka flowed there were no hamburgers available ✳ Following a car chase in Las Vegas, actor-rapper **Tupac Shakur** (*Juice, Above the Rim, Poetic Justice* and the upcoming *Gang Related*) is shot and is in critical condition ✳ **Jeremy Irons** is involved in a second car accident in a week, this time his car plunging headlong into the Nissan Sunny occupied by Richard and Doris Belgrove, both in their eighties. Again, Irons escapes without injury, although the elderly couple are hospitalised, with Mr Belgrove undergoing emergency surgery. Incidentally, Mr Belgrove is the father of a driving instructor for the Thames Valley police ✳ **Jim Carrey** and **Lauren Holly**, who co-starred together in *Dumb and Dumber*, tie the conjugal knot ✳ **Mark Canton**, chairman of Columbia TriStar and the brain behind such lavish ventures as *Last Action Hero* and *The Cable Guy*, is relieved of his duties ✳ *Eraser* grosses $100 million in the US – in 12 weeks ✳ Following an operation to facilitate his circulation, **Dirk Bogarde**, 75, suffers a stroke ✳ **Tupac Shakur**, 25, dies from his gunshot wounds ✳ **Clint Eastwood** is in court, sued by former lover and co-star **Sondra Locke** for deliberately sabotaging her career as a director. According to Locke, Eastwood promised that if she withdrew her palimony suit he would organise a three-year production deal for her at Warner Brothers. He then reneged on his word ✳ After a gruelling eight hours, **Melanie Griffith** gives birth to a baby girl (weighing in at 5lb 8oz) at the Hospital Costa del Sol in Marbella, Spain. The child's father, **Antonio Banderas**, names her Estella Carmen ✳ *Phenomenon* grosses $100 million in the US – in 12 weeks ✳ Warner Brothers announce that they will release *Michael Collins* in Britain ✳ **Elizabeth Taylor** is forced to pay $607,000 to the actress **Cicely Tyson** in compensation for firing her from the Broadway production of *The Corn is Green* in 1983. Ms Tyson had left just one performance of the play in order to attend a tribute to her husband, the jazz legend **Miles Davis**, and returned to find herself without a job ✳ **Sharon Stone** allegedly reveals to friends that she is engaged to the Guess? millionaire Michel Benasra ✳ **Clint Eastwood** agrees to pay **Sondra Locke** $5 million.

October 1996

The Rock grosses $300 million world-wide ✳ After **Tom Hanks** pulls out of *Primary Colors* due, some think, to a request from the President, **John Travolta** signs on for $15m to play the womanising Southern governor. **Emma Thompson** is still hoped to play his wife, reportedly modelled on Hillary Clinton ✳ *Independence Day* grosses $600m worldwide ✳ *Mission: Impossible* grosses $400m worldwide ✳ **Madonna**, 37, gives birth to a 6lb 9oz baby girl, Lourdes Maria Ciccone Leon. The child's father, fitness trainer Carlos Manuel Leon, 30, stands by ✳ *Twister* grosses $450m worldwide ✳ **Angela Lansbury** is 'rushed off' to Century City Hospital and is diagnosed with acute exhaustion ✳ Disney pay **Michael Crichton** a record $10 million for the rights to film his latest novel, *Airframe* ✳ **Stanley Kubrick** starts work on *Eyes Wide Shut*, his first film for nine years. **Tom Cruise**, **Nicole Kidman**, **Harvey Keitel** and **Jennifer Jason Leigh** star ✳ Prostitute Catherine Sheehan files a police report against **Jack Nicholson** for battery, claiming that the actor slapped her up, grabbed her by the hair and banged her head against the ground. Apparently, she was just one of two prostitutes that Nicholson had hired for an evening's recreation, when he lost his temper over the issue of her fee and threatened to kill her ✳ *Independence Day* grosses $300m in the US, making it the sixth highest-grossing film of all time – after *E.T. The ExtraTerrestrial*, *Jurassic Park*, *Forrest Gump*, *Star Wars* and *The Lion King*. However, having sold more tickets than any other movie, *Gone With the Wind* remains the box-office king ✳ **Jodie Foster** is named 'actor of the decade' at the Chicago International Film Festival ✳ **Tony Curtis** is made a Knight of the Order of Merit of the Republic of Hungary by the country of his parents, who emigrated to theUS in the early 1920s. The actormost recently starred in *The Continued Adventures of Reptile Man*.

Jack Nicholson: hard hitter (October)

November 1996

William Shatner is ordered to pay his estranged wife, Marcy, a lump sum of $2 million. He is also to pay her an extra $100,000 a month for the next 20 years, along with such provisions as a condominium in the ski resort of Vail in Colorado, homes in Mexico and Indonesia, and a Volvo ✳ A controversial new biography of **Francois Truffaut** shocks France with its revelations of his early Fascist and anti-Semitic sympathies and affairs with such leading ladies as **Jeanne Moreau**,

Catherine Deneuve, **Julie Christie**, **Jacqueline Bisset** and **Fanny Ardant** ✳ Within four days two shootings erupt outside cinemas in southern California showing the Afro-American crime thriller *Set It Off*. In the second incident two men are wounded and one killed ✳ Investigations into the death of **Tupac Shakur** are set back when Yafeu Fula, 19, a witness to his murder, is found shot dead in New Jersey ✳ Disillusioned with Hollywood life, **Hugh Grant** and his producer, **Elizabeth Hurley**, move to Paris ✳ **Frank Sinatra**, 80, spends over a week in hospital for treatment of an irregular heartbeat, pneumonia and a pinched nerve ✳ **Daniel Day-Lewis** marries actress **Rebecca Miller,** 32, the daughter of playwright **Arthur Miller**, in a private ceremony in Vermont. The bride, who is also a writer and director, has appeared in such films as *Consenting Adults* and *Mrs Parker and the Vicious Circle* and met her husband on the set of her father's latest film, *The Crucible*, which the latter adapted from his own play ✳ **Pamela Anderson Lee** separates from her husband, the musician Tommy Lee ✳ *The First Wives Club* grosses $100m in the US ✳ After his fourth proposal, **Brad Pitt** gets the nuptial nod from girlfriend **Gwyneth Paltrow**. The couple plan to marry in March ✳ **Burt Reynolds** files for bankruptcy in Florida, declaring debts of $6 million.

December 1996

Ransom grosses over $100 million in the US – in under four weeks ✳ Following the traumatic heart operation on his baby daughter, Sophia Rose, **Sylvester Stallone**

Sylvester Stallone: from violence to London and marriage (December, May)

swears that he will no longer star in violent movies ✳ **Michael Ovitz**, president of the Walt Disney company, parts company with the 'Mouse House' after just one year. He receives a £55m golden handshake ✳ At a press conference in London, **Madonna** admits that she's expecting an Oscar nomination for her role as *Evita* ✳ **Clint Eastwood** undergoes treatment for skin cancer at the UCLA Medical Center. He has a portion of his upper left cheek reconstructed ✳ **Chris O'Donnell**, 26, is engaged to kindergarten teacher Caroline Fentress, 23, the sister of his old college roommate ✳ In a stunt to focus publicity on the threat to a redwood forest in California, **Woody Harrelson** climbs the Golden Gate Bridge in San Francisco – and is arrested ✳ **Charlie Sheen** is booked for 'investigation of assault' after a woman claimed that the actor knocked her to the ground, causing a gash to her lip that required seven stitches ✳ **Sylvester Stallone** announces that he will be moving to London to live, to protect his young daughter from the escalating violence in American society ✳ **Clint Eastwood** becomes a father for the seventh time when his baby daughter, Morgan Collette (weighing in at 8lb 4oz), is induced during a routine check-up ✳ **Dudley Moore** flees to Britain to escape his disintegrating marriage to Nicole Rothschild. The couple file for divorce, citing 'irreconcilable differences' ✳ **Don Johnson** allegedly proposes to actress **Jodi O'Keefe**, 18, who plays his daughter on the TV police series *Nash Bridges* ✳ *101 Dalmatians* grosses $100m in the US.

January 1997

Joan Collins receives an OBE in the New Years' honours ✳ **Pierce Brosnan** is the proud father of a baby boy, Dylan, courtesy of his girlfriend Keely Shaye ✳ **Demi Moore** and **Bruce Willis** are expecting another child (to add to their stable of Rumer, Scout and Tallulah). This time the offspring will be a boy – and they know that for a fact ✳ **Heidi Fleiss**, 'madam to the stars,' is sentenced to 37 months in prison for laundering profits from her call girl activity and for cheating on her taxes ✳ **Jennifer Aniston** reportedly answers in the affirmative to boyfriend **Tate Donovan**'s proposal of marriage in a Hollywood parking lot. Donovan, who recently supplied the voice of Hercules in Disney's cartoon, was previously involved with **Sandra Bullock** for four years ✳ Following the death of his wife Linda, **George Segal**, 62, falls for an older woman. In fact, Sonia Schulz, 63, was at school with Segal but had not seen him since. 'It makes you believe in fate and destiny,' the actor noted after the wedding ✳ *Evita* grosses over £2 million in its first weekend in the UK ✳ **Frank Sinatra**, 81, is taken to the Cedars Sinai medical centre in Los Angeles after suffering a heart attack ✳ **Michael Eisner** agrees to stay on as chairman of Disney until the year 2006 – for a basic salary of $750,000 (plus $8 million's worth of share options) ✳ **Sharon Stone** tells friends that she is thinking of adopting a baby ✳ The only son of **Bill Cosby**, Ennis, is shot dead at point blank range in Bel Air, Los Angeles. He was 27 ✳ **Warren Beatty** and **Annette Bening** become the proud parents of their third child, Isabel Ira Ashley ✳ *The Hunchback of Notre Dame* grosses $300 million worldwide ✳ *Mission: Impossible* grosses $450m worldwide ✳ *Independence Day* grosses $772.4 million, making it the second highest-grossing movie of all time, after *Jurassic Park* ✳ After many weeks of procrastination, The British Board of Film Classification postpone 'indefinitely' the UK release of David Cronenberg's *Crash* ✳ *Jerry Maguire* grosses $100m in the US.

February 1997

Following a blood test, **Kevin Costner** admits that he is the father of Liam, the baby of Bridget Rooney. Costner had met Rooney in Aspen where, following the break-up of the actor's marriage, they enjoyed a brief affair. And it's interesting that the actor's new son should be called Liam, as Costner lost the lead in both *Schindler's List* and *Michael Collins* to **Liam Neeson** ✳ **James Stewart**, 89, is rushed to hospital in Santa Monica and given 12 stitches to his forehead. He was found unconscious by his housekeeper, having blacked out after a fall at his home in Beverly Hills ✳ *Ransom* grosses over $250 million worldwide ✳ **Patsy Kensit** and her fiancé, singer Liam Gallagher, cancel their wedding plans at the last minute due to the pressure of undignified publicity ✳ **Emmanuelle Beart** continues her attack on the French government for its draconian immigration laws by heading a 100,000-strong demonstration on the streets of Paris. She is joined by **Catherine Deneuve** and the director **Bertrand Tavernier** ✳ *101 Dalmatians* grosses over $200 million worldwide ✳ Another one bites the dust: production on the romantic comedy *Broadway Brawler*, starring **Bruce Willis** and **Maura Tierney** (Jim Carrey's ex-wife in *Liar Liar*), is abandoned after 20 days of filming – due, according to Cinergi president **Andy Vajna**, to 'grave concerns over the production schedule and the financial and creative elements of the picture' ✳ Meanwhile, Bruce's wife, **Demi Moore**, attracts a wave of media attention after a day out with **Leonardo DiCaprio**. Besides reportedly caressing his head and playing with his hair in public, the actress invited the 22-year-old actor back to her place – the beachside home in Malibu she shares with Bruce and their three children – where she and DiCaprio spent the night together. The next morning the young actor is photographed leaving the house, followed shortly by Demi...

March 1997

As director **Roger Spottiswoode** and his crew are waiting to board a plane to Hanoi to film the 18th James Bond outing, *Tomorrow Never Dies*, they are informed that the Vietnamese government has had a change of heart about letting them film there. The official reason is that the Hanoi authorities feel their country is ill equipped to take on such a major production, although insiders believe the Communist government think that 007 had battled one too many 'pinko bastards' in the past. *Tomorrow Never Dies* was due to shoot in Vietnam for three weeks ✳ **Farrah Fawcett** moves out of the Beverly Hills home that she shares with **Ryan O'Neal**, taking their son Redmond with her ✳ **Don Johnson** really does propose to **Jodie O'Keefe**, the actress who plays his daughter on TV's *Nash Bridges* ✳ The British Board of Film Classification finally makes its mind up and passes *Crash* uncut ✳ **Meg Ryan** and **Matthew Broderick** are reunited in New York to re-film the final kiss in *Addicted to Love*. Apparently, test screening audiences didn't find the original snog passionate or lengthy enough ✳ *Voici* magazine reports that Dior is dropping **Emmanuelle Beart** as its official ambassador due to her involvement in demonstrations against the French government because of the latter's stance on immigration. Not only that, but it was reported that the actress was not wearing make-up at the time ✳ **Jim Carrey** does it again: *Liar Liar* grosses $31,423,025 in its first weekend in the US ✳ *Space Jam* grosses $200 million worldwide ✳ *Ransom* grosses $300 million worldwide.

Emmanuelle Beart: railings, protests and a reconciliation over no make-up (August, February, March, April)

April 1997

Both Dior and its international 'face', **Emmanuelle Beart**, deny that they have parted company over the latter's involvement in anti-government demonstrations ✳ **David Carradine**, of all people, receives a star on the Hollywood Walk of Fame ✳ **Patsy Kensit** and her fiancé, rock singer **Liam Gallagher**, finally tie the knot – in a secret ceremony at a London registry office ✳ **Elizabeth Hurley** is photographed embracing and holding hands with a tall unnamed man at the airport terminal in Los Angeles. One thing is for sure: it isn't **Hugh Grant** ✳ **Will Smith** drops out of Brian De Palma's *Snake Eyes* as Paramount refuses to meet his $12.5 million asking price ✳ *Liar Liar* grosses $100 million in the US in under three weeks ✳ **Julia Roberts**, **Kenneth Branagh**, **Sally Field** and **Lynn Redgrave** add their names to a 10,000-strong petition to Hollywood studios demanding shorter working hours. Due to a combination of tighter release deadlines and directors' perfectionism, working days can often stretch to 20 hours, resulting in untold stress and employees falling asleep at the wheel. The motion is dubbed 'Brent's Rule', after the cameraman Brent Hershman was killed driving home after a 19-hour day working on *Pleasantville* ✳ **Arnold Schwarzenegger** undergoes open heart surgery as doctors replace an aortic valve ✳ *Independence Day* grosses $800 million worldwide ✳ **Brooke Shields**, 31, finally ties the knot with her four-year-old beau, tennis champ **Andre Agassi**, 26, at a ceremony in Carmel, California ✳ The actress **Anne Heche**, whose film credits include *Walking and Talking*, *Donnie Brasco* and *Volcano*, and **Ellen DeGeneres**, star of TV's *Ellen*, exchange rings in a public announcement of their affection for one another. DeGeneres, who was the first to step out of the closet, proclaims that she is 'madly in love' with Heche ✳ **Pamela Anderson Lee** (who is now back with her estranged husband) is sued by the Private Movie Company for pulling out of their picture *Hello, She Lied*. According to the producer, **Ben Efraim**, she made a verbal commitment to the project but backed out just two weeks before start of production. Pambo, on the other hand, expressed her concern about appearing naked on screen in 'explicit' sex scenes. She is replaced by **Kathy Ireland** ✳ **James Garner** is in hospital, having a blood clot removed from his leg ✳ **Chris O'Donnell** and his bride, Caroline Fentress, say 'I do' at a ceremony in Washington, attended by Ted Kennedy ✳ It looks like the six-year on-again-off-again affair between **Al Pacino** and **Lyndall Hobbs** has finally reached its conclusion. Most recently, Pacino has been seen in the company of the actress **Beverly D'Angelo**.

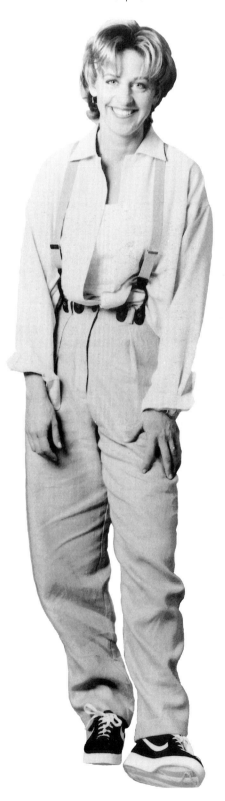

Ellen DeGeneres: lesbian chic (April)

May 1997

101 Dalmatians grosses $300m worldwide ✳ **David Duchovny**, of TV's *The X-Files* and the upcoming *Playing God*, and **Tea Leoni**, of TV's *The Naked Truth* and *Bad Boys*, say 'I do' during a ten-minute ceremony in Manhattan ✳ After 18 years together, **Kathy Bates** and her husband call it a day. They were married in 1991 ✳ **Ryan O'Neal** and **Farrah Fawcett** are reunited after a much publicised separation in March. 'Now we can start afresh and build an even better life than we had before,' O'Neal reveals – after more break-ups with Farrah than this publication can calculate ✳ **Eddie Murphy** is stopped by police while driving down Santa Monica Boulevard. His passenger, Atisone Seiuli, turns out to be a transsexual prostitute and is arrested. Murphy, who had just picked Seiuli up, appeases his fans by announcing, 'I'm not gay' ✳ In spite of his pay-or-play contract on Paramount's *Snake Eyes*, **Nicolas Cage** could win a free pay day when the contract for the former clashes with his duties on *Superman Reborn* ✳ *Liar Liar* grosses $150m in the US ✳ **Dudley Moore**'s fourth wife, Nicole, is allegedly suing the comic actor to the tune of $3 million for implementing a 'campaign of terror and abuse against her' ✳ Two years after his devastating fall from a horse – and 20 months after doctors said that recovery was impossible – **Christopher Reeve** regains some feeling in his arms, hands and back ✳ To celebrate the 90th birthday of **Katharine Hepburn**, a garden in New York – near the United Nations building – is dedicated to the actress ✳ £92,250,000 of National Lottery money is allocated to three consortia of private companies to invest in British film. Of the 34 bidders for the funding, the chosen ones include Pathe Productions (which will receive £33m), The Film Consortium (£30.25m) and DNA Film Limited (£29m). Pathe, an Anglo-French concern tied up with such producers as **Simon Channing-Williams**, **Jake Eberts**, **Barnaby Thompson** and **Michael White**, is committed to produce 35 films, The Consortium (with **Nik Powell**, **Stephen Woolley**, **Simon Relph** and **Sally Hibbin**) 39 and DNA (comprising **Duncan Kenworthy** and **Andrew Macdonald**) 16 ✳ The lawsuit filed by the Private Movie Company against **Pamela Anderson Lee** (see April) is dismissed by a Los Angeles judge. His Honour, David Horowitz, declares that Pam's contract had not been binding ✳ Now **Lesley Anne Down** finds herself in a similar boat

Barbra Streisand: otherwise engaged (May)

as she is sued by producer Frank Monte for backing out of his low-budget picture *The Private Eye*. Allegedly, she refused to honour her contract with Monte when she was offered the lead in the TV series *Sunset Beach* ✳ **James Brolin**, the star of TV's *Hotel*, and **Barbra Streisand** are officially engaged ✳ **Sylvester Stallone** and his bride, Jennifer Flavin, finally tie the knot at a private ceremony in London ✳ After just eight months of marriage, **Jim Carrey** and **Lauren Holly** have reportedly separated ✳ *Jerry Maguire* grosses $250m worldwide – in 23 weeks ✳ *Scream* grosses $100m in the US – in 25 weeks ✳ *The Lost World: Jurassic Park* grosses $100m in the US – in six days ✳ **Jodie Foster** is presented with an honorary doctorate in fine arts by Yale University 'for breaking new ground for women in film through her choice of roles and her success as a director and producer' ✳ Offered $24m to reprise his role as John McClane in the fourth *Die Hard* film, **Bruce Willis** becomes the highest paid star in Hollywood history.

June 1997

Following the success of his *Fifth Element* and the failure of her *Striptease*, **Bruce Willis** finds himself fielding a divorce from his missus of nine years, **Demi Moore**. Of course, her highly publicised friendship with **Leonardo DiCaprio** and his affiliation with the Russian bombshell **Milla Jovovich** can't have helped matters ✳ After 19 years of marriage, **Charlotte Rampling** and musician/composer **Jean Michel Jarre** finalise their separation ✳ **Peter Bogdanovich** is ordered to cough up $4.2m in mortgage payments and punitive damages to the owner of his rented house. Bogdanovich, director of such hits as *The Last Picture Show*, *What's Up, Doc?* and *Paper Moon*, files for bankruptcy ✳ *The Lost World: Jurassic Park* grosses $150m – in two weeks ✳ **John Travolta** and **Kelly Preston** are named Show Business Couple of the Year at a ceremony held at the Friar's Club in New York ✳ **Brad Pitt** and **Gwyneth Paltrow** end their seven-month engagement. Apparently, Gwyneth's need to settle down and Pitt's predilection for parties did not gel ✳ That great London landmark, Battersea Power Station (featured on the cover of Pink Floyd's *Animals* album), is to be turned into a 32-screen multiplex at a cost of £34 million, making it the largest cinema complex in Europe ✳ **Princess Diana** finds herself at the centre of a storm after taking her two sons, William and Harry, to see *The Devil's Own*. Released with a 15 certificate in the UK, the film is deemed unsuitable for children under the age of 15. Prince Harry is just 12 years old ✳ **Stanley Kubrick**'s *Eyes Wide Shut* is still in the midst of shooting and doesn't look close to completion. Even if the film wraps by September (an optimistic projection), it will have exceeded the director's schedule for *The Shining* by 100 days. Meanwhile, **Harvey Keitel** has packed his bags and has been replaced by director and sometime-actor **Sydney Pollack** ✳ **Colin Firth** gets hitched to his 24-year-old Italian girlfriend, Livia Giuggioli, in a secret ceremony in Tuscany ✳ According to the French magazine *Voici*, **Brigitte Nielsen** accepts an 'indecent proposal' from a member of the Saudi royal family – an offer of $1 million to indulge in a '12-hour sex marathon' ✳ **Robert De Niro**, 53, marries his lover of 20 months, Grace Hightower, 42, in a secret ceremony in New York, attended by **Harvey Keitel**, **Joe Pesci** and close family and friends. De Niro was previously married to the actress-singer **Diahnne Abbott** (1976-1988) ✳ Following nine years as director of the British Film Institute, **Wilf Stevenson** announces his resignation ✳ *The Lost World: Jurassic Park* grosses $200 million in the US ✳ According to the *Daily Mail*, **Mia Farrow** and the playwright **Tom Stoppard** are now an item ✳ And, according to *The Express*, **Keanu Reeves** and **Amanda De Cadenet** are now husband and wife ✳ In an interview with *US* magazine, **Rupert Everett** reveals that he used to be a male prostitute.

Film Soundtracks

James Cameron-Wilson

In the first month of 1997, four film soundtracks jostled with No Doubt, Celine Dion and Toni Braxton for the first seven places in Billboard's Top Ten albums' chart. This would appear to be good news for the soundtrack industry, but then the sales of *Evita*, *William Shakespeare's Romeo + Juliet*, *Space Jam* and *The Preacher's Wife* aren't exactly going to put a smile on John Williams' face. *Evita* and *The Preacher's Wife* are as-good-as-damn-it re-packaged Madonna and Whitney Houston vehicles, while *Romeo + Juliet* and *Space Jam* are no more than merchandising opportunities for Twentieth Century Fox and Warner Brothers.

Having said that, it was also a good year for *real* film music, with a large proportion of the best scores arriving out of left field – at least, east of Berlin. While such offenders as Bruce Broughton and Randy Edelman continued to turn orchestras into sonic sledgehammers, some less well-known composers practised the arcane art of musical seduction, notably a distinguished host of Eastern Europeans. Consequently, on this occasion *Film Review*'s Composer of the Year is an amalgam of artists.

Composer of the Year:

THE EASTERN EUROPEAN

In February of this year (1997), **Zbigniew Preisner** was honoured with a special Silver Bear at the 47th Berlin International Film Festival, awarded in recognition of a single remarkable achievement. This was for the composer's music written for the Danish-British-German film *The Island on Bird Street*. Now, film music may be enjoying something of a comeback of late (just look at the success of *Shine*, *The English Patient* and *Braveheart* in the classical charts), but it's not often that a musician is singled out for his work – particularly somebody whose name most film critics can't even enunciate. I can't pronounce Wojciech Kilar, Ondrej

Soukup or Stanislas Syrewicz either, but I know that I love their stuff.

While Preisner, who began his musical studies in Krakow at the age of 15, has forged something of a reputation with his scores for *Europa Europa*, *Three Colours: Blue, Red and White* and *The Secret Garden*, his European peers are less well known. Of the latter, **Wojciech Kilar** is receiving the most recent exposure, thanks to his many scores for such compatriot filmmakers as Krzysztof Zanussi, Andrzej Wajda and Krzysztof Kieslowski, as well as for his work on Coppola's *Bram Stoker's Dracula*, Polanski's *Death and the Maiden* and Jane Campion's *The*

Portrait of a Lady. There is also an excellent CD – *Kilar – Warsaw to Hollywood* (on Milan Classics) – which magnificently exhibits this artist's melodic, powerful range.

And let us not forget the Russian-born, Polish-reared **Stanislas Syrewicz**, whose credits include *Biggles*, *The Holcroft Covenant* and *True Blue*; or **Jan A. P. Kaczmarek** (*Three of Hearts*, *Total Eclipse*, *Bliss*); and **Krzysztof Komeda** (*Rosemary's Baby*). Joining this august assembly is the Czech-born **Ondrej Soukup** who, although a veteran of film music, only recently made his mark on the international scene with his delightfully idiosyncratic score for the Oscar-winning *Kolya*. Finally, I would also like to doff my hat to **Ilona Sekacz** who, besides her celebrated work for the Royal Shakespeare Company and the National Theatre, has scored such prestigious TV productions as *Boys From the Blackstuff* and *Northanger Abbey*. With her delicate, evocative music for *Antonia's Line* (another Oscar winner for Best Foreign Film), she now looks set for a fruitful career in film. Although English-born and a graduate of Birmingham University, Ms Sekacz is the daughter of Polish parents so, in my book, that makes her an honourable member of this most noble tribe.

Zbigniew Preisner   *Wojciech Kilar*   *Ondrej Soukup*   *Ilona Sekacz*

Soundtracks of the Year

Bean
Terrific songs, spurts of dialogue and a dash of **Howard Goodall**'s manic piano make this a splendid keepsake of a thoroughly enjoyable film. And in keeping with the *Four Weddings* tradition, there's even a cover of 'Yesterday' by Wet Wet Wet.

Brassed Off
A fragrant medley of the theme from Monty Python, *Bridge On the River Kwai* and tea on the lawn at the church fete, this is a genuine collector's item. While **Trevor Jones** is credited as composer, his largely sparse melodies are drowned out by a raft of timeless classics from The Grimethorpe Colliery Band, blowing emotion into everything from 'Jerusalem' to the heart-swelling 'En Aranjuez Con Tu Amor'.

Dead Presidents
A terrific roll call of legendary names honour this mighty compilation of 1970s soul. Sly and the Family Stone, Isaac Hayes, James Brown, Barry White, Curtis Mayfield, Aretha Franklin and Al Green are all here, as is **Danny Elfman**'s powerful, distinctive score. Followed by a second album – *Volume II* – with more of the same (and Stevie Wonder).

The Devil's Own
Another fine score from **James Horner**, this time with a strong Irish lilt, plenty of soul-stirring fiddle, flute, uillean pipes and even a lyrical lament from The Cranberries' Dolores O'Riordan.

Emma
Rachel Portman at her playful, melodic best, richly capturing the genteel irony of Jane Austen's social vortex. Lovely music – and winner of the Oscar for best comedic (i.e. light-weight) score.

The English Patient
Wistful, deceptively spartan yet compellingly complex score from **Gabriel Yared** (of *Betty Blue* fame), who draws on the geographical diversity of Michael Ondaatje's book to bring his extraordinary canvas to life. From the unaccompanied Hungarian ballad 'Szerelem, Szerelem' to the solo piano recitals, this is a soundtrack to cherish.

Evita
Superb, lavish realisation of Tim Rice and Andrew Lloyd Webber's dramatic, intelligent and complex opera, including the Oscar-winning 'You Must Love Me', written specially for the film, and Madonna's sublime theft of 'Another Suitcase In Another Hall' (sung by Peron's mistress, not Evita, in the stage version). Madonna has never sung better.

Fever Pitch
Another bright, diverting soundtrack from the *Four Weddings* school, with snatches of playful dialogue ('You can't remember if life's shit because Arsenal are shit, or the other way round'), a morsel of incidental music (from The Bible's **Neill MacColl** and **Boo Hewerdine**) and a healthy variety of upbeat numbers from the likes of The La's ('There She Goes'), The Pogues, The Who, Van Morrison, etc.

Independence Day
Rousing militant suite from England's **David Arnold**. Even if it recycles much of the composer's previous work on *Stargate* and *Last of the Dogmen*, this is a soundtrack to go to war to. John Williams should be jealous.

Kama Sutra
Mysterious, moody and magnificent score from **Mychael Danna**, the most

exciting new composer on the block (hear *The Sweet Hereafter*, *The Ice Storm*).

Kansas City
The top jazz soundtrack of the year – rich, earthy and joyous salute to the Kansas City sound of 1934. Reenacted by a host of contemporary greats, the loose-limbed, swinging blues of Bennie Moten, saxophonist Lester Young and their like is recalled here with zest and affection.

Kolya
Endearingly lyrical and robust score by Ondrej Soukup, with large chunks of Dvorak (his 'New World'), a little opera (courtesy of soprano Olga Seskova) and a Russian variation of 'The Lord Is My Shepherd' delivered quaveringly by the film's five-year-old star, Andrej Chalimon.

Lone Star
The ultimate collection of Tex-Mex (and its musical ilk) courtesy of music man **Mason Daring**, opening with the quintessential tejano ballad 'Mi Unico Camino' by Conjunto Bernal, easing into the blues harmonica of Little Walter and embracing everything from the contemplative guitar of Duke Levine to the plaintive voice of Freddie Fender. A must for Acapulco dreamers.

Madame Butterfly
I don't know much about opera, but I know what I like. Featuring the latest superstar of the genre, Ying Huang, the album makes up in emotion what it lacks in fine tuning (Ying's voice has been dismissed as 'too small and hard' by critics), and emotion can win new converts to an arcane art form.

Michael
Another classic soundtrack to add to your John Travolta collection, an upbeat, polished assortment of MOR numbers with standout tracks from Don Henley, Van Morrison, Randy Newman, The Mavericks, Bonnie Raitt – and even a whimsical turn from Andie MacDowell (!) Enough to wipe away the memory of a fatuous film.

Michael Collins
An epic, melancholy and dynamic score, backed up by some haunting vocals from Sinead O'Connor and Frank Patterson. Tag this **Elliot Goldenthal**'s magnum opus (to date).

One Fine Day
Divinely romantic collection of new and old cuts, opening with **Natalie Merchant**'s soulful reinvention of the title song, Van Morrison's sincerely maudlin 'Have I Told You Lately?' and Harry Connick Jr's smooth and sultry 'This Guy's In Love With You'. A melodic wallow of the first order.

Phenomenon
Cool, good sounds collected by executive producer Robbie Robertson that perfectly reflect the meditative, romantic flavour of the film. While Eric Clapton and Peter Gabriel are a little dull, Aaron Neville's 'Crazy Love' and Jewel's 'Have a Little Faith In Me' are spine-tingling, while exceptional tracks from Taj Mahal, The Iguanas and JJ Cale make this a class act.

The Portrait of a Lady
If there was any emotional texture in Jane Campion's stilted, lifeless film it was supplied by **Wojciech Kilar**'s moody, swooning score, one of the most accomplished in recent memory. Add three sublime pieces from Schubert (including 'Death and the Maiden', last heard in the film of the same name, also composed by Kilar) and you have a soundtrack of classic dimensions.

The Preacher's Wife
Exuberant, joyful and inspirational collection of gospel numbers belted out by Whitney Houston and the Georgia Mass Choir. Every home should have one.

The Secret of Roan Inish
By turns buoyant, meditative and haunting, **Mason Daring**'s extraordinarily picturesque score is always magic. From the seductive eddy of fiddles to the profound lament of the flute and whistle, the music inhabits its own world without compromise. And on top of all this there's Eileen Loughanne's stark, unaccompanied 'Selke Song' to die to.

She's the One
Tom Petty's love letter to Edward Burns, a collection of smoky, edgy and melodic numbers inspired by Burns' witty comedy. While not all the songs here made it into the finished movie, they certainly reflect the feel of the piece.

Shine
Top-selling companion piece to Scott Hicks' exquisite film, not only featuring Rachmaninoff's now-legendary Piano Concerto No. 3 (containing 'more notes per second than any other concerto', according to the sleeve notes), but works by Chopin, Schumann, Liszt, Vivaldi, Rimsky-Korsakov and Beethoven. Furthermore, David Hirschfelder's Oscar-nominated score blends in perfectly with the classical stuff, while most of the piano work is bashed out by David Helfgott himself, the very subject of the film.

That Thing You Do!
Exuberant collection of new songs modelled on the sound of the early 1960s – complete with sleeve notes by Mr A.M. White (Tom Hanks, to you). It's like discovering an early Beatles album in pristine condition – with some wonderfully moody cameos tacked on.

True Blue
Inspirational, get-up-and-go-for-a-jog score distinguished by handsome bouts of regal and ecclesiastical flourishes. Obviously composed with an ear to the *Chariots of Fire* market, *True Blue* works in its own right, which is more than can be said for the film. Little known to soundtrack enthusiasts, the Russian-born, Polish-bred composer **Stanislas Syrewicz** obviously has a great future ahead of him.

The Truth About Cats and Dogs
An impressive line-up of prize acts on exceptionally good form, including Dionne Farris, Cowboy Junkies, Al Green, Aaron Neville and Blues Traveler (not to mention Sting, Suzanne Vega, Squeeze, etc.).

William Shakespeare's Romeo + Juliet
Arguably the hip soundtrack of 1997, a huge hit in the US (where it sold three million units) and a heady leg-up for such diverse, independent acts as Garbage, One Inch Punch and Kym Mazelle, as well as cool cuts from the more established Radiohead, Butthole Surfers and Gavin Friday.

Bookshelf

James Cameron-Wilson

Action! The Action Movie A-Z, by Marshall Julius; Batsford; £9.99; 240 pages.

Marshall Julius makes no bones about his predisposition towards the movies. In his no-holds-barred introduction he insists, 'I'm not advocating real-life violence. I just want to see it up on the screen, where it belongs.' And,'The next time somebody accuses an action film of provoking copycat violence, they're cruising for a bunch of fives.' Indeed, Julius is refreshingly unpretentious, can deliver a neat upper-cut of phrase and is more in touch with his public than a battalion of your regular, tweed-encrusted critics. Above all, Julius is immensely readable. An alphabetical companion of what the author has decided are the 250 key movies in the genre, *Action!* doesn't offer any information you can't find elsewhere so much as a fresh and healthy perspective. Embracing everything from *Woo* to *Waterworld*, the book errs towards the modern (you won't find *The Great Train Robbery* here, or even my favourite action movie, John Carpenter's 1976 *Assault on Precinct 13*) but is packed with quotes, trivia, biogs, photographs and even some incredibly difficult quizzes. It's what action fans have been waiting for ever since Joseph Wiseman announced, 'I never fail, Mr Bond.'

The A-Z of Horror Films, by Howard Maxford; Batsford; £17.99; 302 pages.

The point of any new reference book in such a crowded marketplace is the ability to deliver facts that you can't find anywhere else. Well, horror has been pretty well charted, so it's a brave man indeed to enter such congested waters. What Howard Maxford has done is to compile an A-Z of the genre, embracing everything from the key films and production companies to the personnel who have made their name in horror. Thus, you can look up make-up wizard Rick Baker (*An American Werewolf in London, Wolf*) and find your eye drifting to the entry on Peter Jackson's innovatively tasteless *Bad Taste* and then on to American actress Barbara Bach (*The Humanoid, The Great Alligator*). The credits of the films themselves are suitably comprehensive (although you won't find characters' names) and Maxford's star system unstint-ingly austere (arguably one of the most seminal, perfectly executed horror films, *The Texas Chain Saw Massacre*, isn't even given a single star). Maxford obviously favours atmosphere over gore, but it's the information that's useful. So, should you wish to know the costume designer of *From Hell It Came* or the year of Stephen King's birth, you'll find it here. A major undertaking, *The A-Z of Horror Films* should sate the curiosity of most horror buffs and prove enjoyable reading for the *cineaste* browser.

BFI Film and Television Handbook, edited by Eddie Dyja; BFI; £16.99; 414 pages.

Self-labelled 'the essential reference to UK film, television and video', this compact little number is a cornucopia of titles, addresses, telephone numbers and statistics – with all the magnetism of a tele-phone directory. But, dig lightly beneath the top soil and you find a multitude of truffles. Replete with lists that range from the downright esoteric to the indispensable, the book includes tables of box-office figures, photographic libraries, cinema publications (including this one), TV programmes, film releases, production companies, awards, CD-Roms, cinema circuits, film and TV study courses, international festivals, press contacts, preview theatres and laboratories, libraries and legislation. Thank God, then, for the index at the back. Dry as toast, maybe, but then toast is the roughage that kick-starts our day.

British Television, by Tise Vahimagi; BFI/Oxford University Press; £14.99; 387 pages.

As Larousse is the last word on food and Jane's on battleships, so this handsome, fact-packed BFI publication is the definitive reference work on British television. Having said that, the book doesn't share the scope of its American cousin, *Total Television*, but it is light years more comprehensive than the arbitrary stab at the subject provided by *Halliwell's Television Companion*. Buttressed by an exhaustive index of names and titles at the back, the book spans the entire spectrum of British TV from 1936 to 1995, with entries on the best loved and most seminal programmes, whether they be drama, documentary, soap opera, sitcom or game show. Arranged in chronological order, the shows are accorded a brief synopsis, back-ground story, cast and credits, characters' names, tally of episodes, dates and related programmes. Written in an economical and not humourless hand, the entries not only inform but activate forgotten memories, resulting in a work as nostalgic as it is educational. Embracing over 1,100 titles – each of which is illustrated (a feat in itself eliciting untold admiration) – *British Television* reveals an informed devotion that is nothing short of miraculous. In addition, I had the delight of discovering that my own father had played the role of Sir Lancelot Spratt in the original 1960

TV play *Doctor in the House* (with Brian Rix as Simon Sparrow).

The Companion to French Cinema, by Ginette Vincendeau; BFI; £10.99; 202 pages.

As an admirer and follower of French cinema, I was really looking forward to this guide. While I was familiar with the films of such Gallic stars as Fanny Ardant, Michel Blanc, Francois Cluzet, Bulle Ogier and the incomparable Michel Serrault, I knew little of their background. The more obvious names – Belmondo, Deneuve, Depardieu, Godard, Truffaut – I had already read extensively about elsewhere. Unfortunately, this slim, glossy paperback from the presses of the BFI proves to be neither one thing nor the other. Its A to Z embrace of Adjani to Claude Zidi manages to exclude all of Ardant, Blanc, Cluzet, Ogier and Serrault, as well as such established character actors as Jean-Pierre Cassel, Jean-Pierre Marielle and even Jean Rochefort. And forget such exciting new directors as Patrice Chereau, Mathieu Kassovitz, Patrice Leconte, Pierre Salvadori and the late bright and shining Cyril Collard. Yet the existing entries are disappointingly incomplete, the prose dry, the facts meagre and the filmographies highly selective. You can find much more about the likes of Delon and Rohmer in any number of other film reference books. I had hoped, too – in order to balance the ubiquitous table of Oscar winners in British and American works of reference – that there would be a complete list of Cesars, the French Academy Awards. But even this opportunity is missed. *The Companion* may serve new devotees of French cinema, but it will surely frustrate the real fans.

Leonard Maltin's Movie & Video Guide 1997; Signet; £8.99; 1,614 pages.

In my book still the most complete, accurate and manageable film guide on the market, Maltin's miracle of compactness grows in usefulness every year. Now running to 1,614 pages and embracing more than 19,000 cinema, TV and video titles, the 1997 volume brags 300 new entries, from *Fargo* to *Mission: Impossible*. All the essential bits and pieces are still here: star ratings, video and laserdisc availability, sequel information,

running times (plus allusions to edited and censored versions), alternative titles, extensive cast listings, star cameos (credited or otherwise), screen formats, comprehensive filmo-graphies of stars and directors at the back and the usual, frequently withering wit. The book is also invaluable for getting your facts straight, making a point of inserting the hyphen in Daniel Day-Lewis and Kristin Scott-Thomas (post *Four Weddings*) and excluding it from Helena Bonham Carter.

The Macmillan International Film Encyclopedia, by Ephraim Katz; Macmillan; £35; 1,496 pages.

It is an unfortunate truism that reference books are frequently remembered more for their faults than for their virtues. However, Ephraim Katz's phenomenally comprehensive encyclopaedia is a hard tome to beat, even in our age of information. An astonishing labour of love by any standards, it includes extensive histories of world cinema, chronicles the track record of the major and independent studios and explores the various genres of film (animation, film noir, etc.), as well as containing detailed profiles of actors, directors, producers, cinematographers, etc., exhaustive filmographies (including alternative titles), major Academy Award winners, technical terms and entries on organisations. Thus, under one roof, you can find out what a key grip is, swat up on the history of Czech cinema (beginning with Purkinje's concept of 'persistence of vision' in 1818), discover that Sean Connery started out as a coffin polisher, that Miramax was formed in 1979 and that Helena Bonham Carter was born on 26 May 1966. Furthermore, strange anomalies that popped up in the first edition – published in 1979 – have now been amended (such as the bizarre inclusion of *Massacre at Blood Bath Drive-In* in Kim Novak's filmography). Notwithstanding, there are still the inevitable blunders: referring to Nicola Piovani as a pseudonym of Ennio Morricone is to do an injustice to the talented composer of *Dear Diary, Fiorile* and *A Month by the Lake*. Yet, bearing this in mind, Katz's achievement is close to miraculous and is as useful and imperative a reference as any buff can hope to own.

The Marx Brothers Encyclopedia, by Glenn Mitchell; Batsford; £15.99; 256 pages.

An intriguing format for what is essentially a biography of the anarchic siblings rearranged as a dictionary, *The Marx Brothers Encyclopedia* is a well-illustrated, comprehensive A-Z. An absolute requirement for Marx buffs, this eminently 'dippable' tome covers everything from the comics' stage appearances and co-stars to their marriages and dialogue, all conveniently arranged in alphabet-ical order. Thus, under 'puns' you will find this discourse between Chico and Thelma Todd (from *Horse Feathers*): Chico: 'You sing high, uh?' Todd: 'Yes, I have a falsetto voice.' Chico: 'That's-a-funny, my last pupil, she had a falsetto teeth.' And under 'insults' there is Groucho's famous comment to Chico (also from *Horse Feathers*): 'You've got the brain of a four-year-old boy, and I bet he was glad to get rid of it.' There are also entries headed 'cars', 'censorship', 'continuity errors', 'religion' and 'smoking', which should give a rough idea of the scope of this labour of love. The films themselves are covered in enormous depth, with extensive credits, scene-by-scene synopses and detailed breakdown of the production story, critical reception and nuggets of trivia you won't find in other biographies. My only brickbat: a concise chronology would have proved extremely helpful to the uninitiated, so as to provide an overall perspective. A lot of the time one is forced to rely on initiative in order to find one's way around the book ('births' is a good entry to start with; 'deaths' to conclude).

The Moving Picture Boy, by John Holmstrom; Michael Russell; £39.50; 551 pages.

Not since the aberrant *Cluck!*, an encyclopaedia of chickens in the movies, has an author devoted so much attention and energy to what, it must be said, is a marginal cinematic subject. The last word on boy actors in the international pantheon of cinema, *The Moving Picture Boy* is a profusely illustrated work of enormous commitment. Detailing the very first appearance by a boy actor – 'le petit Duval' in Louis Lumière's 1895 *L'Arroseur Arrosé* – the book ploughs on through the next century until

eventually stopping at Elijah Wood in *North* (1994). Along the way, Holmstrom presents a biography and filmography of each actor, listed chronologically by birth. Following this is an exhaustive index which not only directs the reader to any given entry, but also includes an additional tally of one- (or more-) film wonders, complete with credits and, where possible, birth dates. This is then followed by a supplementary 102-page index of film titles, appended with date, nationality and the name of relevant child star, succeeded by a second index that includes any name (adult or otherwise) mentioned in the main text. Spreading its net to include every actor from the obvious (Mickey Rooney, Mark Lester) to the obscure (Tsai Yuanyuan, Zdenek Lstiburek), *The Moving Picture Boy* stands as a definitive and extremely handsome reference. It's also a must for discovering whatever happened to the spoilt brats, revealing that Fergus McClelland (Sammy in *Sammy Going South*) is now an electrician writing a novel inspired by the Old Testament, and that Matthew Garber, who played Michael Banks in *Mary Poppins*, died in 1977 aged 21.

Quinlan's Film Stars, by David Quinlan; Batsford; £22.50; 510 pages.

Endowed with its most attractive cover to date (featuring Theda, Grace, Kirk, Denzel, Sandra Bullock and others), the fourth edition of Quinlan's magnum opus is as inviting and useful a reference as ever. Comprising a phenomenal 1,850 entries, the tome features a photograph, thumbnail profile and exhaustively comprehensive filmography of each star, from Bud Abbott to George Zucco. Exercising his characteristic stamina, Quinlan has again eclipsed the efforts of his peers by routing out the most shadowy credits of his entrants, whether they be cameo, voice-over or documentary appearance. Thus, you will discover that Whoopi Goldberg not only narrated the obscure 1994 docu-mentary *Liberation* but appeared in both *Star Trek Generations* and *Bordello of Blood*, in which she contributed uncredited cameos. If the job of a critic is to carp, then my only complaint is that a walk-on or guest appearance is not specified. P.S. On top of all this,

you will find no other encyclopaedic work that so meticulously details the hair colour and, where relevant, the cause of death of its subjects.

Talking Pictures, edited by Lucy Johnson; BFI; £10.00; 132 pages.

For anybody whose interest in the cinema extends beyond the effects of Industrial Light & Magic and the dating techniques of Brad Pitt, this modest little book throws up some fascinating insights. A compilation of interviews conducted with inde-pendent British producers, *Talking Pictures* examines the nitty gritty process of making films from the inside out. Far from reflecting the glamour of an industry that brought us *Goldeneye* and *Sense and Sensibility* (both of which were funded in the US), it reveals the sheer graft, love, passion, desperation and bloody mindedness needed to get a coffee budget out of *Camelot*. As Paul Brooks reveals, 'It's incredibly hard, but it's incredibly simple. It funda-mentally revolves around energy. Energy and positivity. Energy will make a bad script happen and no energy will leave a good script lying on the shelf.' Strong on advice and weak on anecdote, the volume is unlikely to appeal to any but the diehard film buff, but is an essential handbook for those contemplating a career in the industry.

TV Times Film & Video Guide, by David Quinlan; Mandarin; £7.99; 801 pages.

In the pantheon of film and video guides, David Quinlan's labour of love slips somewhere between the *Variety* manual and Maltin's. Easy on the eye and physically manageable (an eight year old could hold it in one hand!), the tome includes all the essential information one needs – video availability, copyright date, running time, director, stars and ratings – plus the user-friendly asset of symbols donating a film's degree of viewer suitability. The reviews themselves are readably substantial and loaded with fascinating titbits and it is here that the guide comes into its own. As for the book's scope, the accent is on Hollywood, Britain and the new, but silent and foreign classics are also included.

The Western, by Phil Hardy; Aurum; £25; 416 pages.

The ultimate companion to the western, this Titan of film reference is virtually beyond criticism. Boasting the inclusion of every western produced in the era of sound, the encyclopaedia is a year-by-year study of the horse opera, from *In Old Arizona* (1929) – 'the first major sound western' – right up to *Young Guns II* (1990). Including basic credits (producer, director, writer, cinematographer, leading actors), synopsis, background information and critical comment, the book is workmanlike in its dedication if, at times, a trifle dull. It does, however, bring a perspective and reverence to a genre frequently undervalued as a frivolous 'boy's own' amusement. But in recognising the 'sombre themes' and 'unexpected density' of John Ford's *The Searchers* and defining John Wayne's character as 'an embodiment of the primitive forces that must be quashed before the foundations of civilisation can be properly laid and the desert transformed into a garden', it knows of what it talks. In addition, there are some useful and interesting extras at the back of the book that include a list of the biggest money-making westerns of all time (topped by *Dances With Wolves*), an 'inflation-adjusted' list (headed by *Duel in the Sun*, would you believe?), a year-by-year breakdown of the top box-office cowboy stars (up until 1954), an assortment of critics' top tens (most illuminating), Oscar winners, bibliography and a comprehensive round-up of secondary westerns denied due space within the main bulk of the book. Voluptuously illustrated and handsomely mounted, the volume is a monu-mental undertaking and could, I think, only be improved by one significant step: the addition of twice as many pages. But then the size of the tome would probably kill you.

Who's Who On Television, by Anthony Hayward; Boxtree; £9.99; 280 pages.

While not strictly a film book, this useful compilation contains enough cross-over names to be of interest to fans of the big screen (i.e. Julie Christie, Alec Guinness, Angela Lansbury, Julie Walters, etc.). Com-prising more than 1,300 entries, the volume includes actors, presenters and nebulous TV personalities and lists their birthdays (where possible), comprehensive TV and film credits, major stage appearances and awards. And for devotees of trivia, there are the stars' pets and hobbies (Maureen Lipman notes that her pastime is 'thinking about almost writing something wonderful'). However, I should warn you that the book is a British publication, so you won't find Pamela Anderson, George Clooney, Courtney Cox, Jimmy Smits or Oprah Winfrey within its pages. None the less, a most handy and enjoyable browse.

Other notable books

The Art of Star Wars: The Empire Strikes Back Episode V, edited by Deborah Call; Titan.

The Art of Star Wars: A New Hope Episode IV, edited by Carol Titelmann; Titan.

The Art of Star Wars: Return of the Jedi Episode VI, edited by Lawrence Kasdan and George Lucas; Titan.

The BFI Companion To Horror, edited by Kim Newman; BFI/Cassell.

Bogart: A Life In Hollywood, by Jeffrey Meyers; Andre Deutsch.

Boy Wonder; James Robert Baker's satirical take of Hollywood; Fourth Estate.

Burton on Burton (Tim, not Richard, that is); edited by Mark Salisbury; Faber and Faber.

Buster Keaton: Cut To the Chase, by Marion Meade; Bloomsbury.

Clint Eastwood: A Biography, by Richard Schickel; Jonathan Cape.

The Complete Films of Vincent Price, by Lucy Chase Williams; Citadel.

Errol Flynn: The Movie Posters, Lawrence Bassoff; The Lawrence Bassoff Collection.

Fritz Lang: The Nature of the Beast, by Patrick McGilligan; Faber and Faber.

The Guerilla Film Makers Handbook, by Chris Jones and Genevieve Joliffe; Cassell.

Hamlet Screenplay, Introduction and Film Diary, by Kenneth Branagh; Chatto & Windus.

The Hammer Story, by Marcus Heam and Alan Barnes; Titan Books.

The Hollywood History of the World, by George MacDonald Fraser; Harvill.

I Fellini, by Charlotte Chandler; Bloomsbury.

Industrial Light and Magic: Into the Digital Realm, by Mark Cotta and Patricia Rose Duignan; Virgin.

James Stewart, by Donald Dewey; Turner Publishing.

Jean Howard's Hollywood: A Photo Memoir; photographs by Jean Howard; text by James Watters and Harry N. Abrams; New York.

John Wayne: The Politics of Celebrity, by Gary Wills; Faber and Faber.

Lachapelle Land, David Lachapelle's outlandish showbiz photographs; Booth Clibborn Editions.

Man On The Flying Trapeze: The Life and Times of W.C. Fields, by Simon Louvish; Faber and Faber.

Pierce Brosnan: The Biography, by York Membery; Virgin.

Projections 7, edited by John Boorman and Walter Donohoe; Faber and Faber.

The Real Life of Laurence Olivier, by Roger Lewis; Century.

Roger Ebert's Video Companion, by Roger Ebert; Bloomsbury.

Screen Violence, by Karl French; Bloomsbury.

Sex and Zen & A Bullet In the Head, Stefan Hammond and Mike Wilkins' chronicle of Hong Kong cinema; Titan.

Star Wars Chronicles, by Deborah Fine; Virgin.

Steven Spielberg: A Biography, by Joseph McBride; Faber and Faber.

Stone (Oliver, not Sharon, that is), by James Riordan; Aurum.

Uncaged: The Biography of Nicolas Cage, by Douglas Thompson; Boxtree.

The Undeclared War: The Struggle For Control of the World's Film Industry, by David Puttnam and Neil Watson; HarperCollins.

Under the Rainbow: The Real Liza Minnelli, by George Mair; Aurum Press.

The Unkindest Cut, by Joe Queenan; Picador.

In Memoriam

by James Cameron-Wilson

Lew Ayres

Born: 28 December 1908 in Minneapolis, Minnesota. **Died**: 30 December 1996 in his sleep in Los Angeles.

Lew Ayres is perhaps still best remembered as Paul Baumer, the young German soldier in the Oscar-winning *All Quiet On the Western Front* (1930) who, during the heartbreaking finale, stretches out his hand to reach for a butterfly. In keeping with the film's anti-war message, Ayres went on to court notoriety as a conscientious objector during World War II (although he served as a medical orderly on the front line), a move that severely

Lew Ayres

damaged his subsequent career. He also starred opposite Greta Garbo in *The Kiss* (1929) and Ginger Rogers in *Don't Bet On Love* (1933), Ms Rogers becoming his wife a year later (they divorced in 1941). For MGM he played Dr Kildare in nine films, when the studio terminated his contract in protest of his pacifism. After the war he made an impression as the psychologist involved with good and bad twins in *The Dark Mirror* (1946) and as the amiable doctor who cares for a deaf-mute in *Johnny Belinda* (1948), for which he was nominated for an Oscar. His later pictures included *Donovan's Brain* (1953), *Advise and Consent* (1962), *The Carpetbaggers* (1964) and *Damien – Omen II* (1978). He also directed the Civil War drama *Hearts in Bondage* (1936) and two religious documentaries, *Altars of the East* (1955) and *Altars of the World* (1976).

John Beal

Born: 13 August 1909 in Joplin, Missouri. **Died**: 26 April 1997 in Santa Cruz, California, of complications following a stroke two years earlier.
Real name: J. Alexander Bliedung.

A leading man of the 1930s, John Beal acted on stage, in film and on TV in a career that spanned 60 years. Starting out in the Helen Hayes vehicle *Another Language* in 1933, he clocked up a prodigious list of movies and notched up over 50 stage appearances. His TV credits included

Freedom Rings, the original *Twelve Angry Men*, *Road to Reality*, *Another World* and *The Adams Chronicles*, while his films numbered *The Little Minister* (1934), with Katharine Hepburn, *Les Miserables*, *Laddie* (both 1935), *The Cat and the Canary* (1939), *Edge of Darkness* (1943), *Amityville 3D* (1983) and *The Firm* (1993). He married the actress Helen Craig in 1934 and during the Second World War directed a number of training films.

Jason Bernard

Born: 1938. **Died**: 18 October 1996 of a heart attack (while driving his car) in Hollywood, Los Angeles.

A busy character actor and familiar face, Bernard played deputy inspector Marquetee in TV's *Cagney & Lacey* (1982-83) and most recently starred as Othello in the LA Shakespeare Festival. His films included *No Way Out*, *All of Me*, *While You Were Sleeping* and *Liar Liar*, the last named (in which he played the long-suffering Judge Marshall Stevens) being dedicated to his memory.

Bibi Besch

Born: 1941 in Austria. **Died**: 7 September 1996 of cancer in Los Angeles.
Real name: Bibiara Besch.

An attractive and busy character actress, Bibi Besch emigrated to the US as a child. Her film credits included *Meteor*, *Star Trek II: The Wrath of Khan*, *The Lonely Lady*, *Kill Me Again*, *Steel Magnolias* and *Betsy's Wedding*. She was nominated for two Emmys, for *Doing Time on Maple Drive* and for her recurring role in *Northern Exposure*. She is survived by her daughter, the actress Samantha Mathis.

Anthony Bushell

Born: 19 May 1904 in Westerham, Kent. **Died**: 2 April 1997.

A prolific actor in the Leslie Howard mould (and sometime director), Bushell moved to Hollywood in 1929 to play Lord Deeford in *Disraeli*. After appearing in a number of films there, he returned to Britain three years later to pursue a career as a sensitive leading man. He later

served as associate producer on Laurence Olivier's *Hamlet* (1949) and made his directorial debut the same year with *The Angel With the Trumpet*. He subsequently pursued a career in television as an actor and director, and produced the costume drama series *Sir Francis Drake* (1961-62) with Terence Morgan. As an actor, his film credits included *Journey's End* (1930), *The Scarlet Pimpernel* (1934), *The Miniver Story* (1950), *The Battle of the River Plate* (1956) and *The Wind Cannot Read* (1958).

Marcel Carne

Born: 18 August 1909 in Paris. **Died**: 31 October 1996 in Clamart, Paris.

Best known as the director of the 1945 French masterpiece *Les Enfants du Paradis*, Carne, the son of a Paris cabinet maker, promoted the ideal of poetic realism and was especially skilled at coaxing superlative performances from his actors. After serving as apprentice and assistant to the filmmaker Jacques Feyder (on such pictures as *La Grand Jeu* (1934) and *Pension Mimosas* (1935)), he made his directorial debut with *Jenny* (1936), starring Feyder's wife, Francoise Rosay, and scripted by Jacques Prevert. Carne then embarked on a fruitful collaboration with Prevert, producing such distinguished works as *Drole de Drame* (1937) and *Quai Des Brumes* (1938). Their magnum opus, *Les Enfants Du Paradis*, was secretly filmed during the Nazi Occupation and remains a haunting, intensely moving epic detailing the inter-twined lives of a courtesan, mime, actor and thief. However, with the emergence of the nouvelle vague, Carne quickly became unfashionable, although he continued to direct films until his 66th year. Then, at the grand old age of 83, he started work on a screen adaptation of Guy de Maupassant's *Mouche*, but was forced to abandon the project because of illness.

Maria Casares

Born: 21 November 1922 in Coruna, Galicia, Spain. **Died**: 22 November 1996 in La Vergnes, France.

Real name: Maria Casares Quiroga. A tragedienne of the French stage, Maria Casares was not a fan of the

cinema, even though she appeared in as many as 20 pictures. Seeking asylum in France after serving as a nurse in the Spanish Civil War, Casares made her mark on the Paris stage in the title role of J.M. Synge's *Deirdre of the Sorrows*. Three years later she made her film debut in Marcel Carne's legendary *Les Enfants du Paradis* (1945) as the simple Nathalie, the abandoned wife of Jean-Louis Barrault's mime. Her other notable screen credits included Bresson's *Les Dames du Bois du Boulogne* (1946), Cocteau's *Orphee* (1950), Cocteau's *Le Testament d'Orphee* (1960) and Michel Deville's *La Lectrice* (1989). In 1995 she played Tom Conti's mother in the Franco-British-German *Someone Else's America*. While some criticised her for overacting, others admired her daring, but nobody could ignore her powerful presence or dark good looks. She died just three weeks after the death of Marcel Carne, the director who made her a star.

Virginia Cherrill

Born: 12 April 1908 in Carthage, Illinois. **Died**: 14 November 1996 of unreported causes in a hospital in Santa Barbara, California.

A serial wife and occasional actress, Cherrill will forever be remembered as the flower girl in Charlie Chaplin's *City Lights* (1931). Less well known is the fact that she was forced to do 300 takes to get her scene right. She also appeared in the John Wayne comedy *Girls Demand Excitement* (1931), *Charlie Chan's Greatest Case* (1932) and the British thriller *Late Extra* (1935), with James Mason. Married five times, she was the first wife of Cary Grant (1934-5), himself a quintuple spouse.

Claudette Colbert

Born: 13 September 1905 in Paris. **Died**: 30 July 1996 in Bridgetown, Barbados.
Real name: Claudette Lily Chauchoin.

Arriving in America in 1911 with designs on the fashion industry, the French-born Colbert ended up on the Broadway stage and made something of a success of it. However, it was when Cecil B. De Mille invited her to play 'the wickedest woman in

Claudette Colbert as she appeared in Anatole Litvak's Tovarich *(1937)*

Giuseppe de Santis

Born: 11 February 1917 in Fondi, Italy. **Died**: 16 May 1997 in Rome's Sant' Eugenio hospital – from a heart attack.

De Santis was an Italian filmmaker who injected a powerful eroticism into social commentary, notably with his 1950 hit *Bitter Rice*. Starring a scantily clad, 19-year-old Silvana Mangano (as a city girl who strips down in the rice fields of the Po Valley), the film called for better working conditions for women, but its message was largely lost on the post-war raincoat brigade. The director's later films, however, proved more mundane.

David Doyle

Born: 1925. **Died**: 27 February 1997 of a heart attack.

Best known for his role as John Bosley, the cheerful associate of Farrah Fawcett, Jaclyn Smith, Kate Jackson & co. on the popular crime show *Charlie's Angels* (1976-81), David Doyle was a prolific character actor whose film credits included *Coogan's Bluff*, *Vigilante Force*, *Capricorn One* and *Love or Money*.

Joanne Dru

Born: 31 January 1923 in Logan, West Virginia. **Died**: 10 September 1996 in Beverly Hills, of respiratory failure.
Real name: Joanne la Coque.

Joanne Dru was a lovely, petite leading lady who started out as a model and then became the heroine of three notable Westerns, starring opposite John Wayne and Montgomery Clift in Howard Hawks' *Red River* (1949), Wayne in John Ford's *She Wore a Yellow Ribbon* (1949) and Ward Bond in Ford's *Wagonmaster* (1950). She also played the highly bred, two-timing Anne Stanton in the Oscar-laden *All the King's Men* (1949) and was rancher Babs Hooton in the ABC TV sitcom *Guestward Ho!* (1960-61). She was married to the Argentine-born crooner Dick Haymes (1941-49) and the Canadian actor John Ireland (1949-58), the latter her co-star from *All the King's Men*.

the world' (Poppea) in his scandalous *Sign of the Cross* (1932) that she made her stamp on the public. Although the film was not particularly successful at the box office, her scene bathing in asses' milk became a milestone in erotic history. In Frank Capra's *It Happened One Night* (1934), a film she thought little of, she played a runaway heiress pursued by a nosy reporter (Clark Gable) and got to utter the immortal line (to Gable): 'I just had the unpleasant sensation of hearing you referred to as my husband.' The role was originally intended for Myrna Loy, but Colbert made it her own and won an Oscar for it. Oscars were also awarded to the film, Gable, Capra and scenarist Robert Riskin, marking the first time that one movie walked off with all five major prizes. Over the next 52 years her most noteworthy films included *Cleopatra* (1934), *Imitation of Life* (1934), *Private Worlds* (1935) (for which she was nominated for a second Academy Award), *I Met Him in Paris* (1937), *Midnight* (1939), *Drums Along the Mohawk* (1939), *Boom Town* (1940), *Arise My Love* (1940), *The Palm Beach Story* (1942), *Since You Went Away* (1944) (another nomination), *The Egg and I* (1947), *Three Came Home* (1950) and the TV movie *The Two Mrs Grenvilles* (1987), with Ann-Margret. She was married to the actor Norman Foster (1928-35), but never lived with him, and to Dr Joel Pressman until his death in 1968. It was Mary Astor who commented that Colbert was 'pretty rather than beautiful – she had some rather difficult angles to her face. The right side of her face was called "the other side of the moon" because nobody ever saw it.'

Herb Edelman

Born: 1934. **Died**: 21 July 1996 of emphysema in Los Angeles.

A bald, gangly character actor, Edelman worked extensively in all mediums, winning recent recognition as Stanley, Bea Arthur's irritating ex-husband on NBC TV's *The Golden Girls*. His films included *In Like Flint*, *Barefoot In the Park* (both 1967), *I Love You, Alice B. Toklas*, *The Odd Couple* (both 1968), *The Way We Were* (1973), *The Front Page* (1974), *The Yakuza* (1975) and *California Suite* (1978). He also played salesman Harry Pearlman on the ABC TV sitcom *9 to 5*. Divorced with two daughters, Edelman spent the last 12 years of his life with the actress Christina Pickles (from TV's *Friends*). He died aged 62 in Los Angeles.

Barry Evans

Born: 18 June 1943 in Hampshire, England. **Died**: 11 February 1997 in Claybrooke Magna, near Lutterworth, Leicestershire, England.

Barry Evans was a lightweight English leading man who starred in the 1967 hit comedy *Here We Go*

Joanne Dru

Round the Mulberry Bush, although he was better known for his TV roles in *Doctor in the House* (1969-70) and *Mind Your Language* (1977-79). His other films included *The Class*, *The White Bus*, *Alfred the Great*, *Die Screaming Marianne* and, ironically, *The Adventures of a Taxi Driver*, as he then abandoned show business to become a taxi driver. He was found dead in the living room of his modest bungalow, where he had been living on his own for four years. Police admitted that they were treating his death with suspicion.

Marco Ferreri

Born: 11 May 1928 in Milan, Italy. **Died**: 9 May 1997 of a heart attack in a Paris hospital.

Arguably Italy's most controversial and anarchic filmmaker, Marco Ferreri started out as a producer of commercials (and initiated the short-lived film magazine *Documento Mensile*) before directing his first film, *El Pistino* (1958), in Spain. Attracting some attention at the 1960 Venice Film Festival with his corrosively comic *The Wheelchair*, Ferreri continued in much the same vein throughout his career, regularly prompting outrage and admiration. His most notable films included *The Conjugal Bed* (1963), *Dillinger Is Dead* (1969), *The Last Woman* (1976), *Tales of Ordinary Madness* (1981) and his most famous, *La Grande Bouffe* (1973), in which Marcello Mastroianni, Philippe Noiret, Michel Piccoli and Ugo Tognazzi play four men who make a pact to eat themselves to death.

Mark Frankel

Born: 1962 in London. **Died**: 24 September 1996 from injuries sustained in a motorcycle accident.

Mark Frankel was a young leading man who made his name as the star of Gary Sinyor and Vadim Jean's *Leon the Pig Farmer*, playing Leon, a Jewish lad who discovers that his father is a pig farmer. Frankel then took the lead in Sinyor's *Solitaire for 2* as an arrogant body language instructor who falls for Amanda Pays, an archaeologist with ESP. The actor also appeared in the TNT mini-series *Young Catherine* and *Roseanna's Grave*.

Ronald Fraser

Born: 11 April 1930 in Ashton-under-Lyne, Greater Manchester. **Died**: 13 March 1997.

Ronald Fraser was a distinctive character actor whose porcine features and cheerfully gruff manner brightened many a picture. His innumerable film credits included *The Sundowners*, *Crooks in Cloisters*, *The Flight of the Phoenix*, *The Killing of Sister George*, *Too Late the Hero*, *Rentadick*, *The Wild Geese*, *Let Him Have It* and *The Mystery of Edwin Drood*. He also starred in the comedy series *The Misfit* (1970-71) as Basil 'Badger' Allenby-Johnson, who returns from Malaya to suffer the indignities of seventies' London.

Miles Goodman

Born: 1949. **Died**: 16 August 1996 of a heart attack in Los Angeles.

A film composer and jazz record producer, Goodman wrote the music for such films as *Footloose*, *La Bamba*, *About Last Night...*, *Little Shop of Horrors*, *Dirty Rotten Scoundrels*, *What About Bob?*, *Getting Even With Dad* and *'Til There Was You*.

Walter Gotell

Born: 15 March 1924 in Bonn. **Died**: 5 May 1997.

Walter Gotell was an authoritative, frequently sinister character actor, best remembered for his portrayal of KGB chief General Gogol in six of the James Bond films, namely *The Spy Who Loved Me*, *Moonraker*, *For Your Eyes Only*, *Octopussy*, *A View To a Kill* and *The Living Daylights*. Interestingly, he also popped up in the second 007 outing, *From Russia With Love*, as Rosa Klebb's henchman Mozerny, and played a variety of Nazis in such films as *We Dive at Dawn*, *The African Queen*, *Sink the Bismark!*, *The Guns of Navarone* and *The Boys From Brazil*. On TV he gained further exposure as Chief Constable Cullen in *Softly, Softly: Task Force* (1970-76). Gotell was also a keen businessman and farmer.

Margaux Hemingway

Born: February 1955 in Portland, Oregon. **Died**: 2 July 1996 from an overdose of sleeping pills.

The granddaughter of Ernest Hemingway and older sister of

actress Mariel Hemingway, Margaux made her name as Faberge's 'Fabulous Babe' when she landed a $1 million, four-year deal to promote Babe, the cosmetic company's scent. Then, in 1976, producer Dino De Laurentiis launched her as a movie star in the disastrous rape drama *Lipstick*, which also featured Chris Sarandon, Anne Bancroft and sister Mariel. Her career hardly improved with such pictures as *Killer Fish* (1979), *They Call Me Bruce?* (aka *A Fistful of Chopsticks*) (1982), *Over the Brooklyn Bridge* (1983) and the Spanish-made *Killing Machine* (1986), and she succumbed to a series of physical and psychological disorders, including alcoholism and bulimia. To make matters worse, she was also dyslexic and an epileptic. In 1988 she had put on 60 lbs in weight and in 1994 was admitted to a mental hospital for 'hearing voices'. Then, at the age of 41, she was found dead in her one-room flat in Santa Monica, California, on the eve of the 35th anniversary of the suicide of Ernest Hemingway. Talking of suicide, Margaux's great grandfather, great aunt and great uncle all took their own lives. She was married to the hamburger tycoon Errol Weston (1975-78) and the French film director Bernard Foucher (1980-86).

Ronald Howard

Born: 7 April 1918 in Norwood, Surrey. **Died:** 16 February 1997.

The son of Leslie Howard and a cousin of the actor Alan Howard, Ronald Howard enjoyed some

Ronald Howard

success himself in films, theatre and on television. Following a career in journalism and a stint in the Navy (taking part in the D-Day landing), he was offered (and took) a leading role in the lightweight film *While the Sun Shines* (1946), adapted from the play by Terence Rattigan. Refusing to change his name to Leslie Howard Jr, he retreated to the Theatre Royal Windsor to hone his craft and temporarily altered his name to Ronald Martin. Filmwise, Howard's more notable credits included *The Browning Version* (1951), *Drango* (1956) and *Babette Goes to War* (1959). He also had the title role in the American-produced TV series *The Adventures of Sherlock Holmes* (1954-55), and played Wing Commander Hayes in the ABC TV adventure series *Cowboy in Africa* (1967-68). His autobiography, *In Search of My Father*, appeared in 1980.

King Hu

Born: 29 April 1931 in Yongnian County, near Beijing. **Died**: March 1997.

Real name: Hu Chin-Chuan (or, in Pinyin, Hu Jinquan).

A celebrated Hong King filmmaker, King Hu graduated from art director to actor and scenarist for the Shaw Brothers, Run Run and Runme. Becoming a director in the early 1960s, he brought a fresh intelligence, humour and photographic eye to the martial arts genre, notably in his three-hour epic *A Touch of Zen* (1969). Set during the Ming dynasty, the latter is a celebration of Zen Buddhist philosophy and is enhanced by lively, graceful choreography of the type established by the Peking Opera. King Hu was also a learned scholar of Chinese history and literature.

Richard Jaeckel

Born: 10 October 1926 in Long Beach, New York. **Died**: 14 June 1997 of an undisclosed illness in Los Angeles.

An all-round character actor, Jaeckel played everything from a juvenile delinquent and rapist to an astronaut and gunslinger in his 54-year film career. His more notable credits included *The Gunfighter*, *Come Back Little Sheba*, *Town Without Pity*, *The Dirty Dozen* (as Sgt Bowren), *Pat*

Garrett and Billy the Kid, *The Dark* and *Starman*, while his later years saw him cast in such fodder as *Baywatch: Nightmare Bay* (on TV) and *Martial Outlaw*. In 1971 he played the ill-fated lumberjack Joe Ben Stamper, cousin of Paul Newman's Hank Stamper, in the Newman-directed *Sometimes a Great Notion* (aka *Never Give an Inch*), for which he received his only Oscar nomination.

Brian Keith

Born: 14 November 1921 in Bayonne, New Jersey. **Died**: 24 June 1997 at his home in Malibu, California. **Real name**: Robert Brian Keith Jr.

A gruff, burly film and TV actor, Brian Keith tackled everything from light romantic comedy to outdoor adventure in a career that embraced over 80 films. Occasionally a leading man, he was better known as a character actor of some presence, whether playing a cavalry officer in *Run of the Arrow*, Teddy Roosevelt in *The Wind and the Lion* or the Cardinal in *Entertaining Angels* (qv). Other films include *Arrowhead* (1953), *The Parent Trap*, *Savage Sam*, *The Russians Are Coming! The Russians Are Coming!*, *Nevada Smith*, *Reflections in a Golden Eye*, *Meteor*, *Sharky's Machine* and *Young Guns*. On TV he starred in *The Westerner* (1960), portrayed Manhattan bachelor Bill Davis in the sitcom *Family Affair* (1966-71), was a paediatrician in *The Brian Keith Show* (1972-74) and played Judge Milton C. Hardcastle in *Hardcastle and McCormick* (1983-86). In early May of '97 Keith's daughter, Daisy, committed suicide, and he shot himself six weeks later.

Masaki Kobayashi

Born: 14 February 1916 in Otaru, Japan. **Died**: 5 October 1996 of cardiac arrest in Tokyo.

One of Japan's most celebrated filmmakers, Kobayashi remains best known for his powerful, epic anti war trilogy *The Human Condition*, comprising the films *No Greater Love* (1959), *Road to Eternity* (1959) and *A Soldier's Prayer* (1961). His other more famous works include *Harakiri* (1962), *Kwaidan* (1964) and *Rebellion* (1967). In 1970 he produced Akira Kurosawa's *Dodes'ka-den*.

Dorothy Lamour

Born: 10 December 1914 in New Orleans, Louisiana. **Died**: 21 September 1996 in North Hollywood. **Real name**: Mary Leta Dorothy Slaton.

Dorothy Lamour succeeded in leading two parallel careers, but will forever be associated with her persona as the exotic temptress, preferably in a sarong. A former beauty queen (she was crowned Miss New Orleans at the age of 17), Lamour started out as a big-band vocalist on the radio, making her screen debut as such in a short. Following her feature debut in *College Holiday* (1936), which co-starred George Burns and Gracie Allen, she was signed up by Paramount and put into the leading role of *The Jungle Princess*. The latter, in which she played a distaff Tarzan, set the tone for her future films, including her next, *The Hurricane* (1937), *Her Jungle Love* (1938, a sequel to the first) and *Typhoon* (1940). When Gracie Allen, George Burns and Fred MacMurray dropped out of *Road to Singapore* (1940), they were replaced by Lamour, Bing Crosby and Bob Hope – and a tradition was born, with Lamour lampooning her image as the exotic seductress. In all, the jolly trio made seven highly popular *Road* comedies, although Lamour was consigned to a cameo (as herself) in the last, *The Road to Hong Kong* (1962), with Joan Collins replacing her as the female lead. She also appeared in such films as *Tropic Holiday* (1938), *Moon Over Burma* (1940), *Aloma of the South Seas* (1941), *Rainbow Island* (1944), *Masquerade in Mexico* (1945) and *Creepshow 2* (1987). Later, she turned to nightclub appearances and starred in a triumphant tour of *Hello, Dolly!* She also penned an autobiography, *My Side of the Road*, which was published in 1980. Her husbands included the band leader Herbie Kay and businessman William Ross Howard III.

Laura La Plante

Born: 1 November 1904 in St Louis, Missouri. **Died**: 14 October 1996.

A bubbly blonde star of the silent screen, La Plante's credits included *The Dangerous Blonde* (1924), *Silk Stockings* (1927), *Show Boat* (1929) and, most notably, *The Cat and the Canary* (1927). Entering films at 16, the actress was Universal's top female star by the age of 20 (earning $5,000 a week), later appearing in a number of British features produced by her second husband, Irving Asher.

Frank Launder

Born: 1907 in Hitchin, Hertfordshire. **Died**: 23 February 1997.

In collaboration with Sidney Gilliat (who died in 1994), Launder wrote a number of successful British comedies, including *Facing the Music*, *A Yank at Oxford*, Alfred Hitchcock's *The Lady Vanishes* and *Night Train to Munich*. They also scripted the biographical drama *The Young Mr Pitt* (starring Robert Donat as the British prime minister) and such comic thrillers as *I See a Dark Stranger*, *Green For Danger* and *State Secret*. On his own, Launder scripted the notable *Under the Greenwood Tree* (1929) and *Hobson's Choice* (1931) and turned director with *Millions Like Us* (1943), followed by such projects as *Two Thousand Women*, *Captain Boycott* and *The Blue Lagoon*. Later he became identified with the *St Trinian* films, starting with the priceless *The Happiest Days of Your Life* (1950), which he also directed, leading to four sequels of varying quality, and ending with the regrettable *The Wildcats of St Trinian's* (1980), his last picture. In the latter part of his career he also executive produced the Hayley Mills thriller *Endless Night* (from a screenplay by Gilliat) and the Dick Emery vehicle *Ooh...You Are Awful*.

Jean Louis

Born: 5 October 1907 in Paris. **Died**: 20 April 1997 – of natural causes – in Palm Springs.

Jean Louis was a legendary costume designer whose sensuous creations draped countless actresses, not to mention his wife, Loretta Young, whom he married in 1993. Working for Columbia and Universal before becoming independent, Jean Louis won the Oscar for *The Solid Gold Cadillac* in 1956 and was nominated for a further 13 pictures, including *From Here To Eternity*, *A Star is Born* (1954), *Pal Joey* and *Thoroughly Modern Millie*. Among his more

Dorothy Lamour

memorable designs were Lana Turner's famous figure-hugging sweater and Rita Hayworth's strapless gown in *Gilda*.

Alfred Marks, OBE

Born: 28 January 1921 in Holborn, London. **Died**: 1 July 1996.

A prolific character actor, particularly adept at gruff types, Marks was a regular on radio, television, the stage and in films. Formerly an engineer and auctioneer, he made his professional debut in variety at the age of 25, but never lost his love of engineering, a passion he indulged in alongside model building, photography and riding. On television he presented *The Theatre Quiz* and played Solomon Snr in *Lovejoy*, while his film credits included *Desert Mice* (1959), *There Was a Crooked Man* (1960), *Frightened City* (1961), *Scream and Scream Again* (1970), *Our Miss Fred* (1972) and *Valentino* (1977).

Marcello Mastroianni as the 74-year-old Matteo Scuro – one of his later roles – in Giuseppe Tornatore's Everybody's Fine *(1990)*

Marcello Mastroianni

Born: 28 September 1924 in Fontana Liri, near Rome. **Died**: 19 December 1996 at his home in Paris, France, from pancreatic cancer.

The quintessential Latin lover of Italian cinema, Mastroianni will forever be associated with the films of Fellini and as Sophia Loren's most enduring leading man. Detained in a labour camp during the war, he escaped and made his home in a Venetian attic until the declaration of peace. Two years later he made his film debut in an Italian edition of *Les Miserables*, and two years after that he began his film career in earnest. As the hedonistic gossip columnist at the centre of Fellini's *La Dolce Vita* (1960), Mastroianni became an international star and cemented his reputation in Antonioni's *La Notte* (1961) and Pietro Germi's *Divorce Italian Style*, securing an Oscar nomination for the latter. He worked for Fellini again in *8 ½* (1963), *City of Women* (1980) and *Ginger and Fred* (1985) and won further Oscar nominations for *A Special Day* (1977) and *Dark Eyes* (1987). Equally at home as a predatory male or as a henpecked husband, Mastroianni was also as adept at comedy as drama and became a proficient character actor in his later years. His last film was Manoel de Oliveira's

Journey To the Beginning of the World. Incidentally, his daughter by Catherine Deneuve, Chiara Mastroianni, is also an actor, and has appeared in such films as *Ma Saison Preferee*, *Pret-à-Porter*, *All Men Are Mortal*, *Don't Forget You're Going To Die*, *Chameleon* and, with her father, *Three Lives and Only One Death*.

Brian May

Born: 1934 in Adelaide, Australia. **Died**: 25 April 1997 in Australia, of a heart attack.

A productive Australian composer, May graduated from scoring the lamentable *The True Story of Eskimo Nell* (his first film) to such features as *Mad Max*, *Mad Max 2*, *Gallipoli* and *Freddy's Dead: The Final Nightmare*. He is not to be confused with the guitarist of the same name from the rock band Queen.

Anthony Mendleson

Born: 7 February 1915 in Chiswick, London. **Died**: September 1996.

Anthony Mendleson was the chief costume designer for Ealing Studios, whose credits included *Whisky Galore*, *Passport to Pimlico*, *Kind Hearts and Coronets*, *The Lavender Hill Mob*, *The Man in the White Suit* and *The Titfield Thunderbolt*. He is survived by his partner, the actor and antique pipe connoisseur Brian Tipping.

Greg Morris

Born: 1934 in Cleveland. **Died**: 27 August 1996 in Las Vegas.

Greg Morris was best known for his role as Barney Collier, the electronics expert in *Mission Impossible* (1966-73). He also played Lieutenant Dave Nelson in ABC's *Vegas* (1979-81) and appeared in such films as *The Lively Set* (1964), *The Doomsday Flight* (TV; 1966) and *Countdown at Kusini* (1976).

Christine Pascal

Born: 29 November 1953 in Lyons, France. **Died**: 30 August 1996 in Paris.

A French-Swiss actress and film-maker, Pascal appeared in such pictures as Bertrand Tavernier's *The Watchmaker of St Paul* (1972), *Les Guichets du Louvre* (1973), Claude Miller's *The Best Way to Walk* (1976),

Tavernier's *The Judge and the Assassin* (1976) and *Spoiled Children* (1977), which she co-wrote, before making her directorial debut with *Felicite* (1978). She went on to direct *La Garce* (1984), starring Isabelle Huppert as a rape victim, *Zanzibar* (1988) and, her best work, *Le Petit Prince a dit* (1991). She also appeared in *Coup de Foudre* (aka *At First Sight/Entre Nous*) (1983) and *'Round Midnight* (1986), before throwing herself out of the window of a clinic on the outskirts of Paris.

William Prince

Born: 26 January 1913 in Nicholas, New York. **Died**: 8 October 1996 in Tarrytown, New York, of unreported causes.

A character actor equally at home on stage, in film or on television, Prince was seen on the big screen in such pictures as *Destination Tokyo* (1944), *Objective, Burma!* (1945), *Dead Reckoning* (1947), *Cyrano de Bergerac* (1951), *The Stepford Wives* (1975), *Family Plot* (1976), *Network* (1976), *The Gauntlet* (1977), *Bronco Billy* (1980) and *Spies Like Us* (1985).

Juliet Prowse

Born: 25 September 1936 in Bombay. **Died**: 14 September 1996 of pancreatic cancer at her home in Holmby Hills.

Prowse, who was raised in South Africa, thrived as a spectacular dancer in stage musicals and television specials but made few film appearances. Arriving in the States in 1958, she won a supporting role in *Can-Can* (1960) – starring Frank Sinatra – and became a worldwide celebrity when Nikita Khrushchev denounced the dancing as immoral. She also attracted some publicity with her six-week engagement to Sinatra and a fling with Elvis Presley, the star of her second film, *G.I. Blues*. In 1965-66 she was featured in her own TV sitcom, *Mona McCluskey*, playing a movie star forced to subsist on the salary of her husband, a sergeant in the US Air Force.

Beryl Reid, OBE

Born: 17 June 1920 in Hereford. **Died**: 13 October 1996.

An inimitable character actress and comedienne, Beryl Reid was one of the most beloved personalities of British theatre, television, radio and cinema. Her numerous film credits included *The Belles of St Trinian's, Two-Way Stretch, The Dock Brief, Star!, Inspector Clouseau, The Killing of Sister George* (recreating her triumphant stage role), *Entertaining Mr Sloane, No Sex Please – We're British, Joseph Andrews, Carry on Emmanuelle* and *Yellowbeard*. Known for her love of cats, she was also a keen gardener and cook, and penned a number of books, including *The Cat's Whiskers, Beryl, Food and Friends, The Kingfisher Jump* and, in 1984, her 'official' autobiography, *So Much Love*. She was awarded the OBE in 1986.

Marjorie Reynolds

Born: 12 August 1921 in Buhl, Idaho. **Died**: 1 February 1997 from congestive heart failure in Manhattan Beach.
Real name: Marjorie Goodspeed.

A former child star, first in silents, then talkies, Marjorie Goodspeed changed her name to Marjorie Moore in her early teens at which time she emerged as a proficient dancer and talented actress. In 1937 she married Jack Reynolds and changed her name again and really got going in the 1940s when she altered her hair colour – from brunette to blonde. It was at this time that she landed the female lead in *Holiday Inn* (1942) – opposite Fred Astaire and Bing Crosby – and in Fritz Lang's *Ministry of Fear* (1944), with Ray Milland. Despite her subsequent slide into a series of underwhelming action vehicles, Reynolds retained her

Beryl Reid as the promiscuous Kath in Douglas Hickox's screen adaptation of Joe Orton's Entertaining Mr Sloane

popularity by playing Peg Riley in the popular TV sitcom *The Life of Riley* (1953-58). Having made her film debut at the age of two – in *Scaramouche*, with Ramon Novarro – Reynolds achieved a durable career, lasting 39 years.

Joan Rice

Born: 3 February 1930 in Derby, Derbyshire. **Died**: 1 January 1997 of emphysema in Maidenhead, Berkshire.

An attractive leading lady of the 1950s, Rice graduated to character roles in her later years, but is still probably best remembered for her spirited turn as Maid Marian in *The Story of Robin Hood and His Merrie Men* (1952).

Howard E. Rollins Jr

Born: 17 October 1950 in Baltimore, Maryland. **Died**: 8 December 1996 at St Luke's Hospital, New York, of a bacterial infection (produced by complications of lymphoma).

With his roles in *Ragtime* and *A Soldier's Story*, Howard Rollins looked set to be the next Sidney Poitier. Tall, handsome and unarguably talented, Rollins leap-frogged to the forefront of the emerging black star system but, somehow, failed to capitalise on it. At 17, he auditioned for his first play, *Of Mice and Men*, and won the part, prompting him to realise that 'for the first time in my life I felt there was some sense in being alive'. He then served time in the enduring daytime soap *Another World* before seguing into film roles with the black comedy *The House of God* (1979). For his performance as ragtime pianist Coalhouse Walker Jr, the central protagonist of Milos Forman's *Ragtime* (1981), he was nominated for an Academy Award. He then headed the cast of Norman Jewison's *A Soldier's Story* (1984), playing the military attorney who investigates the murder of a black officer at a Louisiana army base. The latter film, like *Ragtime*, was showered with accolades, including an Oscar nomination for best picture. Then Rollins all but vanished from public view until, in 1988, he landed the lead in the TV series *In the Heat of the Night*, resurrecting the role of the

Howard E. Rollins Jr as Virgil Tibbs in TV's In the Heat of the Night

detective Virgil Tibbs originated by Sidney Poitier in the 1967 film. Then, in May of 1993, the star was defending himself in a Georgia court, appealing for leniency after five arrests for speeding and driving under the influence. Opening his heart to the jury, Rollins claimed that he was broke and was suffering from the death of his father, both brothers and his stepfather. Furthermore, his mother had amnesia and poor legal advice had cost him $250,000. He was jailed for a month and was written out of *In the Heat of the Night*, allegedly because of his drug use.

Alexander Salkind

Born: 2 June 1921 in Gdansk, Poland (then Germany). **Died**: 8 March 1997 of leukemia at the American Hospital in Paris.

A flamboyant producer and private man, Salkind followed his father, Michael, into independent film production, later bragging that he was the last of the great independent showmen. Following his work on the early films of Dietrich and Garbo, Michael Salkind travelled to Cuba, where Alexander joined him before moving on to Mexico and taking up citizenship there (his son, Ilya, was born in Mexico City). Returning to Europe in the 1950s, Salkind made his name as a producer of big-budget co-productions, notably *The Battle of Austerlitz* (1960), *The Three Musketeers* (1974), the *Superman* films and the almighty flop *Christopher Columbus – The Discovery* (1992).

Tupac Shakur as he appeared in Vondie Curtis Hall's Gridlock'd

Joe Seneca

Born: 1944. **Died**: 15 August 1996 of an asthma attack in New York.

Joe Seneca was a black character actor and songwriter whose acting credits included the films *The Verdict*, *Crossroads* and *A Time To Kill*.

Tupac Shakur

Born: 16 June 1971 in the Bronx, New York. **Died**: 13 September 1996 from shotgun wounds in Las Vegas, Nevada.

Named Tupac Amaru after an Inca chief (meaning, literally, 'shining serpent'), Shakur was one of the most notorious voices of gangsta rap, once receiving a caution from vice president Dan Quayle for his trigger-happy lyrics. He was also constantly at loggerheads with the law. In 1992 a civil lawsuit was brought against him when one of his crew shot a six-year-old boy dead, although the litigation was settled out of court (for a sum reportedly somewhere between $300,000 and $500,000). He then served eight months of a four-and-a-half year sentence for rape and, the year he was released (1994), was arrested again for the shooting of two off-duty policemen, although the charges were dropped. Also that year, he was shot five times in the lobby of a Manhattan recording studio, only to recover and enjoy even greater popularity. Breaking into the mainstream with the record 'Strictly 4 my N.I.G.G.A.Z.', Shakur (who also went under the monicker of 2Pac), produced such top-selling, anti-establishment albums as *Me Against the World*, *All Eyez on Me* and the posthumous *The Don Killuminati*. A fan of acting since he was accepted into the Baltimore School for the Arts at 15, the singer later used his fame to win roles in such high-profile films as *Juice*, John Singleton's *Poetic Justice*, *Above the Rim*, *Gang Related* and *Gridlock'd*.

Steve Tesich

Born: 29 September 1942. **Died**: 1 July 1996 of a heart attack in Sydney, Nova Scotia.
Real name: Stoyan Tesich.

Born in Yugoslavia, Stoyan Tesich moved to the US in 1955, aged 14, unable to speak English. Winning a place at Indiana University on a wrestling scholarship, he majored in Russian literature and went on to earn a PhD at Columbia University. As a playwright, he wrote *The Carpenters*, *Division Street*, *The Speed of Darkness*, *Square One*, *On the Road* and *Arts and Leisure*. He then scripted Peter Yates' *Breaking Away* (1979), for which he won the Oscar. He also wrote the screenplays to *Eyewitness* (aka *The Janitor*) (1980), *Four Friends* (1981), *The World According to Garp* (1982), *American Flyers* (1985), *Eleni* (1985), and one novel, *Summer Crossing* (1982). He died of a heart attack in Sydney, Nova Scotia, while holidaying with his family.

Bo Widerberg

Born: 8 June 1930 in Malmo, Sweden. **Died**: 1 May 1997 in Angelholm, Sweden, following an extended illness.

A florid Swedish director known for his lush photography, Widerberg leaped from venerated novelist to outspoken film critic to acclaimed filmmaker in an eventful career. While still best known for his 1967 romance *Elvira Madigan* (which made Mozart's 2nd piano concerto a household theme), Widerberg directed three films that received 'best foreign picture' Oscar nominations: *Raven's End* (1964), *Adalen 31* (1969) and his last feature, *Love Lessons* (see Releases of the Year).

Bill Williams

Born: 10 August 1905 in Slough, Berkshire. **Died**: 3 November 1996.
Real name: Lawrence Paul Williams.

As art director, Bill Williams' most notable credits included *On Approval* (in which his tubular chrome look inspired the Art Deco movement), *Sixty Glorious Years*, *A Yank at Oxford*, Hitchcock's *Mr and Mrs Smith* and *Brief Encounter*. In 1951 he retired to rear cows and pigs on his farm in Oxfordshire.

Fred Zinnemann

Born: 29 April 1907 in Vienna, Austria. **Died**: 14 March 1997 in London.

Arguably one of the finest film-makers of all time, Fred Zinnemann initially dreamed of becoming a musician, then switched aspirations to become a lawyer. However, after being knocked out by the films of King Vidor and Erich Von Stroheim, he set his sights on the cinema, taking work as an assistant camera-man in Paris and Berlin. In 1929 he emigrated to the US and almost immediately landed a bit part in *All Quiet On the Western Front*, then co-directed his first film, a documentary called *The Wave*, in 1934. He was directing shorts regularly for MGM from 1937 and won an Oscar for his one-reeler *That Others Might Live* (1938) before making his feature debut with *Kid Glove Killer*, in 1941. He received a second Oscar for his documentary *Benjy* (1951), set in a Los Angeles hospital, and then won the statuette a third time for his work on the classic World War II romance *From Here To Eternity* (1953). He was also nominated for the films *The Search* (1948), *High Noon* (1952), *The Nun's Story* (1959) and *The Sun-downers* (1960), before winning his final Academy Award for *A Man For All Seasons* (1966). His other movies included Marlon Brando's first picture, *The Men* (1950), *Oklahoma!* (1955), *The Day of the Jackal* (1973) and *Julia* (1977), the latter securing Zinnemann yet another Oscar nomination. While some criticised the director for his lack of artistic invention, no one could deny his all-embracing versatility and his ability for coaxing superlative performances from his actors.

Awards and Festivals

The 69th American Academy of Motion Picture Arts and Sciences Awards ('The Oscars') and Nominations for 1996, Los Angeles, 24 March 1997

Best Film: *The English Patient*.
Nominations: *Fargo*; *Jerry Maguire*; *Secrets and Lies*; *Shine*.

Best Director: Anthony Minghella, for *The English Patient*.
Nominations: Joel Coen, for *Fargo*; Milos Forman, for *The People vs. Larry Flynt*; Scott Hicks, for *Shine*; Mike Leigh, for *Secrets and Lies*.

Best Actor: Geoffrey Rush, for *Shine*.
Nominations: Tom Cruise, for *Jerry Maguire*; Ralph Fiennes, for *The English Patient*; Woody Harrelson, for *The People vs. Larry Flynt*; Billy Bob Thornton, for *Sling Blade*.

Best Actress: Frances McDormand, for *Fargo*. Nominations: Brenda Blethyn, for *Secrets and Lies*; Diane Keaton, for *Marvin's Room*; Kristin Scott Thomas, for *The English Patient*; Emily Watson, for *Breaking the Waves*.

Best Supporting Actor: Cuba Gooding Jr, for *Jerry Maguire* Nominations: William H. Macy, for *Fargo*; Armin Mueller-Stahl, for *Shine*; Edward Norton, for *Primal Fear*; James Woods, for *Ghosts of Mississippi*.

Best Supporting Actress: Juliette Binoche, for *The English Patient*. Nominations: Joan Allen, for *The Crucible*; Lauren Bacall, for *The Mirror Has Two Faces*; Barbara Hershey, for *The Portrait of a Lady*; Marianne Jean-Baptiste, for *Secrets and Lies*.

Best Original Screenplay: Ethan Coen and Joel Coen, for *Fargo*. Nominations: Cameron Crowe, for *Jerry Maguire*; John Sayles, for *Lone Star*; Mike Leigh, for *Secrets and Lies*; Jan Sardi (screenplay) and Scott Hicks (story) for *Shine*.

Best Screenplay Adaptation: Billy Bob Thornton, for *Sling Blade*. Nominations: Arthur Miller, for *The Crucible*; Anthony Minghella, for *The English Patient*; Kenneth Branagh, for *Hamlet*; John Hodge, for *Trainspotting*.

Best Cinematography: John Seale, for *The English Patient*. Nominations: Darius Khondji, for *Evita*; Roger Deakins, for *Fargo*; Caleb

Ralph Fiennes as Count Laszlo Almasy in Anthony Minghella's Oscar/BAFTA/Berlin/Golden Globe/National Board of Review-winning The English Patient

Frances O'Conner and Alice Garner in Emma-Kate Croghan's delightful Love and Other Catastrophes, *for which Garner collected the prize for best supporting actress from the Australian Film Critics' Circle*

Deschanel, for *Fly Away Home*; Chris Menges, for *Michael Collins*.

Best Editing: Walter Murch, for *The English Patient*. Nominations: Gerry Hambling, for *Evita*; Roderick Jaynes (aka Joel and Ethan Coen), for *Fargo*; Joe Hutshing, for *Jerry Maguire*; Pip Karmel, for *Shine*.

Best Original Score (musical or comedy): Rachel Portman, for *Emma*. Nominations: Marc Shaiman, for *The First Wives Club*; Alan Menken (music and orchestral score), Stephen Schwartz (lyrics), for *The Hunchback of Notre Dame*; Hans Zimmer, for *The Preacher's Wife*; Randy Newman, for *James and the Giant Peach*.

Best Original Score (dramatic): Gabriel Yared, for *The English Patient*. Nominations: Patrick Doyle, for *Hamlet*; Elliot Goldenthal, for *Michael Collins*; David Hirschfelder, for *Shine*; John Williams, for *Sleepers*.

Best Original Song: 'You Must Love Me', from *Evita*, music by Andrew Lloyd Webber, lyrics by Tim Rice. Nominations: 'Because You Loved Me', from *Up Close and Personal*, music and lyrics by Diane Warren; 'For the First Time', from *One Fine Day*, music and lyrics by James Newton Howard, Jud J. Friedman and Allan Dennis Rich; 'I Finally Found Someone', from *The Mirror Has Two Faces*, music and lyrics by Barbra Streisand, Marvin Hamlisch, Bryan Adams and Robert 'Mutt' Lange; 'That Thing You Do!', from *That Thing You Do!*, music and lyrics by Adam Schlesinger.

Best Art Direction: Stuart Craig (art) and Stephenie McMilan (set), for *The English Patient*. Nominations: Bo Welch (art) and Cheryl Carasik (set), for *The Birdcage*; Brian Morris (art) and Philippe Turiure (set) for *Evita*; Tim Harvey (art) for *Hamlet*; Catherine Martin (art) and Brigitte Broch (set) for *William Shakespeare's Romeo + Juliet*.

Best Costume Design: Ann Roth, for *The English Patient*. Nominations: Paul Brown, for *Angels and Insects*; Ruth Myers, for *Emma*; Alex Byrne, for *Hamlet*; Janet Patterson, for *The Portrait of a Lady*.

Best Sound: Walter Murch, Mark Berger, David Parker and Chris Newman, for *The English Patient*. Nominations: Andy Nelson, Anna Behlmer and Ken Weston, for *Evita*; Chris Carpenter, Bill W. Benton, Bob Beemer and Jeff Wexler, for *Independence Day*; Kevin O'Connell, Greg P. Russell and Keith A. Wester, for *The Rock*; Steve Maslow, Gregg Landaker, Kevin O'Connell and Geoffrey Patterson, for *Twister*.

Best Sound Effects Editing: Bruce Stambler, for *The Ghost and the Darkness*. Nominations: Richard L. Anderson and David A. Whittaker, for *Daylight*; Alan Robert Murray and Bub Asman, for *Eraser*.

Best Make-Up: Rick Baker and David Leroy Anderson, for *The Nutty Professor*. Nominations: Matthew W. Mungle and Deborah La Mia Denaver, for *Ghosts of Mississippi*; Michael Westmore, Scott Wheeler and Jake Garber, for *Star Trek: First Contact*.

Best Visual Effects: Volker Engel, Douglas Smith, Clay Pinney and Joseph Viskocil, for *Independence Day*. Nominations: Scott Squires, Phil Tippett, James Strauss and Kit West, for *Dragonheart*; Stefen Fangmeier, John Frazier, Habib Zargarpour and Henry La Bounta, for *Twister*.

Best Animated Short Film: *Quest*. Nominations: *Canhead*; *La Salla*; *Wat's Pig*.

Best Live Action Short Film: *Dear Diary*. Nominations: *De Tripas, Corazon*; *Ernst & Lyset*; *Esposados*; *Wordless*.

Best Documentary Feature: *When We Were Kings*, by Leon Gast. Nominations: *The Line King: The Al Hirschfeld Story*; *Mandela*; *Suzanne Farrell: Elusive Muse*; *Tell the Truth and Run: George Seldes and the American Press*.

Best Documentary Short: *Breathing Lessons: The Life and Work of Mark O'Brien*. Nominations: *Cosmic Voyage*; *An Essay on Matisse*; *Special Effects*; *The Wild Bunch: An Album in Montage*.

Best Foreign-Language Film: *Kolya* (Czech Republic). Nominations: *A Chef in Love* (Georgia); *The Other Side of Sunday* (Norway); *Prisoner of the Mountains* (Russia); *Ridicule* (France).

Irving G. Thalberg Memorial Award: Saul Zaentz, producer of *The English Patient*.

Career Achievement Award: Michael Kidd.

Scientific and Technical Award: Imax Corp., for its large-format pictures.

Host: Billy Crystal

Australian Film Critics' Circle Awards, Sydney, 7 February 1997

Best Film: *Shine*.
Best Actor: Geoffrey Rush, for *Shine*.
Best Actress: Judy Davis, for *Children of the Revolution*.
Best Supporting Actor: Noah Taylor, for *Shine*.
Best Supporting Actress: Alice Garner, for *Love and Other Catastrophes*.

Best Director: Chris Noonan, for *Babe*.
Best Original Screenplay: Peter Duncan, for *Children of the Revolution*.
Best Adapted Screenplay: Nick Parsons, for *Dead Heart*.
Best Cinematography: Dion Beebe, for *What I Have Written*.
Best Score: Nigel Westlake, for *Babe*.
Best Documentary: *Rats in the Ranks*, by Robin Anderson and Bob Connolly.
Best Short: *Two Bob Mermaid*, by Darlene Johnson.
Best English-language Foreign Film: *Fargo* (USA), by Joel and Ethan Coen.
Best Foreign-language Film: *La Haine* (France), by Mathieu Kassovitz.
Special Achievement Award: Bryan Brown.

The 47th Berlin International Film Festival, 24 February 1997

Golden Bear for Best Film: *The People vs. Larry Flynt* (USA).
Special Jury Prize: *The River*, by Tsai Ming-liang (Taiwan).
Silver Bear for Best Director: Eric Heumann, for *Port Djema* (France-Italy-Greece).
Best Actor: Leonardo DiCaprio, for *William Shakespeare's Romeo + Juliet* (USA).
Best Actress: Juliette Binoche, for *The English Patient* (USA).
Silver Bear for Single Achievement: Zbigniew Preisner, for his music in the film *The Island on Bird Street* (Denmark-UK-Germany).
Silver Bear for Lifetime Contribution to the Art of Cinema: Ray Ruiz, director of *Genealogies of a Crime* (France).
Blue Angel Prize: Montxo Armendariz, for *Secrets of the Heart* (Spain-France-Portugal).
Alfred Bauer Prize: *William Shakespeare's Romeo + Juliet*.
Golden Bear for Best Short Film: *The Latest News* (Sweden).
Silver Bear for Best Short Film: *Late at Night* (Germany).
Ecumenical Jury: *Under Western Eyes* (Israel).
Panorama Prize: *Brassed Off* (UK).
International Forum: *Nobody's Business* (USA).
Special Prize: *Mother and Son* (Germany-Russia).

Special Jury Award: *They Teach Us How To Be Happy* (Switzerland).
Special Mentions: *Life is All You Get* (Germany); *Get On the Bus* (USA).
Young Actress: Anna Wielgucka, for *Miss Nobody* (Poland-Germany).
Young Actor: Jordan Kiziuk, for *The Island on Bird Street*.
FIPRESCI Prizes (International Film Critics' Association):
Best Film: *The River*.
Panorama: *Wednesday* (Germany-UK-Finland-Russia).
International Forum: *Nobody's Business*.
Wolfgang Staudte Prize: *Landscape of Memories* (Brazil).
German Art House Cinemas: *Get On the Bus*.
Berliner Morgenpost Reader's Jury: *The People vs. Larry Flynt*.
Kinderfest Jury: *Flight of the Albatross* (Germany-New Zealand).
CICAE (international confederation of art cinemas)
Jury:*Mother and Son*.
International Forum: *The Sleeping Man* (Japan).
Panorama Award of New York Film Academy: Simone Horrocks, for *Spindrift* (UK).
Gay Teddy Bear Awards:
Best Feature: *All Over Me* (USA).
Short Film: *Heroines of Love* (Germany).
Peace Film Prize: *Off Season* (Germany).
Caligari Film Prize: *Nobody's Business*.
NETPAC (network for the promotion of Asian cinema) Award: [*Focus*] (Japan).

President of the jury: Jack Lang (former French Culture Minister)

The 1996 British Academy of Film and Television Arts Awards ('BAFTAs'), 29 April 1997

Best Film: *The English Patient*, by Anthony Minghella.
David Lean Award for Best Direction: Joel Coen, for *Fargo*.
Best Original Screenplay: Mike Leigh, for *Secrets and Lies*.
Best Adapted Screenplay: Anthony Minghella, for *The English Patient*.
Best Actor: Geoffrey Rush, for *Shine*.
Best Actress: Brenda Blethyn, for *Secrets and Lies*.

Best Supporting Actor: Paul Scofield, for *The Crucible*.
Best Supporting Actress: Juliette Binoche, for *The English Patient*.
Best Cinematography: John Seale, for *The English Patient*.
Best Production Design: Tony Burrough, for *Richard III*.
Best Editing: Walter Murch, for *The English Patient*.
The Anthony Asquith Award for Best Music: Gabriel Yared, for *The English Patient*.
Best Costumes: Shuna Harwood, for *Richard III*.
Best Sound: Jim Greenhorn, Toivo Lember, Livia Ruzic, Roger Savage and Gareth Vanderhope, for *Shine*.
Best Special Visual Effects: Stefen Fangmeier, John Frazier, Henry Labount and Habib Zargarpour, for *Twister*.
Best Make-up/hair: Rick Baker and David Leroy Anderson, for *The Nutty Professor*.
Alexander Korda Award for Best British Film: *Secrets and Lies*, by Mike Leigh.
Best Foreign Film: *Ridicule*, by Patrice Leconte (France).
Best Short Film: *Des Marjorettes dans l'Espace* (Carole Scotta and David Fourier).
Best Animated Short: *The Old Lady and the Pigeons* (Bernard La Joie/Didier Brunner/Sylvian Chomet).
BAFTA Fellowships: Woody Allen and Julie Christie.

The 17th Canadian Film Awards ('Genies'), Toronto, November 27 1996

Best Film: *Lilies*.
Best Director: David Cronenberg, for *Crash* (his fourth Genie).
Best Actor: William Hutt, for *Long Day's Journey Into Night*.
Best Actress: Martha Henry, for *Long Day's Journey Into Night*.
Best Supporting Actor: Peter Donaldson, for *Long Day's Journey Into Night*.
Best Supporting Actress: Martha Burns, for *Long Day's Journey Into Night*.
Best Original Screenplay: Pierre Gang, for *Sous-sol*.
Best Adapted Screenplay: David Cronenberg, for *Crash*.
Best Cinematography: Peter Suschitzky, for *Crash*.

Best Editing: Ronald Sanders, for *Crash*.

Best Art Direction/Production Design: Marie-Carole de Beaumont/Sandra Kybartas, for *Lilies*.

Best Music: Mark Koven, for *Charm*.

Best Original Song: Michael Turner, Swamp Baby and Peter J. Moore, for 'Who the Hell Do You Think You Are?' from *Hard Core Logo*.

Best Costumes: Linda Muir, for *Lilies*.

Best Sound Editing: David Lee, for *Crash*.

Best Overall Sound: Jane Tattersall, for *Lilies*.

Best Feature-length Documentary: *Bones of the Forest*, by Heather Frise and Velcrow Ripper.

Best Short Documentary: *Maman et Eve*, by Daniele Caloz and Paul Carriere.

Best Short Film: *The Home For Blind Women*, by Christina Jennings and Sandra Kybartas.

The Golden Reel Award for Box-Office Performance: *Crash*.

The 50th Cannes Film Festival Awards, 18 May 1997

Palme d'Or for Best Film: *The Eel*, by Shohei Imamura (Japan); and *The Taste of Cherries*, by Abbas Kiarostami (Iran).

Grand Prix du Jury: *The Sweet Hereafter*, by Atom Egoyan (Canada).

Best Actor: Sean Penn, for *She's So Lovely*.

Best Actress: Kathy Burke, for *Nil By Mouth*.

Best Director: Wong Kar-wai, for *Happy Together* (Hong Kong).

Best Screenplay: James Schamus, for *The Ice Storm* (USA).

Palme d'Or for Best Short: *Is It the Design On the Wrapper?*, by Tessa Sheridan (UK).

Jury Prize: *Western*, by Manuel Poirier (France).

Jury Prize for Best Short: *Leonie*, by Lieven Debrauwer (Belgium) and *Les Vacances*, by Emmanuelle Bercot (France).

Camera d'Or for First Feature: *Suzaku*, by Naomi Kawase (Japan).

Special Mention for First Feature: *The Life of Jesus*, by Bruno Dumont (France).

Grand Prix Technique: Thierry Arbogast, for his cinematography on *The Fifth Element* and *She's So Lovely*.

Fiftieth Anniversary Honour: The Egyptian director Youseff Chahine, for the totality of his work.

Fipresci International Critics' Award: *The Sweet Hereafter*.

Special Mention: *Journey To the Beginning of the World*, by Manoel de Oliveira (Portugal-France).

Jury: Isabelle Adjani (president), Paul Auster (USA), Luc Bondy (France), Tim Burton (USA), Patrick Dupond (France), Gong Li (China), Mike Leigh (UK), Nanni Moretti (Italy), Michael Ondaatje (Canada), Mira Sorvino (USA)

The 41st David di Donatello Awards ('Davids'), Rome, 20 April 1997

Best Film: *The Truce*, by Francesco Rosi.

Best Director: Francesco Rosi, for *The Truce*.

Best Actor: Fabrizio Bentivoglio, for *Witness in Danger*.

Best Actress: Asia Argento, for *Travelling Companion*.

Best Supporting Actor: Leo Gullotta, for *The Sniper*.

Best Supporting Actress: Barbara Enrichi, for *The Cyclone*.

Best Producers: Leo Pescarolo and Guido De Laurentiis, for *The Truce*.

Best Editing: Bruno Sarandrea and the late Ruggero Mastroianni, for *The Truce*.

The 22nd Deauville Festival of American Cinema, 8 September 1996

Grand Prix for Best Film: *The Daytrippers*, by Greg Mottola.

Jury Prize shared by: *Welcome to the Dollhouse*, by Todd Solondz; and *Bound*, by Larry and Andy Wachowski.

Prix du Public: *The Daytrippers*.

Critics' Prize: *Big Night*, by Stanley Tucci and Campbell Scott.

President of the jury: Charlotte Rampling

The 9th European Film Awards ('The Felixes'), Berlin, December 1996

Best European Film: *Breaking the Waves* (Denmark/Sweden/France/Netherlands/Norway), by Lars von Trier.

Best Young European Film: *Some Mother's Son* (Ireland/UK/USA), by Terry George.

Best Actor: Ian McKellen, for *Richard III* (UK).

Best Actress: Emily Watson, for *Breaking the Waves*.

Best Screenplay: Arif Aliev, Sergei Bodrov and Boris Giller, for *Prisoner of the Caucasus* (Russia).

European Critics' Award: *Breaking the Waves*.

Life Achievement Award: Alec Guinness.

Prix Arte: Jerzy Sladkowski and Stanislaw Krzeminski.

The Screen International Five Continents Award: *Dead Man* (USA/Germany), by Jim Jarmusch.

The 'Evening Standard' 1996 Film Awards, London, 2 February 1997

Best Film: *Richard III*.

Best Actor: Liam Neeson, for *Michael Collins*.

Best Actress: Kate Winslet, for *Sense and Sensibility* and *Jude*.

Best Screenplay: Emma Thompson, for *Sense and Sensibility*; and John Hodge, for *Trainspotting*.

Best Technical Achievement: Tony Burrough, production designer of *Richard III*.

Most Promising Newcomer: Emily Watson, for *Breaking the Waves*.

The Peter Sellers Comedy Award: Mark Herman, writer-director, of *Brassed Off*.

Special Award: Leslie Phillips.

The 22nd French Academy ('Cesar') Awards, 8 February 1997

Best Film: *Ridicule*.

Best Director: Patrice Leconte, for *Ridicule*; Bertrand Tavernier, for *Capitaine Conan*.

Best Actor: Philippe Torreton, for *Capitaine Conan*.

Best Actress: Fanny Ardant, for *Pedale Douce*.

Best Supporting Actor: Jean-Pierre Darroussin, for *Un Air de Famille*.

Best Supporting Actress: Agnes Jaoui, for *Un Air de Famille*.

Most Promising Young Actor: Mathieu Amalric, for *Comment Je Me Suis Dispute*.

Best First Film: *Y Aura-t-il de la Neige a Noel*, by Sandrine Veysset.

Best Photography: Claude
  Nuridsany, Marie Perennou,
  Hughes Ryffel and Thierry
  Machado, for *Microcosmos*.
Best Editing: Marie-Josephe Yoyotte
  and Florence Ricard, for
  Microcosmos.
Best Foreign Film: *Breaking the Waves*
  (Denmark/Sweden/France/
  Netherlands/Norway).
Best Producer: Jacques Perrin, for
  Microcosmos.
Honorary Cesar: Andie MacDowell.

The 54th Hollywood Foreign Press Association ('Golden Globes') Awards, 19 January 1997

Best Film - Drama: *The English
  Patient*.
Best Film - Comedy or Musical:
  Evita.
Best Actor - Drama: Geoffrey Rush,
  for *Shine*.
Best Actress - Drama: Brenda
  Blethyn, for *Secrets and Lies*.
Best Actor - Comedy or Musical:
  Tom Cruise, for *Jerry Maguire*.
Best Actress - Comedy or Musical:
  Madonna, for *Evita*.
Best Supporting Actor: Edward
  Norton, for *Primal Fear*.
Best Supporting Actress: Lauren
  Bacall, for *The Mirror Has Two
  Faces*.
Best Director: Milos Forman, for *The
  People vs. Larry Flynt*.
Best Screenplay: Scott Alexander
  and Larry Karaszewski, for *The
  People vs. Larry Flynt*.
Best Original Score: Gabriel Yared,
  for *The English Patient*.
Best Original Song: 'You Must Love
  Me', music by Andrew Lloyd
  Webber, lyrics by Tim Rice, from
  Evita.
Best Foreign Language Film: *Kolya*
  (Czech Republic).
Best TV Film: *Rasputin*, by Uli Edel.
Cecil B. De Mille Award for Lifetime
  Achievement: Dustin Hoffman.

The 12th Independent Spirit Awards, Santa Monica, 22 March 1997

Best Film: *Fargo*.
Best First Film: *Sling Blade*, by Billy
  Bob Thornton.
Best Director: Joel Coen, for *Fargo*.
Best Actor: William H. Macy, for
  Fargo.

Charles Berling in Patrice Leconte's Ridicule,
winner of the Cesar for best film

Best Actress: Frances McDormand,
  for *Fargo*.
Best Supporting Actor: Benicio Del
  Toro, for *Basquiat*.
Best Supporting Actress: Elizabeth
  Pena, for *Lone Star*.
Best Debut Performance: Heather
  Matarazzo, for *Welcome to the
  Dollhouse*.
Best Screenplay: Joel and Ethan
  Coen, for *Fargo*.
Best First Screenplay: Stanley Tucci
  and Joseph Tropiano, for *Big Night*.
Best Cinematography: Roger
  Deakins, for *Fargo*.
Best Foreign Film: *Secrets and Lies*
  (UK/France), by Mike Leigh.
Best Documentary: *When We Were
  Kings*, by Leon Gast.
Someone To Watch Award: Larry
  Fessenden, writer, producer,
  director and star of *Habit*.

Host: Samuel L. Jackson

The 17th London Film Critics' Awards ('The Alfs'), The Cafe Royal, London, 2 March 1997

Best Film: *Fargo*.
Best Actor: Morgan Freeman, for
  Seven.
Best Actress: Frances McDormand,
  for *Fargo*.
Best Director: Joel Coen, for *Fargo*.
Best Screenwriter: Joel and Ethan
  Coen, for *Fargo*.
Best British Film: *Secrets and Lies*.
Best British Producer: Andrew
  Macdonald, for *Trainspotting*.
Best British Director: Mike Leigh, for
  Secrets and Lies.

Best British Screenwriter: Emma
  Thompson, for *Sense and Sensibility*.
Best British Actor: Ewan McGregor,
  for *Brassed Off*, *Emma*, *The Pillow
  Book* and *Trainspotting*; and Ian
  McKellen, for *Richard III*.
Best British Actress: Brenda Blethyn,
  for *Secrets and Lies*.
Best British Newcomer: Emily
  Watson, for *Breaking the Waves*.
Best Foreign Language Film: *Nelly
  and Mr Arnaud* (France).
Dilys Powell Award: Sir John Mills.
Special Awards: Fred Zinnemann,
  Norman Wisdom.

*Presenters: Christopher Tookey, James
Cameron-Wilson, Quentin Falk,
Mariella Frostrup, Paul Gambaccini,
Marianne Gray, Tom Hutchinson,
George Perry, Simon Rose, etc.*

The Los Angeles Film Critics' Association Awards, December 1996

Best Film: *Secrets and Lies*.
Best Actor: Geoffrey Rush, for *Shine*.
Best Actress: Brenda Blethyn, for
  Secrets and Lies.
Best Supporting Actor: Edward
  Norton, for *Everyone Says I Love
  You*, *The People vs. Larry Flynt* and
  Primal Fear.
Best Supporting Actress: Barbara
  Hershey, for *The Portrait of a Lady*.
Best Director: Mike Leigh, for *Secrets
  and Lies*.
Best Screenplay: Ethan and Joel
  Coen, for *Fargo*.
Best Foreign Film: *La Cérémonie*
  (France), by Claude Chabrol.
New Generation Award: Emily
  Watson, for *Breaking the Waves*.

The National Board of Review of Motion Pictures, New York, 10 December 1996

Best Film: *Shine*.
Best Actor: Tom Cruise, for *Jerry Maguire*.
Best Actress: Frances McDormand, for *Fargo*.
Best Supporting Actor: Edward Norton, for *Primal Fear, Everyone Says I Love You* and *The People vs. Larry Flynt*.
Best Supporting Actress: Juliette Binoche and Kristin Scott-Thomas, for *The English Patient*.
Best Director: Joel Coen, for *Fargo*.
Best Documentary: *Paradise Lost: The Child Murders at Robin Hood Hills*, by Joe Berlinger and Bruce Sinofsky.
Best TV Documentary: *Wild Bill: Hollywood Maverick*, by Todd Robinson.
Best Foreign Film: *Ridicule* (France), by Patrice Leconte; *Les Voleurs* (France), by André Téchiné; *Bitter Sugar* (USA-Cuba), by Leon Ichaso; *La Cérémonie* (France), by Claude Chabrol; and *Kolya* (Czech Republic-UK-France), by Jan Sverak.
Career Achievement Award: Gena Rowlands.
Special Awards: *The First Wives Club*, for its ensemble cast.
Outstanding Newcomer: Renee Zellweger.
Special Achievement in Filmmaking Award: Billy Bob Thornton, for writing, directing and acting in *Sling Blade*.

The 31st National Society of Film Critics, New York, January 1997

Best Film: *Breaking the Waves*.
Best Actor: Eddie Murphy, for *The Nutty Professor*.
Best Actress: Emily Watson, for *Breaking the Waves*.
Best Director: Lars Von Trier, for *Breaking the Waves*.
Best Supporting Actor: Martin Donovan, for *The Portrait of a Lady*; and Tony Shalhoub, for *Big Night*.
Best Supporting Actress: Barbara Hershey, for *The Portrait of a Lady*.
Best Screenplay: Albert Brooks and Monica Johnson, for *Mother*.

Best Cinematography: Robby Muller, for *Breaking the Waves* and *Dead Man*.
Best Foreign Film: *La Cérémonie* (France), by Claude Chabrol.
Best Documentary: *When We Were Kings*, by Leon Gast.
Special citation: James Katz and Robert Harris, for their restoration of Alfred Hitchcock's *Vertigo*.

The 62nd New York Film Critics' Circle Awards, December 1996

Best Film: *Fargo*.
Best Actor: Geoffrey Rush, for *Shine*.
Best Actress: Emily Watson, for *Breaking the Waves*.
Best Supporting Actor: Harry Belafonte, for *Kansas City*.
Best Supporting Actress: Courtney Love, for *The People vs. Larry Flynt*.
Best Director: Lars Von Trier, for *Breaking the Waves*.
Best Screenplay: Albert Brooks and Monica Johnson, for *Mother*.
Best Cinematography: Robby Muller, for *Breaking the Waves* and *Dead Man*.
Best Foreign Film: *The White Balloon* (Iran), by Jafar Panahi.
Best Non-Fiction Film: *When We Were Kings*, by Leon Gast.
Best First Film: *Big Night*, by Stanley Tucci and Campbell Scott.
Distinguished Reissue: *Vertigo* (1958), by Alfred Hitchcock.
Special Award: Jonas Mekas, co-founder, president and programme director of the Anthology Film Archives in New York.

The 13th Sundance Film Festival, Park City, Utah, 25 January 1997

The Grand Jury Prize (best feature): *Sunday*.
The Grand Jury Prize (best documentary): *Girls Like Us*.
Special Jury Award: Therese DePrez, production designer for *Going All the Way* and *Box of Moonlight*.
Special Jury Prize (documentary): *Sick: The Life and Death of Bob Flanagan, Supermasochist*.
Best Performance: Parker Posey, for *The House of Yes, subUrbia* and *Clockwatchers*.
Best Direction: Morgan J. Freeman, for *Hurricane*.

Best Direction (documentary): Arthur Dong, for *Licensed to Kill*.
Best Cinematography: Enrique Chediak, for *Hurricane*.
Best Cinematography (documentary): *My America... or Honk if You Love Buddha*.
Audience Award (best feature): *Hurricane; love jones*.
Audience Award (best documentary): *Paul Monette: The Brink of Summer's End*.
Filmmakers' Trophy (best feature): *In the Company of Men*.
Filmmakers' Trophy (best documentary): Arthur Dong, for *Licensed to Kill*.
Waldo Salt Screenwriting Award: Jonathan Nossiter and James Lasdun, for *Sunday*.
Freedom of Expression Award: Macky Alston, for *Family Name*; and Laura Angelica Simon, for *Fear and Learning at Hoover Elementary*.
Latin American Cinema Award: Jose Araujo, for *Landscapes of Memory*.
Short Filmmaking Award: Kris Isacsson, for *Man About Town*.

The 53rd Venice International Film Festival Awards, September 1996

Golden Lion for Best Film: *Michael Collins*, by Neil Jordan (UK-US).
Special Jury Grand Prix: *Brigands* (French-Russian-Italian-Swiss-Georgian), by Otar Iosseliani.
Best Actor: Liam Neeson, for *Michael Collins*.
Best Actress: Victoire Thivisol, for *Ponette* (France).
Best Supporting Performance: Chris Penn, for *The Funeral* (USA).
Best Screenplay: Paz Alicia Garciadiego, for *Deep Crimson* (Mexico).
Best Art Direction: Monica Chirinos, Patricia Nava and Antonio Muno-Hierro, for *Deep Crimson*.
Best Music: David Mansfield, for *Deep Crimson*.
Gold Medal (for a film which emphasises civil progress and human solidarity): *Carla's Song* (UK-Germany-Spain), by Ken Loach.
Golden Lion for Career Achievement: Dustin Hoffman, Robert Altman, Vittorio Gassman and Michele Morgan.

Jury: Roman Polanski (president), Paul Auster, Anjelica Huston, Mirial Sen, etc.

Index